Christian
Systematic Theology
in a World Context

Christian Systematic Theology in a World Context

NINIAN SMART AND STEVEN KONSTANTINE

FORTRESS PRESS

Minneapolis

CHRISTIAN SYSTEMATIC THEOLOGY IN A WORLD CONTEXT

ISBN 0-8006-2515-3

Library of Congress Cataloging-in-Publication Data available

Manufactured in Great Britain   AF 1-2515
95   94   93   92   91   1   2   3   4   5   6   7   8   9   10

Contents

Preface   7
Foreword   9

PART I Setting the Scene
  1. Preliminaries   17
  2. Questions of Method: the Religious Studies
     Context   27
  3. The World Situation and the Phenomenology
     of Religion   54
  4. Philosophy of Religion: Preliminary
     relevances to a Christian Worldview   82
  5. Christian Neotranscendentalism and Some
     Influential Modern Theologies   132

PART II The Vision of Love
  6. The Divine Threefoldness   149
  7. Divine Creativity   201
  8. Divine Embodiment   249
  9. Spirit and Psyche   300
 10. Love and Behavior   359
 11. Patterns of World History   388
 12. Criteria and Conclusions: the Federal Stance   429

Bibliography   447
Index   465

For Alexander and Nadezda

Preface

This book would not have been completed without the excellent help of Cindy Nunn and Sara Duke of the Religious Studies office at the University of California Santa Barbara. We are grateful to Dr Mokusen Miyuki for guidance and the London Society for the Study of Religion for enlightened discussion. We also thank Brian Wilson for help with the bibliography and the charts.

N.S. and S.K.
27 May 1990

Foreword

This book is written in a calm and scholarly fashion, but we view the themes with passion. Its central messages lie close to our heart. What we present is a vision, or as Indians would say, *darśana*, which expresses an articulated version of the Christian faith, but one which, though traditionally based, is written against the background of the modern, religiously plural world. It is a vision which we think reflective people can be drawn to: it is not clothed in ancient categories. It does not sneer at other visions, and it is open to the human condition. We make use of non-Western ideas, drawing on insights from Buddhism, Hinduism and a variety of other faiths. We attempt to delineate freshly the face of Christ in the marketplace of the modern world.

We draw upon our dear traditions: on Orthodoxy and liberal Anglicanism; in this we hope we have woven together motifs from their sources in the Catholic, Protestant and Orthodox ways of looking at the world. The danger of the Roman Catholic way is an excess of authority; that of the radical Protestants is disintegration. Ours is a middle path, open-minded and critical, we hope, and yet drawing on the strengths of sacramental light shining through our particular traditions. We are pluralistic and critical, as befits followers, somewhat, of Karl Popper. We do not think of our Anglo-Orthodoxy in any smug manner: after all, we know that today's Orthodoxy often displays a beautiful face but an empty mind, and Anglicans are often confused and timid. But we are loyal to the Christian faith. Anyway, we consider that we are entering a new phase in the world's history, where fresh vision is needed. While we draw on the past, we look to the present and the future.

The vision we present is easy to share but impossible to

prove. We write at a time when it is more obvious that public certainty is a false idea. No worldview can be proved: from what point of view should we prove it? The epistemological criteria of right vision are soft. This fact destroys our arrogance and we eschew fanaticism. To those who think they have public certainty we may seem not to shout much. But we think that inner certitude in faith is possible without public certainty. We are soft non-relativists. But softness of voice may signal humility, the antidote to the deadliest of the Seven Deadly Sins.

Heaven shielded us from her Light by creating us in this beautiful material world. It is inevitable that we suffer from ignorance and confusion. But this does not mean we need too to suffer from hatred or greed. Where different visions flash their lights before us, let us not rush to protect our own vision, but seek rather to learn from others.

It follows that our stance is different from those of the Falwells and Khomeinis of the world. We do not wish to enter into combat with them: for the good things they have seen, we congratulate them. As to the dangers that publically expressed certainty poses, we hope that reasonable men and women can struggle against their ill effects by following a differently perceived ideal of love.

Our vision flows from our feel for the Trinity. It is our sense of the social Trinity which explains how God is Love. This informs our whole viewpoint and ethos. We consider too that in surveying the sorrows of the world, which run like dark shadows through the beauties of the cosmos, only a God who is willing to come into our life and suffer in the world could contemplate the dread and wonderful task of creating us and all those other creatures who share the pains and risks of living in the light.

The Divine *Īśvara* we follow is Lord of Compassion, is the Great Ultimate, is Kwoth, and shows forth the love which bodhisattvas display. But while we see echoes of our faith in the world's religions and great and meaningful overlaps, we do not hold that all religions are one, or that we are in orbit round the same Sun. We do not follow Radhakrishnan or Aldous Huxley or John Hick. But we take with utmost seriousness the existence and challenges of all worldviews. We think that worldviews can ultimately work together richly through a federal view of our tasks in this world: to develop our spiritual creativity, to feed the hungry, to strive for peace. We think our federalism of the spirit is realistic. From a Christian perspective we can say that God put other faiths there to keep us honest. We can all be friendly critics of one another. There is no Truth without criticism. So we await criticism too of our vision with interest and concern.

We are modern, liberal, scientifically-minded citizens of a plural world. Our Christian vision is a picture of what such persons can believe. We quote Fathers and Bible: but they belong also to a different age. We cannot continue to have an ancient mind in a modern place. But we can kiss the ikon and taste the bread and wine. What lies behind these symbols? That is what we have tried to express.

In the first section which we call "Setting the Scene" we look at the intellectual and living milieu of commitment. In the second part called "The Vision of Love", we delineate our viewpoint. We draw extensively on the published writings of Ninian Smart, but the central message flows from Steven Konstantine's analysis of the idea of the Trinity.

We do not wish to underestimate the great work of former writers of systematic theologies and the like in the Christian tradition: but we believe we live in an age when the cultural tribalism that so often underpinned their learning and their attitudes should be over. Whether our vision seems to the reader to be appealing, consistent and fruitful we cannot yet know. But we hope that it will be: we are ourselves merely vehicles of that vision. It is the Light which we look to see, and we struggle in shadows.

Ninian Smart
Steven Konstantine

Santa Barbara
27 May 1990

PART I
Setting the Scene

1
Preliminaries

Our Approach

We hope that our approach here to articulating a Christian systematic theology is fresh and revolutionary. We think that this is perhaps the first comprehensive attempt to place the Christian faith in its real new context: that is, in the milieu of the plural and postcolonial world, and intellectually in the light of the modern study of religions. Hitherto, Christian theologies have been mostly Europocentric, and though there have in recent times grown up traditions of Asian, African, Latin American and other theologies, these have often neglected the whole-world context, and the reflection of that in religious studies. Also, ours is an age when the epistemological and scientific situation is different from that in earlier ages: we live in the era of a critical, experimentalist, technical and revisionary epistemology. It is not possible artificially to divide religion and faith off from this milieu, and attempts to do so will result in worldviews which are obsolete. There is a crisis of authority in all faiths, and yet this is not in itself bad news: it can encourage the spiritual equivalents of scientific criticism, experiments, technology and revision – namely, search, openness, pragmatism and growth.

In presenting a Christian systematic theology we present what the Indian tradition calls a *darśana*, a viewpoint or vision of reality. For reasons which are perhaps obvious but which we shall spell out anon, we do not intend to attempt to prove our version of the Christian *darśana*. But in presenting it we do wish to be loyal to the Christian tradition as we understand it, without confusing loyalty with mere conservatism (the hermeneutics of this we shall argue). The adoption of a *darśana* has its reasons, but it is also a matter

17

of being gripped by it. Presenting a Christian systematic theology is one mode of expressing loyalty to the faith, and so a word or two about our perspective and institutional traditions will be in order. Though we believe in the richness of our backgrounds in the Christian way (or ways), we do not argue that everyone ought to conform to our *darśana*, but it may be that the vision here presented can have splendid fruits. It is by its fruits that it will be judged in the long run, though we are also very mindful of other criteria, such as coherence and reasonableness, realism as to the world into which it enters, loyalty to our tradition, and beauty.

We are respectively, by affiliation, Episcopalian and Orthodox. Broadly there are four main currents flowing through modern Western Christianity – Orthodoxy, Catholicism and Protestantism, together with humanism since the Enlightenment. We have been deeply touched, in the nature of our affiliations, by all of these. But in addition we have been immersed in the modern study of religion, itself a product of liberal scholarship in recent times. And less academically we both have been immersed in the plural modern world, as seen in the microcosm of California and the macrocosms of Africa, Asia, the South Pacific and Latin America. So while we intend this *darśana* to reflect Christian pasts, we also wish to place it in that plural intellectual and postcolonial context supplied by religious studies. This adds a powerful new dimension to Christian systematics: for post-Enlightenment humanism has hitherto been implicitly colonialist, though containing within it the seeds of world revolution in thinking. Our hope is to be a world vision, which can be shared by humans of the various great civilizations and cultures of the globe.

But it is not intended to be a perennial philosophy, a synthesis of all religions and secular worldviews. It is avowedly a Christian vision: it is equally up to Jews and Buddhists, Marxists and Hindus, Classical African religionists and others to present their own visions. But to be modern such visions have to take cognizance, both intellectually and in feeling, of the other faiths and traditions. Every movement is in the minority in the one world in which we now live and may perish. So Muslims without a good theory of other faiths, or Marxists without a grasp of the history of religions, or Buddhists without an analysis of the great religious alternatives, are all out of date. And so are those Christians who neglect world culture and world history.

For this reason we make much too of the need for a relating of our *darśana* both to world history and to the phenomenology of religion. We have to interpret the preceding histories of the world which have flowed together into world history today from a Christian perspective, but positively. Only if such an interpretation makes sense will the *darśana* seem at all reasonable. Likewise Christian experience must be related to religious experience in general, Christian ritual to other rituals, Christian ethics to other values, and so on.

Religious Studies and Christian Theology

If what we present here is a Christian *darśana*, it has to be written in the right spirit. Before we delineate that spirit, a word, though, is needed about how we understand the study of religion. This as a way of study and thinking has to be quite independent of affiliations: it is in no way subordinate to Christian theology. Although it may be that religious studies cannot avoid philosophical encounters, and to this degree is involved in questions about the truth of religion (if any), its primary focus is the polymethodic exploration of religions and to some degree also secular worldviews. It involves history, phenomenology, sociology, anthropology, art history and various other methods or approaches to the study of religions, without fear or favor. It is thus an absurdity that often the study of world religions is placed institutionally under Christian divinity schools. Its healthiest manifestation is when religions and religion are studied in a "secular" (that is to say, pluralistic) context. So in relating our Christian systematic theology to the milieu of religious studies we wish to affirm clearly that we are trying to make use of results independently arrived at. Because in much of Europe and in the divinity schools of

America the study of religions is so frequently subordinated
to Christian theology, that theology is too much insulated
from the real, that is to say the global, world. Similar remarks
apply, perhaps even more forcibly, to Jewish studies, save
that Judaism as a minority religion has at least to take account
of a largely Christian and Muslim milieu. But it is often the
case that seminaries are places of turning inward. And yet
it should also be said that it was institutional Christianity,
especially in the 19th century German universities, which
pioneered modern scholarly self-criticism. To that excellent
self-criticism we are merely adding a further stage, in exposing
the Christian *darśana* to the demands of religious studies, and
thereby to what we have called the global world.

This may seem a pleonasm; but what we have in mind
is that we have entered, especially since World War II (when
Wendell Wilkie wrote his seminal book, *One World*), into
a period of history when the interaction of cultures, for good
or ill, and the dialogues and clashes of worldviews, parallel
the economic and political interactions of a single world
system. The price of gold, skins, wheat, radio sets and so
forth in Brazil is set by forces in Hong Kong, Southern
Africa, the Middle West, Thailand and so on. Roughly
speaking we are involved in a single, global economic system:
and likewise the major cultural forces of the world including
the religions and secular worldviews are all interacting with
one another. This is what is meant by what we called the
"global world", of which a major mirror is religious studies.
So Christian theology, in being exposed to an untamed
religious studies, is exposed to the plural world of many
religious and ideological movements. So Christian systematic
theology in this context must speak the language of that
world: it must use some of the key concepts of non-Western
civilizations: there is Christian *bhakti* or devotion,
contemplation of *dhyāna*, kenosis or *śūnyatā*, a Christian
tao or way, sacraments or *li*, compassion or *karuṇā*, and
there are the Pillars of Christianity, Christian Sufism,
Christian ancestors. Though we may write in English we
must be mindful of other means of expressing the religious
experience of humankind.

In brief, religious studies can mediate the actual world of religion and religions to us: and in the light of that we must formulate a world or global theology, presenting articulately a way of understanding the faith in this plural perspective, as well as a way of interpreting, in the light of that articulation, the meaning of world history.

The existence of the many movements of the human spirit, including such vast and noble traditions as Buddhism and Islam, is from one point of view uncomfortable for Christian orthodoxy. Because of the nature of worldviews there cannot be proofs or disproofs. Even the question of whether there are proofs of God's existence is controversial, and that means that whatever happens such proofs will not be probative. Thus the epistemology of worldviews is soft: there are soft reasons for holding to a *darśana*. It may be that we claim certitude in faith, but it is no public certainty. The epistemological position which we here adopt is therefore one of "soft non-relativism" — soft because of the absence of proofs and of decisive evidence, and because of the flexibility of organic religious systems; and non-relativist, because we do not draw the relativist conclusions from that fact.

Neotranscendentalism

There is another perspective which a Christian worldview has to adopt. It has to see the world not just from a special angle, amid the world religions and the world's worldviews. It has also to see the world from a transcendent perspective. In this it goes beyond science, beyond historical studies and beyond that agnosticism which the science of religion needs to embrace. It has a transcendent focus, which so to speak underpins Christian experience and the history of the world. We therefore need to evolve some form of two-aspect theory of truth. The vision we present includes that glittering "other world" from which come the rays which suffuse the saints with light. This two-aspect theory is reminiscent of the two-level of Mahayana Buddhism and of Advaita Vedanta, and requires philosophical discussion (which is why Christian theology cannot remain "raw": it needs philosophical

21

treatment). This transcendent perspective has to be presented in the new context of scientific thinking and humanistic enquiry. We call it, because of this new milieu, Neotranscendentalism.

So far then we have sketched the needed properties of the *darśana* which we here present: it is intended as Christian, because we are loyal to the Christian past (or pasts); it is sensitive to the emergency of a world civilization, so it is not parochially Europocentric; it includes an interpretation of world history, not just the "salvation history" from ancient Israel to the modern Church; it is set within the bounds of modern epistemology, and combines soft non-relativism with possible inner certitude; and it reflects its transcendent focus, and so is critical of flat materialisms and humanisms. All these points have, of course, to be worked out and presented in greater detail.

We have called our work "A Christian Systematic Theology in World Perspective": it claims no authority beyond being a way of expressing the Christian worldview. It is an attempt at articulating the belief aspect of the faith. But what we refer to so easily as "the Christian tradition" is itself highly variegated, to say the least, constantly shifting in its outer forms over the centuries and dividing into many different streams. Even at the beginning we can trace diverse trajectories. It is of course a dream that Christians often entertain that there be one universal Church, a single message, a blessed state of ecumenical harmony. But even in these latter days when those of varied denominations are charitable to one another, to a great degree, dissent still exists. There are many kinds of African independent churches which are not part of the ecumenical movement: there are Southern Baptists and others in the United States who remain deeply suspicious of liberal and Catholic alternatives; and so on. So empirically it is best to think of Christianities, and not to assume some normative Christianity which somehow pervades the varied manifestations of the tradition (Smart, 1979). We do not in this sense believe in an essence of Christianity. What we present, however, belongs in intention to a main stream (a main stream that some see as narrowing in the modern world), combining primary motifs from Orthodox, Catholic, Protestant and liberal humanist expressions, and from Christianities of North and South and East and West.

In articulating the belief aspect of the Christian way we do not intend that our doctrines should be seen as abstract and dry. They not only exist side by side with sacred narrative (Biblical and world history) and ethics, including politics; but they are to be seen in the rich context of the other dimensions of religion − ritual or sacramental life; feeling and experience; and the social institutions through which Christian life is expressed and manifested. In addition there is the art and music which helps to form our feelings. In all of this we make use of the six-dimensional analysis of religion, or (if we include the material manifestations of a religious tradition − its icons, vestments, mosques and so on) − the seven-dimensional analysis. A tradition can be seen under the aspects of doctrine, myth or sacred narrative, ethics, ritual, experience and institutions (Smart, 1984, pp. 6-12).

After all, belief has to have both expression and fruits, and they are seen in the spiritual and ethical life of Christians and of others who may gain from aspects of the vision presented. So though this worldview-articulation, being incarnated in marks on paper and unheard sounds in the reader's brain, cannot by itself create worship or heroism or compassion or social activism, it must in part be judged by whether its vision can help to express and stimulate a deeper Christian, and human, life.

So we may see the quest for an articulation of a Christian worldview as involving depth, in the sense that doctrines, narratives and ethical judgments are to be presented within the deeper phenomenology of religion. This itself says something about the spirit in which we approach our task.

Motives Not Primarily Academic

Though we are making use of our "professional" expertise, in the impartial and empathetic study of religions, including the Christian traditions, our motives in presenting this *darśana* are not primarily scientific or academic, even if what we write must be hoped to interest academicians; but spiritual, and indeed ethical. Our purpose is to use intellectual categories as paints with which to create a picture of the world, seen as exhibiting the glories and sufferings of the Lord and of humanity, and seen as leading us towards the blessed vision of the Ultimate. We aim to delineate in a certain fashion the beauty and challenge of the Divine and the divine in our fellow human beings. Our doctrines will be means to such ends, in pointing to the Transcendent, in helping to shape the community who have faith in the Trinity, in synthesizing human knowledge with what has been handed down, in showing the coherence of the collage with which we express our values. We wish to exhibit a Christian vision which humans from diverse cultures can feel at home with, and which modern citizens of the world can hold to, alongside with the cosmology presented through modern science. Our *darśana* hopes to be continuous with what has gone before, but to tell a story which embraces both the narrower take of Jews, Christ and Church and the interpretation of the Spirit's work in the whole spiritual development of the human race. In all these functions of our systematizing we aim far beyond learned categories, though we make use of our own and others' knowledge. It follows that something must be said about the conditions which we need to meet, in addition to the epistemological milieu in which we find ourselves. So it was with the great commentaries on the Vedanta Sutras: they begin by discussing the qualifications of the enquirer (do you need really, for instance to be able, as Sankara said, to discriminate the eternal from the non-eternal?).

The Spirit or Ethos of the Enquiry

We consider that the conditions for searching for an articulate worldview expressing a Christian faith are, on the ethical side, the attitudes of love and humility. We present a vision because we feel it may help others towards the Christian life. If we were Buddhists we would present our vision out of compassion for other living beings. And we present it out of humility, for what can our mere words do? But we do not present it obediently to human authority: we are creatures of today, where loyalty to authority is a chosen commitment, and where knowledge progresses by, among other things, criticism of what has been received. Because of these attitudes, our criticism of other writers in the field, where we deliver it, is not intended as "doing them down". There are many fine insights to be derived from writers such as Karl Barth, Karl Rahner, John Hick and Wilfred Cantwell Smith. But in defining differences we hope to clarify our portrait of the Eternal as best we can, and to remind our readers that no theory is sacrosanct, no doctrine immovable, no text infallible, no narrative uninterpretable, no value unchanging, no experience quite catchable, no sacrament frozen, no institution unchallengeable and no icon unbreakable. But we are at such a vital point in human history, full of such human opportunities and dangers, that we feel the desire to present the golden vision of a Christian faith in a way which will make it more accessible to citizens of the world. We do it because we are privileged, having had the pleasure and challenge of studying religions and worldviews in the modern mode, in being free in the open society and the pluralistic university to wander where our fancy takes us, and in being grasped by the separate insights of Orthodox, Catholic, Protestant and humanistic perspectives: and we repay those privileges by bringing some coherence to vision in a world context. It is in that spirit, then, we write, and we hope that it is in such a spirit too that these words will be read.

We may summarize the main points of the foregoing as follows:

(1) We present a Christian systematic theology, in the new context (since World War II especially) of global interaction – economic, political, cultural and spiritual.

(2) We make strong use of categories derived from the modern study of religion (religious studies), partly because it mirrors the religions, including Christianities, to us, but also because the new Christian *darśana* or systematic vision has to reflect the categories used across the world, and not

merely the dominant ideas of the European and American traditions.

(3) We present as part of our vision an interpretation of world history in which the role of religions and ideologies is viewed positively.

(4) We take account of the modern epistemological situation, which casts grave doubts on traditional ideas of authority, and where it is necessary to present a coherent view of the relation between language about the Transcendent and scientific knowledge.

(5) In combining a modern view of the Transcendent – a view which we call Neotranscendentalism – with a sensitivity to alternative worldviews, we hope to present older Christian teachings and other dimensions of religion in a new light.

(6) We write in the spirit of Christian theology, however much use we may make of the more scientific study of religion, and so are motivated by spiritual and ethical intentions, ultimately: the worth of a *darśana* is not just dictated by its coherence and intellectual elegance, but by its capacity to point to the glory and suffering inherent in the faith and to the spiritual and ethical goals that lie before us.

2
Questions of Method: the Religious Studies Context

The Importance of the Modern Study of Religion
It has been easy for Christian theologians, that is constructors and exponents of a Christian worldview, to ignore or under-value the modern study of religion. It has been easy to be absorbed in the exploration of primary authorities, such as the Bible, the Fathers, the Reformers, the Councils, and to neglect outer challenges. The reasons for such a coolness about the modern study of religion derive from a number of factors.

(1) Institutionally Theological or Divinity Faculties and Schools may only include the study of the so-called "non-Christian religions" at the periphery of their operations, or even not at all. This creates or may create the illusion that Christianity itself does not belong under the plural study of religions (an illusion fostered by the Barthian distinction between the Gospel and religion).

(2) The sense that only Western intellectual debates are important, so that it is only necessary for the Christian intellectually to debate with, and learn from, Western philosophy, Western sociology, humanism, Marxism and so forth, has been widespread, even in the Third World.

(3) Often the study of religion has been identified with the comparative study of religion, or the history of religions, and the emphasis here has often been on ancient and historical manifestations of religion, rather than living religions "on the ground". Conversely the latter have often been studied by anthropologists and sociologists, who may be governed by colonialist assumptions or by some neglect or undervaluing of the doctrinal dimension of religion which has so much interested Christian theologians.

27

(4) Often the positive study of religions has been conceived, kindly enough, under the head of dialogue: but dialogue is at best only a small part of the methods of exploring religions, and often is not empirically based or aimed, but rather a way of doing theology (or buddhology) across traditions. It belongs to a kind of worldview-construction rather than worldview analysis.

But it is not possible for those who present a Christian worldview to avoid the modern study of religions and worldviews – what we call "worldview analysis" in its broader form – that is the analysis of worldviews, both traditionally religious and so-called secular ideologies (Smart, 1983). The reasons are straightforward.

(1) The modern study of religions and worldviews, insofar as it aims at describing the operations and power of symbols, experience, ideas and so on in human history and society, may have much to say about the actual nature of Christianities. The ideals of Christian faith as presented in a Christian *darśana* cannot be divorced from actual Christian history, because at some point or other the latter has to be seen as in some degree incarnating the former.

(2) Comparisons between religions, and contrasts, can be both illuminating and challenging. Paul was, from one perspective, a *bhakti* practitioner, an exponent of Christian devotionalism. Why do we attach so much importance to his example rather than Hindu or Buddhist kinds of devotion? Since all religions and their subtraditions are, despite some resemblances, also unique, what is special about Christian uniqueness?

(3) Human beings in the world live side by side with one another, and Christians cannot ignore their Muslim or Marxist or agnostic neighbors, nor can the Christian traditions escape the challenges of our "one world".

(4) Increasingly in actual practice there are blends and interactions: Christian evangelical patriotism, Catholic Marxist-influenced liberation theology, Christian yoga, Zen Catholicism and so on. We need to have some criteria for judging these phenomena.

(5) The attempt, by such as Kraemer and Barth, to

28

insulate the Gospel from the religions breaks down because to be of any power the Gospel has in some degree to be incarnated in actual Christian practice, and thereby necessarily becomes comparable to actual non-Christian practice (Smart, 1966, pp. 98–100; 1970, pp. 103–112). So there is no way in which ultimately the Christian faith can simply rise above the other faiths and religious expressions and in such an empyrean escape competition. Even if it could it would find the other faiths doing the same thing and we would have upper-region competition. Hindu Dharma could challenge aspects of the Gospel, as could Buddhist Emptiness.

We are, then, citizens of a plural world and if we are conscientious in trying to frame a *darśana* containing the Christian message in that world we have to take the facts of the many worldviews seriously. That is why Christian theology has to operate within the context of the modern study of religion. And what, then, is that?

The Modern Study of Religion

It is a modern thing, and as yet a by no means universally recognized thing, to try to study human beliefs, behavior, feelings and so on as facts within the world – to study them empirically, and as displaying power, rather than studying them as topics for evaluation. We are often more interested in the truth of ideas rather than their power, especially in the case of religions and ideologies. But the primary emphasis of the modern study of religion is on the descriptive and historical mode of approaching the phenomena, without importing into the study normative assumptions (we hope) from any one tradition. The reasons for this range from philosophical considerations to institutional concerns. They are as follows:

(1) Religions are important ingredients in the processes of human history, in that they have effects on human behavior. In order to estimate these effects, and indeed in order to estimate the force of any theories we may entertain about the degree to which religion is an epiphenomenon of other factors, it is necessary to describe religion in a "neutral"

29

way, that is without importing into the descriptions assumptions about the truth or otherwise of the actors' beliefs, etc. This is not to say that in the last resort we might not turn to a (Christian or other) theological interpretation of human history. But we can describe the ways religions work without coming down on any side about the truth or worth of the phenomena, but seeing them as factors, as we have said, in the ongoing processes of human history.

(2) Humanly, we need to understand what religions are as meaning-systems, and so, as the Native American proverb has it, we should not judge a person till we have walked a mile in his moccasins. An important part of modern methods of anthropological exploration in religion is the use of informed empathy: that is gathering the data and mustering the imagination so that we may know what it is like to be the other. It is partly for this reason that people enter into dialogue: one way to find out about the other is to enter into conversation and to begin to see the world from her point of view.

(3) As citizens of the world we ought to be able to empathize with diverse cultures and points of view. It is a defect of much education that it neglects the use of the imagination in trying to understand people of a different kind (for boys to understand what it is like to be a girl; for the white American to understand the thoughtworld of the Native American; for the Muslim to understand the Buddhist, and so on). It is important at the level of politics: know who you are dealing with. But it is also profoundly important in the interchanges of religious people.

(4) Institutionally the modern democratic state typically has a plural population. Greater Los Angeles is the greatest multiethnic conglomeration in the history of the world; but many other Western and non-Western cities possess a strong degree of cultural and religious variegation. The study of religions in our institutions, especially in the universities, needs to reflect this pluralism, out of fairness if nothing else. But also because the logic of the modern approach to the humanities involves cultural and other kinds of openness, and the artificial restriction of the study of religion, either

by eliminating it altogether as in many universities, or by confining it to Christianity, as in some others, in the West, cannot be institutionally justified.

But it is also worth noting that we cannot confine the study of religions to religions (to put the matter a little paradoxically). Our field must extend beyond the boundaries of the definition of religion or of what is a religion, to cover so-called "secular" worldviews and worldview-themes, and this is so for the following reasons.

(1) In practice the various worldviews, both religious and non-religious (that is, given any traditional definition of what a religion is), are in interaction: Marxism and Buddhism in Tibet, humanism and Protestant Christianity in Sweden, and so on. It seems more rational to treat together those things which play, so to speak, in the same league.

(2) The concept *religion* is a Western one. It has rightly been criticized by, among others, Wilfred Cantwell Smith (Smith, 1963). Had the comparative study of religion started in India or China or Africa, the lines would have been drawn differently. If it were *darśana*-s we were considering we would not erect a wall between Christianities and humanisms. Similarly with analogous Chinese and other concepts.

(3) The modern notion of religion has been defined institutionally and has importance in such matters as taxation, education and so on. It may be that from this point of view the relatively narrow conception of religion in Western law is justified: but it itself expresses an ideological distinction, and academe does not have to follow suit.

(4) In any event, ideological motifs, such as the variety of nationalisms that have emerged roughly in the period since the French Revolution, have a symbolic and often an ultimate character. Most people who have died violently in modern times have died in wars, usually of a nationalistic character: so it is common to make the ultimate sacrifice for one's country; and the nation demands of the living huge amounts in taxation. Its symbols are secular equivalents of religious ones, and often combine with religious ones. The analysis of secular worldviews reveals similarities, though not identities perhaps, to traditionally conceived religions.

31

(5) There are three main ways of defining *religion* and they all point towards a stretching of the concept towards secular worldviews. One way is in terms of content. Because of the contrast between Theravada Buddhism and Jainism on the one hand and the Western theisms on the other, and between philosophical Taoism and both arms of this polarity, the best we can do in regard to content is to have a definition which makes use of Wittgensteinian family-resemblance. But then the "outsider", say Vietnamese Marxism, no longer looks quite so much outside. Another way is psychologically and existentially, such as Tillich's famous invoking of the notion of *ultimate concern* (Tillich, 1957): but by such a test the Vietnamese Marxist dying heroically at Dien Bien Phu is as much religious (or more so) as the Scottish Presbyterian who dies in her bed. Then we can define a religion through the use of such formal characteristics as the six dimensions aforementioned. But in this case we can draw attention to the way we find these in Chinese Marxism as well as in Theravada Buddhism. So it is hard to produce a notion which will seal religions off from so-called secular ideologies. (Even the concept of the Transcendent, which we shall find useful in delineating some major traditional belief-systems, cannot be used unambiguously.)

For these reasons we prefer to see the study of religions at the empirical level as non-finite — that is, as stretching out into the analysis of secular worldviews. The concept *worldview* then is used as an umbrella-word for belief-systems, and their accompanying practice, whether religious or secular. Of worldviews there are two species in ordinary English parlance — religious and secular. Our modern study of religion may start with religions, and draw most of its sustenance from there; but it moves also into secular worldviews. At the descriptive level we refer to the study as *worldview analysis*.

We distinguish between doing Christian (or some other kind of) theology and worldview analysis, in that the latter is descriptive, historical, empirical, whereas the former involves the construction, articulation or endorsement of a worldview (Smart, 1973b, pp. 9–52). Much of philosophy is involved ultimately in the same sort of exercise. Both terms "theology" and "philosophy" have grown up in Western universities as parallel terms. But they both stay silent about their origins. This is one reason why often "theology" secretly, or not so secretly, imports a view of the world in which Christianity is the norm. This can no longer be the case. This is why we consider that "theology" ought always to have a prefix: "Christian" or "Catholic", "Jewish or "Reform Jewish", and so on. Basically you can only do theology from within a community, or in relation to a community. It is not a neutral thing: it involves expressing one's faith, and typically that of the community to which you belong. So in our task of constructing a Christian theology we are going beyond worldview analysis or the strict history of religions. Yet in so going beyond we also are starting the process of translating our words into data. What we produce is an instance of the doctrinal dimension of religion. Likewise when we worship we are part of the ritual or practical dimension of religious life. In this sense our work has piety, and is meant to stimulate reflections which will help to uncover the vision of the Divine in which we believe.

It is of course true that Christian theology may make a lot of use of worldview analysis, history of religions. The Christian theologian may use tools and techniques which are the same as those of the analyst and historian. But she is still building up a system and a vision, and doing that is manifesting faith and manifesting religiousness. But because she is making religion, she is part of the data, in the long run, of the modern study of religion as worldview analysis.

Not everyone is agreed about the scope of religious studies, but we here take it to exist at two levels, at what may be called for short the descriptive and philosophical levels. At the first level, we are primarily focusing on descriptions, histories, empirical explanations, of religious and more generally worldviewish, facts. What led Augustine to his conversion? How many Sikhs are there in Canada? What

33

are the relations between modern Hinduism and Indian nationalism? What have been the causes of anti-Semitism in Europe? What changes are happening in Romanian interpretations of Marxism? Is worship declining among Muslims who have migrated to England? Such questions belong to the descriptive analysis of religions and world-views. At the philosophical level there are such questions as: By what criteria can we judge the truth as between religions? Which of Gandhi's ideas seem to be the most fruitful in struggling against war? Is Christ the Son of God? Such questions more directly concern values and truth. There are some scholars who are uneasy about admitting these questions into the academic study of religion; but we consider the main reason for this is that they fear a recurrence of establishmentarianism, the reduction of the study of religion to a Christian, Jewish or other enclave again. But there is no doubt that some at least of these questions emerge not only in the minds of students, many of whom are involved in their own individual long searches, but in the minds of anyone who begins to reflect about the data of religion. Now those who are happy enough with such philosophical reflections in the study of religion occasionally think in terms of using "theology" *tout court* to cover such reflections. We do not think that this is wise, and prefer therefore to use the phrase "religious reflection" for the process of judging worldviews and perhaps even constructing a new worldview on the basis of what emerges in knowledge about the religions.

A word too is necessary about the term "secular". It is a word which conceals great ambiguity. One sense of it (as in "the secular State") is "pluralistic". India is a secular State in this sense, but it happens to be a very religious place, and not secular in the other sense. In the other sense "secular" means roughly non-religious. Now naturally this is as hard to define as the concept of the religious. But we think of many modern industrial workers in the West as being secularized in the sense that they have lost the traditional worldviews, they do not involve themselves much in traditional rituals, except perhaps at weddings and funerals;

and so on. It was this second sense of "secular" that Harvey Cox celebrated in *The Secular City* (1963). It may turn out that pluralism leads to secularism, though we doubt it. It is true that the pluralism of certain modern democracies owes a lot to the Enlightenment which helped also to generate modern industrial society. But basically the two ideas are not really related. And it is by an irony that the chief place where the older conception in Europe of the relation between Church and State persists is where secular worldviews – Marxism in particular – hold sway. As the 18th Century Englishman had to affirm the Thirty-Nine Articles if he were to go to Oxbridge and pursue a successful career in Government or the Army, so now preferment in China and until lately East Germany depends on affirming the Marxist articles. But of course a secular ideology can be pluralistic: in principle liberal humanism is. It is in this pluralistic framework of the open society that the university chiefly flourishes, and it is in that same pluralistic university that we would expect the study of religion to take its modern, plural form.

It is in its descriptive, historical form that the modern study of religion mirrors the world with its many and often overlapping worldviews. We need to say more about it than that it is non-finite, that is that it reaches out into the analysis of secular as well as religious worldviews. It is also polymethodic – bringing to bear the disciplines and methods of history, sociology, anthropology, phenomenology and so on (Smart, 1983). This is so because of a number of factors.

(1) Religions and worldviews are both ancient and modern. Modern ones can be explored anthropologically, but it is hard to do this at all in regard to the past. We therefore need documents, texts, inscriptions, ruins, remains, skulls, pictures and so forth. So we need philology even more, and archaeology, and iconography, etc., in order to diagnose the actual religion of the ancients.

(2) Because of the existence of the six dimensions we find that different disciplines must significantly be brought to bear. Doctrines and myths have to be explored through texts;

but rituals cannot so easily be explored that way, and religious feeling and experience may require other methods to get into.

(3) The existence of similar and dissimilar motifs in differing traditions stimulates the comparative method and phenomenological typology.

(4) In looking at the religious aspect of human behavior, feelings, institutions, and so on we are abstracting from the whole of human existence; just as in economics we abstract from the totality of human life that aspect which is economic. So we are cutting the cake, so to speak, horizontally, and for the vertical slicing we need the languages and histories and sociologies which go to make up area studies – the investigator of Graeco-Roman religion needs to be a classicist in some degree; the explorer of Hinduism and Indian Buddhism an Indologist; the documenter of Chinese religions a Sinologist; and so forth.

So, in brief, the modern study of religion is non-finite, plural, and polymethodic. If it has an emphasis in its descriptive expression, that emphasis is upon informed empathy: walking in others' moccasins. Its descriptive emphasis is also upon the power, rather than on the truth or value, of ideas and religious practices. Evaluation can come later. It tries to depict the multifarious world of worldviews, and the symbols and institutions which give them dynamism and solidity. It reflects the plural world in which the modern citizen of the globe finds herself, and it provides the immediate context for the creation of a Christian theology sensitive to the global city's nature.

The Study of Religion and Christianity
Does the modern study of religion make a difference to the way we look at Christianity? And does that affect the way we may set about constructing, or reconstructing, a Christian worldview? On the first question there are several important things to say.

(1) Because modern religionists have become a little suspicious of the reification implied by such notions as Buddhism and Christianity, there is much greater emphasis

upon the pluralism of any tradition. Either we should stop using the singular abstraction "Christianity" or we should simply break out into the plural and talk of "Christianities". The resemblance of Ethiopian Christianity to the Christianity of the Baptists of Arkansas is not great, and like divergences can be seen up and down Christendom. It is true that modern times have seen a certain convergence, partly because of the ecumenical movement. But there may be limits to this convergence, and the ethos of the ecumenists themselves is towards a more federal approach, so that individual denominations do not have to give up their separate styles and identities. So though the modern study of religion, so alive to regional variations and the proliferation of subtraditions, does not compel us to adopt a particular worldview, it does encourage a certain *federalism* in theology. The Indian example, of the modern Hindu ideology which seeks to see all faiths as pointing somehow towards the same truth, should not in our opinion be followed in too exact a fashion (for it is at the end of the day so difficult to square with the facts of most religious life); but it does point towards an analogous federalism of spirit with which we might approach the varieties of Christianities.

(2) The modern study of religion can exhibit through a variety of examples ways in which religions are highly selective about their pasts. In an important sense modern Hinduism is indeed modern, a new religion of the 19th and 20th centuries: though for a new religion it has very ancient roots. What has happened is that modern exponents of the Hindu way of life have produced a kind of retrospective synthesis, largely under the aegis of a modernized Advaita Vedanta. But similarly what now passes for Christianity is often the result of a selective blend of ancient and modern motifs. As we shall see there is nothing necessarily wrong with this: indeed such selectivity about the past is inevitable. But it raises of course questions about whether the categories we use about the past have not outlived their value. Thus it is common to use such divisions, in thinking about Christianity in the academic context, as New Testament,

Patristics, Church history and so forth. But of course what counts as Church history is determined in part by what counts as the Church, and that involves a normative judgment. And many students study the New Testament (rather than the emergence of Christian movements among the religions of the Roman Empire, including whatever it was that is now retrospectively categorized as Judaism) because the New Testament is regarded as a normative book, rather than just one (though the most important) source book for the earliest days of the new religion. Now all this suggests that we should be more conscious about our own resource selectivity in picking out those things from the various pasts of Christianities which we consider to be the most authoritative and significant. As we shall see, there are deep epistemological questions about the status of Biblical and other sources of doctrine.

(3) Because the modern study of religion is less inclined than traditional studies to be so oriented to texts and is more eager to look at "religion on the ground" it is liable more clearly to see ways in which Christianities are shifting South. In fact a major part of Christian adherents belong to the Southern continents – to Africa and South America. It happens that recent political and economic events have bred Christian theologies of protest from those parts of the world, and this would reinforce our concern that the vision which a Christian systematic theology can offer takes account of these Southern perspectives. (Incidentally, another recent theological lobby, not now primarily from the South, comes out of feminism, and that is important too to embrace in our "federal" theory.)

(4) As we have indicated any modern *darśana* has to be relevant to the "other" religions, and here religious studies can supply the data of world history if we are successfully to tell the Christian story in the full ambience of world history. It is of course in no way the task of religious studies to offer some agreed criteria for determining what are the signs and actualities of the work of the Spirit, that *antaryāmin* or Inner Controller, in world history. But reflection upon the data of the religions, once we have entered into their various

meanings, and into the spirit of each (and all this is the proper task of the modern study of religion) may assist us to draw a picture of that process of the Spirit. To anticipate in brief: the other religious traditions are ways in which the Divine keeps us as Christians and them too honest. They are mutual critics and examples. Not everything about Buddhism, of course, is good: but neither is everything about the Christianities to which we are heirs.

(5) The six-dimensional analysis of religions can help us to keep our *collage* which points to the Transcendent anchored in the realities of the spiritual and ethical life. For by applying the analysis we can always ask what the implications are of a given doctrine for the moral, social and religious life; and how the narratives of the Bible or of world history which we re-express help to illuminate private and public worship and social action.

(6) The phenomenology of religion helps crossculturally to illuminate various facets of Christianities. Sacraments, negative theology, worship, the mystical tradition – these and many other motifs are clarified by seeing them in action across the board. So we can proceed to review Christianity itself anew from this fresh and wide perspective; and this will have effects on the formulation of our *darśana*.

(7) Given, as we have seen, that the modern study of religion branches out to become worldview analysis, we become clearer about the pervasiveness of syncretism. It is a strange thing that the Churches have so often been worried about religion-religion syncretism but relatively blind to religion-secular worldview syncretism. Is it worse to turn Isis into the Virgin than to inject nationalism into Christian faith? It happens that blending (to use a better and less stirring word) is inevitable: but we should be alert to it. This is where the modern study of religion may help us in self-analysis. If we are to espouse a blend of the Gospel and modern liberalism (for instance) it is well to be clear about it.

The Nature of Doctrinal Schemes (Smart, 1958, pp. 11–16)
Essentially, in constructing a new Christian worldview, incorporating the varied accents and motifs which we have

briefly touched on above, we are producing a doctrinal scheme. As we have said, such a doctrinal scheme has a practical aim: it incorporates both one vision of the Divine and an encouragement to spiritual development and ethical action. It has as far as possible to be both realistic to our real world, in this postcolonial epoch, and coherent, though not necessarily altogether free of internal tensions. But what kind of coherence can we expect? It is not reasonable to suppose that in any important sense a doctrinal scheme functions like a deductive system, though there are systems, such as Aquinas' *Summa*, which have an almost Euclidean appearance. But this is misleading, for though as a philosopher Aquinas felt he had to produce a systematic account of the reshaped Aristoteleanism that underlay his worldview-presentation, his scheme also depended upon revelation, i.e. mainly upon Biblical sources (as well as some of the Fathers). Indeed the fact that insofar as a worldview is expressed through a set of propositions (utterances with varied properties − I include performative utterances which do not rate as candidates for being true or false as possible members of the class of propositions that express a worldview), that set of propositions does not except trivially interconnect deductively, is the main reason why I use the looser-sounding word "scheme" rather than "system". Since such a large swathe of terms used about God or nirvana are used analogically, that is not in their literal "this-worldly" sense, even their normal this-worldly entailments will not apply: that "God is our Father" entails that he is male is, to say the least, doubtful − since this is so, then there are very great restrictions upon the absolutely systematic character of any worldview taken as a whole. Even the most philosophical and rigorous aspects of Mahayana Buddhist thought are embedded in a wider worldview with non-rigorous elements (respect for the Buddha, for instance, and the Bodhisattva ideal). In brief a doctrinal scheme is a *scheme* rather than a rigorous system, and this is one reason for the flexibility of a doctrinal scheme in itself. Often ecclesiastical authority may impose external rigor, but that is another story: there may be severe social restrictions upon what is interpreted as the "true" doctrines of a given group.

Another way we can look at a doctrinal scheme and its accompaniments by way of narrative and ethico-legal judgments is as a kind of organism. The reason for this metaphor is that the way parts within a scheme function will depend on what other elements are there. Thus though the dog's nose is analogous to a human nose, the role played by a dog's nose is in all sorts of ways different from the way the human nose operates. Again vertebrae in an upright animal have a rather different function from that which they have in a four-legged creature. Similarly, elements in a doctrinal scheme will have an organic placement. Thus the opening lines of *John* in the New Testament echo the opening of *Genesis*, but now the scene of creation is greatly altered by the fact that Christ is seen as the Creator. The two accounts, obviously, overlap: but they are also organically different because of the other elements in the respective systems of pre-Christian Judaism and Christianity.

Another metaphor one can use is of the *collage*. A doctrinal scheme brings together into a coherent whole (though what coherence means in *collages* needs thinking about), (Smart, 1973b, pp. 20–52) a series of often very disparate elements which the tradition has picked up along the way: fragments, one may say, of revelation, glimpses of the Divine. Woven into that *collage* will be assumptions from the dominant culture, though the history of the Christian tradition has seen many disputes as to how much attention one needs to pay to surrounding worldviews and worldview themes. What has Athens to do with Jerusalem? What has Cambridge to do with Calvary? We shall, as it happens, argue that our collage should incorporate elements not merely from the major Christian pasts – Orthodoxy, Catholicism and Protestantism – but also from liberal humanism: and to this we shall add by way of mixture themes from world cultures. In this we are leaning more to the tradition of natural theology, though we shall argue that it must be conceived very differently – rather as a "natural theology of religious experience". The metaphor of the collage underlines the disparate source of the elements in a scheme, as often the collage may use such diverse materials as paint, wool, cotton, metal, cardboard and so forth. Similarly our collage will pick up pieces of history, metaphysics, texts, experiences, ritual patterns and so forth.

But it may be argued that secretly we are involved in a contradiction. If adding "Christ" to creation makes a difference, so does adding humanism to the Gospel, or ideas of *bhakti* to the Christian life. So we are altering the Gospel, perhaps beyond recognition (it may be objected). There must of course be some sense in which things have changed and did change earlier at whatever point we stop. Is the writing of St Gregory Palamas really in the same key as the Gospel as first preached? Would Paul have quite recognized Aquinas? Would Peter have understood Calvin? The question is, however, whether the spirit remains the same: And here there is a vital way in which in order to stay the same you have to change. This is an important hermeneutical principle.

Change and Hermeneutics (Smart, 1973b, pp. 9–52)
Before we expound this principle let us put in one disclaimer. We do not say that we just have to accept everything that Paul or the Biblical texts have to say. We are committed to the self-critical character of Christianity. But we shall argue in subsequent passages about how we need to change to stay the same on the assumption that we *do* want to stay the same. We certainly of course wish to be loyal to the Christian tradition as we understand it and this of course implies loyalty to the thinking of the earliest Church, insofar as we can penetrate to it.

In order to make the points we need to we shall construct an admittedly oversimplified model of a religious tradition. Thus we can think of Christianity (as we have seen the very use of the singular involves a simplification) as comprised by a population of believers and practisers, not to mention a penumbra of semi-believers; and these for simplicity again we may call the Church. This Church is incarnated in such things as buildings, rituals, the formal and informal behavior of believers, and so on. Now in order that we may understand their behavior we need to pay attention to the values and beliefs transmitted through the institution. We find that these – whether abstract-sounding doctrines, or mythic narratives, or ethical and legal teachings and inclinations – are hooked up to a central Focus. That is, they are essentially *about* that Focus: the doctrines delineate him or her, the narratives tell its story, the values express service to him. That Focus can be called "God in Christ". So singing a hymn, or giving to others, or reciting a creed or thinking about the Trinity – all these activities are ways in which Christians in their lives reflect the Focus, or (to put it another way) paint a picture of the Focus.

Now for the sake still of simplification let us suppose that each age possesses a dominant picture of the Focus – a dominant way in which both in their thoughts and in their lives Christians express the Christian Gospel. Let us divide the time from Christ to now into centuries, which we shall represent by Roman numerals. Thus XV stands for the 15th century of the Common Era. We can now look upon the Christian Church or tradition as an institution (a group of people) housing, so to speak, a gallery of pictures – the pictures are numbered from I to XX. Now it is the task of the historian to try, among other things, to reveal these pictures. There are considerable problems of course in the way of his conveying adequately what it was to believe certain things in Paul's day or Augustine's or even Leo XIII's. For insofar as he uses the language of Paul or these others he is in the XXth century using it in a different context. Since the context enters into the situation do we not change the picture by expressing it in such a different milieu? Is this not what follows from what we said earlier about the organic nature of doctrinal schemes? Let us consider the problem.

If I simply affirm the text of the Bible (for instance) but in a greatly changed milieu – if, that is, I affirm the Ist century picture in the XXth century – am I not in effect presenting a picture which can be written as I (XX); or if we affirm the picture presented at Nicaea, am I not really affirming IV (XX)? So even if we use the exact words of the Bible, as many so-called fundamentalists love to do, then

43

we are already changing the picture. But if in order to deal with the problem of milieu-transformation we change the picture, though conforming it as best we can to Paul's message, we are producing XX (I). We are changing the picture. In brief, if we do not change the picture we change the picture and of course if we change the picture we change the picture. So we change the picture.

It could perhaps be thought that there are ways of changing the picture which really allow it to stay the same. Is not the person who changes the picture at least aware of what he is doing? The so-called fundamentalist may be blundering into changes he cannot perceive.

Now there are various reasons, as it happens, which we need to spell out later why we need today as Christians to be adventurous in getting away from an uncritical acceptance of the scriptures as they stand. So in this work we take a position far removed from the so-called fundamentalist. The saints and scholars of the tradition are for us as much a source of authority as the canonical texts. From that perspective it is not possible for us to take the "evangelical option", though we adhere to the principles of feeling enunciated in the beginning, that we should treat out fellows with loving respect. In fact the very Biblically centered option is just one among the possible pictures in the Church's gallery. The so-called fundamentalist is exercising one of the choices in resource selectivity. He is looking on the Bible – and that too interpreted according to certain principles – as the most central resource.

In one way we are more traditionalist. As far as we are concerned the Christian tradition's doctrines are *all* the pictures. But though we wish to draw sustenance from all these, we also feel that to do justice to the spirit even of early Christianity we need to change the picture. If Paul wandered into our house and spoke like Paul would he not seem bizarre, indeed unhinged? To be true to what he was trying to put across we would have to put across a different picture. This is why *milieu-transformation itself dictates content-transformation.*

This is a continual source of hermeneutical trouble. It

would be disingenuous, having transformed content, to say that what we say is what Paul said. If we are altering the message in the interests of staying with the essential spirit of what went before, yet we must make it clear that our message is not the I-message or the IX-message: we live neither in the I nor the IX century. So though we may aim to be loyal to the spirit of Paul, we are shifting from his collage, and producing our own collage.

Which Are the Right Changes?

But the fact that we have to change does not of course guarantee that the changes which we do make are the right changes. The same applies to the past. This is why it is not always enough to be traditionalist. The traditionalist is himself forced to change, but he incorporates as much of the gallery of pictures I-XX into it as possible. But suppose the Church took some wrong turnings? Naturally, this possibility cannot be excluded by any Protestant: but even the most traditionalist Orthodox must admit it (and anyway he thinks that the Western Church took a wrong turning with the *filioque* and subsequent events). By contrast with the traditionalist, there is the prophetic type: the person who produces great criticisms of the past and of the pictures which both past and present produce. She may delineate a fiery new picture, let us call it XXa, which claims to be nearer the spirit of the faith, for whatever reason, than the conventional picture XX. Now for the historian of religion – the Religious Studies descriptivist – it is easy enough to cope with the problem. She claims to be a Christian: she is criticizing Christianity from a Christian perspective. She is in some continuity with the rest of the tradition. So we just add her Christianity to the other Christianities. And even if the rest of Christians think that she is heretical, no matter: from our angle, normative questions of whether a person is a heretic do not worry us. They simply have to be registered as further facts about the situation. Norms transform into data – that is, so long as we are looking at matters descriptively.

But as Christian *collagistes*, as worldview-constructors,

we have to make judgments about those who in affirming and endorsing tradition value it one way and those who prophetically value it another way. Now since, as we shall later indicate, it is an essential ingredient in scientific and other kinds of exploration of the truth about the world that we need to be critical of received opinion, it should not be surprising if we cannot avoid a critical stance about the tradition which we wish to interpret. A special need in today's world, and not just in regard to religions and worldviews, is the evolution of a critical theory of traditions. For after all, traditions nurture our psyches and anchor us in time as well as in space: they help to form human identities. But we need to be critical of them, for they can be affirmed too easily in an obscurantist way, and they can generate such strong inner ties that groups may be tempted to be hostile and paranoid about one another.

So in constructing a *darśana* we need to be critical. Part of that comes naturally from within, since there are obvious tensions between certain elements in Christianity, for instance the call to love, and certain collages which have dominated sections of the Christian faith, such as the too easy synthesis between Christianity and nationalism. Part of the criticism can come from without: if the advance of science shows us certain things about the scale of the universe then the puny cosmologies of erstwhile times need to be jettisoned; and if they themselves depended in part on Papal backing or Biblical texts, then so much the worse for our uncritical acceptance of authorities, whether paper of otherwise, in the Church.

But it should be noted of course that the prophetic and critical stance is not directed just to inner problems. The Christian may well have her prophetic criticisms of our times. This is why it is important for us to see clearly the nature of the Transcendent, for the Christian has that higher vantage point from which to criticize the shallow materialisms of the world, and the blindness to glories which might help to transform our ignorance and errancy.

We have still left unanswered the question about, given that we need to present a collage which is different from its predecessors in order to express continuity with them, *which* of the possible collages is truest to the spirit of the faith. We cannot easily answer this, though arguments about the question of priorities among the elements of Christianity as found in the mass of Christian traditions will emerge from time to time. We shall be satisfied if our *darśana* can prove to be, at least for some, appealing, coherent, challenging and critically loyal to the tradition. We present a picture. It is for others to admire it or detest it.

The Bible

Because we need to change the message in order to repeat it, and because we are not always solely interested in repeating it, since the Church from earliest times may have taken wrong turnings, our attitudes sit fairly loosely to Biblical or other authority. It happens that critical enquiry into the Biblical texts has reached such a point that there is no general agreement on precisely what Jesus said, or what the early Church believed about him. The liberal-academic solvents have gnawed away at the rusts of Biblical certainty. It therefore seems nonsense to pretend that the Bible has doctrinal or narrative authority. We accept of course its central liturgical place in the Christian life as it is usually understood. But we shall not, in this attempt at a Christian *darśana*, cite Biblical proof texts as if the critical work of the last century and a half did not exist, nor will we cite them as if there were any kind of absolute agreement as to what they reveal about Jesus. They are testimonies to what the Church subscribed to when the canon was being formed, of course, and this is important to us as a segment of Church history. But we do not even subscribe to that Jaina thought that the further we get from Christ the less enlightened we are. The development of the Christianities itself may be an important testimony to Christ, and there is no reason to be excessively servile to the ancient in the traditions. All this creates epistemological problems for us, of course; and we shall address them later. But let us make one observation about belief, which is relevant to the whole Christian-theological enterprise.

47

Belief is a disposition to do things, think things, respond to questions in a certain way: but simplifying, it can be seen as the disposition to affirm a statement. If I believe that there is cheese in the refrigerator I will be inclined to say if relevantly asked "There is cheese in the refrigerator". Now with complex and practical beliefs, we may know what to say but not know fully what it means. That itself may be elucidated more fully in the future, perhaps under crossquestioning. So it is with the beliefs of the tradition: their meanings may be revealed under history's crossquestioning. For instance, despite Paul's remarks about slaves, Christians may come to feel that slavery is incompatible with the true brotherhood and sisterhood of humans, under God. So it is not as though revelation ceases in the earliest days. We can see already of course in the tradition how the community's beliefs about Jesus as partly recorded in the New Testament were taken to imply the Trinity doctrine. In a sense of course the beliefs of the community underwent a change, but they were seen retrospectively as being somehow contained in a nutshell in the original attitudes toward Christ. From this perspective, then, there is what could be called developing revelation. Those who merely look to the past for authority forget that maybe the best is yet to be. The tradition is in geological time very young indeed, and in historical time not all that old. The future may shine more gloriously than the past, and the meaning of the faith may be becoming clearer as we pass forward in history, even in advance of that Last Trump which promises what Hick has called "eschatological verification". (Actually, it is in the nature of transcendental worldviews that they should be mysterious, so even the sound of the Last Trump may prove ambiguous, and when we see "face to face", the light may be just as blinding as the darkness.) So early beliefs themselves may undergo developments and qualifications, often as our beliefs about people may develop when we see their characters unfold.

We can indeed make use of biography as a metaphor. If we consider the life of Roncalli up to just before Vatican

II, we would get a good idea of his character; but there is no doubt that the event of Vatican II and beyond – the whole unfolding of his practical concern with Aggiornamento – would make a difference to the way we viewed him, though without overthrowing what we knew before, necessarily. So it may be with the Christianities. Their possibilities may become more apparent as their trajectories reach into the future. The character of Christianity may become more conspicuous. In all this, then, we need to be sceptical of a fixed view of the past.

This somewhat relates to contemporary debates about texts and hermeneutics. A certain subjectivism has been expressed by Gadamer about entering into past minds, the minds of authors in their context and culture; and the attention of some has shifted towards an interest in the way literary critics often deal with texts, as participating so to say in the life of the text way beyond the intentions of the author. Our position about traditions has greater affinity to the latter position, when it comes to our worldview construction. But in regard to the pursuit of descriptive religious studies we are on the side of those like Dilthey who stress the possibilities of empathy and entering thus into other people's worldviews, both ancient (difficult) and contemporary (much easier). But in that as worldview constructors (rather than worldview analysts) we ride loose to origins, we acknowledge that we are not just interpreting the Bible or any past texts, but are developing a picture. We consider it is disingenuous to present worldview-construction simply as interpretation. Interpretation should stick to re-presenting the meanings of texts, as they were conceived or as later they have been used.

In brief, we take up the option of content-transformation within the context of the changing world milieu of the Christian message, and we shall be involved in worldview-construction in the light of the modern study of religion, partly because it is into that wider context that the Christian traditions are now projecting themselves in today's "one world".

Worldview Analysis as a Prelude to Worldview Construction
We have looked at some of the characteristics of worldviews
considered as doctrinal schemes and value-systems. It is
useful to conclude this chapter by summarizing the
characteristics of worldview analysis as we have delineated
it, and to show the usefulness of this approach as a context
within which to do some worldview-construction. The
modern study of religion can be seen to have the following
characteristics.

(1) It is plural, dealing impartially with the many secular
worldviews and religions of the globe, whether old or new.

(2) It is not finite, in that it includes consideration of
belief-systems lying outside the frontiers of traditional
religions: it is open-ended in the direction of political science,
so that it includes political ideologies, especially forms of
nationalism, in its scope, and in the direction of philosophy,
so that it also sees existentialism and scientific humanism
as possible competitors of traditional religions and as among
worldviews to be analysed.

(3) It treats of worldviews both historically and
systematically, and tries to enter into the viewpoint of
believers through structured empathy.

(4) It makes thematic comparisons which form the basis
of a phenomenology which will among other things yield
some of the basic crosscultural concepts to be used in a world
language about religions and worldviews and which can be
used to rid the study of religion of its too Western clothing.

(5) It is polymethodic and uses many disciplines, partly
to illuminate the various dimensions of religion.

(6) It aims to show the power (and sometimes the lack
of power) of religious and other ideas and symbols in
interaction with other aspects of human existence.

(7) It can set the scene for an educated understanding of
our world, and also for personal pursuits of truth and
growth.

Since any new Christian doctrinal scheme has to be
realistic and fit in with the real world, it has to have plural
outreach. Since it will blend ideas drawn from religious
tradition with themes from modern worldviews, it is

important that it is not confined intellectually to the ghetto of religion or the parish of the West. Since structured empathy is not only a method of religious exploration but also a preliminary to other attitudes, it has something important to say to Christians and others about the right way to deal with human beings who have different values from ours. Since in order to enter the wider world, and also for philosophical reasons related to the challenges to Christian belief in a plural world, it is necessary to pay attention to phenomenological categories, it is vital that these crosscultural types be made use of in constructing a modern Christian *darśana*. Since the doctrinal dimension is only one among many it is important that worldview-construction be sensitive to the various ways in which doctrines relate to ethics, experience, ritual, narrative and institutions. Further, though worldview-construction has an overtly truth-seeking and value-affirming role, it cannot neglect power: ultimately if a Christian theology lacks power to move people it has little importance. So the fact that the modern study of religion can set the scene for the baffling but exciting pursuit of truth and spiritual growth in the modern world means that it has peculiar relevance to those who perhaps have not yet made up their mind, but wish to have presented to them a vision of the real world and of what perchance exists Beyond.

We now turn to some matters of content: a sketch, first, of the world and its worldviews, and then, more significantly, a preliminary account of the phenomenology of religion with which we shall be working and which will provide some of the categories for clothing our Christian doctrinal scheme.

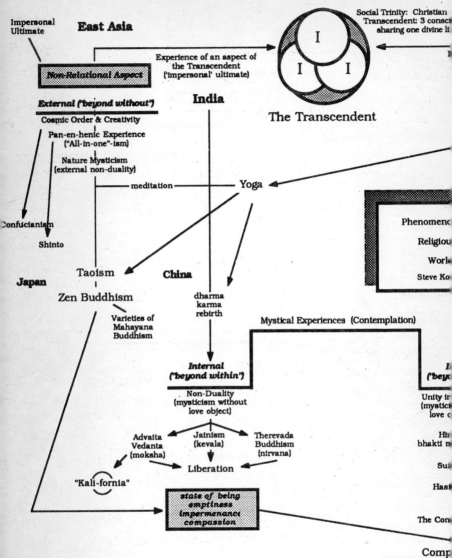

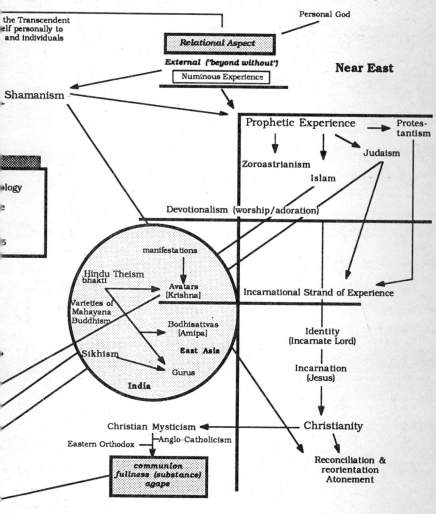

(The Yogi and the Devotee)

3

The World Situation
and the Phenomenology
of Religion

The World Situation

It is important that a Christian worldview be presented in
the real context, which is relevantly found in the mental
geography of the world – the various religions and secular
ideologies which set the scene of human activities. There
are, of course, other factors that we need to see clearly –
the new economic structure of the world, political
polarizations and so on. But as we come towards the end
of the XXth century, it is useful to bear in mind the main
configurations of belief. It is among these configurations that
our argument will dance. One may simplify the world
situation by seeing our globe as divided into so many
"tectonic plates" of belief, with many of the strains and
earthquakes running along the divisions between them, and
other strains occurring where older configurations have been
overlaid in the contemporary power distribution. Before we
list these main areas and kinds of belief, it is important to
remember two rather opposite tendencies in today's world:
the division of the planet's land surfaces, and some of its
sea, into nation-States; and the emergence of the transnational corporations, which are a main factor in the
creation of a (roughly speaking) single world economic
system. The tendency to nationalism has covered the earth,
save the Antarctic, with a complete array of nations; and
generally speaking there is a sentiment, e.g. in the United
Nations, that no one nation should interfere in the territories
of another – even though of course all countries are bound
together most dramatically in the threat of universal war
and less so in the interchanges between different parts of

the economic system. But bearing these tensions in mind, let us now turn to consider the main blocs into which the world as a whole is divided.

(1) For convenience we begin with Western democratic states of primarily the North of the planet, which we may call the *Transchristian West*. It is Transchristian because the dominant past culture of Western Europe, North American and Australasia has been Christian, with a varying Jewish admixture (culturally very important since the time of Napoleon). This religious culture has greatly faded, though it retains vigor in North America especially; and it has been transformed through the power of the Enlightenment and liberal democratic humanism. Now it is entering a new phase because of the influence of certain Eastern ideas since World War II and because of the blending into such societies of many non-Western migrants, who boost the already established pluralism of democratic societies.

(2) The next main bloc to consider, logically, is in part another offspring of European thought, the *Marxist bloc*. Since World War II Marxist governments for various reasons (Soviet occupation, successful guerrilla warfare, Vietnamese conquest, etc.) have been established in a large number of countries from the Elbe to Kamchatka, and from Ho Chi Minh City to Warsaw. Although there are tensions between some of the regimes, e.g. between Yugoslavia and Moscow, Albania and most everybody else, and between China and the Soviet bloc, the patterns of political rule are much the same. They involve the imposition of Marxist ideology, and the restriction (and sometimes the attempted suppression) of traditional religions. These regimes are the successors of the establishment systems of post-Reformation Europe, and operate the principle *cuius regio eius religio* in a new form: *cuius regio eius ideologia*. Despite this the older religions survive in milder and stronger forms – vigorous in Romania, Poland and Tibet, for instance; less so in Russia, Czechoslovakia and China; and weak or underground in Albania. This bloc also has one or two "outriding" instances, notably South Yemen and Cuba. In 1989 the Marxist bloc

has undergone great changes, towards the ideas and institutions of the Transchristian West.

(3) A great swathe of the middle planet is occupied by predominantly Muslim countries, ranging from Indonesia, through Malaysia, Bangladesh, Pakistan, Iran, the Arab lands as far as Mauretania, and on to West and East Africa. This *Islamic crescent* has a strong presence in international politics, and because of the large number of migrants in some Western countries, shows itself as an important factor even in the Transchristian West. Also India, though predominantly Hindu, has a very substantial Muslim population and must count as one of the major Islamic countries in the world.

(4) There are traditional Asian societies which have not been overcome by Marxism and which maintain a generally plural religious situation, with dominant motifs such as Hinduism in India and the Himalayan States, Buddhism in Sri Lanka, Burma and Thailand, Chinese religions including Buddhism in Taiwan, Hong Kong, Singapore and South Korea, and Buddhism and Confucian motifs in Japan. We may call this the *Old Asian grouping*. There are diaspora versions of Indian, Chinese and other cultures in various places such as Fiji, Guyana, South Africa, California, Malaysia, Indonesia, etc.

(5) South of the Islamic belt across much of northern Africa from Somalia to Northern Nigeria, there is the culture of *Black Africa*, which today is predominantly Christian, but underlain and interwoven with classical Africa religion in the great mosaic of small-scale ethnic groups. The nations of Africa are largely artificial, because they represent mostly arbitrary colonial boundaries; but nation-building proceeds, laid upon top of the diversities below. In addition to the predominant Christianity, Islam makes progress; and there are some ten thousand or more independent churches and new religious movements, reflecting new ways of seeing ethnic identities in the light of Christianity, but not under the domination of the old missionary churches. Also, at the Southern tip of Africa is the largest White minority in Africa, with its own deep problems and its conflicting forms of Christianity.

(6) There is *Latin America*, from Southern California to Patagonia, with its diverse regions and mixtures – often of a dominant Spanish culture superimposed upon Indian civilizations and tribes; sometimes involving this plus a variety too of migrants, Black or other, as in Brazil; and of largely European migrants as in Argentina. As an adjunct to Latin America we can perhaps include *the Caribbean*, with its Spanish, British, French, Dutch, African, native American, Indian and other elements. Latin America is of course predominantly Catholic, but its mingled culture is hospitable to other varieties of Christian and pre-Christian motifs.

(7) The other great region of the world is *the Pacific*, where the many island cultures, Polynesian, Melanesian and Micronesian have become mainly Christian, but look back upon older paths as contributing to their identities. Into this region have intruded the Americans, as in Hawaii, and Northern Whites in Australia and New Zealand.

(8) It is unwise also to forget that through much of the Transchristian West and the Marxist bloc and to some extent elsewhere, there exist enclaves of smaller-scale societies struggling for survival under the surrounding impact of Western-style economies and technological methods: such as the Inuit, Siberian tribes, and Native Americans in the USA and Canada. We might call these peoples *Minority Smallscalers*. Their problems, however, are not in principle very different from smallscalers elsewhere, e.g. in parts of Africa, where the new ways pose a threat to traditional values, or among the Australian Aboriginals.

These groupings are a convenient way to survey the cultural varieties of the world. Each grouping may of course conceal very great divergence, for instance between Sri Lankan and Japanese cultures, despite their both being mainly Buddhist countries; or between Chinese and Soviet Marxism; or between White Uruguay and nearby mingled Brazil. But they are a convenient arrangement by which we may have an overview of the world's diverse cultures in the postcolonial epoch.

Many of the cultures have to wrestle with the problems

of ethnic plurality, sometimes within the Marxist context, but most often within the general framework of a capitalist or semi-capitalist economy. In countries such as India and Kuwait, Belize and Japan, non-Western cultures are blended with liberal institutions and democratic forms. In many nations, capitalism blends with varieties of authoritarian regimes, from Lee Kuan Yew's relatively polite dictatorship in Singapore to more fascistically organized systems such as until recently in Chile. Experimentation with new forms of plural politics, but in an authoritarian framework, are typical of Black Africa.

Because some degree of modernization is necessary to survival, and quite a lot for economic prosperity, and the relationship between modernization and liberal institutions and ideas, though ambiguous, is perhaps closer than alternative socialist methods, many of the older traditional cultures find themselves having to deal simultaneously with the need to assert national identity in the face of the preceding colonialism and with the need to import liberal notions which act as solvents on tradition. Part of the impetus of new religions and reform movements within older ones is to try to reconcile these rather conflicting demands.

At any rate it is against the background of these blocs and kinds of religion in the modern world that a Christian *darśana* has to be framed. And since we wish to set the scene also in terms of the varying major religious themes of human history, we shall now turn to sketch such a phenomenology, and for ease of arrangement we shall deal with it in relation to the differing dimensions of religion, including the "hardware" – the external manifestations of religions in the world.

1 The Phenomenology of Doctrines

(1) Naturally, the most familiar idea for the Christian reader is the concept of God as Creator. This notion of a creative, omnipresent sustainer of the cosmos is found of course in the sister-religions of Judaism and Islam; but it is, not surprisingly, important in other mighty religious traditions.

It is in its own way the dominant doctrinal underpinning of Hinduism. It is true that the Hindu tradition in recent times has so often been interpreted through non-dualistic Vedanta, but the practise of people is largely *bhakti*, devotion to a personal *Īśvara*. And the one Lord is refracted through the various more local and particular gods with which the Hindu tradition teems. The creative aspect of *Īśvara* is often perceived as female, *śakti*. So that God is refracted as both male in character and as female. By subordinating a kind of polytheistic melange to the demands of divine unity the Hindus manage to give personal qualities to the various properties of the Divine.

But it is an important motif in the various theisms also that there is an unspeakable aspect of God, often figured as non-personal, or at least in less personalistic terms than the *Īśvara*: the *nirguṇam brahman* of the Advaitin tradition, the En Sof of the Jewish mysticism, and T'ai Chi of Neoconfucianism, etc. Such an ineffable aspect of the Divine or of the Ultimate may or may not be given priority over the personal aspect. Thus in Advaita, it is; but it is not a necessity. In its most radical form it appears as *sūnyatā* in the Mahayana. This is a radical form because it is doubtful whether it can be considered as a sort of "substance" underlying the world: whereas the other systems think of the Divine as a being or Being itself, and given some kind of substantial atmosphere.

However, the ultimate may not even be seen as something somehow pervading or underpinning reality, like the Tao, but rather as a culmination of a quest: a transcendent goal, like nirvana. Nirvana is in no sense (in the Theravada) a principle underlying process, but yet it lies "beyond" the world of processes. In the last resort, Theravada has at its heart a transcendent, but not God or Ultimate Reality. This fact is of profound importance in the history of religions, and is vital for Christians to take account of. For Theravadin Buddhists, the Christian faith in a Lord, *Īśvara*, is intelligible only at the lower level, where gods abound: at the highest level there is the true spiritual goal, which is nirvana. Since Theravadins are in no sense theists, they serve as the great counterexample to the old (false) platitude that all peoples worship God in diverse forms.

So we have various concepts of the Divine and the ultimate which we may wish to deploy in the course of framing a world Christian theology: the *Īśvara* (personal Lord); the non-personal *Brahman* (the Divine's ineffable aspect); a monistic Principle underlying all things – the T'ai Chi, the Tao, a monistic quasi-Principle, Emptiness as in Great Vehicle Buddhism; and the ultimate conceived as indescribable liberation, nirvana.

In the various traditions the Divine may manifest itself in human form, so it is thought: the ultimate truth manifests as the Buddha; the Lord as Krishna; and so on. But we shall deal with this under the next head (the narrative or mythic dimension).

Also important are various ways of conceiving of *Īśvara*'s creative activity, and her or his relation to the cosmos. One that may prove important in the exposition of Christian doctrine is the notion, found especially in Ramanuja, that the world is the Divine body. The doctrine is not monistic, but it relates the ongoing activities of the cosmos to divine intentions; and it links with the conception of the Lord as "inner controller" or *antaryāmin* of events, important for an exposition of the Spirit in history.

Many smallscale cultures have the conception of a Divine Being who presides over the world as a High God, sometimes seen as a *deus otiosus*. Although Father Wilhelm Schmidt's thesis that such a High God is a universal aspect of smallscale religion as exhibiting a carry-over from the earliest stage of human religion is open to criticism, it is a thesis that has helped to draw attention to the frequency at least of a kind of theism in such societies.

All this implies (1) that theism in differing forms – aniconic to what we have called "refracted" – is very widespread in world religions; but (2) some major religious traditions, notably Theravada Budhhism, have no *Īśvara* or even a Great Ultimate, not to mention (3) there are consciously atheistic and non-religious versions of secular ideologies. The fact of (1) and (2) suggests that we need an explanation of why this is so, and we shall return to that question under the head of the experiential dimension.

There are of course a large number of other doctrinal issues about which the religions overlap and disagree: but the diverse notions of the ultimate are the most crucial, and we have sketched here a few of the alternatives.

2 The Mythic Dimension (Smart, 1973b, pp. 79–110)

The huge diversity of the world's myths is hard to sort neatly into differing baskets: but we may look to some important motifs. Narratives which have divine or transcendental significance can translate us to *illud tempus*, as Eliade has well attested, where we are in a time which is timeless, especially where we are being pointed to "origins", the "in the beginning" of our life. Such myths often have an ambivalent status, for they include reference often enough to real features of the world: they are not just taking us beyond the familiar existence in which we are plunged. Important for our purposes are those stories of creation and the beginnings of the human race which give an account, somehow, of the relation between the world and the ultimate and more particularly of us as humans and the ultimate. It seems characteristic of such stories (for instance of the Fall, according to the Christian interpretation of *Genesis*) to become transformed in modern and in more analytical circumstances into symbolic ways of affirming metaphysical or doctrinal truth. God's *fiat* that brings the cosmos into being becomes a way of symbolizing the dependence of the world on the Divine (it has a more dramatic symbolism than the notions of emanation or transformation, which alternatives are found in Neoplatonism, some Hindu accounts, etc.).

As soon as we begin to talk about the symbolic values of myth, or its parabolic nature, and to substitute as its "real meaning" some other frame of reference than the, so to speak breathlessly asserted, narrative, we are involved in the process of demythologization. Adam's story becomes symbolic of the human alienated condition. In some cases it involves "de-narrativization" – we substitute analytic accounts for narrative sequences. Mara gives place to the

Abhidhamma abstractions. The myths of creation and preservation and destruction give way to Ramanuja's analysis of dependency as analogous to that of the human body and soul. The stories come to have a primarily pedagogical function: though in fact they may have a deleterious educational effect, since the backlash against liberal demythologization is a kind of literalism: and stories once told literally and believed may have to be unlearnt.

It is commonly asserted that many cultures have had a cyclical view of time, as opposed to the linear view which (supposedly) is the prerogative of the Jewish and Christian traditions, and via them, of Islam. Much is made of the contrast. But it is not so: the Western religions are not the only ones that have laid stress upon historical sequence. It is true that the Indian tradition espouses differing forms of a cyclical cosmology, and various versions of a cyclical view of history were tried out in China. But at the same time, historical sequence was stressed in Chinese writing, and a sign of this is the way events are so easy to date in early Chinese history, and so hard in India. But not all of South Asian civilization had such an apparent undervaluing of historical change: the Buddhist chronicles of Sri Lanka testify to the contrary. So though we can make a rough and ready contrast between cyclical and linear views of time, that contrast does not coincide with the East-West divide, nor for that matter with the North-South distinction.

A cyclical mode, of course, comes in with calendars, themselves dependent on the recurring nature of the seasons. Religious festivals may turn out to be regularly or irregularly calendrical: and here we have the notion that (let us say) Easter is the same one year and the next – that is that different times are the same time, as different spaces may be the same space. Thus, each bathing tank in India is also the Ganga: so on each Easter it is "today" that Christ is risen. This mythico-symbolic concept of time-travel and space-travel through ritual is a vastly important feature of nearly all religion. The ritual abolishes temporal and spatial distances, making Christ's Last Supper present to us *here* and *now*. The there is here, the then is now. This is a different conception from the idea of cyclical time, though it may, as in calendrical rites, be tied in with recurrence of the seasons. It is part of the mythico-symbolic idea of time that the same date each year is indeed the same, so that my birthday recurs, and abolishes the time gap between my now and my then. But this abolition of distances is not the same as the cyclical idea, for it can occur alongside and arising out of linear time.

There is also a notion of recurrence in the ideas of rebirth and karma: but though this has its effect on ideas of time, since the rebirth of the individual is mirrored in the rebirth of the universe, etc., it is not in itself instrinsically tied to notions of cyclical time.

The linear mode in one sense belongs to all narrative, but where the story has a "once upon a time" atmosphere, we can agree with Eliade that in effect we are transferring the action beyond ordinary time to *illud tempus*. But the modern world has been pervaded by the modern historical mode of thinking, which has its alternative in fiction (of which in religion the parable is parallel). But modern fiction mimics real time, as it mimics the real world. It presents events as being such that they might have happened. These parallel universes are meant moreover to throw light on our universe – to illustrate human reactions and predicaments as they actually are. Fictions then are make-believe about events, but not (on the whole) make-believe about the world in which the events are set. Even science fiction normally supposes that the creatures and worlds depicted may exist in the future, or elsewhere in the cosmos. So the predominant motif of modern thinking is historical and realistic.

And this has its effect on the demythologization process. Those myths, such as that of Adam, which can hardly be sustained as actually historical, are re-presented as allegories of the human condition, or as complex symbolic tales which throw light, from the depths of psychology, upon human life (think of all those tales about Siva). The story after all, despite our previous caveat, is a good pedagogical vehicle, and from earliest times the human being is comfortable with and eager for the story mode. But the other tendency is

63

towards prizing the historical, the real way in which revelation or enlightenment had unfolded in history. So there is a systematic attempt to clean up the narratives, to penetrate to the history behind the Buddhist stories or the Christian narrative or the Moses saga. The old myths are slit like a fish: you have on one side the flesh of "pure history", and in a metaphysical background the doctrinal interpretation of that history.

By an irony "pure history" (suitably selected of course) reinforces the myth of the modern nation-State. What is taught in history textbooks to American children, to French, to Thai and so on is in each case the myth of the group — how we came to be (e.g. the American Revolution), the growth and glory of the nation, the fine individuals who incarnate its spirit. A new set of calendrical festivals is drawn up: Washington's Birthday, Independence Day, Memorial Day and so forth. The dead are celebrated as though living still, and their heroic deaths add substance and depth of value to the nation's substance. So *history becomes sacred narrative*, just as in the religions *sacred narrative becomes history*.

The telling of a story makes the past present to us, and perhaps is the most basic performance in the ritual dimension: but when such telling is overlaid with the demands of a fixed rite, as in the communion service, then we have a very strong re-presentation of significant event. This can occur out of linear time, as we have said, so the ritual abolition of time is not, as we have noted, the same as the cyclical concept.

So far we have distinguished some happenings to the mythic dimension:

(1) A myth may be de-narrativized and seen as a way of symbolizing some structural feature of the world, for instance the alienation of human beings from the Ultimate.

(2) A myth may be "slit" into straight history and a heavenly interpretation thereof — such as the story of Jesus or the Buddha seen as reflecting divine intentions or dharmic novelty. Such an account may or may not allow for some miraculous events as part of real history, but even if it does this is far removed from that seamless mythic mentality in

64

which, so to speak, dreams and realities are thoroughly interwoven, and anything may happen.

(3) We have noted too that selectively "pure history" may become the sacred narrative of a nation as a human group of ultimate concern.

We no longer have a choice: we cannot treat the fanciful stories of Hindu mythology or classical African religion as if they are merely historical: we have to see them as setting forth symbols of the human condition, and this is a form of de-mythologization. To see the configurations of a world religious view we need to interpret world history: our task is the construction of a *sacred narrative of the world*.

A bridging notion between the transcendent and historical realms is that of the holy person – the prophetess, the shaman, the mystic, the incarnate deity, the Enlightened One, the sage, the sacred practitioner. It is in some ways (as we shall observe in our treatment of the experiential dimension) the shaman who is the most seminal figure. But the idea of a holy person as telling forth or as exhibiting in her or his life the nature of the Transcendent is an important one in the narratives of the human race. Generally such persons fall into two, not always easy to distinguish, forms: as the prophet or teacher, who while not himself divine, can tell you authoritatively about the Transcendent; and as the *avatāra*, embodiment or incarnation of the Transcendent – e.g. Christ or the Buddha of the Mahayana who incorporates the transcendent Dharma in his own person, or many gurus who are thought of as real manifestations of the Divine. The advantage of our using here the term *avatāra* is that it admits of degrees. In the Christian tradition Christ is the only full *avatāra*, and saints are just reflected *avatāras*, subsidiary, but sources of inspiration to the Catholic or Orthodox believer: but in Hinduism there is a multitude of divine incarnations. We may call the former kind of holy person a *nabī* and the latter, then, an *avatāra*. These two types are important in modern interpretations of sacred narrative, which emphasize the historical aspect of sacred narratives and therefore the human protagonists. Also, modern emphasis upon religious experience means that the most luminous spiritual persons are important for they have "tasted" the Transcendent.

One final comment about the mythic dimension concerns cosmologies. It happens that the modern discovery of the true and immense scale of the cosmos pulls in an opposite direction, mythically, from the formulation of evolutionary biology. The latter reinforces stress upon the linear view of history. Now we see "nature into history": the whole story of the planet exhibits a transition from the flow of biological into human events, a kind of directionality made much of by Aurobindo and Teilhard de Chardin. But linear myths in the past have existed within tiny frameworks – very inadequately small mythic cosmologies. By contrast the cyclical cosmologies of South Asia have revelled in huge statistics. Thus a *kalpa* or cosmic period was reckoned as 4,320 million terrestrial years and corresponds to a day in the life of a Brahma, who live 100 years. Such staggeringly large figures are set against a background of infinity, for there is no ultimate beginning of the cosmos, and there are an infinity of world-systems (some modern cosmologists compare this to modern discoveries of billions of galaxies of staggering scale). So the cyclical cosmologies go with hugh size and the paling into insignificance of the minor distortions of symmetry induced by linear histories within the cosmos.

The linear cosmology of our immediate environment – via geological and biological evolution through to human history – exists, then, against a background of immense scale; and here traditional South Asian ideas are closer to recent ideas than are the punier world-pictures of other traditions, notably the Biblical tradition. We shall be returning in more detail to some of these issues in presenting our Christian worldview, for, obviously, cosmological issues affect the way we understand soteriology and the conception of Christ's status as *avatāra*.

3 The Ethical Dimension

Every tradition incorporates some universal ethical values, such as love, brotherhood and compassion; but these may or may not be tightly integrated into a structure of religious law. Thus Hindu *dharma* and Jewish *Torah* bridge the areas of ritual, ethics and law. Although there are some points where Christians similarly hold a ritual view of ethics, e.g. in regard to marriage as a sacrament, for the most part Christian ethics are not tied down to the particularities of right conduct. There is, that is, no detailed system of law. An intermediate position is to be found in Confucianism, where emphasis upon *li* or proper behavior, covering matters ranging from moral action through etiquette to certain religious rites, opens up to us the importance of performative acts as an ingredient in our world. (We shall return to this point later in depicting a performative analysis of the notion of a person as vital for a Christian understanding of the ethical dimension.)

It appears to us that though moral values are universal – that is, they are found reflected in all societies – the function of a worldview is to add to accepted values a depth of interpretation which integrates morality into a wider vision. So, from a theistic point of view, doing good is itself a major part of worshipping God, and from a Buddhist perspective showing compassion is a major ingredient in the pursuit of the Bodhisattva ideal; while in Confucianism exhibiting proper *li* is a main part of the life of the Sage. Where a moral system is tightly integrated into the total ritual life of a society, then the difference in practice between morals and law tends to disappear, and insofar as the ritual reflects piety, morality and piety become indistinguishable. This is only the extreme case of the interpretation of moral norms as the fulfilling of transcendentally-oriented goals, which is a feature of all traditionally religious systems. In a general sense, therefore, a worldview has to show something of the *dharma*-nature of morality: to see, in other words, the practice of what is good as rooted in the very constitution of our universe.

Conversely, moral criteria may also be important in trying to shape a worldview. Sometimes ritual requirements may become divisive, and they may also, for whatever reason, run contrary to that kind of morality which seems proper to a modern society. Thus a certain openness and freedom is demanded by the fabric of modern searching for knowledge: and this may be somewhat in conflict with some religious attitudes to authority. What we here will seek is an interpretation of *li* or proper conduct in a wider-than-ethical sense which nevertheless accords with the openness required of modern world civilization.

4 The Experiential Dimension

In many ways this is the most important dimension of all, for diversities of doctrines in the world's religions forces us to ask whether these do not significantly arise from diversity of experience. This is not the only factor, but it is a crucial one. It is also in practical life of great moment: after all, religion has to speak to feelings, and it has, to be thoroughly meaningful, to be experienced in the heart as well as figured out in the head: and it has to conduce to inner illumination as well as control outer acts. The question of the nature of human experience has therefore played a most important part in recent philosophy of religion, from the time of Schleiermacher onwards.

In this discussion we shall content ourselves with a very brief sketch of complexities which have to be supplemented by our interpretation of world history. Moreover the typology of central religious experiences here presented has to be laid down somewhat dogmatically.

A seminal place in the history of religions is held, in our opinion, by the figure of the shaman, for out of shamanism various motifs emerge which lead us towards the prophet and the mystic, and divine possession together with the ideal of the suffering *avatāra*, and indeed the notion of triumph over the forces of death, sickness and adversity.

The shaman belongs most typically to a hunting and gathering society, such as among the tribes in the circumpolar region of the world, from the Inuit to Siberian peoples. So his or her expertise relates partly to the discovery of abundant supplies of relevant animals, fish and so on. But leaving this aside, the shaman is a person who acquires, often by the practise of suitable austerities, visionary powers which fit him or her for the role of healing the sick and in other ways ensuring the welfare of the group. His ecstasies involve possession by, though sometimes control over, various divine spirits; and often a journey (in inner experience) to the world of the deceased to rescue the soul of a sick person. Such a journey is itself a kind of death of the shaman – his dismemberment, for instance, and then his final reassemblage and the restoration of health to the person whose soul he has rescued. In all this we perceive a number of motifs important in the development of the classical great religions (Eliade, 1964).

The austerities and preparation for vision foreshadow the spiritual training of mystics, whether in the yogic Indian traditions or in later developments such as Sufism and Hesychasm in the Western religions (or the techniques of Taoism also). So one motif that we can draw from shamanism is the mystical quest. Since the primary notion of contemplation is called *dhyāna* in the Indian tradition, we shall use this term to cover this major area of practise and experience.

The possession by the divine foreshadows the nature of the prophetic experience, that of the *nabī*, as we shall call him, from the Semitic languages. The *nabī* may or may not be professionalized, but when he or she combines his ecstatic knowledge of the Divine with ethical attitudes, we have the classical critic of society, so important in ancient Israel and in later times (e.g. John the Baptist, Jesus and Muhammad). The notion of possession gives the initiative, so to speak, to God, and God is the overwhelming object of the *nabī*'s vision. So we may call this kind of experience, the numinous, with Otto (he however wrongly conflated the consciousness-emptying type of mystical experience with the numinous).

Dhyāna experiences and numinous experiences each involve diverse emphases. On the one hand there is an experience of pure consciousness and emptiness in the dhyanic category which helps to account for the non-theistic character of Theravada Buddhism, etc. On the other hand there is a *dhyāna* of love, which is aware of a personal subject so to speak alongside the human, and representative of divine love. This helps us to understand certain aspects of theistic mysticism. Now likewise there is a polarity in the numinous. On the one hand the fearful awe-inspiring side of the numinous other issues in the *nabī*'s call. On the other hand because of the divine initiative in bringing holiness to the devotee the latter can experience the Transcendent as love. The response is *bhakti* religion, which is warm, but involves adoration, prostration before the Divine − but not so much out of fear as out of wonder at God's love. So we can see a double aspect in each case. Thus we have the contrast numinous-dhyanic (numinous-mystical), and within the numinous the religion of the *nabī* and the religion of the *bhakta* (devotee); within the dhyanic, the religion of brilliant emptiness and the *dhyāna* of love. The two sorts of love converge and produce theistic mysticism.

If the ethics of the *nabī* are critical and draw upon divine commands, the ethics of the yogi who pursues *dhyāna* are often those of "giving up". This chimes in with the mystagogic life of the shaman, who dies in order to save others. He or she harrows hell. The dismemberment and restoration of the shaman foreshadow other ideas of self-sacrifice − the service and sufferings of the bodhisattva, and the death and resurrection of Christ. So it is too with some of the prophets and leaders of new religions, that they suffer and through their suffering lead their people upwards to new highlands of prosperity and renewed identity.

The *nabī* and *bhakta* religions emphasize duality − the gap which is placed between the human worshipper and the God who creates her, between the individual and the Transcendent. Such dualism, when taken strongly, fights against the idea of the *avatāra*. Also, there is another tension in religious experience and so in doctrines − between the non-personal aspect of the Transcendent and the personal Lord as object of numinous experience and the *dhyāna* of love. How can the path of the Theravadin and of the Calvinist meet? We consider (but later shall spell this out) that for various reasons, including the demand for the richest kind of religion which will testify to the types of experience evident in human history, both sides of the Divine are important, but they must be kept in balance. So there is one side of the Transcendent which is unfathomable, unspeakable, empty of human concepts, beyond worship; and there is another side which is full of personal qualities, above all love and creativity. On one side gazes Gautama the Buddha, and on the other Jesus.

There is a further kind of experience not comprised precisely under the foregoing. That is the experience sometimes called *panenhenic*, again impersonal, but comprising in its grasp a sense of intense unity with nature and what lies unseen within nature. Its most beautiful literary expression is in the classic of *Tao*, the *Tao-teh Ching*. This sense of rapport with nature may also be foreshadowed in the shamanistic life, for the shaman's society is one where the human merges with his or her environment, where he or she has as much reverence for the surrounding powers as for members of the human community. It is a constant motif of modern interpretations of Native American and Australian Aboriginal religions that they do not incorporate that severe cleft between humanity and nature characteristic of modern technical culture. There is a unity between all powers. This notion chimes in with the panenhenic feeling, which in various forms has been echoed in modern literature (Wordsworth being the most conspicuous example). The panenhenic or *tao* experience, as we may call it, reinforces the sense of a nameless non-relational non-personal aspect of the Transcendent.

The two aspect theory of the divine will in this work be related, of course, to the Trinity doctrine in chapter 6. It helps to illuminate some important features of Christian faith – but as phenomenology it helps to explain the enigmas of religious history: how (without the *nabī* and *bhakta* traditions) Theravada Buddhism can exist as a non-theistic, nirvana-oriented religion; how we can in parallel have Taoist motifs, including Ch'an and Zen; how the Mahayana developed with the injection of numinous *bhakti* religion into the non-personal fabric of the Buddha's message; how Advaita represents the dominance of the mystical over the ritual and *bhakta* side of the Hindu tradition; how Ramanuja

71

is the reverse – and so on. It explains too the vicissitudes of some Sufis, the waywardness of Eckhart, the mysteries of the Kabbala. So as a phenomenology it has enough richness to explain something of the variety of doctrines to which we have briefly alluded, and to which in due course we shall return. It is important that the prime use of this phenomenology is explanatory, within the context of the history of religion: it is accidentally important that it helps with the expression of a Christian worldview – or is this providential?

With pure *dhyāna* you get the disappearance of subject and object. With love *dhyāna* you get unity through love. With *bhakta* you love the Other, with the faith of the *nabī* you get fearful vision of the Good, and with the *tao* experience you return to unity, with, now, the outer world of nature, behind which the Transcendent is concealed. The rhythms of these relations of identity and difference of course chime in with some of the main motifs of the *avatāra*, who stands beyond both *nabī* and *bhakta*. Beyond prophecy and devotion, but not necessarily in contradiction with these roles – is this not the role of Christ, who was critical of many in his own day, but went through with his death on behalf of alienated humankind? The connections are suggestive.

We can see echoes of the varied types of religious experience in some of the Western writers of this century, each rather incomplete: Barth, who emphasizes the religion of the *nabī*; Buber the *bhakta*; Alan Watts, the *tao*-experiencer; and Thomas Merton, walking through the Cloud of Unknowing.

5 The Ritual Dimension

Differing kinds of religion are nurtured by, and expressed by, differing patterns of ritual activity. Here we must take the word "ritual" in the widest possible way – to include some very informal performances at the one end, and to include, at the other, stylized forms of practical training, such as yoga. In between stand the heartlands of worship, sacrifice, propitiation, at the interface between the visible world and the unseen world of the Transcendent and of the spirits of nature and living beings. Thus the religion of *bhakti* involves adoration, warm worship, so to speak. Thus, *bhakti* expresses humility and love in face of the Other's love and blessedness. Yoga is the practice which helps to promote and reinforce *dhyāna*. Prostration is the worship of the fearsome numinous. Generally speaking we can divide the main forms of ritual activity into worship and yoga, then. But various other forms remain important, and can exist within the framework of the above two types. Thus sacrifice is one typical mode of worship: the slaughter or destruction of some valuable thing, particularly a domesticated animal, as an offering to the numinous Being with whom one is in contact. Sacrifice itself establishes contact, and opens a path of mutually favorable attitudes: humility and proper abnegation on the part of the sacrificer, and graciousness on the part of the Deity. We shall have more to say on some of these issues later on.

As we have indicated, it is possible to superimpose the practical values of ritual on ethical values, so that doing good, looking after our sisters, controlling our passions and so forth are seen as themselves forms of worship, self-sacrifice, yoga and so forth.

It should be noted that differing kinds of ritual will demand differing kinds of religious specialists. The more technical demands of ritual, especially sacrifice and sacramental kinds of ritual, need a priestly class. The practice of yoga demands those who somewhat withdraw from the world, and they may be organized as monks, or more loosely arranged as hermit, wanderers, and others. The continuation of a *nabi* tradition may be achieved through the preacher. The ethical dimension with its outreach into the community may indicate the importance of a pastoral function – which can blend with the others: the monk as pastor, the priest as pastor, the preachers as pastor. In such ways the exigencies of differing styles of religion have their institutional implications, so let us now turn briefly to that dimension.

6 The Social-Institutional Dimension

We have noted that the planet has become divided up on the principle that each nation should have its State, and conversely. Hence there is the modern territorial imperative. Of course the ideals of such ethnicity are not realized, and the many forces of secularization, migration and ideological change mean that an older ideal of the social integration of religion in a group is seriously weakened, and where revived, revived consciously and so rather aggressively. Thus it is no longer true that to live in Sweden is (virtually) to be Lutheran. Where in older tribal societies there was a coincidence between religion and culture (so that to be Nuer is to practice Nuer religion), now there are choices because of the intrusion of mission, education and other factors. Increasingly therefore religious institutions are becoming denominational, though some are also transnational. The existence of a strong priestly tradition, or a monastic tradition, or both, gives coherence to transnational denominations. But even without these there may be unifying factors: in Islam, in modern times especially, the *hajj* is a vital factor, for it is at Mecca in the *hajj* season that men and women from all ends of the earth meet together, and reinforce one another's piety in times when piety is under attack from foreign and world influences.

There is tension which arises from the contradictory demands of ritual and belief. Ritual means the maintenance of certain traditions, especially in sacramental religion. So the behavior of priests and monks may over time become very stereotyped. On the other hand in a plural world there is increasing looseness towards authority, and much experimentation. How can religious institutions both retain traditional behavior and a greater openness to ideas? We have already noted that this question of a theory of critical traditionalism is a vital one in our religious quest, and we shall come back to it.

We may note that certain religions are more open to non-traditional transformations than others, partly because of the nature of the religious specialists. In Hinduism, for example, there has long been the institution of the guru, of the holy teacher who gains his reputation in an informal way, as he may gather disciples and as the word of his insight may go around. There are no formal tests of who is a guru or whether a guru is good or bad. Within the overall conservative structure of Hindu society, of which the brahmins are the chief guardians, for they control so much ritual and with it who or what counts as pure or impure (thus they become guardians par excellence of the caste system), gurus perform often in new and experimental ways. Again, among Christians groups the Protestant Biblical preacher is another type who can come up with new methods and messages. The preacher also like the guru is judged by success in gaining followers, and not by more formal criteria of wealth. It is partly for this reason that evangelical preachers have been successful in the United States in gaining a television following. Such figures who can set up as gurus on a free-lance basis help to explain some of the new religious movements which are flourishing in the Western world, and elsewhere, at the present time. Our view, however, of the Christian message is that it needs to be presented in real continuity with the mainstream traditions, even if the form of the worldview presented may be novel and its impact revolutionary. We cannot escape the fact that the institutions of religion are profoundly affected by the development of one world. The pressures on traditions are great: authority cannot be what it once was; yet the visions of the past do not need to be thrown away, and we are led back to the all-important epistemological question as to how in a doctrinally permissive age, and an era of advance through questioning and not of simple acceptance of what is handed down, we can retain the stamp of the past together with the approval of the future.

The Phenomenology of Six Dimensions and the World Situation

Finally it may be useful for us to comment on some of the contributions of the various worldviews and worldview-blocs, as delineated at the beginning of this chapter, to the formation of a world Christian outlook which can make positive sense of the various traditions, ancient and modern. These comments are in advance of the more detailed treatment of world history which we shall deliver later on.

Though we have referred to Western democratic societies as Transchristian, because the major religious culture of their background has been what is now a fading Christianity, and Protestantism, as being able to stimulate and absorb new patterns of libertarian thinking and scientific endeavor, it also contains as a minor, but highly significant, motif, the Jewish heritages, especially in the United States. It is necessary for Christianity to come to terms with its Jewish counterpart, its alter ego. Both religions draw on the *nabi* tradition and this is profoundly important (for it links up with Neotranscendentalism and the stance "in the other world" from which we can evaluate the things of this world); but Judaism contains also the most striking claims to particularity, through the maintaining of the identity of the people and the adherence by many to the complexities of the Torah. We need to pay attention, then, to the interpretation of the Law from the perspective of a religion which (largely perhaps for *bhakti* influence) does not hold that adherence to the Law to be important for salvation or for daily life.

The kind of society pioneered by the Transchristian West sets the scene for our worldview, mainly because of its being important for the development of knowledge, religious freedom and a possible two-aspect theory of the relation between religion and science (though the formulation of this two-aspect theory of the relation between religion and science and between religions and scientific language will owe a lot to Mahayana Buddhist dialectic). The conception, so important in modern Western society, that religious conviction is for adult decision owes much to the Anabaptist tradition, so crucial in the development of the Protestant Reformation. This, paradoxically, can make it easier for us to accept, critically, the more conservative traditions of the Catholic and Orthodox Churches, purified by their liberation from old forms of triumphalism.

The Marxist ideologies which hold so much of Asia in their grip do not in our opinion present much to us to weave into a Christian worldview. It is in our view contrary to the spirit of the age and to the spirit of Christian freedom that people should be pressured politically towards an official ideology. Nor do we consider that the nationalist ideals to which in fact Marxisms have so often been instrumental are of great interest to Christian worldview-construction when the communities of greatest concern to us – the Church and the human race – transcend national boundaries. The chief lesson from Marxism is that the social and economic problems which have given socialism its attractions have to be taken with the greatest seriousness, but on a global basis. Poverty now is redistributed, so that it is no longer a majority phenomenon in so many northern countries, but is something which has its greatest showing in so-called Third World countries.

There are non-official Marxian analyses, however, which may be very vital in formulating a Christian ethic of the global city. Given the world distribution of poverty, we need now to look upon world problems in a way which transforms the old class-analysis into a global perspective. This is where some of the deliverances of liberation theology are relevant; but we attach importance both to the view that the Christian picture is not to be tied too closely to particular fashions; to the observation that an open epistemology derives from vital non-Marxian elements in the modern reflection about the nature of science and knowledge in general.

Here we attach great weight to a reconsideration of the Mahayana Buddhist "two-truth" perspective, as a way forward in formulating the difference and mutual inherence between the spheres of science and religion (Smart 1983, pp. 162–172). On the front of theistic reformulation we attach equal importance to Ramanuja's doctrine of the God-cosmos' relation being like that of soul to body (Smart 1966, pp. 113–125). This seems to us the easiest formulation for bringing out the intimate way in which God's glory is discoverable in every aspect of the world; it also, as we shall see, resolves some of the problems about revelation (for just as my smile tells you more about me than the movement of my ears, so some parts of God's cosmos are more revelatory than others). There are also elements of the South

Asian traditions which are very important for understanding
the non-personal aspect of the Divine Ultimate.

Of all the concepts in the Chinese tradition the most
crucial is, in our view, that of *li*, which brings together ideas
of ritual and performatives under one head (Smart, 1981).
For us, the concept of the person has to be explained
performatively, or *li*-wise; moreover, the engagement with
li helps to explain the connections between worship, daily
living, atonement and salvation, so vital to traditional
Christianity. But both Taoism and Hua-yen have a role to
play in explicating the doctrines of creation and of the
cosmos, as we understand them. We shall draw too upon
Japanese and Chinese Pure Land Buddhism in drawing out
the meaning of grace in the Christian tradition.

It follows from the way in which we expound the
Christian *darśana* that we are sympathetic to the Sufi
movement in Islam, and we see that as pioneering in a
different context the solidarity between numinous and
mystical experience, which is an element in our "natural
theology of religious experience". For, we argue, it is not
reasonable, given any one major type of religious experience,
to claim validity for it and not for alternative major types.
From this it follows that (other things being equal) numinous
and mystical religion have to be given equal weight: and
this is in our opinion done better in Sufi theology than in
recently more fashionable systems such as Advaita Vedanta
(though we do not undervalue the positive contribution by
modern Advaita to a theory of the compatibility of religions,
important in the evolution of modern Indian nationalism).
We have strong reservations, naturally, given the "soft non-
relativism" implied by our epistemological stance, about
Islamic attitudes to the Qur'an, and though we recognize
the importance of the Qur'an in the formation of a very rich
Islamic civilization, we consider that there are real obstacles
for the creation of a lasting Muslim modernism – but this
is a problem for Islamic rather than for Christian theology.

The small-scalers and the ethnic cultures of the world's
South have many riches to offer out of their classical cultures,
e.g. the possibility of a reappraisal of shamanism, a new

look at who our "ancestors" are in a new world culture, the close ties between myth and ritual; and they have in our view a vested interest in pluralism, if there are to be important elements of their indigenous cultures which are to survive the pressures of the world system. Thus the concept of a "federalism of the spirit" which in one aspect of the Christian *darśana* which we shall present will be reinforced by this natural interest of such societies.

These are brief indications of some of the ways in which we shall fashion a worldview which draws upon world civilization as we find it today. The aim is not of course a universal synthesis; but it rather is to give the Christian faith an expression which is not irrevocably tied to one of the older civilizations. There are whole aspects of the Western heritage which we do not adopt: for instance, the Aristotelian cosmology, the traditional concept of natural theology, acceptance of the Biblical text itself as revelation, Protestant exclusivism, Existentialist categories, the colonialist perspective of much modern theology, etc. We accept the creativity of Western culture in helping to shape Christianities, but we look to a new destiny for the faith now that we have embarked on a global civilization.

Western exclusivism has often been fostered by the appeal to the scandal of particularity. It is true that we have to face up to the problem of the uniqueness of Israelite history, of Jesus and of the first days of the new community. This problem of particularity has become more acute in a vast cosmos which may well harbor life elsewhere. But it may be that we can in the life of people like Gandhi see a way in which a particular faith can serve as a light for all, without either throwing away its own particular vision or demanding the submission of other great spiritual traditions.

These are some brief hints of the way in which we shall weave in ideas drawn from the various traditions and cultures into a comprehensive Christian worldview. But these interweavings need to be exhibited in a sketch of world history: in this, in a sense, we go beyond Toynbee's project, but will owe much to his example. We shall in this combat neo-triumphalist interpretations of world history such as that of van Leeuwen and Kraemer. These examples, by the way, throw light on the dangers created by revelationist exclusivism.

Although we think of the community of ultimate concern as being humanity and although it is vital that we stress our common human nature, the presupposition of our approach is that the great and little traditions will retain their influence upon people, and it is not for us to ignore the riches which the varied cultures can contribute to a Christian, or indeed any other comprehensive, *darśana*. So we need to take seriously various sections of humanity: often undervalued in older theologies – ordinary people and not just the literate elites who have transmitted sacred texts to us; women; the South as well as the North; and smallscalers as well as the members of traditionally great cultures.

We have, then, sketched something of the phenomenological framework within which we shall be composing our world-picture. Already some reference has been made to some of the philosophical issues which arise, and to these in the next section we shall turn. But before that we need to add a brief note about struggles within Christianity itself, between the various motifs and subtraditions – for our interpretation of history must itself throw light on the Christian past itself.

From the point of view of method we of course owe so much to the critical post-Enlightenment tradition of Protestant scholarship, especially those endeavors undertaken in the Protestant faculties of Germany in the 19th century, but reinforced by the individualist and liberal leanings of the English-speaking democracies. These liberal motifs themselves stem in part from the radical Reformation, notably the Anabaptists, and in part from one major strand in the Enlightenment. But it has been the Roman Catholic tradition above all that, despite its suppression of Modernism and other highly conservative instincts, kept a positive attitude open to other civilizations (the danger both of Protestantism and of liberalism has been a standardized view of humanity which has effectively modeled all human beings on the Westerner: the Catholic kept more alive that opening to the religious variations in the world which has its logical culmination in the kind of approach we are adopting). Orthodoxy has not been so creative in thought over many centuries; but it has preserved two things of great importance for balance in the interpretation: a strong spiritual investment in the mystical path – and this makes Orthodoxy a bridge to the further East – and a sensitive and passionate concern with the doctrine of the Trinity which is reflected in our work and which registers this, of course, as the most vital aspect of Christianity distinctiveness. The terrible divisions and struggles within Christendom are in part consequence of unstable elements at the heart of the faith, which have generated an inner dialectic. Hegel was right in seeing such rhythms of contradiction as important as an engine of historical change, and this may be a clue to the enigma as to why science should have arisen in a Western Christian culture dominated by an Aristotelean cosmology and philosophy both on the whole inimical to the truths of science. For within the dialectical process and the interaction with classical humanism there could develop that critical sense which, coupled with the thought of a rational Creator, encouraged new scientific enquiries. So already the very doctrine of the Triad suggests a shifting, stirring center of struggle within the varied strands of Christian belief and practice which trigger both harsh conflicts and imaginative ventures into new worlds.

We now, however, turn to some of the philosophical prolegomena to our task of worldview-construction.

4

The Philosophy of Religion: Preliminary relevances to a Christian Worldview

The Philosophy of Worldviews and Religious Epistemology (Smart, 1964, 1970)

The custom has grown up of treating of certain problems, such as the validity of Aquinas' Five Ways, the problem of evil, the meaning of terms like "God" and so on, under the head of the philosophy of religion. As we have already shown, we do not need to, and indeed should not, draw too clear a line between religions and so-called secular worldviews. Ultimately we should look to a new category: the philosophy of worldviews, dealing among other things with the criteria for judging between alternative worldviews, including religious ones. It is evident that there are problems about how to resolve worldview questions. The problems can be set out as follows:

(1) Whether any religious worldview is true in part depends on whether we can affirm the existence of a Transcendent Being or state (Brahman or nirvana). Here we take belief in the Transcendent as definitional of religious belief. Now there are some problems in turn about the definition of "Transcendent", but let us take it as involving at least the idea that some Being or state exists which is not part of, but lies "outside of" the cosmos. We leave out of account for the time the thought that there might be parallel cosmoses, but if we did entertain this thought then the Transcendent would lie "outside of" all cosmoses. But to simplify our discussion let us suppose that this cosmos is the only one and that it has, as it were beyond it, a Transcendent Being or state – perhaps as Creator in the former case, and as "place of liberation" in the latter case.

Now, does such a Transcendent exist? Looked at nakedly so to speak (for invariably in practice the Transcendent is clothed in a doctrinal scheme), how could be have evidence for that which admittedly and even brazenly lies outside the scope of empirical investigation? You could not send a space probe to discover the Transcendent, for space is the woven texture of the cosmos, and the Transcendent supposedly lies outside the cosmos. To be of religious significance the Transcendent would no doubt have to be an object of a religious experience (say, Otto's the numinous). But in that case, the question of whether we take the experience seriously in part depends on whether we entertain the possibility that such an experience is *of* the Transcendent. So though it is meaningful to postulate a Transcendent there can be no *proof* of its existence.

(2) Again attending to the case of religious worldviews, it might be that – as according to the Indian philosophical tradition – the existence of the Transcendent is known by *śabda*, that is, by verbal testimony (scriptural revelation). But we find that there are in the world alternative scriptures – the Qur'an, the Jewish Bible, the New Testament, the Vedas, etc. So even if you thought that there was a Transcendent of some sort, you would not on that basis know how to choose between alternative clothed Transcendents.

(3) Even if you tried to resolve this problem by saying "All the *śruti-s* point to the same truth", in a manner reminiscent of Radhakrishnan or Hick, this would not resolve matters, for there are also reasons for doubting this: religions after all differ seriously about various things, rebirth, the importance of *bhakti*, the speakability of the Ultimate, etc. And so the unified religion of all scriptures would be opposed by many adherents of the particular worldviews, so your move would only add one more worldview to the competing alternatives.

(4) Alternatively, you might have a rigidly secular worldview and reject belief in the Transcendent. In doing that you would be neglecting the fact that so many serious and good people have actually followed religious

worldviews. You might have a theory of projection: that factors in human psychology and society project Gods and the like "out there", whereas they relate to human beings, who thus suffer from the illusion that their Gods are real. But no projection theory, be it that of Feuerbach, or Marx, or Freud, or Durkheim, can be said to have proof, for various reasons (mainly on the one hand, that projection theories themselves form parts of worldviews and do not take the history of religions properly into account and so are culture-bound). So though projection theory may be plausible it does not have empirical proof.

(5) Even if you were convinced that some secular view or other were true, there is still the question of which one – some kind of Scientific Humanism, or of Marxism, or of Existentialism? Varieties of Marxism, for instance, depend upon the controversial analysis of great quantities of historical data, as well as on philosophical arguments for a special version of materialism, and so on. So which worldview one adopted, even if secular, would arouse some measure of controversy and doubt.

(6) So-called proofs regarding the Transcendent such as the classical "Five Ways" and other varieties (whether in the Western or Indian traditions) are themselves subject to debate, to put it no more strongly. The attempted rehabilitation of the Teleological Argument by Swinburne is recognizably not probative; and our (Smart's) attempts to rehabilitate the Cosmological Argument professedly only introduce considerations which may influence people but cannot have a compelling character. Thus the question "Why does anything exist at all?" is important in generating a sense that we need to postulate a Transcendent, but there are doubts about the legitimacy of the question, which can be argued to and fro. So proofs wither into hints at best. They may also function as arousers of experience (e.g., in the manner argued by I.T. Ramsey), but this is a "soft" function, not a hard one.

(7) Though some religious worldviews are open in theory to empirical disproof, because for instance they make historical claims, they often display great flexibility in

adapting to criticism. Now this may earn the disapproval of Popper: one should not avoid disproof by artificial manoeuvres. However, deep-seated beliefs can in fact bend themselves around, and so avoid counter-evidence. It may be that after a while such bending seems artificial and absurd, and for those for whom it thus appears, it loses plausibility. It is like a fading paradigm. And we certainly do not want to deny that worldviews do fade away. But this fading is not straight disproof, and the reasons for it may be themselves greatly complex. What seems obvious or unobjectionable in one generation may look very different to the next. But again we are not here speaking of disproof.

(8) Even if a person be "born again" and converted to a particular worldview in a manner which gives her certitude, it does not follow that she has proof, save to herself. She cannot convince others on the basis of her experience unless the kind of thing she claims to know is already uncontroversial. If a person says she saw a mutual friend in the street yesterday I trust her experience and her word. But if she claims to have seen Christ, and I do not believe in Christ (or believe in Christ but not in *her* Christ, for there turn out to be many Christs), then I am not simply going to accept her word for it. In any case, between an experience and its interpretation there lies a gap, according to the degree of ramification of the claim made on the basis of it. If her claim is very ramified, that is, involves a number of concepts themselves embedded in a wider doctrinal scheme, then there is a large gap. Since a worldview is typically complex and so ramified, we cannot base proof on a worldview on any one experience: even if for the "born again" person, already half-convinced on other grounds of the worldview the experience is a clinching "proof". In brief we have to distinguish private certitude and public proof.

For all these reasons, then, we have a soft epistemology of worldviews. This is an important conclusion in the philosophy of worldviews. There are some similar things to be said in regard to subtraditions, for instance of Christianity. Let us look at Christian worldviews from a somewhat different angle in order to bring this out. We have already noted that the Christian tradition presents us with a gallery of pictures, ranging from the Ist Century to the XXth; and also laterally through the various denominations and subdivisions and "heresies" through which the faith has refracted itself. Are there criteria for determining which is the "true" picture, or which are the "true" pictures? If there are they are not very clearly marked out in this case, for various reasons:

(1) You might say that any correct interpretation of the Christian worldview must be grounded in the Bible. But it is obvious that there are quite diverse interpretations of the Bible, and that appeal to texts rarely settles arguments. There may be no doubt that there is a fair amount of agreement at any one time about some main outlines of the Biblical message; but the Biblical input is at best only part of the substance of actual Christian worldviews.

(2) Even if it can be shown that a particular position faithfully reflects the thought of Saint Paul (allowing already for context-shift because of milieu-transformation), why should we simply accept what Paul says? It is open to you to respond that Paul was inspired by the Holy Spirit and could not err in his writings. But is this belief itself an essential or desirable element within a Christian worldview?

(3) It might be argued that authority lies with the community of believers: and this was the feeling of the Church and still is in many parts. But from this nothing follows as to the locus of that authority in a more particular way. It need not be agreed that the Councils of the Church are the locus of canonical authority, even if we were to agree upon which ones were the true Councils. And there is no agreement about the infallibility of the Pope, or about its scope, even among Catholics. So having the agreement of the body of the adherents is hard. It seems that, without serious sanctions or without proofs, then if a person locates authority in scripture, or the Church, or the Pope — or in any combination of these — that location is a form of *adopting* authority.

The conclusion that we might draw is that any location of authority cannot itself be proved, and is itself a kind of choice. It might thus be called "Canonical Adoptionism" – the adoption by the believer of what counts as canonical in the determination of what is a "true" Christian worldview. Thus also within the ambit of these worldviews which we may provisionally think of as Christian there is a epistemological softness, however much a person may have inner certitude. In this worldview-construction we attempt to stay loyal to some main themes which have been important from Biblical times through some of the main streams of Christianity – the Trinity doctrine, the Eucharist, the atonement by Christ's life and suffering on the Cross, and so on. But we regard it, of course, as useless to try to "prove" these things. We consider that there are reasons for out belief, and in this sense we are not relativists. But our main concern is to *present* a worldview, which is congruent both with this outline Christian tradition and also with modern knowledge – of science, of the plural character of global religion and worldviews, etc. We hope that the picture presented has charismatic features and may appeal both to Christians of the mainstream but also to anyone outside that orbit. In effect we are meaning to add another picture to the gallery of pictures which the Church houses through its past and its wide spread.

It has to be asked why it should be so, that worldviews are not more obvious. The reasons are various, and are worth noting.

(1) A worldview includes both factual and valuational elements, and they are not held together by a necessary relation: in general, in fact, worldviews are a kind of *collage*, containing disparate elements drawn from different spheres of experience.

(2) Worldviews, in interpreting the whole of reality, typically include claims which must go beyond the possibility of direct empirical verification: they reach the limits of experience, so how can their truth be decided by experience?

(3) Since often worldviews are cultural composites which have been worked out over a long history, with continuous milieu-transformation, it is not easy to determine the degree to which any two are really in conflict. So, though

Christianity and Buddhism appear often to be in conflict, examination shows areas where the disagreement may be more apparent than real.

Of course, it may be pleasing ultimately that our human fate and condition are not more clearly presented to us: the very obscurity of worldviews allows us freedom in our existential interpretation of reality. Incidentally, there are, of course, whole swathes of science shrouded in obscurity too, where future knowledge remains to us an enigma. Neither the Spirit nor Nature yields her secrets lightly.

Soft Epistemology and Non-Relativism

So far we have deployed arguments as to why it is that we can have no clear proof, even in the most informal sense of that term, of a worldview. We only have soft reasons at best for choosing between worldviews. It is usually tempting at such a point to opt for relativism: to say that in the last resort in fact all worldviews have equal claims (equally empty). But we do not wish to make the step from softness into relativism, nor even into that lesser morass, namely agnosticism. We do not wish to be agnostics, apart from our loyalty to the Christian tradition, because life in fact demands, pragmatically, the adoption of a worldview. Closed agnosticism is equivalent to nihilism, while a genuinely open agnosticism continues the "long search", and still implies hope of finding an acceptable worldview.

At this point it may be that the Christian (or Pure Land or other) reader might object that we are making the spiritual life involve the "adoption" of a worldview (already we have spoken of canonical adoptionism, in regard to authority). But this is misleading in the case of theism: it is not that we adopt a worldview, but rather there acts upon us the divine grace. We are adopted by God, not *vice versa*. To this we reply: indeed it is so, but it does not at all follow from this that we do not adopt a worldview, if you like, under divine influence. For if the claim that God chooses us is based upon experience, then that experience is one of the things that perforce we try to interpret against the background of our culture and knowledge. It is the consequence of such interpretation that we fashion or adopt a ready-made worldview, part of which consists in the claim that the Divine adopts us. The very concept of grace is something which figures both in our doctrinal scheme and in our experience, in our worship and in our ethical outlook and behavior, etc. It is part of the incarnation of our worldview.

The mention of the experience of grace reminds us that our worldviews are held for reasons, and they themselves may relate to the six dimensions we listed as typical of worldviews as incarnated. Let us look briefly at some examples of these reasons.

Reasons for Faith

There may be metaphysical reasons for holding a theistic worldview, for example, that the existence of the cosmos represents a problem, and the postulation of a Transcendent, suitably connected to positive features of the cosmos, such as its beauty and relative orderliness, constitutes an advance in understanding over the brute affirmation that it simply exists and that is all that there is to it. But there are some contrasting reasons: that nothing decisive can be known on the "other side", so it is best to limit our conception of the Transcendent (the Buddhist move); or to stick to the solider basis of scientific reasoning and method of sources of our knowledge (scientism). Such metaphysical debates themselves related to the doctrinal dimension (though not all doctrines of course may be grounded in metaphysical thinking but will owe much to revealed or other sources).

At the mythic level there first of all arises a metaphysical thought about narrative: is it right that our view of the world should be determined at all by myth? Perhaps the narratives of the past owe themselves either to rather childish ways of dealing with nature, or to depth symbolism, or both: and the deeply symbolic contents of the human psyche as explored and revealed by such as Jung and Eliade are, after all, simply part of the rather accidental products of evolution. We attach no great cosmic importance to the shape of the human nose or the fact that foreheads wrinkle, so why should we attach any deep importance at all to the quirks of human dreaming or symbolizing? Yet, incidentally, and by an irony, the very appeal to evolution as a conception involves us in telling a story – the history of prehuman into human times. Perhaps the narratives of the human past can tell us something about the acquisition of various spiritual as well as cognitive powers, and these may well be relevant to worldview-construction. Did evolution produce consciousness as a mere by-product? Is knowledge itself without significance in the cosmic scheme of things? Are human spiritual capacity and human love themselves of no wider meaning for the cosmos? In such questions we are plunged into narrative questions about the growth and provenance of such human factors in history, so at least we may think of the narrative dimension as furnishing us with reasons for holding a worldview which exhibits some loyalty to the Christian past and to the manifestations of spirituality in human history.

In the case of the Jewish and Christian traditions there is also the fact that particularity, and particularity of historical detail, is an important ingredient in the understanding of the Ultimate's dealing with human beings: so the narrative becomes of the essence. We shall later have to consider the meaning of such particularism; but at the moment it is enough to point to the narrative dimension here as incarnated in historical events. Although the appeal to such events is not at all decisive (for we may begin from other assumptions about the importance, or not, of human history in the ultimate scheme of things, and there may also be other narratives than the Jewish and Christian ones to consider as central), it may nevertheless enter into the fabric of reasons which you might give for holding your faith. Conversely you may have reasons for doubting the historicity of some religious claims.

If you spurn history altogether, and glory perhaps in the non-historical character of your faith, as might be the case with a Mahayana Buddhist who thinks that it is an advantage that Bodhisattvas and celestial Buddhas are in the last resort creative projections of the human spirit, you would still be in the position of commending crucial narratives on some ground or other: for instance, their edifying nature.

Which brings us to the ethical dimension; "By their fruits ye shall know them". It is one reason for having faith in your religion that on balance it seems to make people better – and better than other alternatives do, perhaps. Of course, what counts as better may be in dispute, in part because what is a good fruit is determined somewhat by the rest of the religion or worldview. Thus, humility may loom large among Christians where the root sin is pride or ego-inflation: but it may not be important for Muslims or Brahmins, and indeed may be thought counterproductive in a number of cultures. So we are, in comparing fruits, in the business of setting persimmons and nectarines side by side. Still, even if we do not know the relative worth of persimmons and nectarines we can at least see if the religion if properly followed actually does produce persimmons, and whether its rival actually produces nectarines. *Effectiveness* in relation to fruits is a relevant criterion. And if it be true that some virtues are in conflict, there may be relevant reasons here too for argument. For instance it could be argued that humility conduces to gentleness and gentleness to peace: but the rival may claim that gentleness lets villains get away with evil, and actually may increase the chances of violence. Such reasons about virtues are relevant in comparing fruits; and although of course they are unlikely to prove to be decisive, they do constitute, after all, *reasons*. Moreover, they indicate that over some virtues and rules we can have some agreement crossculturally or cross-traditionally. So direct comparison of fruits in some areas is possible.

As for the experiential dimension: here comparisons are somewhat problematic, but a phenomenology of religious experience is, as we have already shown, feasible. And appeal to experience as interpreted by the subject is often cited as an important reason for holding the worldview one does. Paul relates his experience in part in this context, for instance, and such appeals are notable in many areas of Buddhism, in Advaita Vedanta, in Vivekananda's Neo-

Hinduism, in parts of Neoconfucianism, and so on. It is by experience in part that the shaman is selected. We recognize too the "what is sauce for the goose is sauce for the gander" argument: if a Christian affirms his faith because she is "born again" she ought to pay attention to those who have apparently similar experiences from within the Islamic or Mormon or whatever tradition.

Regarding the ritual dimension of religion, you might hold that ritual action conveys or expresses things which words cannot (as music also does, and music is often deeply woven into the ritual fabric). It is the setting also of profound feelings, which you might think as relevant to the interpretation of the cosmos. We once met a Romanian nun who ascribed her conversion to Orthodoxy from "scientific socialism" as due to the feelings brought on by even passing a church and the meaninglessness (or feelinglessness) of Communist Party meetings for her. It may be that religious practices gives strength and courage, etc.

Finally, arising from the institutional presence of religion there are reasons which have to do with political fruits, or wide-ranging social fruits. If it be the case, as is sometimes claimed, that Buddhism has not been responsible for any religious wars, and if this fact is ascribed to the peaceable nature of the Sangha, then that prima facie is a reason for commending the Buddhist worldview as incarnated in among other things the Sangha. There are analogous arguments appealed to on behalf of other traditions and subtraditions. It is, likewise, a serious criticism of Marxism if, as seems to be the case, there is not a single Marxist-dominated country where various human rights, such as freedom of opinion, are incarnated. At some point or other it becomes impossible to shrug off a bad record just on the basis that there is always among humans a gap between the ideal and the real.

The above brief account of the dimensional expression of reasons for holding or not holding a worldview is sufficient I think to rebut relativism. It is true that it is hard to be decisive: but the existence of reasons creates the ultimate hope of "being right": and though it does not follow from this that it may turn out that only one worldview is true, for an "inner truth" may run through more than one worldview, there is some point at which some one worldview or set of worldviews turns out to be more likely, or less unlikely, than the rivals.

It is for these reasons then that we characterize our position as "soft non-relativism". However, there remains a dim possibility of some ideal tending towards the disappearance of all worldviews in a Habermas maneuver: a possibility dependent on a pejorative evaluation of all "ideologies". The Eastern analogy for this is a thoroughgoing program of emptiness in the manner of Nagarjuna. But we have already argued that in practice such an "empty" outlook (or non-outlook) has practical consequences which themselves have an interface with genuine worldviews and so pragmatically itself constitutes a kind of worldview.

Private Certitude and Public Uncertainty

It does not follow from the position that we have here called "soft non-relativism" that the individual cannot have inner certitude about her worldview: it is just that in the arena of public debate and reasoning, there is no worldview that can be proved. It may be that private certitude can in some cases be extended to groups: after all a group may have its normative sources of authority, which, given certain shared premises, provide ways of deciding issues for the community. It is of course hard in fact to insulate a community, and for this reason the solvents of modernity are likely to enter in, and the authority within the community becomes individualized – it is a matter of a group of individuals agreeing to recognize a given authority. But the fact that at a public level, whether between groups or individuals, proofs are impossible, does not in any way mean that a person may not be sure of her position and passionate about expressing and defending it. It thus is possible to envisage what we shall call "private certitude" in the midst of public uncertainty.

It thus may turn out that many arguments which on the surface appear to be apologetic ones, that is, arguments addressed outwards into the public debate, have more to do with explicating some of the reasons held by "insiders" for their faith. Thus, the arguments for the existence of God are perhaps best seen as modes of filling out faith and connecting up different parts of the worldview. For instance that famous lines at the end of Aquinas' ways – "and this all men call God" (or words to this effect) – helps to show that a link is being made between experience of the ordered world about us and the Divine Being revealed through the Bible and other founts of the Church. What putative proofs end with is a Being with some resemblance or analogy to the revealed God, to make it reasonable to think of cosmic orderliness as having the same source as does revelation.

We have seen in the history of philosophy many cases of common sense belief (the existence, for instance of other minds) which under the scrutiny of critical arguments seem to crumble: so we should in principle have no difficulty with the notion of beliefs in which we have certitude and yet which do not have public certainty. Moreover, our position of Canonical Adoptionism can help to explain how it is that even with such a recognition of public softness there can be authoritative communities: for it is easy to see how a group can find the locus of its authority within itself, and exercise that authority over its members, while knowing that the members' belonging is a matter of individual choice. In short, the epistemology which we advocate here as realistic to the world and the way in which worldviews are actually held is itself congruent with the concept of a free society, in which the tag *cuius regio eius religio* does not apply. We shall later have to explore the political consequences of our position: but there is surely a solidarity between soft epistemology and the open society. This involves a revolution of thinking: no longer is it appropriate to think of our society (whatever it may be) as a Christian or a Buddhist society, unless we contravene the spirit of our epistemology. That is, it is not for society in general (and this means in practice today the nation-State) to impose upon its citizens the requirement to believe in a determinate religious worldview. And because there is public freedom to differ, it follows that at least pragmatically (but also for good logical reasons) there are no public certainties about religion.

All this stems in part from the Enlightenment, in the West, and from the preceding Anabaptist tradition: for the Anabaptists, in demanding adult baptism, effectively argued for individual choice in religion. Thus however much we owe, in our worldview construction, to the classic or mainstream Christianity to Catholic, Orthodox and magisterial Reformation traditions, e.g. the Anglican, we also are greatly indebted to the individualism of the radical Reformation and the libertarian traditions stemming from the Enlightenment. Thus the American Constitution's stand on the establishment of religion we believe to be a fine model. In practice such a separation of worldview and State means that the private certainties of the faithful must not be represented as public and universal truths. All this, of course, may present us with a problem of the interpretation of the Christian past, where authoritarianism has often been at the norm in Christian denominations. And many Christians may feel uneasy at the apparent loss of any *magisterium*, any determinate authority, which the rather permissive atmosphere of our soft epistemology seems to allow. This brings us to the question of how we do treat actually of the sources of the Christian faith.

Revelation: Canonical Adoptionism and the Sources of Christian Faith

Our aim in this work is, as we have said, to articulate and present, in a radically new context, a Christian worldview, which is both congruent with modern scientific method on the one hand and the pluralism of today's global city on the other. But why should one accept the "given" of the Christian faith? We have already touched on the reasons we might have for adopting a worldview. But though there may be *reasons* for such adoption, it does not follow that the worldview is solely the product of *reason*. That is, the worldview is itself a kind of *collage* of a number of givens. Practical life requires, of course, more than intellectuality to command it. And if we look, as humans whose thoughts aspire beyond the seen, to the Transcendent, then where is that extracosmic something manifested within the life of the cosmos? We can draw inspiration from the beauties of the world, and those numinous beauties can reflect something of what lies Beyond. That itself is a kind of revelation, through nature (this is one reason why there is not a simple divide between revealed and natural theology). But there can also be the unveiling of the Transcendent through the lives of those who express its nature well (whatever that is): for the Buddhist the nature of nirvana is to be seen through saints and through the Buddha himself. For Christians the nature of the Divine is seen supremely in Jesus (though obscurely also). In each case there is a problem, perhaps, of particularity. But though there may be a question "Why follow Christ?" or "Why follow the Buddha?", it may in fact be reasonable to think of the Transcendent as giving itself through a human being. For, at least in our part of the cosmos, humanity exhibits the purest form of consciousness: and the cosmos has these two aspects, of the conscious and the material, so that it would not be surprising if it revealed its inner nature through incarnate consciousness, that is in and through a human being. But you do not discover these self-revelations of the Transcendent in the abstract: but concretely they are "given". For the Christian Christ is the "given" one.

So revelation as a category applies to the notion of the manifestation of the Transcendent in whatever mode, and concretely to the given from which and through which the community develops.

From this point of view the given consists in those persons, notably Christ, who constitute the mainstream ancestry of the community, and whose doings are partly covered by the Biblical writings. There are, of course, other items than stories about these spiritual and ancestral heroes in the Bible. There are theological reflections, liturgical material and so forth. It is consonant with the practice of the community as it developed to treat holy persons within the Christian tradition as new sources of revelation (that is, of the

96

manifestation of the Transcendent); and it seems to us that this is an attitude that ought to be carried all the way through history. One of the worst things about treating the Bible itself as alone canonical is that it cuts off the interpretation of Christian salvation-history. From this perspective, though the words of the Bible might secondarily be given, like anything else which may be literary and liturgical means to stir awareness of the Divine Being, they are important chiefly from their relative nearness to the two main motifs of the historical manifestation of the Transcendent, namely the creation of the people of Israel and the incarnation of the Divine in the being of Jesus and his work. Our approach therefore to the problem of revelation is to view the primary importance of Biblical texts inductively: they can help us in the induction to the self-manifestation of the Transcendent. They are not a set of propositions from which we can deductively frame a set of doctrines and ethics defining the Christian life. Ours is therefore a variant on the non-propositional account of revelation.

Moreover, there is no canonical limitation upon revelation. Thus revelation, that is, the making manifest to the eye of faith the nature and activity of the Transcendent, is not confined to the Biblical texts, but is evident in the life of the community, and beyond. This in a way is recognized in the practice of canonising saints, for it gives community approval to following certain particular heroines and heroes of the community. They are more manifest appearances of divine Power than the texts themselves.

From a certain point of view, our "adoption" of this mainstream ancestry of saints leading back to Christ and of prophets and other heroes who were important in the formation of Judaism is arbitrary. We shall be – in the course of this work – helping with the task of reducing this arbitrariness by presenting a Christian worldview in an articulate manner. But however great the meaningfulness of Jesus' life and of his words, so far as we know them, a good case could be put up for having an alternative ancestry: why not Confucius and Mencius; or Muhammad and Ali; or the Buddha and Bodhidharma? There are plenty of fine ancestors elsewhere. Now we shall eventually be arguing that even from within a generally Christian framework these other heroes can be our heroes – for are we not citizens of the world as a whole? But for the moment let us consider these people as alternative "givens": from their angle our choice of Christ and the saints is arbitrary, even willful. Well, the justification for choosing these people as the major manifestation in our world's history of the Transcendent can only be gradually unfolded: to some degree we shall be unfolding it here. But of course there can be no proof that Christ is divine (as was evident already in the New Testament texts). But in as much as we treat Jesus as our major "given" – as the Focus of our earthly loyalty – we are making a choice out of human history. We are assuming (what itself has to be argued for) that the Divine is manifested in the nitty-gritty of human life: She is not just to be perceived in the heavens and in the swirling atoms of the inward world, but also in human life, that is in the ongoing processes which we know as human history. And what we are doing is fixing our eyes upon this Focus and participating in the part of the flow of events known roughly as the Christian community. We are seeing the manifestation of the Divine as particularly evident in the flow of Christian events. This is not, of course, to deny that the Divine is elsewhere in history. In fact, there are many givens, we believe, for the Christian in what is often perceived rather negatively as "non-Christian" history. But in articulating a worldview our primary given is the story of Christ and his followers down through history. In short, revelation is itself an aspect of the traditions which go to make up what loosely we call Christianity.

Now obviously we have to have criteria for determining what are the clearer manifestations of the Divine in human history. Much of Christian history is black; and many of those saints actually canonised by the Church both East and West have after all rather doubtful characters. The best perhaps that we can do here in evolving criteria is delineating a consistent ethos which pervades both the life of Christ and of the developing church.

We are, in anchoring our worldview in revelation, not tying this concept to the words of the Bible, even if they are central to the ritual dimension of Christian living. From the perspective of Christian living, anything is revelatory which conduces to the experience of the Transcendent. The Eucharist itself, then, is a mode of revelation, and so in certain circumstances are the words of doctrines. Indeed, revelation can occur in any dimension of the Christian life, and in any human beings in the ongoing process of history.

The adoption of a Christian perspective on world history can be seen also in the context of Jewish thinking: for Judaism a vital question is how the people who have been chosen to walk with God through the world can serve other peoples, who also have their own divine destinies. So the Christian should think about what service this particular gleaming band of history can perform for the globe as a whole. So, looked at in this light, we do not so much need a justification for revelation, but rather a sense of loyalty to the given, and a feeling for ways in which the community, with this given nature, can serve the world. The root of the Christian faith has to do with Israel and Christ: but it functions for the Christian much as the highlands and the lochs do for the Scot. They are the Scot's heritage, and she is loyal to it; she thinks them wonderful, and does not diminish their claims. But they are there as brute givens: they help to define the character of Scottishness.

So what has been called revelation is, on our account, broader than the words of scripture, which are secondary in that it is what they point to which is, in part, revelation. Christ and the early community are part of the given through which the Transcendent manifests itself to us. This is an inductivist account of revelation, but it is also a stretched version. We stretch the concept to that which is illuminatingly given to the Christian in the processes of history and, for that matter, in the recesses of human experience and the brilliance of Christian ritual. It is artificial to cut Christian history as though beyond the time of Peter and Paul − that is, roughly the period of the writings of the early community and the events that they describe, more importantly − there is no revelation. Whether the Church was right in closing the canon where it did is open to debate. Since we only regard the Bible as *primus inter pares* to genuinely Christian writings, and only as secondary to the human events through which, properly speaking, the Transcendent is revealed, we do not think that it was wise to draw so sharp a line as the Church did; and the Bible should be set in the context not only of later writings, but also in the lives of holy people in later history. The best thing about the Canon is that it forced the community to decide which were the documents most in accord with the spirit of the faith as conceived at that time.

Perhaps we would be wise then to draw a distinction which occurs in the mainstream Hindu tradition, between those things called *śruti*, the primordial revelation, and those summed up as *smṛti* or secondary revelation. Or better still to follow Buddhist practice and ask ourselves what the Dharma is as preached by Christ and extended in the community.

It should be noted, though, that modern ideas of the very central importance of the Bible as revelation arise largely from a particular circumstance: that it was studying the Bible in a restless age that led to the perception, by Luther and other Reformers, of the gap between primordial teaching and primordial community life on the one hand and the actual behavior of the Church on the other. The Bible became a bomb under the establishment. It was the angle from which the official doctrines and practices could be criticized. It became that higher ground from which the swamps of ecclesiastical life could be surveyed, and on which the new faithful could find a safer existence. Thus the Bible became, in the days of the Reformation and afterwards, a key to the prophetic critique of the Church that claimed too to be faithful to the Gospel.

But we have witnessed a second wave of criticism: it is true from a more secular direction, but valid nonetheless − the criticism of rigid interpretations of the Gospel by those who do not perceive that the Bible can be studied and explored like any other set of ancient documents. The critical investigation of the Bible has largely exhausted itself, and most results that can be achieved have been. The endless working over of the texts yields a degree of scepticism about how much we know in a hard way about the historical Jesus, and an array of rival scholarly interpretations so various, that we can no longer use the Bible for proof texts. We can no longer even be "conceptual revelationists", taking the concepts as given even if the historical facts are not; or symbolic revelationists, taking the symbols as sacrosanct even if the concepts and the facts may be in doubt. This revolution in our thinking has yielded liberal Protestantism, Catholic modernism and other movements. That they have had a profound effect is obvious; and yet the community has continued because for many the real revelation is not the Bible itself but the ongoing life of the Church.

The Sources of Revelation

We have already sketched how revelation can occur in several dimensions. We here oppose that view that only through revealed scriptures is there revelation. The reasons we do so are as follows:

(1) The main reason why Protestantism has taken the *sola scriptura* position is to preserve the principle that all knowledge of God is saving knowledge, and all salvation comes from God: so we must reject the pretensions of human reason to be a source of knowledge about God. We do not at all deny the premise. But of course on the Christian view all things, including our own powers, flow from the Divine. If the principle is "Only from God", no restriction is thereby placed upon the actual sources of revealed truth. We may call this principle the principle of *prasāda* or divine favor. It is best to think of the point made as *prasāda* only, not *sola scriptura*. For divine favor permeates the whole of creation. Naturally, however, this principle is not a primary one, for how do we know that the Divine is a personal being and the sole source of holiness? That claim is itself something that has various sources.

(2) As we have indicated there are epistemological

weaknesses pertaining to the Bible and to any other scriptures, but let us spell the two primary ones as far as the Bible goes. In spelling these out we are talking about how we know things. Questions of how inspiring, or stirring, or subversive the Bible is are separate. First, there is the problem of the uncertainty of the real narrative: modern critical studies undermine aspects of the historicity of the Gospels, etc. – or to be more precise, though the Gospels, etc., may be historically rooted we cannot proceed as if every incident is actual. Thus there arises a pervasive uncertainty when we quote the written texts. Second, the Church's decision to adopt what is now canonical may have been well justified, but there must be plenty of room for argument because primarily of modern knowledge of alternative texts, etc.

(3) Notoriously differing groups have different interpretations of the same texts. This suggests that it is texts multiplied by interpretation that are the true source of doctrine. But interpretation means persons or some group. What if we think that the group has bad fruits? This suggests that the true sources of revealed truth as we perceive it are much wider than the *scriptura*.

(4) The idea of a sacred book is in world-historical terms a strange one. Of course having such a thing has the advantage that your tradition is liberated from the mechanical repetitions of those who specialize in exact oral transmission (typically a priestly class involved in ritual, since ritual is often thought to involve exact repetition). A book can also, as has the Bible, sit like dynamite beneath the innovations and possible corruptions of the tradition. But it is itself no guarantor of purity, because of the text-interpretation-group tryad mentioned above: in the hands of a bad group the text becomes poison, not salvation.

So we think that it is best to be straight about it. We accept the texts of the Bible as part of our loyalty to the tradition. We adopt the texts as canonical, and in a sense they too adopt us, since we are made in the image somewhat of the tradition which has taken a grip upon our lives and imaginations. We shall have occasion to argue from time to time that our treatment of key issues (e.g. the notion of divinization of *theosis* is suggested by and consonant with the Biblical texts). But we do not pretend that the Biblical texts are sufficient by themselves for our understanding of the faith. Our concept of the sources of revelation is much wider. In effect, as we have mentioned, revelation can come through any of the dimensions of religion: so let us sketch how this is.

The Doctrinal Dimension: Abstract "Proofs," Concrete Doctrines

There are several ways in which the doctrinal dimension presents the Ultimate to us.

(1) We consider that two of the so-called proofs of God's existence are suggestive to us (Smart, 1964, pp. 80–115; 1970, pp. 140–157). The question "Why is there a cosmos?" (which is a better formulation than the more haunting "Why does anything exist at all?") remains a question even when all the science has been done, and whether we consider the empirical cosmos to be everlasting or to have had a finite beginning in time (e.g. something over ten billion years ago). Even if it be everlasting we would still be able to ask a question about it. So although no one could ever show that you have to go outside (i.e. "outside") the cosmos for a Cosmos-Explaining Being the notion is still suggestive. If such a CEB is filled out with some properties (derived from revelation in some other mode), then there is an advance in explanation in ascribing the cosmos' existence to the Divine. But no one would think of this as *proof*. It is just an argument that has some potency. It is a reason for belief, not by itself very powerful, but not devoid of plausibility either. Second, the universe is orderly enough for life. It is not unreasonable to see the evolutionary emergence of consciousness as significant. It may be coincidence, and how could we prove otherwise (even juggling with statistics in the mode of Richard Swinburne)? But there is some basis in the argument from enough-design-for-consciousness for belief in the Divine, especially given our weak form of the Cosmological Argument. And, by the way – we shall say

more of this later – a Divine Being who brings consciousness into existence by evolution or other means creates suffering in the cosmos: could he or she decently refuse to be part of that system? We believe not merely that the Ultimate is a complete *avatāra* and so identified with our sufferings; but also that the Spirit is the inner controller or *antāryamin* within all individual consciousnesses, no doubt including animal ones, and so finds reflected in her life the sufferings and joys of each; so in causing joy in ourselves and others we cause a fragment of joy in the Divine and in causing suffering, some suffering.

(2) The doctrinal dimension yields Christian theologies or *darśana*s. The function of these is to present a vision of the Divine. Consequently the chief use of a Christian systematic theology, such as this one, is to present an intellectual vision. Its being intellectual will not diminish its existential impact: indeed, hopefully the opposite is the case. For it is lack of plausibility that saps the sense of inspiration among many intellectual constructs – as older sets of ideas fade (for instance Neothomism). More concretely, a view of the relation between religion and science which seeks somehow to synthesize two different approaches to the Reality "out there" may help to give us a sense that differing aspects of our lives are not to be separated. We can see God's mind at work among the quarks and gravitons, and in the waves and particles interwoven with mathematical formulae. Or again, the notion that the Divine can be seen as three centers of consciousness helps to let us see the diversity of her operation in and through history as a unity. So the concrete systems have a practical outreach in the visions interpreted through our lives.

(3) In any case every doctrine has to be seen in its setting in other dimensions. A God is a Being who is to be worshipped. The impermanence of the world is something to be experienced. The doctrine of the Incarnation has obvious ethical significance. The Spirit is to be seen, among other places, in the institutional setting of our ongoing communities.

The Mythic or Narrative Dimension: A Prime Locus of Self-Revelation

Modern scholarship, in prying loose the texts of the Bible from their sacred monumentality and subjecting them to ordinary historical scrutiny has driven us onward, through the texts, to what they are about – and what they are about is a whole flow of events, interpreted in various ways, which constitute part of wider human history. There are, for instance, the prophets of the Hebrew Bible and Jesus and Paul among others in the New Testament. It is of course Jesus above all who shows the Christian the divine nature and performs that ultimate act which we see as salvation. And so in an important sense it is a historical person whose narrative gives us the central insight into the nature of the Divine. But that is not all. There are in our opinion at least three levels at which the Divine behind history shines luminously through the events of history.

(1) There is the primary locus to which we have already referred: the life and words of Jesus, which is the central point of reference of the scriptural writings. But Jesus is embedded in his times and those times include also his followers: the people round and beyond Jesus also reflect his nature, and it is quite artificial for us to give unique status to those who happen to be mentioned in the New Testament and inferior status to the saints outside those documents. And so we come to the second level of biography in which we see God displayed.

(2) At the second level are the "saints" of the Church and of the Christian community at large. We put "saints" here in quotes because we do not need to identify these figures with those whom the main Christian organizations have given the title to: but we mean those whose lives have conspicuously reflected Christ and the whole Christian message. They represent in a living way a revelation of what the *darśana* means. As the Christian tradition grew and expanded through the Roman empire it was these saintly figures who stood beside the written words and were equally, or more, inspiring, and equally, or more, the *śabda* or testimony to the Highest. They range from Paul to Bon-

hoeffer and from Peter to Teresa; from Andrew to Ruys-
broeck, and from James to Gregory Palamas. So revelation
occurs in narratives far beyond the Biblical ones, but
including them. This is the second way in which revelation
occurs within the mythic dimension.

(3) There are the stories of great heroes and saintly
persons of other traditions, from Hallaj to the Hasidim, and
from Buddhaghosa to Ramanuja, from Shinran to
Confucius, from Muhammad to Gandhi, whose lives also
illuminate us and who reflect, imperfect though they may
sometimes be, like all "saints", the Divine nature. It is part
of our thesis that it makes no sense to view Christian truth
as cut off from global history; and there seems no good
reason at all to think of these personages as not telling us
something about the Ultimate. So we include these as a third
strand in the people of history who are part of our "sacred
book". We read the hand of Īśvara in the pages of world
history as well as in the Gospels and their companions in
the New Testament. Already we are of course committed
to such divinely-revealing heroes in the pages of what we
call the Old Testament: the figures of the pre-Christian
tradition sparkle with the gleams of the Beyond.

Should we go beyond these three levels? What are we to
make of mythic beings who do not exist, but serve yet as
archetypal inspirations? We think of the innumerable
bodhisattvas of Buddhism, of Lao-tze, of Rama and Krishna,
of primeval persons in African tales – there are many such
fictional heroes embedded in the world's myths. And there
are also the true fictions of modern times – Alyosha in *The
Brothers Karamazov*, the Saint of Fogazzaro, and other
revelatory persons who tell us something about the Īśvara
(the personal Ultimate) and yet who are sometimes despised
because they lack reality. Well, they do not exist, but they
are real persons in the minds of many faithful people. They
have the power of reality even if they lack the accolade of
existence. They can be accounted a fourth source of narrative
or mythic knowledge about the Ultimate. So we can in these
matters adopt a doctrine of levels of source in the narrative
dimension: where for the Christian Christ is primary, and

Christ is of course identical with Jesus. (To foreshadow our later discussion of the Incarnation, the difference between Jesus and other illuminating spiritual heroes lies in the fact that he is identical with the Divine Being, when seen from a Christian perspective).

Naturally, a narrative of good people does not by itself make up revelation. It is when the narrative is told and reveals the person and when she who contemplates the person sees behind her the Person that revelation takes place, and faith is stimulated.

The Ethical Dimension: Critical Values

To some degree we have of course already dealt with the realm of ethical and political values by considering the saints as exemplars. But the more systematic ways in which moral values are set forth through the history of Christianities, whether in communities or in textbooks, can represent challenges to us which may stimulate greater imitation of Christ. There is a prophetic strand in Christian thinking about what is socially and individually right and wrong. Because of this we need to be stirred from Beyond: the prophet speaks her message from the ramparts of another world. Such prophecies thus are intimations of the nature of the Ultimate, as Love.

At the same time other traditions can help to put Christianities in perspective. We have already said, as an apophthegm, that the Īśvara arranged for there to be rival religions in order that they might keep one another honest. Thus Buddhist non-violence, Islamic brotherhood, Confucian courtesy, Jewish orderliness, Black liberation and other values stand as silent criticisms of much that goes on in Christian hearts. There is no call to derive our values exclusively or even primarily from Christian sources.

The Experiential Dimension: Patterns of Spirituality

Lying behind many of the prophetic challenges, saintly lives, creative encounters, ethical challenges, etc., there are, of course, attitudes and quests, visions and patterns of self-training which come under the general rubric of the experiential dimension of religion. We do not need at this juncture, then, to stress ways in which yoga, bhakti and other experiential contexts can be revelatory of the Great Ultimate. They are concretized in patterns of spirituality which point beyond themselves. It may be that we look primarily to the Christian traditions, as we have noted in the foregoing. In principle the four levels of revelation apply in this context too.

The Ritual Dimension: The Sacramental World
The Christian *darśana* is profoundly sacramental. Jesus is Christ's body; the cosmos is the body of the Heavenly Father; each consciousness is as it were the body of the Spirit as inner controller or *antaryāmin*; the central ritual of Christianity as we understand the Christian dharma is the thanksgiving, the Eucharist. But the very idea of sacrament is a ritual or more broadly a performative act (an expression which though redundant is meant to tie in with the notion of performative utterance, for a performative act is an act with specialized meaning − of which we need to talk more later). Not all religions prize ritual in quite the same way: and some are remarkably informal. But *li* as we understand it is primarily an interpersonal act of communication (but not of information, save secondarily). At the heart of the Christian *darśana* is the notion of the Ultimate communicating itself through a life, and then conveying that life through a sacramental ritual. It is quite artificial to think of Christian experience as divorced from ritual: and therefore ritual means are used to convey revelation to the individual and to the group. And can the Christian not at one remove learn something from Muslim prayer or Hindu yoga?

The Institutional Frameworks of Revelation
The various communities of the religious world exist to respond somehow to the Ultimate. They are bearers of the other dimensions which we have considered: they provide a milieu for *darśana* reflection; they give us the stories which are handed down; they provide the values of the faith-traditions which they represent; they are nurturers of

experience and are shaped by *li*. In being loyal to a revelation we are loyal to, though one hopes we are not uncritical of, a set of institutions. It is again artificial to think of revelation as existing outside of institutional frameworks entirely, however the prophet or the individual seeker may be a loner.

Implications of the Foregoing

Our loyalty to a particular line of "saints" does not exclude learning from many other sources, including of course so-called secular thought and action. We have made use of the notions of levels of the divine self-revelation, and more needs to be clarified on this score. But it is already obvious that we have a positive evaluation of much in human history and in human religions others than the Christianities of our tradition. Not only is there much good in other faiths; but there is also much that is bad in the Christianities to which we are heir. This rather positive view of the "others" springs from the fairly obvious effects of studying the religions. We shall shortly consider an objection to this stance, from a Barthian direction. But let us first note that on the view which we have here presented, revelation is something of a wide category. Why not? If it be the way the Lord stirs us into response, then there is no reason why it should not be through any aspect of what embodies her in the cosmos or in human life. If we have an anchorage in Christ and to that degree the Bible as reflecting his life and meaning, that is because we are gripped by the Christian *darśana*. There may be, as we have seen, reasons for holding to this vision, but no proofs.

Yet a strong motif in the Christian tradition has been the sharp line drawn between the Gospel and other messages, and between Christ and other teachers, and between the Christian path to salvation and other prescriptions for liberation. Even those who held that there might be knowledge of God outside of revelation, through natural theology, so-called, did at least draw a clear boundary round revelation. This we refuse to do, both on logical and human grounds. If there is a line drawn it concerns Jesus' identity.

We affirm the identity-statement that Jesus is God (and we do not make this statement about anyone else, though many men and women manifest Ultimacy). But we do not in other respects make hard and sharp divisions, e.g. between revealed and natural theology. It is no longer plausible to do so not only because once we have refused to identify revelation with Biblical texts, there can be no ground for hardness beyond the texts, or in the texts. The texts too become human constructs of course, and why should we single out these texts from all others?

Barth, however, and Kraemer who followed him somewhat, wished to draw a sharp line. For all religion is a human construct; but the Gospel in Christ transcends all religion and religions, and as divine self-revelation is that to which Christianity is a response. All religions come under the judgment of Christ (so argued Kraemer in his influential *The Christian Message in a Non-Christian World* though he modified his position later). The trouble of course with this view is that anyone can turn it the other way: the Dharma transcends all religions, as do the Tao in itself, Buddhahood . . . and so on. If the Christian jumps a logical level so can anyone else. One is reminded of the famous scene in "The Great Dictator" when the two dictators wind themselves up in barbers' chairs in order to transcend each other. We do not deny that the Focus of faith transcends the arrangements of religion, but which is the true Focus? The rivalry just breaks out again at the transcending level. The stubborn claim to follow Christ beyond all religions becomes simply an affirmation, without reasons.

The scriptural and experiential basis for wishing to express the inadequacy of human intellect and judgment in relationship to what is revelation is, in the monotheistic traditions, that there is but one source of the holiness which liberates people: that one source is the one Holy Being. Or to put matters in other language, it is by divine grace that we are saved – indeed enabled to do anything excellent. It is for this reason that we affirmed earlier the principle that all saving knowledge of the Ultimate comes from the Ultimate. But as we earlier stated, this says nothing to us

110

about natural theology, or the theology of religious experience, etc. For as Creator, the *Īśvara* pervades our whole existence, and generates in us the vision by which she herself is perceived or experienced. There are, then, religious reasons behind the position of Barth and Kraemer but they do not have the exclusivist consequence which they imagine.

The epistemological situation is complicated. If we say that knowledge of the Ultimate comes to us by "revelation", we have to make out this case: it is because of certain features in the general structure of Divine-human relations. If we appeal to grace, then that itself flows from a special kind of experience, namely the numinous experience, and from devotional or *bhakti* religion. Since that, as a dominant motif, has to be defended, there is much groundwork to do. But even if the concept of divine initiative has been established, a whole lot of other things have to be grounded as well: for instance, that the Ultimate's grace comes to us in one way rather than another. Just to appeal to revelation is to point to something brutely given. In fact defenders of a given mode of revelation have usually reasons for identifying it as such – the extraordinary circumstances of the composition of the Qur'an (if "composition" be the word), etc. If there are reasons for the claim that Jesus is alone an *avatāra* in the fullest sense, then these are the grounds for seeing him as supremely revelatory. And so on.

But once again we can't talk about proof. There is never clinching evidence that some set of writings is revelatory and that others are not. There can be no proof that they are the handiwork of the Divine.

In brief, we may have reasons to think of knowledge of God as self-revealed, of coming from the Other: but this in no way implies exclusivism. Nor does it imply the related irrationalism which merely presents revelation on a take-it-or-leave-it basis.

Very often the most conservative presenters of the Christian revelation have good, but not by themselves wholly adequate, grounds for affirming revelation: they say that study of the Bible in the right spirit will bring about a

111

transformation of character, that they have experienced being "born again", that they have achieved peace. These are taken by themselves in an exclusivist way: but they are in fact testimonies whose equivalents can be found in other faith contexts. The events in themselves are significant fruits and relevant to the truth of a religious position; but taken exclusivistically they are of course quite inadequate to establish what they purport to establish.

To sum up the gist of this part of our discussion: that God somehow has the initiative in revelation is an important view, and we are highly sympathetic to it; but it is a view which has to be supported in the crosscultural framework. It forms no basis, however, for an exclusivist position, whether that be formulated in a rather sophisticated theological manner in the style of Barth, or whether it be formulated at a gutsier level, as "fundamentalism".

The wider notion of "natural theology" chiming through the varying dimensions of religion which we have briefly indicated means that we can maintain a non-relativist position, have a positive view of other traditions and give soft reasons for our adopting the Christian tradition. So we may call our kind of appeal to wider grounds for our faith the "transChristian appeal"; when we are simply relying upon selected notions and values from our adopted tradition we can call it, of course, "Christian".

It may be objected by supposed purists that our method means that the Christian tradition will be deeply affected by non-Christian values. Our answer is double – first, because a value is not in the primary historical sense Christian it does not follow that there is anything wrong with it: it may be that the Christian tradition as we have hitherto understood it leaves out some elements of goodness; and second, all statements or formulations or livings of the Christian life involve syncretisms or blends. Fundamentalists often blend more easily because their blending is unconscious. There is no way in which we can protect ourselves from blends with values which are new in history – and it is right that we should so blend, because of the hermeneutical situation discussed earlier: to stay the same we have to change. There are no hard criteria for doing this, and so we doubtless have to rely upon Ultimate-given virtue — we need to try as far as possible to be true to our vision of Christ and to exclude feelings of malice or egotism. We also ought to be clear-thinking, so far as this is possible. But we cannot settle any issue simply on the basis of some hard external criterion, like "what the Bible says", for much depends on how we interpret it, the reasons why we have chosen the Bible and the correctness of the Bible itself.

Naturally we subscribe to the belief that the primary Christian revelation, which we find illuminated in the Bible, is the life of Christ. But it is time for us to make quantitative rather than qualitative distinctions between the sources of truth as we see it — that is, things do not belong to separate categories as sources of truth, but range in plausibility and weight from the more central to the more peripheral sources of knowledge of the Ultimate.

Insofar as we subscribe to a canon, the answer is that the canonical history of the Israelites, their successors, and of the budding Christian church and its aftermath, is what we "adopt" as canonical. Insofar as we are in the grip of this vision of the Ultimate, we might say also that we are adopted by this stream of divine action.

Some Other Classical Philosophy of Religion Questions

We have touched on some primary issues in the philosophy of worldviews, but there are others, such as the so-called problems of evil and freewill, and the possibility of immortality, etc., which have been very much the staple of Western philosophy of religion. We shall deal somewhat with these issues in a more theological context. For instance, the so-called problem of evil has to be seen in the context of the doctrine of creation, and in turn this has to be seen in the context of the idea of incarnation and of the Divine as being "inner-controller". Thus a God who undergoes the sufferings of her own creation is different from an aloof impassible Creator.

The Concept of Transcendence (Smart, 1958, pp. 34–45; 1966, pp. 113–125)

It is important to recognize that the traditionally-religious worldviews wield the concept of transcendence and have belief in some arm or other of the Transcendent. This is a prime mark of the distinction between a religious and a non-religious worldview, according to the canons of Western usage. It is necessary for us to be clear about what this concept amounts to, since it bears on some important philosophical issues, notably on the status of the cosmological argument (e.g. in its weak form adumbrated earlier).

First, we must note that the Latin word "transcendence" enshrines in a jargon-ridden way the conception of something which is "beyond". That is what "trans-" means. But often there are different things that the Ultimate is said to be *beyond*. Sometimes God, for instance, is said to be beyond thought or beyond speech. Roughly, it is correct in our view to say that there must be at least an aspect of the Ultimate which is ineffable, and so cannot be thought or described. Of course, there are different ways of going beyond speech too, so that this concession may have multiple meaning. But it appears to us contradictory to hold that there is no respect in which the Ultimate can be spoken about or at least indicated or pointed to: since then there would indeed be nothing about which we were concerned. However, it is not this sense of transcendence which is primary. The primary sense in which the Ultimate is said to be beyond something is that in which it is "beyond the world", or "beyond the cosmos".

The concept of *cosmos* seems to us clearer than the concepts of *world* or *universe*. "World" sometimes is used in a rather existential sense, as in "the world of Paul Slickey" or "the world of Mikhail Gorbachev". This is a useful mode of locution, but it is not the sense in which God transcends the world since anyone else transcends Gorbachev's world. And anyone else is not God, necessarily. The notion of "universe" is sometimes defined as "everything that there is" – and if God is then he or she cannot transcend everything that there is: she is part of the universe. (You can be both part of the universe and beyond it, no doubt: but this is not applicable here.) So we think it best to think of the world as the cosmos, i.e. the object or complex of objects studied by cosmologists. To complicate matters there is some talk in modern cosmology of parallel cosmoses and the like: let us just say that if you need anything beyond what hitherto has counted as this cosmos to explain some aspect of it then that is part of a wider supercosmos. We thus are either talking about this cosmos or this supercosmos. We shall leave on one side the empty thought of possible parallel cosmoses having no relation at all to this cosmos. So to say that God or nirvana is transcendent is to affirm that God is "beyond" the cosmos.

But that at first sight seems to be a contradiction, since the very idea that one thing is beyond another implies that they both are in space, but different parts thereof relative to the speaker. But space is coterminous with the cosmos. So in saying that the Transcendent is beyond the cosmos we are saying that it is beyond space. But this is meaningless, if taken literally.

Unless, that is, the concept of "beyond" is analogical. It may be that the Transcendent is non-spatial. We may note that even when we say that the Divine is "within" all things we do not mean this literally. We cut the wood and in a sense God perchance is there, but not literally in the sense in which maggots might be in there, or grains of wood, or even molecules or atoms or quarks. So the Divine is not literally in anything but might be working in all things in some analogical sense. This notion that both within and beyond in some contexts may refer not to literal directions but to analogical ones might suggest that apparent differences of direction may not actually be so. The Transcendent beyond may lie in the same place as the Immanent within. But we should note that when some writers refer to immanence they often mean something like "manifesting itself in some particular place or being within the cosmos", as when it is said that God is immanent in the sacraments. But in the more general sense in which it is

115

claimed that the Divine is within all things, it may be that the locus of immanence and transcendence is the same. Moreover, the infinity of the Divine Being can be expressed through the concept of non-spatial extension. We shall discuss this in the Chapter on the Divine Embodiment.

However, there is more to the idea that the Divine transcends the cosmos than that the Divine is non-spatial. It means at least that (and God might of course be timeless as well): But if that were all, why say that God is beyond the cosmos? One notion implied in the beyond, as it is usually meant, is that the Divine is behind the cosmos. It is as if the cosmos is a sort of screen which conceals behind it the Divine. In fact with the concept of Isvara there is usually also the thought that God is not just behind in the sense of being hidden, but behind more pregnantly as the mover, the dynamic energy behind all created things. So here "beyond" ties in with the context of Divine Being as Creator.

And not just creator when, if ever, there was a Big Bang: but always the sustainer, that is to say the continuous creator, of the cosmos. Even if the cosmos has been everlasting, either cyclically through an indefinite series of Big Bangs and Big Crunches, or in some other manner, there is no reason why God should not be continuously keeping the cosmos in being. It would be as if she were a violin player who has always been playing a cosmic tune upon her instrument, or a singer for whom we are the song, for ever. So the notion of Creation does not, of course and as many have perceived, depend on the idea of a beginning. (In any event the time of "In the beginning . . ." is unusual – as Eliade has rightly observed.) So in the case of a theistic picture of the cosmos, there is an element in the "beyond" or "behind" which is lacking in some other systems. One does not want to say, for instance, that nirvana is behind all things (though some Mahayana ideas come close to this).

To say then that the Divine transcends the cosmos is to imply three things at least – that she is non-spatial, that she is hidden by the cosmos, and that she is creatively active behind the cosmos. All this implies that she is different from the cosmos. This fits in with the model of the God-person relationship that typifies *bhakti* religion and Otto's notion of the Other. The holiness of God is seen in the way in which she is concealed by the world, as if in a temple by a curtain or an iconostasis. And being beyond the visible world she is also in herself unseen. But to say that she is different from the cosmos is not necessarily to say that she does not differ from us – this depends on one's doctrine of the self. But for our purposes we shall here assume that the Divine has an extra dimension – being beyond the self, that is more inward than consciousness – the *antaryāmin*, or inner controller. If God is closer to me than my neckvein, at the summit or abyss of my soul, then she is beyond in a different analogical direction. So, as we have noted, it may be that the God beyond there is in the same place as the God within here.

It seems to us that this complex of ideas contained in the notion that the Divine is beyond the cosmos is not contradictory. That he is non-spatial, causative of the cosmos, holy, Other from us, but working in us and in the cosmos – all these notions hang together. It is not the same list of properties which you would identify with Transcendence in some cases, e.g. Theravadin nirvana. There nirvana is non-spatial, not "in" the empirical cosmos; but not causative or dynamic as sustaining the cosmos. Nor would it be natural to worship nirvana or even nirvana as "incarnated" in the Buddha (though Mahayana and other influences have affected practice in Sri Lanka and elsewhere). So some cases of Transcendence have, in context, more content than do others. But from the angle of our Christian concept, and more generally the theistic notion, to say that the Divine is beyond the cosmos makes fairly rich sense: moreover, the idea that God is beyond does not differ markedly from saying that she is *within* all things – for this too in context implies dynamic creative activity in the whole cosmos, though perhaps especially within us as conscious beings. We account for this through the notion of non-spatial causation.

There might be an objection to the model we have laid out: namely that we have left unexplained how it is that God might have a continuous causative effect upon the cosmos. The image which we can use is very close to us – indeed it *is* us. That is, I can as a conscious being raise my arm or put forward my foot without further intervention by bodily means. The human being illustrates the interplay between conscious and material events. So can we not think of God as (so to speak) the soul of the cosmos? We shall later explore this analogy. But it seems a consistent conception, and though some traditional theists might suspect this of being a "pantheistic" concept, this is actually an illusion. If the cosmos' soul has control over it, then functionally this idea is equivalent to others, such as creation from nothing, which have been advanced to preserve the Divine freedom, and holiness.

The picture which we have here drawn of Divine Transcendence has some peculiar philosophical consequences which it is worth remarking on fairly briefly. The first has to do with the way the Divine in being beyond the cosmos is reflected within the cosmos. To give the notion of an X outside the cosmos substance it is necessary at least to see some events within the cosmos as more clearly reflecting that X than do other events. What, after all, is the stamp of the Ultimate upon its cosmos?

The point of a *darśana* such as this one here presented is to give a geography, so to say, of the Great Ultimate in the cosmos – where it is reflected in the stars and the moral law, as Kant averred; where it is seen in the serene face of the Buddha and the body of Christ; in the scores of Mozart, and in the Analects; in the dark waves and the numinous clouds of the Irish sea; in the gold of altars, and the still voice of noble suffering – wherever that Ultimate is to be seen, where the cosmos and history are experienced as reflecting the divine, there our map is supposed to point. But in thinking about the philosophical questions let us not for the moment look to the particularities of our anyone else's *darśana*, but to the form. Now the *form* consists in this – that a given manifestation of the Great Ultimate is in the cosmos, but the Great Ultimate itself lies "beyond" the cosmos, as we have noted and analysed.

There is no way, at least in this life (and note that the "at least" suggests that it is an easy thing to make the transition to some other life, and yet it is not, for how do we know there is another life *there*?) to swing round to the back of the cosmos and have a look. Behind the holy screen there may be the Ultimate, but we cannot remove the screen. Gertrude Stein went to Oakland from New York and when asked what it was like there she said "There is no there there": but there is for us no passage from our New York, the cosmos, to the Great Ultimate, our Oakland. There are of course ways in which we may wish to speak of what lies beyond: but for the time being (so to speak) there is no bursting forth from our cosmic home. Consequently, the Ultimate manifests here, but lies like a noumenon beyond experience itself.

The point, ironically, was well appreciated by the great phenomenologist of religion, Gerardus van der Leeuw, who was much criticized by some for integrating his phenomenology (supposed to be value-neutral) with his Christian theology (supposed to be espousing particular values). He thought of the objects of theology as lying in that other world, and so the study of its manifestations could itself be phenomenological. The step beyond the experience of Christ to the affirmation of Christ was a step into the noumenal world.

There is truth in this position, though it in no way washes out the distinction between the plural and objective (if that is not too misleading a word) study of religion and Christian or any other brand of theology. But the noumenal character of what lies Beyond can be affirmed. And because of this the analysis which we have given of the Beyond means that our *darśana* in going Beyond does not so to say *add* power to the Christian faith: the experience of Christ has whatever effects it has whether or not Christ exists in the Beyond, and so on with the powers of the various dimensions of religion.

Nevertheless the idea of the Transcendent is of the utmost importance in explicating theism (and other religious positions). We cannot reduce God down to experiences. We need the notion that she lies in the Beyond.

All this implies that the doctrinal affirmation that there is a Divine Being does not point to some further area of power which is added to God beyond experience. All power that we experience manifests itself in and through the cosmos. It is true that a particular individual, in affirming that which is Transcendent, links up her own experience and ritual responses, etc., with those of others, and insofar as God is creator and continuous sustainer of this whole cosmos, with all other events in the world. That of course is a great claim: our point is merely that in this world we can only experience the cosmos and our experiences *as* emanating from God. We cannot go round the back to see the Great Ultimate as it really is. It really is of course what is presented to us, but beyond these presentations it becomes so to speak unfathomable.

It is not thus quite how we imagine it. We tend to picture heaven as a place where we can at last "get round the back" and see God as she really is. We read with fascination of the saints in heaven as depicted in the Book of Revelation. But these images we project are themselves in the here and now: they themselves are cosmic materials through which the Divine is manifest. What they amount to in themselves we can hardly say.

Because of this extracosmic character of the point of reference of our talk about the Great Ultimate, there is for this reason if for no other (and there are other reasons in this connection) a large unspeakable aspect of the Divine. This is for ever a limitation upon what we can and cannot say. This is an important point in trying to explain a Christian outlook, for it means that we have to regret those simple expositions of the Bible which plunge with unabashed anthropomorphism into details about what God intends. These observations may lead us on to the distinction between what is "real" and what "exists".

Reality and Existence

To say that something exists and to say that it is real are often used as equivalents in modern English. But we wish to separate out the two phrases and use them differently.

If I am walking along a path and see a snake, then my heart will start to beat; I shall back off. Now I may later discover that it was not a snake at all but a piece of curving wood. In that case of course I revise my judgment. I thought I saw a snake, but actually there was no snake. But that does not detract from the fact that my heart-rate had increased. I was alert, scared, careful. So we need language to describe the status of the snake independently of whether it really existed. It is convenient for us to use the world "real" for this. For me, the snake was for a time real. Similarly in phenomenology we may wish to say that for Hindu ladies by the Ganges in Varanasi, Vishnu is real, whether or not we believe in Vishnu. One reason for thinking that Vishnu might exist is that for many people he is real: but we can distinguish clearly between the two judgments.

As presenting a Christian *darśana* we wish to affirm and to sketch that which, for us, exists; and indeed we would hold, though we cannot prove this, for reasons which we have already sketched, that the picture we present actually delineates things which exist independently of our faith. But we also wish in presenting a *darśana* to make it existential, that is to delineate it in a real way − as having practical and experiential outreach. The way it is real is something which we can describe phenomenologically: But in the claim that it describes what exists we go beyond phenomenology to make metaphysical-type or Christian-theological claims.

Without reality (in this special sense) a Christian or indeed any other *darśana* has no power and no relevance. But without its existence claims it has no purchase on the universe. The person who feels the power of the Divine will have no choice but to affirm the existence of the Ultimate, save that such a person has to recall the exigencies of criticism and the facts of soft non-relativism. But the existence-claim also has a reality-aspect. In affirming the reality of God's power we may be gripped by faith, and faith is driven to affirm God's existence − and so part of the power of the Great Ultimate manifests itself in humans' willingness to go beyond the empirical cosmos and to make faith-claims about what lies Beyond.

Creation and Transcendence

There is one point about the affirmation of Transcendence and of the divine creativity which needs to be grasped because it modifies what we said above about the lack of extra power assigned to God because of the claim that he or she exists: for as far as personal power channelled through experience, the sacraments and so on is concerned then indeed it is all there, on the hither side, in the working out of this power in the lives of the faithful. But it is of course part of the notion of Creation that the Divine is also "behind" the working of the whole cosmos. In linking personal religious experience to this wider claim the Christian is of course extending vastly the scope of the divine power (but the power in this case too has its instantiation and its working out on the hither side, through the processes of the cosmos).

This has religious significance, in that it means that we can search the cosmos for the luminous signs of the Divine presence. There is nothing around us which does not bear the stamp, whether more clearly or more dimly, of the Ultimate. Wherever we turn in this world we face towards God, and every place stands in her presence. This is itself implied by our picture of creativity and immanent inwardness, that the Divine Being is omnipresent: present in every locus of the cosmos to us. Everywhere there pervades the secret omnipresence of the Divine. We can add this as a notion to the complex of ideas suggested by the ideas of Transcendence and its twin brother Immanence. The only difference between these two ideas is that the one hints that the cosmos is already here (so that God is immanent in it), while the other hints that even if there were no cosmos, the Divine would still be "there". Then we can express God's creativity in part as follows: That if there were no God there would be no cosmos; but the converse does not hold (no cosmos, no God) – except perhaps in the minor context that since God is to be worshipped by us, and we would not exist without the cosmos, God would not in the full sense be "God".

These ideas prepare the way for our recasting of a

Ramanuja-type theology as part of our presentation of a Christian *darśana*: the cosmos is seen as God's body and individual conscious beings are specially luminous places of divine manifestation because our souls are so to say the bodies of God insofar as she appears within us as the *antaryāmin*. Given that God unlike us is thought of as having perfect control of his body, this model is, despite a misleading appearance of "pantheism", a fine way of expressing both the divine ruling of the cosmos and at the same time intimate implication with it, and with us. It flows from this idea that it is important for us to take up a theme of recent process theology, namely that God is affected by the world she has made. It seems to us that this is an inevitable consequence of the doctrine of the Incarnation. We see the Trinity as triply incarnate: as Christ, of course, and as God in the cosmos, and as God among conscious beings. If we picture her as reflecting about the world about to be created we cannot avoid the thought of the divine willingness to enter into the sufferings that inevitably are created for conscious beings in a spatio-temporal world. *Dukkha* or illfare is unavoidable, because joys wither, time for biological beings runs out, old bones creak, and children are snatched from parents by disease and accident, as the living forms of the cosmos necessarily prey upon one another, and as also moral beings slide towards corruption and cruelty. For all the beauties of the dawn gold, and the sweet rain upon tropical leaves, and the majestic mountains and grey deserts of this lovely planet, and the wonders of the cold-seeming stars, furnaces in the infinite blacknesses of the cosmos, there are sufferings also. How could a Creator not be affected by the pain and *dukkha* bound to be caused by meshing nature's glory, consciousness, into the weaving processes of the world? It seems to us that the Christian idea of incarnation profoundly speaks to this aspect of the so-called problem of evil: and process theology is right, with its frank admission, or claim, that God suffers too and is affected by the cosmos in which she incarnates herself and throughout which she is omnipresent. Would not impassibility be cold? And God as love glows with tender warmth.

The Relevance of Transcendence to Criticism of Values
   (Smart, 1981)

We have tried to present a coherent view of the Transcendent which links together a "soft" natural theology (incorporating soft versions of the so-called Cosmological and Teleological arguments) which also points to a conception of the Transcendent providing an anchorage for religious experience, etc., as describable in the phenomenology of religion. There is also as we have seen a spiritual significance for this idea of God as "behind" or "within" everything. There is, too, an ethical and social meaning, as we have hinted already, conferred by the notion of the Beyond. For in discerning within this world the gleams of glory which point to the Beyond we are given a feeling of being at the interface between earth and heaven. As humans our dignity is immeasurably strengthened by seeing ourselves in the light of the Beyond, of the Eternal. We are not just living creatures, but we are living creatures in contact with the Ultimate, and so we participate in that Ultimate reality. We gather some of the gold which shines from the glow of transcendental darkness. But not only that: though in gaining Christ we gain nothing, for Christ has sacrificed everything in his incarnate life, we also gain everything, since we ourselves share in Divine power. Metaphysically, the doctrine of the Transcendent we have sketched reflects the mythic or narrative dynamic of the Gospel. The Other lies beyond this life, this cosmos. In gaining it and in somehow participating in the transcendent substance of the Divine we do not gain the good things of this life: we do not gain some cheerful extension of existence. The nature of existence in the Beyond is wrapped in darkness, and we cannot promise ourselves a well-watered, fruitful paradise, a heavenly Taj Mahal, a delicious reconciliation on jewelled couches, a bathing in the glassy sea where the saints cast down with a grateful sigh their crowns. We can use these images when we sing hymns: but the Transcendent place is not a place in this world, nor is it a place like this world, but with the teeth of this world's suffering drawn. No: in gaining the Eternal we do not know what it is we gain, save for the symbols that throb through our life of service.

124

But being at the interface of heaven we have no need to fear. And we have no other way than to proclaim the dignity of human beings and of other conscious creatures. Ours then is a higher humanism than that afforded by just a scientific humanism. Ours is a transcendental humanism in which we see sketched on the features of every human being the signs of transcendental Love. Being at the interface of heaven and earth, then, we can be fearless in criticizing those ethical arrangements and social configurations which dehumanize our fellows, and which fight with love. So we have a place, so to speak, from which to criticize this world. This represents a way in which we have a prophetic vocation.

This critical function ties in with the epistemology we have espoused. It is not that we can prove our point of view: but purified by spiritual practice and clinging to right intentions, we can honestly proclaim what our vision gives to us as the true destiny and rights of our fellows. The critical ethical stance chimes in with the more general need for criticism in science and in the wider pursuit of knowledge. So there is a harmony between our accent on a Popperite epistemology and our joining with it our conception of the transcendental Other lying beyond the spiritual and other experiences which not only empower us but also reveal the shape of a Christian vision of the world. There is, then, a harmony between the different sides of our philosophical analysis as providing at least the framework for that more particular vision supplied by the tradition which we have adopted, and which has adopted us.

The Transcendent and the Theory of Two Kinds of Truth
(Smart, 1983, pp. 108–112, 162–172)

In certain ways we owe a lot to the pluralist attitude of the later Wittgenstein, that religious life, like other forms of life, retains its strength. The situation is of course fairly complex: for a religious worldview may incorporate scientific elements, in that it may absorb the current cosmologies. We cannot draw a hard line therefore between religious language and other forms. But insofar as traditional religious worldviews point to what lies Beyond, and indicate ways in which the Beyond leaves its traces, so to say, in the world about us and within us, they point beyond the sphere of operation of empirical and scientific language. Provisionally there is some attraction in the Buddhist notion of two levels of truth – *vyāvahārika* or conventional, ordinary truth; and *paramārthika* or higher truth. The one covers this world as we experience it and think about it ordinarily; the latter represents the higher insight and experience that the enlightened persons reach. Now as indeed some Great Vehicle adepts remarked, maybe the value of one position as higher than the other is misleading. For the Zen Buddhist, for instance, the here and now world has as much importance as anything beyond. The polarities are washed away in the end. Well, we can accept this from a Christian point of view: there is nothing which should demeans this world – it is God's body, the scene of Incarnation, the glorious manifestation of divine power and so forth. And can one thing really be truer than another? If there are truths about lapwings and sunsets they are just as true as any portentious truths about the Divine. So let us abandon that scaling implied in the most typical Buddhist formulations, and settle for the idea just of two kinds of truth – truths in which the Beyond is inherently entangled, and those that can be affirmed quite independently of whether we believe in the Beyond. We may add to language aimed at the Beyond worldview language in general: that is, insofar as we have already observed, worldviews "go beyond" the empirical because they have to fit the empirical in general into a wider scheme (even the wider scheme that there is only that which is empirically discoverable). Transcendental language, however, which points to the Transcendent is of chief concern to us here.

It is a good first approximation to distinguish between two kinds of truth, coequal in value. But there are some extra levels, in effect, which need to be sketched in. Thus there are some truths which we wish to affirm which are about events in or aspects of this world which we perceive as revelatory – as shining forth, as guiding our lives and our sense of the nature of the Divine Being. Thus the narratives of Christ's life belong obviously to this category. But there are plenty of other instances: for the Christian all sorts of worldly events point their fingers towards the moon Beyond. Then there are affirmations about the Divine Nature, for instance, how she works as Creator constantly causing the events around us to flow, who paints, so to speak, the colors onto the screen about us. That which is describable in the Divine Being belongs to this realm.

Rejection of a Certain Kind of "Secularizing"
The foregoing analysis of the idea of the Beyond implies that we reject those forms of Christian theology and philosophy of religion which overtly or otherwise reduce religious talk to this-worldly utterance. Thus some analyses became attitudinal, notably Paul van Buren's *The Secular Meaning of the Gospel* (1963) – the doctrine of creation thus boils down to a world-affirming attitude. Other analyses, notably D.Z. Phillips' neo-Wittgensteinian account of religious language, see the latter wholly bound up in a form of life. Outside of the context of religious practice the language becomes meaningless: and the implication is that no ontological claims to what lifes "Beyond" can be made.

In general there are problems with this position. First, it treats religious language as a separate language-game, when in fact it is a whole tribe of language-games: in other words it neglects the pluralism of religions. Also it appears to make inter-religious dialogue impossible; but in fact it happens. As for the Wittgensteinian comparison of worldviews to pictures, there may be merit in it, but it does not dispose of the question of the truth of such pictures. Finally, Fideism makes understanding an all or nothing affair, that is, you have to be inside a language to understand it and outsiders can have no understanding. This is wrong, and would imply the impossibility of the comparative study of religion. It is a wrong view, for there are degrees of understanding.

The "death of God" movement too destroyed the Beyond in Christian faith. Many of these analyses and attempts at reformulating faith had the admirable intent of bringing Christianity into living contact with the so-called secular world. The faith was celebrated as a secular faith. But the attempts rested on some confusions.

First, there was confusion between the empirical and the secular. That human beings of our age are specially bound up with the empirical world around us is nothing new: but to treat this world as "secular" is already to experience it in a special way — to see it in the light of secularism as a worldview. This worldview, which denies a Beyond, is neither necessary nor compatible with the Christian faith. If the point of the "secular city" is that it can get on perfectly well without faith, that judgment is open to question, because the nature of reality is essentially debatable, and so is the very concept of human happiness. Second, the movement was too scientistic: and perhaps was over-impressed by the attitude of much English-speaking Western philosophy in the sixties, namely a form of scientism. Since then there is increased realization of the way science changes (e.g. Kuhn and paradigm shifts; the work of David Edge and others in the social context of science, etc.), of the importance of criticism (Popper) and of the untidiness of science (e.g. exploited in Feyerabend's anarchistic epistemology). Moreover, there is the realization that some aspects of modern cosmology lead somewhat in a Buddhist direction, as the mathematical models spin webs beneath the solid-seeming surfaces of things. It is wise then for us to be more confident in pointing to the Beyond.

We can moreover take care of some of the concerns of the secularizers, that our God should be everyday: that religion should not be cut off from the grime of work, the litter of the inner cities, the magic of the silicon chip, the everyday milieu of people living in modern conditions. It is part of the way religion functions that more narrowly experienced realities have a certain transfer, in principle, to everything. It is perhaps the genius of orthodox Jewish law that by debating the minute applications of the Torah to the smallest details of life it has promoted a real sense of the pervasive relevance of the Divine to all aspects of life. In the Christian faith, which has less worry about law, it is easy to forget that the vision of Christ applies everywhere.

We should see Christ not just in the golden liturgy and taste him in the bread and wine, but see him in the many human faces about us. He is everywhere where there are lips and eyes. And the very doctrine of Transcendence which we have here been expounding implies the immanence of Brahman in everything. The Lord's handiwork is silently there in every single thing we experience. Heaven is all about us, and the *antaryāmin* lies behind every thought, every pang, every taste, every ache. The empirical may be seen neutrally as not having anything to do with our commitments and feelings: but it can also be seen in the glory of the Christian worldview, as marked in every place and at every time by the imprint of the Isvara's creative endeavour.

In short, there is no need to impose a "flat" vision on the empirical. A scientistic outlook happens to be quite important in present times, partly because of the diffidence of traditions in speaking frankly about the human condition, that is about how all worldviews are currently, and now indeed perhaps forever, open to question, including secularism.

Summing Up
The main points we have argued for in this chapter are: soft non-relativism among worldviews; the possibility of private certitude (whether of group or individual) amid public uncertainty; the need for a doctrine of canonical adoptionism to describe our attitude to Christian revelation, which lies beyond scripture; the importance for us of the narrative dimension of religion; the possibility of a multidimensional soft natural theology; the importance of the concept of transcendence, here analysed as involving otherness, non-spatiality "outside" the cosmos, creativity and concealment; and the need for us to see the empirical world as illuminated by the religious experience of the Beyond.

The Relevance of the Foregoing to the Construction of our Worldview
A number of the themes in this chapter will be dealt with in more detail in later ones, where we come actually to

present our variety of a Christian worldview. We shall begin at the heart of faith, namely in our elaboration of the doctrine of the Trinity, where the Brahman appears as *Īśvara, avatāra* and *antaryāmin.* We relate the Trinity also to religious experience and strands of language. As *Īśvara,* God is numinous, overpowering; as inner controller she is the personal presence met with at the depths of mystical experience; as incarnation she shows forth the nature, and also the splendor, of the Ultimate. In order to deal with the Trinity we of course have to see the Divine not just as summing up some of the most profound of human experiences, but also as appearing in the "shining strand" of history which for us is canonical. From there we turn more generally to a narrative interpretation of world history, seeing different great movements of history as complementary to the "shining strand": the wonderful spiritual experiments of South Asian history, the encompassing pragmatism of China, the dynamic sorties of Japanese spirituality, the shamanic and power-laden messages of Africa, and so forth. In this interpretation of world history we shall see how some of the secular forces of our time contribute to the new federalism of the human spirit that is called for in the present human crisis. In the succeeding chapter we shall give a revised interpretation of the concepts of atonement and salvation, in the context of the world religions. We shall delineate also so far as we can discern it the creative functions of the Spirit in present world events and in the vital meaning of the mystical path in modern culture.

We shall discuss in more detail the Neotranscendentalist interpretation of creation and the two-aspect theory of truth to delineate the relations between religion and science. From this we shall to go to diagnose our modern sense of the past and to sketch a gallery of our ancestors as world citizens. Our epistemology implies the federalist approach not just to worldviews but also to the differing strands of Christian denominationalism.

We stressed in our discussion in this chapter the importance of the concept of Transcendence to the critical character of prophetic Christian speaking about current values. Neotranscendentalism will provide a framework for criticizing materialisms of the present era: and also a strong motivation for social action. This will introduce a consideration of the criteria for sifting the positive from negative elements in the plural presence of alternative worldviews.

5

Christian Neotranscendentalism in relation to Some Influential Modern Theologies

A Brief Survey

It may be useful to give our readers an orientation by seeing Neotranscendentalism in relation to some of the important strands of thought among "mainly" Twentieth Century Christian theologians. The more detailed engagement with the particular issues arising in the construction of a Christian worldview will further illuminate the relationship of our position to that of others. Briefly we may discern the following, often overlapping positions.

There is liberal Protestantism, by which we are of course deeply influenced. Of the modern or relatively modern exponents of such a position we shall mention Schleiermacher, Bultmann and process theology. Though using liberal scholarly methods, Karl Barth put forward a neo-orthodox position, and we shall define our views over against his partly because he is not only the most striking exponent of a kind of theological conservatism, but is arguably the greatest of the Twentieth Century theologians. On the conservative front also are evangelical and fundamentalist Christians, about whom we shall also have a comment.

In the sixties there was the great wave of secular theology, expressed notably by Paul van Buren, Thomas Altizer and Harvey Cox. In the Jewish context we should mention also Richard Rubenstein. Though not so rigorously "secularist", the hope-oriented theologies of Moltmann and Pannenberg also need our attention.

The seventies were perhaps chiefly characterized by the influence of various kinds of Christian liberation theology (including Black theology, etc.). Somewhat different, but not uninfluenced by these more political aspects of Christian thinking is feminist theology.

In the Catholic tradition the moves have been made towards a more pluralist understanding, in the thought of such as Kung and David Tracy, partly as a result of that upheaval known as Vatican II.

We also need to define our position over against recent dialogically oriented thinkers such as Hick, W.C. Smith and Raimundo Panikkar – but because their thought is so integral to some of the concerns throughout this book we shall leave our consideration of some of their claims till later. In this excursus we wish rather to indicate our position in regard to some main trends in more traditionally modern theology.

Schleiermacher and Bultmann

We deal here with Schleiermacher largely because he represents the first most important thinker in the Christian tradition who shifted attention from text and doctrine to religious experience. While we have a much more complex perception of the nature of religious experience – of its various types – we welcome the shift in emphasis. The comparison of experiences in the dialogue between religions is much more fruitful than the mere comparison of allegedly sacred texts. So we affirm the Schleiermacher heritage not just positively but also negatively: it enables us more easily to cope with the problems posed by higher criticism and the comparative study of religion. As a main founder of the liberal Protestant position, moreover, Schleiermacher is one of our most vital ancestors. We do not believe in the feeling of absolute dependence as the most satisfactory mode of expressing the inner nature even of the numinous experience (and so importantly we follow Otto here): but the main shape of Schleiermacher's interpretation of religious faith we regard as epoch-making.

It may be that later liberal theology took too optimistic a view of human nature. The confident hope in progress up to World War II went with a "human potential" movement inside liberal Protestantism. Much of this optimism went with a sense of human power: yet we meet the paradox that though we now as humans have immense power over external forces in nature we still feel helpless in taming the impulses in human nature that find expression in social injustice, vast and murderous weapons and political repression. We might think therefore that Barth's protest during World War II, and his affirmation of a new orthodoxy stressing the great gap between heaven and earth, was justified. But we can save much of the liberal Protestant ethos by seeing the problems of human nature against the background of religious experience. Although in the liberal perspective we should not ignore the good things in human nature (here we are impressed by the doctrines of Mencius: What person would not start forward to help a little child tottering on the edge of a well?), we are also well aware of the chief human failings, which Buddhism sums up as *lobha, dosa* and *moha*, namely greed, hatred and delusion (or ignorance, *avidya*). These relate to the classical Christian notion of sin or alienation from God. Greed can be considered to be the desire for material things, but basically out of a drive for aggrandizement. It features in Christian myth in the rebellion against the Creator. Hatred of persons is, from the Christian perspective, the opposite of the religion of love: and love is summed up in Christ. Ignorance or delusion is the opposite of insight, which is what we find in the pursuit of inner truth and in the creative work of the Spirit. We need of course to analyse more deeply why it is we have such a thirst for egotism, hatred and delusion. But it is no part of the liberal perspective as such to be overoptimistic. Ghazali said that reason is God's measure upon earth, and there is no special cause to think that the discontinuous irrationalism of the Barthian position is the only antidote to such human evils as Nazism.

Position Theory and Varieties of Christian Theology
At this point, if we may digress for a moment, a modern analysis of religion and worldview helps to throw some light on the various positions that can be adopted. It is what we

have elsewhere called Position Theory. It sees traditional religions as combining with various intellectual and other living movements, and analyzes the various positions which can be occupied (roughly any position that can be occupied soon or later will be, even if at first you might think its blending components to be incompatible). Liberal Protestantism is a blend of Protestant Christianity, liberal scholarship and liberal political elements, for instance. Liberation theology is a blend of Catholicism, Third World alienation and Marxism. The Moral Majority is a blend of Christian evangelicalism, conservative politics and American patriotism. Though liberal Protestantism was also influenced by the theme of progress (sometimes seen as evolutionary progress), it does not need to be, and it is from this point of view that we treat our own particular liberal Protestant heritage.

But there are elements in the Protestant tradition which we necessarily reject. Since Christian faith is transnational, we reject the identification of Christianities with nations, as in the classical European Lutheran and other magisterial blends. We reject the establishment of religion as inappropriate to the times, and inimical to the free spirit of faith. We are more concerned with the liberal scholarly heritage, which cannot in our view be avoided (we should in any event welcome it), and which is compatible with certain kinds of Christian theology. So of the various forces of the modern world – scientific advance, scholarship, nationalism, capitalism, etc. – we accept some and not others. Why? Because in this case the Christian faith is self-evidently transnational, in which there is neither Jew nor Greek, nor Turk nor Sri Lankan, that it cannot easily combine with nationalism or its polite face, patriotism. Maybe we ought to love our countries (though is *ought* the word?) but if so, not too much. One of the great causes of hatred is groupism, of which nationalism is the most potent political form.

Returning to Bultmann
Bultmann is the major face in modern Christian thinking of the liberal tradition. But his adoption of existentialist

personalism involved blending a rather particular cultural ingredient into his project of making the Bible accessible to modern folk, through demythologization. We do not dissent from demythologization as a project, but we shall note below our attempt at "remythologizing". Nor essentially do we dissent from some emphasis upon Christian personalism. But we still find his outlook very culture-bound.

The personalism of Bultmann provides of course one account of the difference between religious and scientific thinking. The latter "objectifies", whereas in the other we have a kind of I-Thou relationship to other human beings and above all to the Divine. His position is in many ways closer to that of Buber than Heidegger. We would add to his psychologistic account of human relations, the element of *li*. In large measure treating another being as a person is performing in certain ways towards her. We wish to affirm that deep personalism (concern for the feelings and rights of others, and an appreciation of the joys and sorrows of personal relations) is the cure, so to speak, for hatred, and it is that which can reach across the barriers of groupism. It is part of the central message of the incarnation.

But we object to the narrow cultural setting of Bultmann's discussion. Why should other cultures have to start from Heidegger? Moreover we need a different way of looking at his major project. It may be that in modern times it is not easy to believe in some of the supernatural and miraculous events recorded in the scriptures. But it is not possible to abandon the Beyond as shining through the events of Jesus' career. It is not precluded by modernity that we should see Christ in the light of eternity. The mood of modernity is more metaphysical, abstract in orientation, than the story-telling ambience of the New Testament perhaps allows. Yet we are also profoundly influenced by narrative, and in some ways we have more of this now throughout the world – via the media – than has been usual in the past. But for seriousness we prize history: the rest is significant, perhaps, as allegory, or is in fiction realistic enough to pass as history that did not happen.

But Marxism, which has had such a gripping effect on

the world's imagination, wields abstract rhythms beneath the surface of historical narrative, and this may lend it its power. There is a metaphysical ballet of economic forces, classes, varieties of alienation and so forth which gives history a sense of depth. The weakness of Bultmann, and perhaps Schleiermacher too in clinging so much to religious experience, is that his underlying personalism has so to speak no motion. There is not in Bultmann a sense of the onward march of history. This is partly because of his so close attention to the scriptural norm.

By contrast we would like to apply a principle for the conservation of richness to the process of demythologization. If we have to abandon some things in the texts, because we no longer can believe them, we have at the same time to lend extra depth to the story of Christ's life, death and resurrection. In our view this is best done by reemphasizing the metaphysical Transcendent. For a kind of historically rooted set of myths we now have mythic history underpinned by a clear notion of the Beyond. This is one among a number of reasons why we set great store by our analysis of the Transcendent as being clear and coherent (though allowing room to our sense of the mysterious Other, too). We see, in other words, a ballet in history: not just Christ as revealing light upon what lies Beyond, but history as a whole having something to tell us about the divine person Beyond. And beyond the story of Christ is the story of the Church and of Christian, and non-Christian, communities, all of which tell us something of the working of the *antaryāmin*.

A Further Comment on Barth

Barth's wonderful discontinuity between the Gospel and religion enabled him very decisively to reject the Nazi challenge to the faith. But we consider two points in Barthian theology to be wrong. One is his coupling of a liberal attitude towards Higher Criticism to an unintelligible insistence on the unity (and supernatural character of) the Bible. This seems to us simply to be implausible in the light of modern scholarship, and it insulates Biblical history from all other branches of human history. Second, we find his extreme emphasis on human sin defective: first because Mencius is not altogether wrong in his optimistic assessment of human nature, and because it led to the complete devaluation of human reason in giving us insights into the Beyond. The narrowness of neo-orthodoxy has, moreover, occasioned a continuation of the colonialist mentality in regard to other faiths.

But Barth is right to affirm somehow the concreteness of revelation in historical event, the "Christ-event". In agreeing on this emphasis we go beyond the Schleiermachian appeal to experience. Our view is: patterns of religious experience, plus the "incarnation strand" – plus historical events, in other words. Although we recognize the alienated nature of human beings from their Source we do not consider the "natural" sources of insight into that Source to proceed from anywhere else but that Source.

We consider, really, that the *bhakti* character of much of the New Testament lies behind this notion that holiness proceeds only from the Holy, that knowledge thus comes from the Divine. But grace does not need so extreme an interpretation that we artificially condemn all that is natural in human nature. And we think of that Spark within, the divine Source controlling us from beneath our consciousness, and we think of human insight and creativity as a synergistic blend of the divine and the human forces at work in the world: as a kind of incarnational manifestation, then.

You might call Barthian theology as the acceptable face of Biblical conservatism. We ourselves recognize conservatism in quite a different form, that is in the preservation of Christian sacramental religion. We believe that once the heart of the Christian praxis was shifted to preaching, as the chief sacrament, it placed some intolerable burdens upon the underlying theology. For preaching had to have a special kind of urgency and certainty that almost inevitably led to a fundamentalist or near-fundamentalist attitude. What is positive in the evangelical movement is the emphasis upon experience, e.g. the "born-again" experience typical of Christian *bhakti*. It is only unfortunate that hangups about past history lead evangelicals to underestimate the power and importance of other forms of religious, and Christian, experience.

Fundamentalist interpretations of Christianity can of course be accounted for by Position Theory. They represent a typical backlash against the infusion of academic liberalism into Christianity.

The challenge of Barthian theology is most important to us in placing a question mark over the blend of bourgeois liberal attitudes (including academic liberalism)and Protestant faith. There are dangers of self-satisfaction in the blend, and a neglect of the needs of the poor in this world. The attempt to draw a sharp line between the Christian Gospel and human culture raises the issue of the endemic porousness of Christianity. The tradition is easily penetrated by outside forces.

Christian Secularism

We do not need to spend much time in reaffirming the need for a clearly thought out conception of the Beyond. It was a feature of secular Christian theologians of the sixties that they thought they could combine, without contradiction, some of the ethical challenges of Christianity, together with following Jesus, with an absence of God as transcendent. The movement turned out to be ephemeral, but it paved the way for others, notably liberation theology. More, it celebrated the Christian's engagement in the secular affairs of this world.

Part of the meaning of the "death of God" lay in the sensation that the cosmos was unresponsive – that we live, as it were, in a cold world in which it seems that God does not hear us. No echo of our anguish is detected. Rubenstein could thus write that we

> stand in a cold, silent, unfeeling cosmos, unaided by any purposeful power beyond our own resources. After Auschwitz, what else can a Jew say about God? (*After Auschwitz*, 1966, p. 152)

Not just a Jew, we would guess. A Christian might be able to say even less.

139

But in delineating a Christian systematic worldview, we are speaking from encounter, fragmentary though it may be. The cosmos is not just silent. Do the terrible events of this century strike us dumb about the Ultimate? Later we have to explore more deeply how we respond to evil and the so-called "problem of evil". But for many of us the right stance is confessional: you do not just look at evil, as though it were a force "out there", but rather we see it as part of ourselves, as we belong to the very human race that both inflicted Auschwitz and suffered it.

We do not think that Christian secularism speaks from the same condition that this worldview-construction does. It is, or was, a loss of the articulation of religious experience and of faith. But it reminds us that the everyday world is also the sacred world. It may also remind us that we have to account for the role of the faith in the ordinary ongoing processes of history, especially in modern times. It cannot thus be divorced from the political coloration of our times — which is where we come to various forms of liberation, and allied, theology.

These forms have an intimate relation to the oppressed regions of the world — those parts of the planet which have emerged from colonialism and two world wars with a heavy yoke of poverty and social division. They are also intimately related to those who are embedded, one way or another, in the First World, but as special cases of victims of the system (such as Blacks and Native Americans).

Much of liberation theology has a Marxist base of one sort or another — relatively orthodox in the thought of Gustavo Gutierrez and Jon Sobrino and unorthodox in that of Hugo Assmann. From the perspective of position theory, this is a possibility to be realized. There are notable virtues in the various theologies of the oppressed. But there are problems, too, of which we consider the following two to be the most prominent. First, you cannot generalize the Latin American scene to the whole world. Its problems are greatly to do with the heady combination of Spanish feudalism, racism and capitalism: but the same ingredients are not universal. Second, the Marxist tools of analysis are insufficient, since revolutionary violence itself affects the liberated situation: and experience shows that oppression and poverty (though not the most grinding form) are the virtually universal concomitants of Marxist rule. In other words it may be that the oppressed will be exchanging one form of misery for another.

Rather, the message of Third World theology is that we now need to look at the economic and political situation of the world as a whole. Just as in the past we brought in the socialist critique to help with the redistribution of income and the eradication of many of the social problems of certain societies, i.e. within nations, such as Sweden, France, Singapore and so on; so now we may bring in social-democratic measures to adjust the conditions of the North-South world with a view to the establishment of some form of global justice. In other words, the new liberation motifs themselves help to reinforce globalism as an attitude.

They also suggest a kind of federalism. There are different voices that speak to us from their condition – the voices of Asia, of Africa, of the Blacks of the Western World, of Latin America, of the South Pacific and so on. These are different voices with differing social, political and economic problems: they are also regions in search of dignity within the whole-world scene. We should not in all this forget, though, the other oppressed – the Buddhists of Tibet, the Muslims of Soviet Central Asia, Christians in Marxist countries.

Terrible as poverty can be, we should not forget that containment of the spirit which renders Marxist countries, on the whole, such grey areas. But still, the call of the South is powerful, and we need to sketch out a policy for all the world.

Feminism and the Gospel

A somewhat different style from liberation theology is modern feminism, especially when used as a critique of traditional religions, and of Christianities in particular. It has brought some radical changes of attitude towards the exegesis of scripture among other things, adding further weight to the thought of the provisional nature of scriptural authority. If there is sometimes (as in the writing of Mary Daly) an element of male-hating in the movement, it is not surprising but it is not for us – Christian faith centers on love. But the critique of many of the traditional images and institutions of religion is, to our mind, just. This is why in this volume we do not stick consistently to any one pronoun in speaking of the Divine being. There are various spinoffs from the feminist position: a greater concern for the "ordinary folk" (many women) in doing the history of religion, a modification of male macho attitudes (surely consistent with the heart of Christian ethics), a scepticism about the literal application of any images to the Divine, etc.

Yet if we ask about any of these liberation theologies, we can ask whether the groups singled out (Latin Americans, Africans, women) are anything more than provisional ones. It is natural for the groups who feel oppression to underscore their different way of experiencing the world. It is tempting to think that only Blacks can understand Blacks, women women, and so on. But are these different species? In fact the difference between human beings is only provisional and cultural: so we are driven back to see the various liberations as to be interpreted federally.

But we need to think like *bodhisattvas*. We cannot be happy or satisfied to live a relatively free and prosperous life while others still suffer from poverty and oppression. The bodhisattva is restless in his concern for others until all are free. Once again, our conclusions are globalist. But it is important that the different major cultural regions should think of their own past or future contribution to the universal welfare of the human race. It seems to us that the Marxist element in Liberation Theology should spur us towards a kind of global social democracy: that is to see both capitalist methods and welfarism as complementary modes, but to be applied on a global scale to benefit the whole of humankind, and so to get involved in creating a productive but also just economic order.

Towards Process Theology

In certain respects so-called process theology, associated with such figures as Hartshorne, Cobb and Shubert Ogden, belongs with the "secularist" Christianities we have been discussing. In its most classical form, it is underpinned by the metaphysics of Whitehead, though the general principle of God being both involved in and affected by process does not depend on this particular way of supporting process theology. Actually, the form espoused by Hartshorne eschews such notions as divine omnipotence. Evil is part of the cosmic process in part because God is not in full control. Such a finite God is not necessary, either. But the Divine Being could be continuously affected by the processes of creation – as we have already noted, we agree with this notion. For us, the implication of continuous creation and the concept of the cosmos as the Divine body both imply the perfect power of God over what does and does not happen. We shall not duck the issue: it means that the Ultimate is responsible for the evil in nature as well as the good. But the independence of creatures places some limitations on her style of action.

The general principle we applaud. The cosmos is a vast adventure, in which the Divine not only enters into human history at a special point, and is identical with the Jesus who experiences the joy of wedding parties and the pains of the cross, but also is implicated deeply in the conscious living forms which arise within and through nature. It is consonant with this incarnational theology that the Divine is indeed passible, and suffers with the ongoing life of her cosmos.

Process theology has a future orientation not unlike a motif in the thought of Moltmann and Pannenberg, and the theology of hope. This notion of the Divine as somehow lying in the future expresses a vital theme in Jewish and Christian thought and feeling. It is as if the future attracts us forward, drawing us on by its holy magnetism. We are not uninfluenced by the image depicted by Teilhard de Chardin. His concept of the noosphere daily becomes more relevant, as the various parts of the world are in virtually instant communication.

Some Roman Catholic Theology

In the various seachanges of the last forty years since World War II, there is scarcely a more influential Roman Catholic thinker than Karl Rahner. His anthropology, in part drawn from Heidegger, is Europocentric: but his notion of the "anonymous Christian" (though admittedly controversial) is a useful one in helping to destroy that dangerous principle, enunciated from Cyprian onwards, *extra ecclesiam nulla salus*. This loosening up of Catholic theology, from a position beyond the once-prescribed Neothomism, played a role in the formulations of Vatican II. We place our own work somewhat in the spirit of Vatican II; but our standpoint is necessarily more sceptical and critical than that of Catholic orthodoxy. Our epistemology is thus nearer that of Hans Küng, who significantly not only has challenged the concept of papal infallibility, but also has published a book under the somewhat sceptical title of *Does God Exist*?

Towards a World Theology

Already there have been others, notably Wilfred Cantwell Smith who have begun thinking about a world theology. We wish in this work to carry this project forward. To some degree we are building on older openings towards other religious traditions – the writings for instance of Catholics like Heinrich Dumoulin, Thomas Merton and Raimundo Panikkar, Protestants such as J.N. Farquhar, John Hick and John Cobb, and other religious writers. These authors have pioneered an outreach to other traditions from within the Christian tradition which is important as part of the task we have set ourselves. We are also mindful in particular of the shape and spirit of Orthodoxy as in its own substance providing a bridge to other religious traditions, and of the pluralism and internal tolerance which has often marked Anglicanism, itself a bridge between the various kinds of Christianity.

These brief remarks placing Neotranscendentalism among some trends in Christian theology are only intended to set the scene. Some more detailed evaluations of other Christian systems of thought will emerge in the actual presentation of our worldview. We also need to stress that our presentation of a *darśana* is more than the presentation of an intellectual construction. It is the putting forward of a Tao, a form of *bhakti* and *jñāna* "or knowledge", a life clothed in sacramental *li*, a stimulus to *dhyāna* and *karuṇā*, an invitation to eschew *shirk*, and to be called by the power of the *avatāra*.

PART II
The Vision of Love

6

The Divine
Threefoldness

The Mythic Background of the Trinity Idea
The historical and experiential basis of the doctrine of the
Trinity, as it later became clarified, lies in the important
events of the life of Jesus and of the early Christian
community. It is true that it is hard to penetrate to the
historical Jesus. But certain motifs are very crucial to the
narratives of the Christian scriptures, and these we shall treat
in relation to some of the phenomenology of religion which
we have sketched elsewhere. The events in question are
highly suggestive of a Trinitarian vision of the divine, and
they provided the data for subsequent Christian reflection
upon the nature of God. We shall try to show that the
classical doctrine of the Trinity as social is the best interpretation of Christian origins. It provides perhaps the only
comprehensive and coherent account of the key data as
presented in the New Testament writings.

We shall begin here by looking at, in the light of the study
of religions, the extraordinary character of Jesus' own
religious experience (or at least his experience as it was
conceived of in the early community) and of the impact
which this made on his own close followers. Its importance
for later Christian reflection is much enhanced when we can
see it from the perspective of our typology of religious
experience. This is not, these days, a usual way to approach
the life of Christ, since skepticism is prevalent among so
many liberal-minded scholars, while conservatives tend to
ignore the crosscultural approach to religious phenomena.
But it can be said that, viewed from this angle, Jesus' life
takes on a new range of meanings and connections with
world religions. The types of experience which manifest

149

themselves as aspects of his existence can be summed up as follows.

Some Diagnoses of Jesus' Experiences

If there is one thing which is striking about Jesus' teaching it was his use of the term *Abba* of the Divine Being: "my dear father". The Gospel narratives indicate how he would use this formula in prayer, and was accustomed to withdraw to pray in solitude, and spent long hours communing with his "dear father" (Luke 6:12; Mark 1:35). The language implies a loving communion which we can confidently treat as a kind of *bhakti* – intimate devotion to God. His meditation is a variety of love *dhyāna*. This, then, is one vital and prominent aspect of Jesus' own religious experience, which he conveyed to his followers in the injunction to use the same language of "our dear father".

Closely related to this sense of intimacy with the Divine, there seems to have been a sense of being a prophet and of having a prophetic vocation. There is a sense of continually attempting to do the will of his heavenly father through the guidance and power of the Spirit: as we might say, the *antaryāmin* or inner controller. As we shall see it seems to have been his desire that his followers should share his experience, in the communal bond of the Spirit (Hodgson, 1944). At any rate, in his quest to fulfill the will of "his dear father" he blended the ethical concerns of the prophet and the intimate sense of the presence of the Divine. We shall later see how we need to interpret this motif.

According to the scriptural sources, the power of the Spirit enabled Jesus to perform various kinds of healing and exorcisms. Here his work is reminiscent of the shaman. But unlike the cases of shamans and the prophets of the Israelite tradition we probably cannot speak here of total possession. Jesus' personality was not just the vehicle for divine action or that of supernatural powers. His prayer in Gethsemane and his struggle with Satan in the wilderness are indicative of a rather different state than that of mere possession. (Maybe there are those who are sceptical of the account of the wilderness temptations: to us it rings true as delineating an important sort of religious experience.)

We may note that Jesus has resemblances to the prophet, the shaman and the *bhakta*. It is as if the Spirit unifies these roles in his person. But he is not an ordinary *bhakta*, etc. This is an aspect of the logic of Jesus' position. He encountered various categories in his tradition and various concepts, such as that of Messiah: but he transcended these categories – so, while being in the *bhakta* mold he yet was beyond ordinary bhakti, and so on with the other analogical categories used to describe him. (Such *category-transcendence* helps to explain the puzzlement of some of his followers and the difficulties found in using various terms for him.) If the Spirit unifies the prophetic, devotional and other aspects of Jesus' spirituality, the Gospel narratives nevertheless indicate a difference in Jesus' consciousness drawn between his awarenesses of the Father and of the Spirit.

Other narratives in the Gospels point to some important modes of Jesus' religious experience – namely profound numinous experiences, both visionary and auditory at crucial times in his public career. These were supposedly witnessed by his close followers. Thus, at his baptism he experienced the Spirit descending on him and a voice saying that "this is my beloved son". It is as if the heavens opened: this conventional phrase can be visualized as pointing to some kind of splitting of the sky, a solemn, even terrifying, vision of the "Beyond". The disciples had a similar experience when Jesus ascended to the mountain top and was transfigured. Some have thought of this as a displaced resurrection narrative: and it is Jesus as object rather than subject of a numinous experience that is depicted. But there is at any rate the auditory event, and the suggestion that Jesus too could be aware of the thunderous glory of the Divine Being.

All these aspects of Jesus' life together with his speaking with authority, concerning his Father's will, and his exercising divine prerogatives in forgiving sins, form a suggestive picture. It is one which depicts a close and unique relationship of sonhood to his Abba.

This relationship need not, as yet, be thought of as a

metaphysical one. For the moment we can understand it in terms of religious experience. The *bhakti* beyond *bhakti* moderated that sense of division so typical of the numinous experience, and reinforced that sense of possession and inward participation which occur in the shamanic and mystical strands of religious experience. It is important that traces of his religious life are left in the Gospels and that at least the early Church could place Jesus' life and that of his followers in a religious and experiential milieu of meaning. Similar importance attaches to the Resurrection appearances, as throwing light on the early community's understanding of the impact of Christ.

Resurrection Narratives

We do not need here to go into the very complex tangles of discussion about the historicity of the Resurrection. What we are concerned with is the phenomenology of the experiences recorded in the stories. We shall come to this in a moment but first let us comment (not very originally) on the general question of what happened.

That the early followers had a number of dramatic numinous experiences of the living reality of Jesus in his glorified form cannot be too reasonably held in doubt. The death and resurrection of their leader was the central affirmation of the earliest Christian community as expressed in their *kerygma* or proclamation. Peter and others died for this faith: it is unlikely that they could have become martyrs on behalf of what they perceived as a fabrication (this argument, by the way, can be plausibly employed about Joseph Smith Jr.: we do not intend it as proof of any metaphysical position, but merely as tending to confirm that some numinous event or experience befell some at least of the apostles). It seems that there was a dramatic new awareness that Jesus still lived, despite his death, and this gave his followers hope after a period of shattering disillusion, one supposes.

In our view, believing that Jesus lives on in his glorified divine life as the savior is quite compatible with a certain degree of hesitation and scepticism about many aspects of the narratives of the New Testament concerning his resurrection.

Thus, it must be admitted that the historical details put forward in the Gospels about the resurrection appearances prior to Pentecost, and their chronological sequence, contain inconsistencies and are difficult to harmonize. Moreover, the accounts are not altogether straightforward about the supposed nature of the resurrection event or events. Thus, Jesus is presented as having some kind of revivified body and he is made to eat broiled fish; and yet also the body can disappear instantly. So they seem to show his body as both material and immaterial; or at least solid and subtle. But if we stand back a bit from the details, we see that the general drift of the narratives is that Jesus' revivified body was transfigured gloriously and became immortal, and at his "ascension" dematerialized: but yet somehow its form is forever imprinted into the consciousness and identity of Jesus' divine life. These are mysterious words, and we can best approach the matter through consideration of the experience of the disciples.

So, in contrast to the bodily resurrection accounts, there is supporting evidence for the following view: that the early followers of Jesus experienced, through exterior and interior visions, the living reality of Christ. In these, their consciousness was illuminated, and they gained cognitive spiritual awareness or *gnosis* of Jesus, by participating in both mind and body in the divine life of Jesus long after his death.

This experientialist account seems to us to be sufficient both to account for the subsequent behavior of the early followers and to form the basis of an adequate Christology, as the jargon has it. There are those who are strong for the physicalist theory. They are so because it means so much to them in their own experience. In either case the route returns to religious experience. But we do not wish to quarrel with the physicalists: let them affirm bodily resurrection – but it does not seem to us to make much difference. But if you get too literalist about the resurrection you begin to lose the point.

If we now turn to the account of Paul's conversion (so crucial an event in the history of the new religion), we find that in Paul's numinous encounter Jesus appears as a brilliantly shining ethereal light, through which he speaks (again we have both visionary and auditory aspects of the experience). In his *First Letter to the Corinthians* written in 54 C.E. he presents, as we know, a list of those to whom Jesus has appeared, beginning with Peter, the other disciples, many brethren and lastly him, Paul. Now there was an ideological or doctrinal point here: it was on this basis that Paul rested his claim to be an apostle. It was on this basis that he was accepted by Peter, James and the others. This suggests that it was in terms of *visions* that the others apprehended Jesus, as a majestic immaterial figure, as in the case of Stephen, or as a felt presence of shining light, either individually or collectively. Since Paul's testimony is relatively early, we can ascribe some of the contradictions in the Gospel narratives to the fact of an evolving tradition. That tradition in incorporating the notion of bodily resurrection fell into tangles, which no doubt the community rightly retained, for they enable us to give varieties of response to the events of those fargone days.

Our experientialist account enables us to place these occurrences within a longer and continuing framework of events proliferating throughout the Christian tradition, in which Jesus Christ appears within human experience. In the contemplative tradition, both Catholic and Orthodox, Jesus has been experienced as light, in interior experience, in a kind of love-gnosis, as Lossky called it (Lossky, 1957).

Our experientialist account is not incompatible with physicalism. Both sides may have occurred; but our hermeneutical principle is to accept the historicity of events in the New Testament to the degree necessary to provide a coherent account of the beliefs and actions of Jesus' early followers and of members of the early church community (Noss, 1974, p. 418).

Effects of Belief in the Resurrection
As previously noted, the disciples' encounters with Jesus alive in glory filled them with new hope and vitality. They once again, though in a somewhat different mode, experienced

154

the companionship of their master, who was now with them always. This itself led to their sharpened vision, in retrospect, of the meaning of Jesus' life and death. They now began to see in them a fulfillment of the prophecies of Deutero-Isaiah concerning the figure of the suffering servant. This meant that previous categories concerning the person and work of the Messiah and deliverer in contemporary Jewish thought and imagination were transcended. Jesus was seen by Paul as a more than human Messiah; he was pre-existent Son of God and the Lord of Creation in glory together with the power of the heavenly Father.

Jesus was experienced as divine savior in these numinous encounters. Salvation could only be accomplished by God, and it is for this reason that we here stress the he is *divine* savior. This saving was seen as due to his death and self-sacrifice on the cross, liberating human beings from their alienation from God and therefore from death. His resurrection was a visible sign of this victory. As we shall see, this vision of Christ was expressed through worship. It thus appears that from very early times, Christians experienced Christ as divine and yet as a distinct entity from his heavenly Father.

We now turn to the reality of the Spirit in the experience of the early Church.

The Nature of Pentecost
The outpouring of the Spirit at Pentecost is the key factor giving rise to the distinctively Christian experience of the Ultimate and to the distinctive new way of life. We have already seen that, at least judging from the Gospel accounts, the Spirit was important in the devotional and prophetic dimensions of Jesus' own spiritual life. It seems that he wanted the disciples to share his relationship to his Father in the communal bond of the Spirit. So it is that in Mark's Gospel, he promises the disciples that in times of crisis on his behalf the Spirit would somehow given them power and guide their speech, and so enable them to share in Jesus's own experience. In *John* he says that he and his Father will send another, a heavenly Helper.

At Pentecost, the early community, at least according to the later account, began to feel these promises' being fulfilled. The descent of the Spirit filled his followers with new life and power, and they were in this unified into a new community, a koinonia of mutual giving, of agape. In the ritual of baptism (which of course reflected Jesus' own, and reflected too the numinous experience of that event), they were given new identities as adopted daughters and sons of the Ultimate. By the rite they were united to the risen Lord, and could now address God, as he did, as Abba. It was thought that it was from the Spirit that they gained new levels of ethical and spiritual creativity: so, they gained spiritual gifts, such as the power of ecstatic prophecy and the capacity to heal. They were, moreover, impelled by the Spirit to go forth to proclaim this new *kerygma* about their living leader.

In these events a new power within emerges. God has presented himself externally as Lord, both as the immeasurable Yahweh and as the numinous risen Lord. Now there comes a power which transforms them from within.

The disciples also saw in their experience of the Spirit a fulfillment of prophecies about the outpouring of the Spirit in the new age, and about how it would be the inner principle of life in the community of people who live under the new arrangement, the new covenant.

First, the Spirit brings about, and is the unifying factor in, the living organism of the mystical (or sacramental) body of Christ, who is the head of that organism. Fellowship of agape is the special characteristic of the Spirit who is shared in common by the members of the new community. Second, the indwelling Spirit gradually transforms Christians who are adopted sons and daughters of the Heavenly Father, into the image and likeness of Christ. Within this setting, the Spirit helps to produce Christian virtues which are the fruits of his holiness-making activity. Through this sanctification process, people are ontologically united with the living Son, and so progressively share in the divine life. They become deified. Third, Christians are also supposed, according to the early narratives, to receive special gifts from the Spirit, helping them as individuals to exercise their own creative talents within the context and in general for the benefit of the community. From all these experiences there emerged in the consciousness of Christians a conviction that the Spirit was somehow a personal living entity distinct from the living Son, and guiding them individually from within. They worshipped this entity, as we shall see, together with the Father and the Son. Worship is a more important index of who is "god" than just doctrines, which it precedes. It is important for us to recognize that in the apostolic letters, as well as later in the Gospel of *John*, the Spirit is not just thought of as an energy or power or activity of God (rather like grace, which is on the contrary so conceived as in the Hebrew Bible though even there, there are occasional drifts into hypostatizing the Spirit). Moreover he is looked on as having his own center of consciousness, and is typically referred to as "he" rather than as an "it". Nor can the Spirit simply be identified with the risen Lord.

In his masterly work *The Incarnate Lord* (1928, pp. 322–325) the Anglican scholar L.S. Thornton has convincingly argued that the key passages in the New Testament on the topic imply a clear and consistent distinction between the Holy Spirit and the risen Lord. The activities or functions of each are distinct, as well as the modes in which they are supposed to dwell together within the Christian and to be experienced by her or him. Thus, as indicated previously, it is through the Spirit that the Christian is transformed into the image of Christ. It is never vice versa: that is the Christian is not transformed by Christ into the image of the Spirit. The Spirit is the agent and creator of the new life of being adopted son. Christ is the content or form of that life. Thornton's careful textual analysis and evaluation of the key experiential data make it clear that the important phrases "the Spirit of Jesus/Christ/the Son" refer to the power and the dynamic indwelling presence of the risen Lord, and not to the Holy Spirit. Unfortunately Thornton's work has not yet received the widespread attention which it deserves. Some other Twentieth Century Christian theologians have neglected his main thesis. Thus Karl Barth has made the confused identification of the Holy Spirit and the spirit of Christ by means of his exegesis of the rather obscure sentence in Paul's second letter to the Corinthians (3:17): "The Lord is the Spirit" and allows this to control his interpretation of the phrases mentioned above. As we shall later show, Barth's exegesis of this passage is faulty (see p. 336); and his internal modalist account of the Trinity is untenable both upon philosophical and Christian-theological grounds. As we said above, it is not only from certain doctrinal passages that we can see the beginnings of the Trinity doctrine, but more importantly it is from the practice and worship of the early community that we can infer their implicit attitude to the Trinity. To this aspect of the matter we now turn.

Early Christian Worship and the Apprehension of the Trinity
In this section we shall focus on the central significance of the ritual dimension of the early faith: and in this ritual context we shall concentrate on worship and the sacraments. It is from this practical and spiritually live context that the idea of the Trinity gains its meaning (Wainwright, 1980).

First, it is clear that from the very earliest times, the Eucharist was the most distinctive and solemn rite for followers of the risen Lord. It was intended not only as a memorial of his life and work, but also as an expression of his living presence among the faithful. It was also conceived as the primary expression of the sense of fellowship or *koinonia* among the members of the Spirit-united organism. It therefore reinforced the attitude of self-giving love which was so central to the early Christian ethos. The meaning of the Eucharist was apprehended in a very realistic way: in almost a physical sense. By partaking of the bread and wine the celebrants partook of the body and blood of Jesus. He real presence in the Eucharist was analogous to his embodiment during his lifetime. The same healing and other powers which flowed forth from Jesus' body were now conveyed to the faithful. Ignatius of Antioch in about 115 C.E. referred to the Eucharist as the medicine of immortality. Through the ritual, Christians were united with one another in the glorified humanity of the risen Lord.

They were by the same token gradually incorporated into the Divine identity of Christ. This process had begun in the rite of passage of baptism, through which people were initiated into the life of the new community. People died to their old nature and identity, and rose with Christ into sonship.

So it was through the whole framework of the sacramental life of the community that Christians came to experience the transforming and sanctifying effects of the Holy Spirit. Similarly, when the ideal of martyrdom came to be widespread in the Church, in the days of persecution under the Roman Empire, the "baptism of blood" was associated with the activity of the Spirit: martyrs were incorporated into Christ's self-sacrifice in an ultimate act of worship. All this is reflected in the community's liturgical texts, important portions of which were already to be found in the New Testament (Reynolds, 1977). It is here that we most clearly see the early evolution of a Trinitarian consciousness, though, naturally enough, the later doctrinal and philosophically expressed formulae were not in evidence. But the experiential and ritual basis for the idea of the divine threefoldness is already apparent, and this needs to be underlined. Here are the formative influences lying behind the explicit formalism of the doctrinal dimension. Here we can capture something of the early spirit of the Church's recognition that divine power operates in a complex way, through the three persons of the divine Ultimate.

Thus, the community's experience of Jesus as the savior is to be discerned in a number of Christological hymns in the New Testament. He is acclaimed as possessing equal status with God, as being the agent of the creation of the world, as effecting salvation through his death upon the cross, as defeating, by his rising to life again, the cosmic powers of darkness, and as reigning, as exalted Lord or Kyrios, over all of creation. His redemption of those who follow him was seen as being at the very heart of the divine drama of salvation taking place in the whole scheme of history. These are all very extensive claims for Jesus, and imply a remarkably exalted status which is made the more apparent precisely because so many early Christians were drawn from the synagogues of the Roman Empire and so from groups who took monotheism so seriously. The fact that these liturgical acts involve the worship of Jesus indicates in principle the recognition of his divine nature.

The baptismal formula (in the name of the Father, and the Son, and the Holy Spirit) appears already in St Matthew's Gospel and could reflect the liturgy of the community about 80 C.E. But even if it were later it is still relatively archaic, and well before the formal adoption of a doctrinal formula. Earlier, Paul's second letter to the Corinthians, in the late 50's, contains a trinitarian phrase, and seems to reflect the practice of worshipping the Spirit. Such ritual facts can be set side by side by the more expected prayers of thanksgiving and praise which are addressed to the heavenly Father for his love and mercy, and for the gifts to his Son and of the Spirit.

It should be noted that in the eucharistic prayers of the church, according to such writers as Hyppolytus of the 3rd and Chrysostom of the 4th century, the Holy Spirit is called on to transform the elements into the body and blood of Christ. Again, the threefoldness of God is reflected in prayers of the martyrs, such as Polycarp in 155.

The result of this brief survey of the relevant material is to establish ways in which we have to root the Trinity teaching in the experience and ritual life of the community: and this is so from the earliest times.

Motivating Factors in the Development of the Trinity Doctrine

The factors which impelled the Eastern Orthodox church fathers to formulate the classical doctrine of the Trinity at the Council of Nicaea and beyond were two-fold. First, and less importantly, there was the philosophical or rational concern to be able to present the doctrine of Christ and the Holy Spirit without contradiction, and still within the general rubric of Christianity's inherited monotheism. It was necessary to show how it could be that there is a single Divine Being which yet consisted of three distinct identities. Second, and far more vital, there were the soteriological concerns. There was the desire to preserve the distinctively Christian experience and to keep sight of those factors in teaching and liturgy which that experience implied. It was necessary to give an account which could be handed down to later generations and thus preserve the real meaning of those events the participation in which was the mode through which human beings were to be saved. In brief, the chief motivation of the Fathers was practical and spiritual. The events of salvation had to be analysed correctly. The dry formulae were meant to shine with the glory of the events that they described.

The first concern was with Christ's status and nature. It was needful to hold together two positions in order to make sense of Christ's redemptive work. They had on the one hand to preserve the notion of Jesus' divinity, and this against Arius and others who sought to demote Christ to less than divinity. Arianism subverted the Christian faith in at least two ways – by subordinating Christ to the Father (as also some of Origen's followers did) and by denying his eternal nature: hence their famous formula "There was when he was not". But if Christians in fact, as we have argued, worshipped Christ from early times then they were guilty of idolatry if Arius' view was to be maintained. It cut against the Christian experience of Christ as expiating their sins and overcoming their alienation from the heavenly Father. It also did not make too good sense of their experience of union with the risen Lord in the sacraments and the liturgy. Were they to be expected to continue worshipping a being who was other than the one true God?

The second concern was with the reality of Christ's human nature. Here the Fathers had to contend with the docetic strand in Christian thinking. It was one way to preserve a kind of unity to the Godhead: but it did so at the expense of the central and distinctive Christian affirmation. If Christ's incarnation was only an appearance, this reduced Jesus to a kind of experience, a kind of phantom theophany. One reason why the Gospels had sought to maintain the bodily resurrection (despite the other, visionary, elements in the accounts) was to make sure that Christians thought of Christ's saving work as involving a real incarnation. To put the matter in more modern terms: the redemption of the human race implied that Jesus was acting in solidarity with humanity. He was both divine and fully human. For how else could he both forgive and expiate human beings' alienation? We develop this point further in the chapter on divine embodiment.

There is another point which weighs with us, though it is not stressed in the ancient sources. It is that Christianity gives a wonderful vision of Creation and of the Creator's attitude to suffering. Knowing that he in creating freedom will bring about suffering: and knowing too that the whole splendor of life is bound to be shot through with misery, ignorance and despair, she as Creator judges the whole process to be nobly and tragically worthwhile. But she does not stand back and set the process in motion, without being willing herself to enter into that process and to experience in her own person, as the incarnate Son of God, that suffering, ignorance and despair. At the first shining dawn of the world there already was Gethsemane. We attach importance therefore to the reality of Christ's human life. We remain in question about the reality of Vishnu's *avatāras*. In Christ's *avatāra*, all the divine eggs are put in one frail basket.

Apart from the question of the reality of Christ's both divine and human nature, the Fathers were also motivated by a desire to do justice to the divine status of the Spirit. The Spirit had been perceived, as we have seen, as the cause of sanctification and of the implanting of the spiritual charismata in the early community. So that Spirit was seen as an originator of holiness, and therefore indeed herself divine. In other words, the community felt that their new life together, their individual experience of sanctification and their exercise of new powers of spiritual charismata were all manifestations of the working of a distinct divine entity. This latter claim had to be affirmed against those who struggled against the doctrine, namely the so-called "pneumatomachians".

It may be said here in passing that secret or implicit pneumatomachianism is very widespread among people of otherwise impeccable orthodox credentials. There is often a leaving out of the Spirit in the actual life of the Churches, and there is much less personal prayer and cultivation of reverence towards the Spirit than towards the other two members of the Trinity. The teachings of the Church are not always backed up so richly in the prayer life of the communities of those who call themselves Christians.

In any event, by the time of Nicaea there was a felt need for some exercise in skill in words and concepts to deal with two great impulses, struggling against each other, within the life of the community. One was the powerful tradition of monotheism. This had been if anything reinforced during the days of persecution and martyrdom in the Empire. After all, many Christians had gone to their deaths just for refusing to burn incense before the image of the Emperor. From a non-Christian point of view it was a very small concession. It was a sign of the obstinacy of Christians and Jews that they should refuse: an obstinacy even more obvious among Gentile Christians who had adopted part of the Jewish practice in becoming baptized into Christianity. If individuals voluntarily denied the Emperor-cult and risked their lives for monotheism, this made the doctrine, and the purity of Christian practice in this respect, all the more formidable. So on the one hand monotheism was essential to the faith. But on the other hand Christians saw salvation history as having these three moments or phases: the work of the Father, the coming of the Son and the outpouring of the Spirit: and behind these phases were three distinct personal beings. So how could God be both one and three?

The synthesis was of course achieved at Nicaea using the abstract vocabulary which has become so familiar: that Brahman is composed of three hypostases (or as Latin put it *personae*) in one *ousia* or *substantia*. These concepts point to an eternal and triple structure within the Divine Being. They point to the threefoldness in the inner or immanent nature of Brahman. They do not merely point to three modes or phases of divine self-manifestation. In later jargon, they

THE VISION OF LOVE

do not refer merely to the economic Trinity. The Fathers used other terms to explicate the unity of the hypostases by saying that the Father alone was the single source or principle: as *Īśvara* he is a kind of anchorage of divinity, and from this the Son is begotten, and the Spirit proceeds. These relations are conceived as being eternal. They have no origin in time. Their manifestation in history is of course time-bound: the Son was born at a certain date, and the Spirit was poured forth from Pentecost onwards. But the interior relationship to the Father is eternal, part of the unchanging structure of the Threefoldness. (The fact that the relation is eternal does not by itself guarantee the divinity of the persons: the Qur'an is held to be everlasting, and expresses the mind and will of Allah, but it is not itself a divine being. What ensures that from a Christian point of view Christ and the Spirit are divine is that they are both objects of worship.)

However, the Cappadocians strongly emphasized the plural and social character of the three-in-one. They used the analogy of the human family. St Gregory of Nazianzen used the simile of Adam, Eve and their son Seth as three persons yet they shared a single human nature (whether we can ourselves use this example is open to question, since we do not think of human nature as a substance in the same way). But this sense of social plural existence is reflected not only in the liturgy but also in the later iconic representations of the Trinity. Consider for instance Andrei Rublev's famous Old Testament Trinity.

For its times (the 4th century C.E., at Nicaea and Constantinople) the classical formulation of the Trinity doctrine succeeded in its aims. It provided a credal summary of the focus of the Christian faith. It provided a norm of orthodoxy, and by its emphasis upon soteriology it challenged alternative views, which might be held in one way or another to undermine the logic of the faith. But as it stands it does contain difficulties. One of the problems is that we have used the classical formulations in a rather frozen way to maintain continuity with the origins of the faith and with the thought of the Fathers. This can eventuate in an unfortunately uncritical attitude: a kind of patristic fundamentalism.

Difficulties with the Classical Formulation

The most obvious problem, of course, is that we live in a quite different world: a new global civilization which, though it has analogies with the world of the Roman Empire, is immeasurably different in various ways.

For one thing, the available Greek philosophical terminology which the Greek Fathers had to deploy was technically not adequate fully to express their position. For: (1) the categories and concepts were culturally limited and are rather oblique to contemporary understanding. It is not just that the words derived from the Latin translations of the key items, namely the words "substance" and "person" have very different meanings in ordinary English. More importantly, in their classical uses the words *hypostasis* (the individual subsistence of a thing) and *persona* (face or mask, and so the role performed by an actor in a play) do not imply a distinct center of consciousness, and of purposeful activity. Yet it is in this modern sense of persons or agents, i.e. willing subjects, that the Cappadocians meant their term *hypostasis*. This point has been recognized not only by many historians but also be some important modern Orthodox theologians, e.g. Lossky (1957) and Ware (1980). Oddly, hypostasis is better reflected in the modern word "person" than in the Latin from which the latter is derived – though the fact that the Latins used the word *persona* with its partially personalistic implications (its meaning being close to "character" in a drama) was significant.

Incidentally, a number of modern theologians have overlooked this point, among them Karl Barth, whose own rendering of *hypostasis* was "mode of being" (*Seinswesen*), which he uses to construct his own internal modalist view of the Trinity, while claiming continuity with the Fathers. Barth overlooks that a subsistent entity is something which exists: a mode is the *way* in which something exists. In our stronger interpretation a hypostasis not only exists, but is a center of consciousness.

Furthermore, the category of *ousia* or substance has an impersonal and static air. It is true that sometimes in religion we wish to use such terms as Being and Emptiness partly to indicate the way in which the ultimate lies beyond concepts, including personalistic ones. We need the more abstract Brahman as well as the personal Īśvara. But in the present case we are trying to explicate the personal side of the divine Being: we are trying to make sense of the coexistence of the "dear Father" and the Son, and the Holy Spirit, all given personal interpretations in the early tradition. So the terminology does not do its proper job here, of conveying the personalistic aspect of the Trinity doctrine. The static flavor is inappropriate to the portrait of a dynamic God throughout the scriptures. The Divine Being is active throughout the processes of history and in the events of the cosmos.

In regard to the concept of God as person, the modern idea of a person implies both a center of consciousness and a body. The person is so to speak a fusion of the two. But as we note in our discussion of the doctrine of Creation it is useful to use the conception of the cosmos as God's body. Of course it is not like the organic bodies exactly which are fragments of the cosmos. But then God is not absolutely like a human being. But the analogy is there and can be exploited. So though in this discussion of the Trinity we stress the notion of center of consciousness as basically constitutive of the person, we do not wish to deny that the Trinity is incarnated not only as Christ in a human body, but also in the cosmos as a whole. But these are other discussions and raise other issues.

Finally, the terminology used to describe the distinctions and relations between the divine *hypostaseis* remains somewhat problematic. By maintaining that the Father was, as ingenerate and unbegotten, the single source of principle from which both the Son and the Spirit derived their respective identities, the Eastern Fathers admitted that they could offer no coherent reason why the Spirit was not also a "second Son" except by saying that the Spirit proceeded while the Son was begotten (or as the Council of Toledo averred from the Latin end, "came out of the womb of the Father"). The concept of procession, moreover, derived from John's Gospel, could mean either the fact or the mode of origin – either on the one hand the fact that the Son originates from the Father, or on the other hand the mode in which this origination occurs. In these ways, then, the classical formulation is not wholly satisfactory.

The Western theological tradition particularly from Augustine onward clarified the Eastern account by saying that the Spirit proceeded from the Father *and the Son* (*filioque*). Augustine held that the Spirit was the *bond of love* (*vinculum amoris*) between the Father and the Son. As we are so well aware the *filioque* became a bone of contention between East and West, both in itself and more importantly because of issues of authority from the unilateral Western insertion of it into the creed. Eastern theologians thought that the formulation endangered the unity of the Trinity either by implying that there were two primary principles of origin or else by confusing the distinction between the Father and the Son. Lossky felt that referring to the Spirit as the bond of love reduces the identity of the Spirit to that of a relation. But as will be seen we consider this objection to be unconvincing. We now, having surveyed some of the data that have been important for the Christian tradition, turn to our contemporary representation of the classical ideas.

A New Presentation of the Classical Doctrine
Here we shall bring together some of the data already mentioned and material derived from the crosscultural phenomenology of religion. First, let us recapitulate some of the classical evidence within the Christian tradition.

(1) There is the essential relationship of mutual self-giving love between Christ and the heavenly Father in the communal bond of the Spirit, during Jesus' earthly life, as depicted in the Gospels. That this loving relationship or threefold life pattern is also the eternal and essential feature is supported as follows: both Christ and the Spirit were recognized and worshipped as divine on the basis of the

salvation effected, as experienced by the early Christians. It pointed to a transcendent pattern of divine organization.

(2) This trinitarian life pattern is reproduced in the life of adopted sonship, in the fellowship of agape in the new community (Thornton, 1928; Hodgson, 1944). It is within the sacramental life of the church that Christians were united with Christ and divinized. They came to share the bond of love and assimilated to the divine life: this is what is meant by deification. This experience of the Trinity as social was the essence of the distinctively *Christian* apprehension of the Ultimate.

Our reformulation of the classical doctrine involves the following:

(1) We suggest replacing the abstract, statis and impersonal category of the divine substance into that of *divine life*. This divine life is common to the three identities. In this we follow the thinking of Leonard Hodgson in his *The Doctrine of the Trinity* (1944). He sees the divine unity as an organic life unity which includes plurality, rather than as a mathematical unity which excludes plurality. Thus, an organism exists by unifying various constituent elements which contribute to its being into a single life form. Among living forms the higher the organism in the genetic scale, the more complex is the unity. So the human body is much more complicated than is that of an amoeba. But Hodgson notes that this complexity is also marked by a scale of intensity of unifying power, according to which the more complex is the inner structure of an organism the greater is the identity of unifying power. So a living organic unity is an internally constitutive unity.

Hodgson believes that this type of organic life unity is the way to understand the divine life. "The divine unity is a dynamic unity actively unifying in the one divine life the lives of the three divine persons" (Hodgson, 1944, p. 95).

We believe this to be an important insight. There is no possibility of this being construed as tritheism, since the intensity of the infinity of the divine life exceeds anything we can experience or fully conceive. But, by analogy: who would say that Winston Churchill was several people because he had two feet, a liver and so forth?

Hitherto in our discussion we have been using the term "identity" to refer to the three persons, and this was intentional. We shall here develop the inwardness of this usage.

We noted earlier that while the Greek and Latin Fathers understood the divine realities to be conscious subjects, the terms which they used, namely *hypostaseis* and *personae*, do not bring out this idea well. It happens though that the modern theologians whom we shall criticize think that taking person to mean an autonomous center of consciousness leads inevitably to tritheism, and therefore reject not only this analysis but the social trinity as well.

Here, we make use of a novel idea propounded by the Sri Lankan Christian writer Lynn de Silva. In his work, *The Problem of Self in Buddhism and Christianity* (1974), de Silva developed the notion of *anatta-pneuma* combining notions from both Theravada Buddhism and Christianity: *anattā* signifies "non-egocentric" while *pneuma* (spirit) is self-conscious personal life (on the latter see our chapter nine, Spirit and Psyche). Taken together, de Silva's notion signifies "non-egocentric mutuality" or what John Hick calls a "mutually open center of consciousness" (Hick, 1976). If we define each of the divine identities as selfless spirit, then it is clear that each does not exist over against the others as self-enclosed centers of consciousness, as with human persons (thought even with us there can be modes of transcending ourselves through love, and bonding our consciousnesses), but rather each dwells in the others through a kind of inter-permeation. The consciousnesses are fused but not confused. This is a modern way of stating the old idea of *perichoresis* or circumincession, as stated by such Fathers as John of Damascus, who refers to the mutual coinherence of the hypostases.

These biological analogies are in harmony, of course, with the New Testament idea of the sacramental body of Christ, in which Christians are like cells within a divine organism. Note too that the divine life circulates through the selfless persons as the life processes do through the cells and limbs of an organism. We can think metaphorically of the centers of consciousness as being bounded by permeable membranes through which the fluids of the divine life pass. The divine life is, of course, not some fourth entity like the Godhead beyond God. Though some writers have thought like this (Eckhart and Shankara, for instance), this introduces priorities and an ontological distinction which we do not wish to adopt.

We shall now relate this organic model to the relations of origin in the divine life. We believe that our previous analysis of the key experiential data supports Augustine's view of the Spirit as the *vinculum amoris* or bond of love between the Father and the Son. Augustine marshalled additional Biblical support for this view, in his *De Trinitate*, by weaving together material from St John's first epistle (4:7–19) and *Romans* (5:5). John states that Love is of God and is God, and that Christians can recognize that they are God's children and dwell within God in love by the fact that she has given us her Spirit. Paul also says that the love of God is poured into our hearts through the gift of the Spirit. So, for Augustine, this love which is and comes from God is the Spirit. Augustine's view is of great value to us. Thus, God is love – as a proposition – relates to our organic conception: the very nature of the divine life is a process of self-giving love. The first divine identity, the Father, out of the necessity of his/her nature of self-giving life and love eternally engenders, by divine parthenogenesis, the second identity, the Son, through a self-communication of the divine life. In turn, the Son communicates back the very same divine life through a responsive love which brings forth the third identity, namely the Spirit, as blissful love. This divine life process expresses the related notions that goodness is diffusive of itself and that agape/love is the self-communication of the good, i.e., the fullness of life.

There are parallels, though not quite exact, elsewhere. The famous formula of *sat, cit* and *ānanda* as the three pervasive characteristics of Brahman, correspond, up to a point, to the three Identities in the Trinity. The Son is the acme of self-consciousness, both beyond the world and in the incarnate condition of a human being: the Spirit is blissful love which (so to speak) binds the other two constituents together. The Spirit is the *anattā-pneuma* (to revert to de Silva's language) who is the communal bond and mediates between the Father and the Son.

It may be noted also our account indicates how gender in any literal sense does not come into the divine life (save that as a human being Jesus was a male – though if we assume that he was unmarried and yet had a close circle of women friends, both unusual traits at that time, he could be said to have transcended the usual male and female gender roles, as part of his pervasive "category-transcendence" to which we have earlier referred). The divine identities are so to speak androgynous or bisexual life forms, or if you prefer go beyond gender distinctions. The Father engenders the Son: the Spirit is the kiss exchanged between the Father and the Son (as Bernard of Clairvaux put it [Sermon No. 7]), and the two fuse to bring forth the Spirit.

Augustine's account gives us a way of understanding the relationships of the Three and indicates why the Spirit is not a "second Son" or "Twin". We can put our position, then, in the following way:

God is Love

Father: lover	Son: beloved
engendering love	responsive love

Spirit: co-beloved
blissful love

Response to Criticisms

Our analysis enables us to respond to criticisms directed against this view .

(1) Both the Father and the Son together are the source of the identity of the Spirit (cp. Council of Florence, 1438–9). But the Father is still the ultimate source. But we may note in any case that the infinity of the one divine life precludes the possibility of any separation of the Father and the Son ontologically. The distinction between the three centers of consciousness in the Trinity is from one perspective

an analytic one which allows us to perceive the inner structure of the divine life, but it does not mean that we can in the Christian context think of the possibility of the Father existing and the Son and the Spirit not.

(2) Our account does not lead to confusion between the Father and the Son, since the Son receives his identity from the Father alone, while the Father is self-possessed.

(3) The Spirit is not reduced to a relation or affect or adjectival quality. The Spirit's identity is the expression of a process of mutual self-giving love and communication of divine life between the Father and the Son. In other words, we see the Spirit as being a living conscious identity who receives his identity from that process. As Richard of St Victor said, the Spirit is the co-beloved of the Father and the Son. The Spirit knows her or himself to be the "fruition" (as St Hilary said) of the love of the Father and his only Son who ever leans upon his breast. We may note that the love within the Trinity is both ontological, in that it is the divine life: but it also expresses the personal affection between the identities.

We propose also to replace the classical terms *generation* and *procession* as follows. The Son eternally *flows out* from the Father and the Spirit flows out from the Father and the Son.

Comments on Augustine and Richard of St Victor
Augustine's view is further developed in the Trinitarian theology of love of the medieval theologian Richard of St Victor. He argues that since self-giving love is the perfection of human nature it must also be in some mode the perfection of divine nature. This is exactly how God's nature indeed is defined through John's formula that God is love. But how can there be any such *agape* if God is so to speak a single individual? It is true that God is creator of the world, and this gives him objects of self-giving love, i.e. living creatures. This is true: but the world might not have existed. It is the consequence of a kind of decision on God's part. So his or her intrinsic nature must be such that there are within the divine being more than one identity. If God only loved

himself intrinsically (as implied by Karl Barth, Paul Tillich and Spinoza) this would fall short of the perfection of self-giving love. Richard goes on to argue that perfect love needs three, not just two persons. The argument is: the love of two persons would not be perfect unless each was willing to share that love with a third person. The lover desires that her beloved have the happiness of loving and being loved by another person. Her love is so secure that she can, without fear or worry, allow herself a "rival" to share the same friendship with her beloved. If this degree of unselfishness is possible among human friendships and within the human family, then it must also occur within the divine life. Thus, perfect self-giving love seems to demand three identities within the one divine life. The Father and the Son love one another with mutual love from which comes the co-beloved Spirit who is loved together as shared love by the Father and the Son. The Spirit in turn loves the Father and the Son together as a pair, as a child loves her parents.

Richard's theology represents a certain advance over that of Augustine in that it shows that the Spirit is definitely a self-conscious identity. So the Spirit is not just to be thought of as the *vinculum amoris* but also as the *condilectum* or co-beloved. This then includes the idea of a double flowing-out, while making clear that the Spirit is not simply a relation or mode.

The Trinity and Phenomenology

We are now in a position to look at the way we conceive of the Trinity as social enabling us to give a coherent account of the major types of religious experience and the kinds of doctrines correlated with them. We do not say that our schema represents the only way to view the phenomenology of religion. But we are concerned to argue that the Christian faith as we express it does have a perspective which makes sense of the varieties of religious experience.

As well as being conscious of themselves as divine identities the Persons possess together a common divine consciousness through which they are aware of sharing the divine life and love and in which they act together in perfect harmony. This sense of common consciousness reminds us of, let us say, two people, close to one another in life, who together watch the sun set; or jointly create a garden. So the divine Persons are in such harmony in regard to the cosmos (and this is the meaning of the Cappadocian idea of the three Persons sharing a common will). Through the common divine consciousness the identities form a communal or corporate self, an I within the We.

We can make a distinction too between the non-relational and the relational aspects of the Trinity. There is, first, the infinity of the divine life as it circulates through the selfless spirits. This is the non-relational aspect. Then, second, there is the plurality of the three Persons. Third, there is the communal life – the shared ego of the three. These last two aspects are relational (the first to one another, the second towards creatures).

External and Internal Non-dual *Dhyāna*

Meditation of this contemplative kind (involving, e.g. Eastern methods of yoga and *dhyāna*) can be said to put the person in contact with a non-relational aspect of the infinity of the divine life through the medium of the finite world of space and time. Here there is no awareness of being in relationship with a distinct divine identity. This gives these experiences a non-personal quality.

Externally apprehended, the infinity of the Transcendent gives rise to the penenhenic experience, and this is marked particularly in Taoism and Zen Buddhism. The infinite is given, in such cases, rather impersonal descriptions, such as Tao, *Dharmakāya*, Emptiness.

Internally apprehended the non-relational is experienced as some form of non-dual consciousness. The person arrives so to speak at the base of her soul or consciousness, and becomes one with what is also the essence of the divine life, insofar as it is not relational. In the Vedanta this impersonal experience is interpreted as the realization of identity with the one Divine Being Brahman, which is characterised as being, bliss and consciousness. This transformation involves, from the Advaitin perspective, liberation and penetration

174

through the illusion of the world, regarded as a separate entity or complex of entities.

In Theravada Buddhism this contact with the infinite is seen as a transcendental state of liberation, and is not given that more ramified interpretation found in the Advaita and (in a curious way) by Mahayana Buddhism (which of course deeply influenced Sankara). So we here have a minimalist interpretation of the Transcendent. The Buddha rejected a creator God, of course; and chiefly on ethical grounds, it seems. Anyway, nirvana functions as a fifth dimension, so to speak, beyond the space-time world. Our account enables us to show how the Theravadins can experience the transcendent (or an aspect of the Trinity from our perspective), but without having to characterize it in terms foreign to their own understanding. We do not, that is, to have to do what Zaehner attempted, by smuggling souls back into Buddhism, because he thinks that all the Theravadins are doing is experiencing the unity of their souls; nor do we need to think as Radhakrishnan as if they explicitly experience the Self. These interpretations are deeply contrary to virtually the whole of the Buddhist tradition, and make the Buddha a good deal less original than he was. All that we need to do is to show that our more complex view of the Transcendent (as the Trinity) contains an element which taken by itself can quite reasonably be interpreted in the Buddhist minimalist manner.

In Mahayana Buddhism the internal dhyanic experience is subject to different interpretations of the ultimate as being non-personal (chiefly symbolized by the concept of emptiness), and in some way (in Pure Land, Shingon, etc.) as personal: it should be noted that in the dominant non-personalist interpretations, and in Vedanta, the contemplative experience contains affective states such as "peace" and "bliss". We suggest that these are also experiences of the Holy Spirit, who as we have seen is characterized by these states. The sense of the timelessness or permanence of these experiences, giving rise to the notion that there is an unchanging transcendent state beyond the flux or mirage of events in "this" world derives (from our perspective) from

175

the inexhaustibility and stability of the divine life processes in the Trinity.

We can now contrast the Trinity doctrine as social from the *Saccidānanda* doctrine of Advaita Vedanta and the *Trikāya* (Three-Aspect Doctrine) of later Mahayana Buddhism. In the former, the three qualities of being, consciousness and bliss characterize a single, ultimately indefinable entity, Brahman (the "Trinity" of Shiva, Vishnu and Brahmā has a rather different logic and reflects three different modes of divine operation rather than as real members of an abiding Trinity). The Three-Aspect Body describes two levels of existence, the *Dharmakāya* or Truth-Aspect of the Buddha being the impersonal ultimate, which at the lower level manifests itself in visions and ritual as the celestial Buddhas (the Enjoyment-Aspect) and as the Transformation-Aspect in the body and life of the historical Buddha, the Teacher. Though there are some reflections and resemblances to the Trinity, this doctrine has some essential differences. First, it is "two-level", and so regards the personalistic aspects as "lower". We do not accept this kind of priority in the Trinity doctrine, which we see as synthesizing both personal and non-personal aspects all at the one level. Second, there is a docetic strand in the Mahayana formulation which again we reject in the case of Christ. So though there are echoes as between the Eastern doctrines and the Trinity, the resemblances are rather superficial. We do not in this say that the Trinity doctrine is necessarily superior: it is, however, the vision of the truth that we are presenting. We repeatedly have stressed that we cannot expect proof of the one worldview over others. The Buddhist Mahayana has a breadth of vision which makes it most attractive, as does the modern Hindu interpretation of the Advaitin tradition. We just wish to make it clear that our conception of the divine Threefoldness diverges from other threefoldnesses in the history of religions.

The common divine consciousness of the Trinity is encountered also in the *bhaktism* of various religions – the devotionalism of Hinduism, of Sikhism, of Pure Land Buddhism, etc., and of the "Western" religions (e.g.

Methodism, Hasidism and Islamic pietism). Internally, such personalistic faith is found in much of Christian mysticism, Hasidism and Sufism.

This personalist aspect of the Trinity is encountered also in the strongly numinous and prophetic visions of leading religious figures, and the internalization of such dramatic experiences in conversions, shamanistic visions and the like. Contact with the Trinity in its unity accounts for these events: even if those who have such experience may not know that they are also in contact with the divine three-foldness.

This threefoldness becomes manifest to Christians through history, insofar as the Jewish people and the early Christians had encounters, so they considered, with a divine Creator, and then with Jesus Christ and with the Spirit, from Pentecost onwards. It is obvious that in some sense or other all "revelation" or self-manifestation of the Transcendent must occur through historical events, if for no other reason than this, that every experience of human beings is qualified by being placed within the historical process. Still, the Jewish and Christian traditions have also seen linear strands of history as significant for the ongoing manifestation of providence. But it is unavoidable that revelation should appear phenomenologically within temporal experience. It is thus very easy to place the Transcendent at a high level and think of divine revelatory acts at a lower level, and as merely relational. It is important, however, to realize that the Divine occurs as transcendent in the midst of history. We have resisted a view of the Trinity which sees the trinitarian perspective merely in the "economic" activity of the Divine. We have tried to penetrate into the inner structure of the Trinity: and this is something externally manifest also in the historical acts of God. There is a great advantage, we believe, in this way of dealing with the enigmas of our faith, not only because it makes for a greater solidarity between the nature and the actions of the Divine, but also because it shows us that we can embrace the phenomenology of religious experience worldwide and so give an account of other religious traditions which sees them too as containing apprehensions of the same Transcendent that we have depicted in this discussion. Again, we do not wish to say there are any proofs here: but at least it is an indication of the richness of Christianity that we can explicate its central doctrine in a manner hospitable to the diversities of religious experience across the world.

We shall now turn to wield a critique of some other modern accounts of the Trinity. Our desire is to further clarify our own position. We think that the alternatives lead in principle to unfortunate practical consequences, or can do. Once again we stress that the point of a *darśana* is to supply the vision which will guide spiritual and practical activities.

Some Alternative Views: External Modalism

We are here chiefly concerned with 20th Century Christian theologians. We need to explore not just their analysis of the Trinity but also the implications for Christology – since of course different "theories" of the Trinity are correlated with differing views as to the nature of Christ. The most important relevant alternative analysis is "external modalism".

According to this standpoint, God is a single self-conscious identity who manifests himself in three external modes of operation. They are external because they are related to humankind (and more broadly to creatures). Thus, the Father acts in creation and the work of providence. As the Son, God acts as Redeemer (a concept which only makes sense in relation to fallen beings, and not to God himself). God acts, thirdly, in the work of sanctification and in guidance through the Spirit. These modes of operation are not simply successive phases of activity in the history of Israel and of the New Israel, but ways in which God is continuously related to his creation. But this is where we take issue with this standpoint.

For on this account the Trinity doctrine does not delineate the eternal structure of the Divine Being, but instead depicts God's relationship to the cosmos. But we have been at pains to underline, in our treatment of creation and in accordance with virtually the whole of the mainstream Christian tradition, that even if the cosmos is everlasting (though most Christians have thought it to begin a finite time ago), it is not *necessary*. Even if everlasting it is the deliberate creation of God. There might have been nothing. So if a doctrine is essentially about God's relationship to the cosmos it is not about the inner nature of God, but about her activities towards this externally related universe. In other words the doctrine concerns the so-called "economic Trinity", not the "immanent Trinity". We may ask: is it justified to worship God as instantiated in a mode of operation? Our conception of the social Trinity applies the innermost being of God, and we regard this structural description as normative for the whole range of Christian life and teaching.

The type of Christology correlated with the "external modalist" alternative is some form or other of adoptionism. From a logical point of view, of course, Jesus of Nazareth is a person from the midst of the created world, chosen as God's incarnation, and in this sense we may talk of "logical adoptionism", which is a harmless outlook: but it is in a deeper and more radical sense of the term that "adoptionism" is typically used, and used here. On this view Jesus was not eternally the Son of God in his identity, but a person adopted or chosen by God to be his Son or servant, at his baptism. Such a "low" or "adoptionist" view is aptly classified as a form of "spirit Christology", according to which God's presence in Jesus is considered to be analogous to that in Old Testament prophets. The difference is only that in Christ the divine Spirit is present "without limit" (as Tillich affirms [1963]). It is this which makes him the Messiah, on this view. The Spirit, moreover, is considered not a separate entity, but rather the indwelling presence and power of God that was manifested in the life of Jesus and is continued in the life of the Church. This way of looking at the Spirit makes it scarcely if at all distinguishable from grace. The external modalist view and its correlated adoptionism have been defended by a number of liberal Protestant theologians, and notably by John Hick (Hick 1973, 1982).

Hick rejects the classical formulation of the Trinity as

social and the high or identity-Christology that goes with it. He states that the Trinity as social is a sophisticated form of tritheism and indeed a limited polytheism inconsistent with the God of monotheism – the heavenly Father to whom Jesus prayed and whom he worshipped. He and his fellow authors in *The Myth of God Incarnate* appear to regard the classical identity doctrine of the incarnation as untenable, and the Virgin Birth teaching (held to underpin it). They do so on two main grounds: first, there are historical reasons derived from modern scholarship concerning Christian origins; and second there are philosophical reasons, supposing that the notions in question are contradictory and unintelligible. Hick treats the doctrine of the incarnation as myth or metaphor (but by the way no satisfactory account of myth is given in the book, a great omission given its title). It is metaphorical and expresses the intensity of the presence of God's self-giving love in the life of Jesus of Nazareth. Hick here puts forth his own quasi-Arian account, according to which Jesus' self-giving love is continuous with the universal patterns of activity of God's self-giving love. Not *homoousia* but *homoagape*. Jesus' life therefore displays God's characteristic attitude towards humankind. As regards the atonement: Jesus functions as redeemer or mediator in that he reveals God's forgiving love towards humankind, which overcomes alienation from him. From this point of view, Jesus is an exemplar: one whose activity is essentially to manifest the divine qualities. He is just one of a number of mediators, of whom we can count the Hebrew prophets, Muhammad, Gautama, Kabir, Nanak, Lao-tzu, and so on. All these serve as mediums of the eternal One. Hick in this follows Toynbee in holding that the essence of world religion is contact with a transcendent Reality or divine noumenon. The Reality is of course the Sun of his "Copernican revolution": the various religions are so to speak in orbit around it. It contains both a personal and an impersonal aspect. The religions are historically and culturally conditions, mediums which encourage people's transformation from being self-centered to being Reality-centered. Thus, Hick's stance is really what may be called "Unitarian Universalism". This in itself is no bad thing: it is a position to respect, and though the usual criticisms can be made of any attempt to reduce religions to a single essence, it is a noble vision in its own right. But is it Christian? It seems to us to sacrifice the heart of the faith.

From our perspective, the external modalist view and adoptionist Christology are quite unsatisfactory, since they do not account for the key experiential data in the life of Jesus and the early church community. It was these data that the classical Trinity doctrine tried to explicate and on which it rested. Hick's view, for instance, undermines the soteriological basis upon which the distinctively Christian experience of God and the new way of life on earth rest. It is not for nothing that so many of those who came to be regarded as saints, martyrs and fathers of the Church strove vigorously against Arian and similar views as being destructive ultimately of the life of the Church. Such views, of course, undermine traditional understandings of the Eucharist. This is tied, necessarily, to a high Christology, for the concept of the real presence of Christ in the sacrament does not add up to anything if Christ is not himself divine. The fact that the Christian liturgy contains as a crucial element the worship of the three divine identities is surely significant. The notion that Jesus was a man in whom God was specially present does not make sense of the practice of Christian worship. It seems to put the Christian in the position of idolatry.

Hick tries to parry the charge of idolatry by saying that Christians worship *through* Christ, and that human beings can only worship the divine noumenon through mental, symbolic or anthropomorphic images of God. For Christians, Christ is the image of God, while for Hindus there are images such as those of Rama, Krishna, Durga, Kali and so on; and for Buddhists various bodhisattvas and celestial Buddhas such as Amida. He thinks that it is entirely appropriate and indeed necessary that people should approach the Transcendent through these mediators. They are so "vastly higher" and "immensely spiritually nearer" to the Eternal than the rest of humankind. His position here is both phenomenologically false and psychologically untenable.

In particular, Jews and Muslims are aniconic and very strict in their monotheism. They do not rely upon mediators as perceived in Christianity or the Hindu tradition. Hick would be open to the charge by Muslims, of *shirk* – treating that which is not divine as divine, namely Jesus, and associating someone who is other than God with worship which is due only to the Divine Being. Moreover, Christ is phenomenologically somewhat different from the Bodhisattvas, *avatāras*, etc., of the Indian tradition, since he was from earliest times worshipped as himself constituting a divine identity and on a par with the heavenly Father: it was not a question of worshipping the Father through him (but if you like, *with* him). Moreover, his historical anchorage raises some issues which do not arise with the more symbolic figures of the Bodhisattva Avalokiteśvara or Rama and so on.

His picture is psychologically untenable, we would argue, because he states a splitting paradox: that we can worship God with one side of our brain using mythological and liturgical language, while not worrying about what the other side of our brain tells us, that from the analytical and intellectual perspective the language is literally false. If the language is analogical its literal falsity would not matter: but Hick seems to think that we can in an emotional stance take what we know not to the case to be true. If Christ and the Holy Spirit are not divine identities, then it is surely wrong for us (from a Christian theist perspective) to worship them. It is not that mythologically they are divine but literally they aren't: we use mythic language equally for all Gods. A further implication is that somehow God has revealed himself under differing names that do not correspond to any identities, and so there are severe problems for Hick in relation to his view of revelation. (But to be fair: everyone has problems with that.)

Regarding the idea of the atonement, we have already noted that if Christ was not himself divine he could not effect salvation: the latter requires that he be an embodied divine identity acting on behalf of, and indeed in a state of solidarity with, humankind. He expiates their sins through suffering, but if he were only trying to do that as a human being the atonement would be inexplicable. There are of course many others who have suffered on the cross, but the special character of Jesus' death has to do with his divine status. After the revolt of Judas the Galilean in 6 C.E. some two thousand Jewish men were crucified, but though no doubt they were admired by sympathizers with their revolutionary spirit, none of them was subsequently, of course, worshipped as Lord and savior, distinct from the one God or Heavenly Father. We need not belabor this point: suffice it to say that many, many Christians have conceived themselves to be experiencing the risen Lord, and would have been greatly mistaken were Hick's view right. It is of course consonant with our epistemology that we do not hold that we can show or prove Hick's position to be wrong by some incontrovertible proofs. But we do argue that he cannot coherently account for the beliefs and behavior of Jesus' followers, nor can he make real sense of the uniqueness of Christ. So his vision may be noble, but is it, to repeat our question, Christian?

Ours in not a mere appeal to tradition, but rather to a hermeneutical principle, that our account should correspond to the experiential data as phenomenologically accessible to us from the early writings.

Before discussing the next major relevant alternative view, we should note that the external modalist position and adoptionist Christology are held in varying ways by liberal process theologians such as John Cobb, who make use of the general philosophical categories of A.N. Whitehead in order to articulate a modern theistic worldview. Their work is attractive, and its dynamism we accept. It makes use of categories which are dynamic – such as becoming, events, possibility, relativity, novelty and so on. These are most useful in trying to express a view of the cosmos in this post-Einsteinian age (though it must be said too that Whitehead's language is often very difficult and to employ it to *clarify* a theistic position is sometimes self-defeating). Anyway, such process theologians use these ideas to guide their interpretation of the New Testament, and a little like the 19th century Hegelians may be seeing Jesus in the light of their philosophy rather than the other way round. Anyway, for Hartshorne, the Trinity is a symbol of God's social attributes such as love and sympathy in relation to his creatures. For Whitehead God is the supreme exemplification of an actual entity: such entities are units of experience which make up the cosmic process, and God must be conceived as a single identity of which every other actual entity is a reflection. Hartshorne also denies personal immortality, holding instead that all events are eternally preserved in the memory of God. So he, Hartshorne, will have a sort of immortality in that God will remember him for ever. (But we hold that God is specially present at the root of human consciousnesses, and is inner sustainer – so if God remembers us he will also give active sustenance.) John Cobb has sought to modify some of these ideas in a more personalist direction, and also within the pluralistic context of the world's religions. But he too tends to subsume classical Christian doctrines under the framework of the process categories. He for example with regard to the Incarnation calls the single conscious identity of God "Christ" and says that Christ was incarnate in Jesus. This seems to us very misleading. There are still two identities, the Christ principle and the man Jesus, and Cobb's position turns out to be another version of unitarianism (Cobb, 1983). His position is reminiscent too of Neo-Vedantist views of Christ, which also do not give adequate recognition (from a Christian point of view) to the separate divine identity of Christ. The same objections raised against Hick's adoptionism apply, then, also to Cobb.

Whitehead's system does not, it happens, lend itself to a high identity Christology, because of his bipolar panentheism, according to which all actual entities are ontologically manifestations of God's primordial nature (this is where too we glimpse Whitehead's panpsychism – as distinguished from our doctrine of divine omnipresence and our distinction between material and conscious processes). God's presence therefore in Jesus is not ontologically different in principle from his presence in other actual entities. Hartshorne makes use of a biological analogy, and states that human beings are like cells within a divine organism, and that the cosmos is God's body. This differs from our *darśana*. Ours is a kind of social-trinitarian panentheism, which is eschatologically expressed, in a way whereby people are gradually assimilated into the divine life. Ramanuja's notion, which we make use of, of the cosmos as God's body is an instrumentalist and spiritual notion, according to which God is the inner controller of the cosmos as well as of individual consciousnesses. In our perspective, consciousness arises out of cosmic energy (or matter) under the influence of divine creativity in the evolutionary process. We thus reject the panpsychic notion that implicitly consciousness is always there. Note too that in process thought creation is necessary to God from eternity. God must have a set of relational alternatives with which to interact and with which to be socially related. From our social trinitarian perspective the divine life of agape shows that love is eternal, and that it is from this love freely given that the creation springs. It is not necessary, but flows from the Father's love of the Son in the bliss of the communal bond of the Spirit. Here the Father desires to create other self-conscious beings through an evolutionary process and in a free environment. Only by veiling herself will the divine Being give finite creatures freedom. They need a stable environment in order to be "free-ranging" beings, and yet this material milieu is bound to be noxious and confusing as well as supportive and luminous. The Creator in bringing into existence such free and conscious beings wishes to share their responsive love with the Son: together with the cosmos as a whole they will be united with the Trinity and progressively incorporated into the divine life.

Internal Modalism

The next major alternative view of the Trinity which we wish to consider is what we call "internal modalism". According to this perspective, God is a single self-conscious identity who internally exists in three modes of being. This immanent Trinity then manifests herself through three distinct ways of acting in her self-revelation in history. This view is important, for it is espoused by a number of prominent Christian theologians of this century, including Karl Barth, Karl Rahner, John Macquarrie and Paul Tillich. They are exercised by what they see as errors in the other main views.

(1) They do not like external modalism since they see it as implying that God is so to say incommunicado behind his modes. He is unknowable behind his ways of manifesting himself. He becomes so to speak a behavioristic Divine Being: it is not him in himself that is seen in his outer actions. For Hick perhaps the situation is much worse: because the behavior is only symbolic and there are alternative behaviors, none of which, however, reveals the inner nature of God. This view is vigorously rejected by the theologians we have listed, but at the same time they are worried that Christianity should seem to be tritheistic.

(2) They see, then, the doctrine of the social Trinity as tritheistic. They all say that the notion of three centers of consciousness, three "I"s, is tritheism. So they underline in a very emphatic way the thesis that the ancient words *hypostasis* and *persona* do not imply centers of consciousness. They conclude, but in our view erroneously, that the Church fathers did not mean the terms in this way. However, these theologians all agree with us that these old terms are indeed archaic and need replacing to be intelligible in today's world. But their own terms, such as Barth's and Macquarrie's *modes of being* and Rahner's *distinct manners of subsisting* (Rahner, 1970) are too abstract, and have other faults.

We shall focus our critique on Karl Barth as he has written in his massive *Church Dogmatics*. He still remains the single most influential Protestant theologian of this century. And with his view of the Trinity we shall evaluate his Christology. It is a "high" one, but we may note in passing that internal modalism can be combined with a low or adoptionist view of Christ, as in the cases of Paul Tillich (with his Spirit Christology) and John Macquarrie ("Jesus was the man fundamentally open to the Father", 1967, p. 210). While this fact enables them to avoid some of the critical points directed at Barth, they are still open to other elements in our critique of internal modalism, which is a kind of monistic view of the Trinity. Let us first, then, summarize Barth's position.

In formulating his approach, Barth focuses on the term *hypostasis*, which he translates in effect as mode of being. He claims that this is precisely how the Greek Fathers understood the term. He then links this up with his powerful treatment of revelation: for him, God reveals himself as Lord, and this is taken to imply that God is a single self-conscious subject, who exists in three modes. He is first of all the Revealer; then he is the one revealed; and then he is the self-impartation of his revelation. In the first mode, of course, he is the Father; in the second, he is the Son; and in the third, he is the Spirit. For Barth, these modes, of course, are more than manifestations in the historical process. They are eternal modes whereby God reveals himself to himself. He loves himself through himself. But Barth is emphatic that God is not three separate identities or "I"s but a single "I" in an eternal threefold repetition (*repetitio aeternitatis in aeternitate*). So God is in himself as he is towards us (*Dogmatics*, p. 351).

In regard to Christology Barth follows through this logic. God's Word is God himself in his revelation, and Jesus Christ is God's Word. In this way, Barth wishes to maintain a high Christology. He is quite successful, of course, in affirming Christ's divine nature. His is an identity Christology in which Christ is one of the three divine modes of being. Moreover, he goes on to equate the Holy Spirit with the risen Christ. He thinks that it is a mistake to think of the Spirit as a distinct entity which is separable from Christ. He thus says "the Holy Spirit is nothing else than a certain relation of the Word to man" (1959, p. 138). He speaks of the Spirit indeed as being "the Spirit of Jesus". His exegesis, however, is based on a single, and somewhat unclear, passage: "The Lord is the Spirit", which occurs in Paul's Second Letter to the Corinthians (3:17) (Barth, 1959, p. 139). He uses this passage to control his interpretation, as we have already seen in the discussion of Thornton's view.

The relevant passages are as follows: "Now the Lord of whom this passage speaks is the Spirit; and where the Spirit of the Lord is there is liberty" (3:17); "And because for us there is no veil over the face, we all reflect as in a mirror the splendor of the Lord; thus we are transfigured into his likeness, from splendor to splendor; such is the influence of the Lord who is Spirit" (3:18) (New English Bible [NEB]).

Now in the first verse the Lord who is the Spirit is clearly the Holy Spirit, as brought out earlier in this chapter (vv. 2, 3, 6): here the reference is to the ministry of the Spirit as the inner principle of life in people living under the New Covenant in whose hearts the Spirit writes his law. In the first part of the second verse the glory of the Lord refers to Christ who in Chapter 4, vv. 4–6, Paul calls the image of God and in whose face the glory (or splendor) of the Father shines. In the second part of the verse the Lord who is the Spirit is again the Holy Spirit who gradually transforms Christians into the likeness of Christ. Our exegesis here is in agreement with L.S. Thornton's analysis, according to which one of the key activities of the Spirit is holiness-making. This distinguishes her from Christ in whose image Christians are conformed. Paul's thought, moreover, is in this letter clearly social-Trinitarian by implication (Chapter 1: vv. 20–22 and Chapter 13: v. 13 which expresses his formula: "The grace of our Lord Jesus Christ, the love of God and the fellowship of the Holy Spirit be with you all").

We consider that internal modalism as expressed by Barth and others, and the high or identity Christology correlated with it, are untenable. Our reasons are theological and philosophical (but of course ultimately difference of view on these matters have ethical and spiritual consequences, a fact we need constantly to bear in mind: we do not mean to criticize these, our fellow Christians and fellow humans, just to establish an improved theoretical stance).

(1) Barth's rendering of the term *hypostasis* (*Seinswesen*), which is rendered here as "mode of being" is derived from the Neo-Hegelian theologian I.A. Dorner, in his Systematic Theology published in 1874. The great Christian revelationist, so scornful otherwise of the effects of Hegelian

interpretation of the Gospel, makes a strange bedfellow for Dorner. It is a mistaken account, for *hypostasis* clearly means a subsistent entity. We could, if we wished, translate the Trinitarian formula as "three entities in one substance". We have preferred to use "identity" to bring out even more strongly the idea that here there is a self-conscious centre, as the Cappadocian fathers implied. This point is borne out by many comments by historians of Christian doctrine. But there is more to add than a mere point about translation.

(i) If God were only a single identity existing in three modes then the important disputes which raged in the Church about the subordination of the Son to the Father (Arian dispute) and about the procession of the Spirit (*filioque*) would be inexplicable. They could hardly have arisen historically unless the apologists and Church fathers thought the hypostases as distinct conscious identities.

(ii) Barth's Christology involved what may be dubbed Christocentric unitarianism or Monochristism. For he looks upon Christ as the single identity of God in one of his modes of being. But this also makes no sense of the impressions conveyed by the Gospels, above all of the intimate loving communion between Jesus and his dear Father. This is quite central to the Gospel narrative. It pervades the religion of Jesus, from his baptism to Gethsemane and the Cross. There indeed appears to be a logical contradiction in Barth's view. Insofar as he is influenced, realistically enough, by the idea of *kenosis* or the self-emptying of the Divine Being in Christ, then Jesus' knowledge becomes limited. But how can one and the same Being simultaneously be omniscient in one mode and not in another? (This argument does not depend on the concept of omniscience but only upon the idea of a divine attribute discarded by Jesus upon earth.) It is of course possible for a divine identity to have a "career", both involving heavenly and earthly episodes. It appears to us that a high Christology requires a social Trinity, but this point was not realized by Barth and Rahner. Let us continue further along these lines.

Barth's outlook not only appears to nullify the picture of the earthly bonds which drew the Father and the Son together in the communal life of the Spirit; but it also seems to chip away at the edifice of the transcendent *koinonia*. It does not square with the communal *agape* of the divine identities towards each other. This was, as we have seen, the source of, and perceived as the source of, the new fellowship in the life of adopted sonship in the new Israel. There is nothing truly relational in the picture given of God's love, according to the internal modalist theology, for it implies merely that God loves himself (and loving oneself is not entering into any relationship, except perhaps in a merely technical sense). God is supposed to be Love, but this Love turns out to be a rather poor thing. So a much richer view of this pivotal idea in early Christianity is given by our social Trinitarianism. It also has a much richer echo in human experience of fellowship as itself reflecting the divine nature. The family becomes a kind of sacramental reflection of God's life, and that ineffable human togetherness which we experience at the deepest and often the tragic passages in life is a way of understanding the heart of Divine life. Self-love is not the perfection of love, for that involves self-giving. Perhaps Barth and others have been too scared of the possibility of tritheism. They may also have been unduly influenced by a theme in Greek culture which has got itself absorbed into the Christian tradition – the idea that perfection is self-sufficient and impassible. Our God is self-sufficient but in a self-giving way, and she is not impassible. Self-giving puts self-sufficiency at risk, for in loving her creatures God has to suffer with them, both in Christ and as the deep consciousness beyond our consciousnesses, registering our joys and hopes, and pains and fears. Aristotle's God, pure thought thinking itself is repeated in a new form, pure love loving itself. But is that love? Is it what Christians meant by *agape*?

It happens that Barth also seems to misconstrue the position of Augustine: he seems to see Augustine's social trinity merely as incorporating the love whereby God loves himself. It is not the *vinculum amoris* binding Father and Son together. Spinoza we may note held a similar view: God affirms his being through self-love. But understandably he held no Trinitarian belief.

Although Barth wished to ground his doctrine of the Trinity in revelation, his approach was not as empirical as he thought it to be. His interpretation of scripture and of later reflection by the Church was colored, we claim, by his *a priori* anxiety about tritheism, his use of Hegelian categories and his lack of feel for Patristic thinking.

In contrast we hold that our view, following both Thornton and Hodgson, sees the plurality of divine identities as the only adequate picture based upon the data of the early Church and the religious experience of divine togetherness which characterized (and may still characterize) the Christian fellowship. But Barth had other agenda, and though we have been strong here in our critique of his account of the Trinity, we are appreciative of his attempts to give independent vigor to the Christian faith in a terrible period of European history.

Other versions of the doctrine of the social Trinity

It may be noted that various other people, some of whom we have discussed and to whom we are indebted (notably Hodgson and Thornton in modern times), have espoused the social Trinity doctrine. But sometimes their language and conceptions have not been adequate. As we have argued, the older Greek and Latin formulations need radical revision in language. The fact that it can be so misunderstood, as we have seen in the previous section, is problem enough. The leading Protestant theologian Jürgen Moltmann has defended the idea in his *The Trinity and the Kingdom* (1981). He continues to use the classical vocabulary without trying to develop new language. But he defends the Eastern Orthodox view of the Father's being alone originative (he rejects therefore the *filioque*), and he backs up this view in the following manner. He states that the Father utters his eternal Word (*logos*) through the breathing out of his eternal Spirit. There are problems, however, with this analogy of the voice, the spoken word and breath.

First of all, the analogy does not seem to connect with the idea of the loving relation of self-giving which to our mind is the essence of the divine process. Elsewhere of course Moltmann is very eager to emphasize this idea. Still, it is unclear what the bearing of the speech analogy has on the mutual self-giving of God. It also does not give a very clear picture of the separateness of the identities of the Son and the Spirit. Nevertheless Moltmann's work is valuable in its penetrating critique of other theologians, particularly Barth and Rahner, and it contains fine insights into the suffering of the Trinity in and through the Incarnation (and to this point we shall be returning in the next chapter). His work is, though, Western in orientation, and he does not wish to see the Trinity embedded as we do in the phenomenology of the religious experience of the human race.

Some comments on the Hindu view

There are, of course, many religions which are a good deal less exercised than we are about the possibility of polytheism. Of the great world religions, the position of simultaneous monotheism and polytheism is pioneered above all by Hinduism, especially as understood in modern times. The many gods are really one Reality, says the modern Hindu; but nevertheless from a limited perspective, like that of a simple peasant, the gods appear to be different entities, each with her or his own role to play in the economy of the cosmos. Additionally, the Hindu tradition has also the conception of many *avatāras*. But in this discussion we are more concerned with the divergent representation at a heavenly level of the Divine Being – Shiva, Vishnu, Kali, Lakshmi, Ganesh and so on.

It might be called a kind of *refracted* theism. Each God is a refraction of the One. It means that the divine attributes are so to speak personalized and given stories; so that they can interact with one another in myth. The Creative Power of God is a female, who can consort with her spouse. It gives dynamic to the aspects of God. Is this similar to our view of the social Trinity?

It is in a way. It of course presents a much more extravagant picture. The air teems with gods and spirits, and temples abound and multiply. Even Gandhi and Victoria and Mother India become objects of cults. It is this extravagance rather than the formal structure of refracted theism in this case that we do not agree with. There are too many compromises made, we would think, in the synthesizing of the many myths of the diverse parts and parties of the whole Indian tradition. The Christian social Trinity is by contrast austere. But it is also logical. The Creator must feel drawn to her creation; and unites with his *avatāra* through the bond of love. But beyond that God is love and has the closest possible family in himself.

In our view, the doctrine of the social Trinity gives a coherent account of the incarnation, according to which Jesus as one of the divine identities undergoes a kenotic self-limitation in contracting so to speak his divine consciousness and life. The doctrine is part of a picture which we present from the angle of monotheism. We respect the Hindu vision, but it rather is a social multiplicity of the Gods, seen initially through the lens of polytheism, and unified through reflection and spiritual experience. The Hindu multiplex idea has had important development in recent times, as it can provide a framework for tolerant interreligious understanding.

But we stand at a point of revelation which we regard as in line with human needs and experience: God is Love. That means in a way that her Being is refracted. It is because the Trinity makes sense not merely of the given, the early Christian community, but also of our reflections about the logic of creation and the requirements of love that we place it at the center of our *darśana*.

The Spiritual Meaning of the Trinity.
In this section we shall show how the doctrine of the social Trinity relates to Christian life as it is lived. One major difference between the doctrinal dimension of religion and mere metaphysics is that the former is aimed not just at delineating the nature of reality but is at the same time concerned with the way we respond to the Divine Being in practice.

As we have already emphasized, it was through the ritual aspect of liturgical celebration and the sacraments that the early Christians experienced the saving character of their new community life. Thus it was through the ritual dimension that they came to feel and understand the nature of the Divine: in this they had inklings of the Divine as Trinitarian. So we need to see that the early community was from the earliest days a sacramental worshiping community. The doctrine of the Trinity therefore arose from the vision and experience of the Divine as tripersonal, apprehended in worship. It was on this soteriological basis that the Eastern fathers insisted on the spiritual necessity of sound doctrine. So doctrine and worship came to be seen as inseparable. It was thus that "orthodoxy" meant both right belief and right praise. Unsound views about the Trinity and Christology have the negative effect of alienating Christians from truly experiencing the fullness of the Īśvara. They can distort their religious consciousness. In modern conditions we cannot use such dogmatic language. People have of course a choice of values. But we wish here to present as part of our vision the practical consequences which flow from it. Ours, however, is a mainstream vision, and we consider that a wrong view of the Trinity does undermine important features of the Christian life.

From our perspective Christianity is a social Trinitarian vision of the Divine Reality and a lifestyle based on that vision. Through the Christians' new life as adopted daughters and sons, they share in the joy of the divine life – a family life, to use an image which is the favorite of many Orthodox and Anglo-Catholic theologians. Here we shall offer some suggestions which we hope will help people to attain to a more intimate and loving awareness of, and communion with, the tripersonal divine Love.

Together with Hodgson we believe that in addition to the regular partaking in the sacrament of the Eucharist, it is vital for Christians to enrich their spiritual life to the fullest by consciously cultivating a distinct personal relationship with each member of the Trinity, through devotional prayer and contemplation, by a process of *bhakti* and *dhyāna*. As each person is a personal self-conscious life form, prayer may properly be addressed to each of them singularly as you or as Lord. Of special importance here is the Eastern Orthodox practice of personal prayer to the Holy Spirit, under whose guidance and protection devout Orthodox believers place themselves, at the beginning of each day, with the following prayer:

> "O heavenly King, O Comforter, the Spirit of Truth, who are everywhere present and fill all things, treasury of good gifts and giver of life, come and dwell in us and cleanse us from all impurity, and save our souls, O Gracious Lord."

Such personal devotion to the Spirit as loving and heavenly helper is an antidote to that functional Pneumatomachianism which is very prevalent among Christians today. Without this fellowship with the Spirit, devotion can become very easily a form of Unitarianism or Christocentrism through exclusive focus on the personal Jesus. Such can be done explicitly, as among the "Jesus only" group within Pentecostalism. Similar conclusions follow from an exclusive focus on the Father. We might mention at this point that Paul Tillich rejects such tri-personal devotion as being a kind of Tritheism. He says that ultimate concern cannot be directed towards more than one divine hypostasis (*Systematic Theology*, Vol. 3, 1963, p. 289). But this is in our view a greatly mistaken view and ahistorical. It is of course the Trinity as a whole which is the focus of ultimate concern, but there is nothing wrong (on the contrary there is a spiritual merit) in establishing a strong sense of personal tie not only to Abba, but to Jesus, and to the Spirit. The cumulative experience of mainstream Christianity is in this direction, even though there is often in practice a very feebly developed sense of the identity of the Holy Spirit. The intensity of the organic unity of the divine life is important to recall, and it is the Christian's guarantee, so to speak, against polytheism or tritheism. Gods are distinct and finite beings, and save in the refracted theism of the Hindu tradition, cannot be considered at all like the three self-conscious identities of the Trinity, bound together with a love of limitless intensity.

Let us clarify our language at this point. When we use

the word "God" in worship we mean it, typically, to refer to the entire Trinity as a single divine Being. Christian prayer therefore which is addressed to God is clearly aimed at the common divine self or superconsciousness shared in *koinonia* by the three open consciousnesses who together form the perfectly harmonious corporate self. Here, the tripersonal devotion helps Christians to experience the unifying power of love. So the divine love communicates to the Christian *bhakta* the elements of the divine life: harmony, peace, stability, perfect benevolence. So Vladimir Lossky (1957) says that the Trinity as social is really the foundation of all Christian thought, experience and practice. But out of fear of tritheism many Christians cut themselves off from this source of the Christian life. Naturally, the Christian, because of this elevation of the interpersonal social life to the highest point in her devotion should cherish and stimulate similar harmony and deeply felt relationships in this life. This is one reason why the family has been so important an item at the heart of Christian ethical thinking particularly in relation to the control and beautification of sex. But there can be no easy stereotype of truly deep and loving relations, and this is to be prized as reflecting something of the divine nature wherever it occurs. Love as a human relationship, and especially sexual love, is something which is creative, is blissful and merges consciousnesses. It is an image of the life of the Trinity.

The Jesus prayer, which has such a long and effective history in the Eastern Church, is something which can form the core of the spiritual life, and it too – as we shall see in a moment – is replete with Trinitarian implications. We may note first that the verbal and mental recitation of the Jesus prayer along with the natural rhythm of breathing in and out (and also various bodily postures such as sitting cross-legged) links Eastern Orthodoxy to Indian breath control practices: "O Lord Jesus Son of God" (inhale) "Have mercy on me a sinner" (exhale). What we have here is a blend between Hindu control of *prāṇa* and Western devotion. This kind of Trinity-oriented yoga has also been explored by Asian Christians and emphasized too in the thinking of men like Thomas Merton and Bede Griffiths. The Trinitarian aspects of the Jesus prayer can be summed up as follows: no one can confess Jesus as the Lord except by the power of the Spirit (I Corinthians 12:3), while to say "Christ, Son of God" is to affirm something which can only be revealed by the Father (Matthew 16:16–17); and to say "Have mercy on me a sinner" (in the style of the publican in Luke's Gospel, [18:13]) expresses the boundless mercy towards sinners as exhibited by Jesus' life. This prayer in the Spirit also prepares Christians for the experience of the divine Light. This illumination and deifying vision brings to a person a partaking in the love and splendor of the divine life, a merging in the love which constitutes the heart of the life of the Trinity. Thus the devotee has communion with the Three-in-One.

It may be noted that the traditional life style as recommended by the Eastern Fathers, for example through that anthology of spiritual practice which is known as the *Philokalia* (or the Love of Spiritual Beauty), has affinities with Asian practice: e.g. fasting, the use of an experienced guru or spiritual guide (the Starets), but it is also based on the Eucharist and liturgical worship. Because of the ultimate concern with social and personal values, our doctrine should never lead us to totally being out of touch with society on the ground, and even the more austere practices of self-control should not be isolationist. At any rate, we have here a model of a Christian ethos or Trinitarian life style: we are all sons and daughters of a loving Father with the companionship of the Son, and under the guidance of the Spirit.

The Trinity as we have depicted it has other lessons for social practice. The fact that there are differences in the Three-in-One, but that these divergences are held together by the bond of love, provides for a highly relevant pattern of living today. The different genders and ethnic groups, the different kinds of persons, old and young, who go to make up the social order, the different nations which exist side by side in the world need to recognize mutuality. Love does not demand conformism, but delights in independence, freedom, difference. Any system which allows humans to trample on one another and binds them together in a tyranny of fear and hatred, is at odds with the Trinity. So as in marriage, which was seen by Christians as a sacramental fruit of the Spirit's activity, and as a gift, so in social life generally it is our task to devise the attitudes and structures which will allow plurality and unity to coalesce. Wherever human beings act in self-giving love they, whether they know it or not, are participating in the divine life. We see, then, the Trinity as a model for a relaxed loving attitude, in which we can allow other people to retain their uniquenesses and otherness. We do not need to force homogeneity, or if we do it is merely to allow the creativity and deepest feelings and aspirations of others to flower. So we have traffic regulations, but it is understood that this is to make life safe for otherwise divergent and unique individuals.

The Trinity also reminds us that though we are individualists in stressing the importance of each individual and in facilitating for them as much freedom as possible, we are also personalists: the person is not the atomic individual, but someone who gets and finds her meaning through interpersonal relations. Ultimately our human rights spring from mutual acknowledgement of one another's sacredness. We are not just made in the image of God, we are protected by the love which should reflect the divine love in the lives of human beings here on earth.

The social conception of the Trinity chimes in with our view (later to be articulated more fully) about the creativity which is precipitated in human beings by society. We are imaginative beings whose freedom in great measure comes from our capacity to acquire new insights into both nature and ourselves, and we could only achieve these levels of imaginativeness as members of groups and traditions. Thus, though we are born with language capacities these are only actualized through participation in a community. Basically it is as social beings that we acquire the wideranging imaginative powers to go beyond our immediate condition. It is thus only in society that we can get the rationality to become moral beings and only through language can we acquire characteristically human freedom. Our life then is a warp and woof: the warp of our individuality as persons, and the woof of corporate placement. In so far as our freedom is creative, even alas in dark and evil matters, we reflect the nature of the *Iśvara* – the Lord whose light lurks below the surface of the world and behind the light of consciousness.

Jürgen Moltmann (1981, pp. 202–212) has well expressed the situation: the sociality of the Trinity means the end of all forms of monarchianism and political monotheism – that is secular ways in which leaders model their own power on that of God. God in herself is utterly self-giving. So the political ideal needs mutuality and equality. We should not then so readily conceive the *Iśvara* in the image of the political supreme king. Christ is king, but it is an ironic rule, for the crown he wears is made of thorns. He is one who gives himself for others, including his divine "companions" in the Trinity. And if he follows the will of the Father, that father is not seen as family despot, but as "dear Father", *Abba*. And although we favor the open and plural society and recognize that this only so far in modern history has come to be in capitalist or partly capitalist societies, we do not favor that over-emphasis upon consumption which leads to the ideal of individualistic self-rule, or if you like possessive individualism. The welfare of the person has to be balanced by her recognition of the needs of others. So though economic competition may be important and productive, this does not mean we should glorify that hardness of heart to which it can too easily lead. As we have said so often, our ideal is of a self-giving mutuality as displayed by the Trinity herself.

In due course we shall also outline ways in which our Trinity doctrine relates to the values of healing and personal growth, and to an account of personal immortality and the evolutionary development of the cosmos.

In brief we wish to hint here that this at first rather abstract doctrine has warm significance when we look into others' eyes and see the bond of love.

The different theories of the Trinity are illustrated in the chart on the next page.

7
Divine Creativity

Social Trinity and Creation
Before we get into the main part of our discussion of creation it is appropriate to give an overview of the manner in which our thinking about creation is affected by the doctrine of the social Trinity which we have already explored. From that perspective the creation of the world springs forth continuously from the Father's love of his eternal Son in the communal bond of the Spirit. As the blessedness of *agape* consists in self-giving, the Heavenly Father desires to create other self-conscious beings to share in the joy of the Divine Life by being ontologically united with his Son, within the love-bond of the Spirit. This she does through an emergent evolutionary and historical process which the Divine Son enters during his human embodiment (This social trinitarian plan of creation is beautifully expressed in the Ephesians letter, 1:3–14). The reason that free creatures are to be material in their origin and arising is that matter serves so to speak as a veil by which screening the blinding light and love of the creator protects creatures and allows them freedom (but it also alas brings suffering). The dynamic matrix of space-time and the whirling equations which gave rise to the exploding complexity of this cosmos are brought into being *ex nihilo* by the Trinity. While the cosmos has relative independence and operates according to the laws of physics, such as the second Law of Thermodynamics it is continuously dependent on the sustaining power of the Trinity, which alone has absolute ontological independence. Within this dynamic framework we see the continuous creativity of God, operating to bring forth new levels of being through emergent evolution.

This process takes place when something genuinely new,

that is an emergent, comes into being. Such an emergent is not just a regrouping of what has gone before. Rather the pre-existing factors are gathered up into a new nexus. These new living emergents display, as higher levels of complexity are attained, also greater intensity in the unifying power of the organism. Thus the evolutionary process makes the transition from various complicated forms of material energy to the higher levels of consciousness. As each new level is reached, and we have novelty of kinds of behavior and consciousness, we can regard the Divine Being as being coproducer of the novelty. And so it is that in the created order we see the achievement of a high level of self-consciousness in the human race which is yet embedded in and so not wholly alienated from the material environment.

It is through self-consciousness that human beings are able to apprehend the divine Reality through the various types of religious experience that we have described as well as through joy in the color-drenched splendor of creation.

In our view organic existence occurs at differing levels. In the animal kingdom consciousness first appears at various dim stages, and with the evolution of human beings from the ape-family higher levels of intelligence and self-consciousness (spirit) develop. As spirit, human beings are able to experience the Divine Reality and realize the highest values (we develop this in Chapter 9). Together with William Temple (1934) we view the process of emergent evolution as ascending through four levels – matter, organic life, mind (intelligence), and spirit. On our account the sustaining creativity of God means that in the widest sense the "cause" of any new emergent is not wholly physical, so that there is no need to postulate panpsychism to account for the emergence of consciousness out of inorganic matter.

We know more now about the supposed mechanisms through which human beings emerged into history. But our vision of creation was sparked off by the myths which have controlled Jewish and Christian thinking and feeling about our origins. Thus we hold to what may be called theistic evolution as against purely naturalistic evolutionary theories on one hand, and fundamentalist views of creationism on the other.

A View of the Myths of Creation

It is of course for us a perpetual temptation to tie creation too closely to the myths which are found in the Bible and elsewhere. That draws us sometimes to a misleading separation of creation and preservation. This is one reason why Ramanuja's analogy of God-creation to soul-body is important. It gives us a nice picture of the cosmos as continuously dependent upon the Divine Being, and of the latter as immanent in the whole vast process. We shall here adopt this same picture, in order to explicate a vision which is essentially also Christian.

The myths of creation in the Biblical narrative are, of course, important to us even if we read them often too literally. Since they deal with the interaction of the beyond and the cosmos their words cannot be taken in too literal or this-cosmic a fashion. But there are some things important for our *darsana* which the narratives emphasize. First, they underline the utter dependence of everything upon the Divine will: this is *creatio ex nihilo*. Second, in *Genesis*, they are edited into a place which sees a continuous line from creation to human history. Third, they emphasize the importance and central role, in the creative outworking of the myth, of the human race. Fourth, they emphasize something about the damaging consequences of human choice. But about the last we shall speak more later on.

The second and third of the narrative lessons listed above are at first sight undermined by the development of modern cosmology. There may or not be an absolute beginning to our cosmos, but at least there is an apparent point of commencement, a Big Bang: but the distance of this from the emergence of the human species and therefore of human history is staggering. The old myth looks rather naive from this angle of vision. Moreover, the central role of humanity may be undermined by the great scale of the XXth Century cosmos. The vast number of galaxies, the billions of stars in each, and the possibilities of hosts of planetary systems scattered through each galaxy combine to make our planet look peripheral. In a way the picture is misleading: every point of the cosmos is equally central or peripheral according to taste. Still, being one raft of living creatures among many is not very impressive. Why should we think of ourselves as central to the cosmos? The days are gone when we lived in a potty little cosmos with the earth (or the sun) at the center.

There are several things to be said in comment. (1) However much we may doubt the mechanisms of Darwinian or Neo-Darwinian theory, the actuality of the long evolutionary process is beyond doubt (see *The New Biology*, Augros and Staeuciu, 1987): and this gives a new dimension to narrative. We have to tell the story of life at length and of the continuity between humans and the rest of the animal kingdom. This is the appeal of Teilhard de Chardin: he told the story of salvation from the deep past and into the future, using a modern cosmology. So we need not be hung up with the details of *Genesis* or the *Upanishads*. We need to think of our story in the wider, longer perspective. (2) The modern thought that there is life elsewhere in the cosmos depends on the wedding of two ideas: one, the immensity of the cosmos; second, the natural way in which life evolves. These jointly suggest that where life can be it will be, and where conscious life can be it will be. Now this in turn leads to a metaphysical reflection, that there is no need to evaluate the cosmos by reference to its material nature, however subtle and ingenious, and however important physics may be. We can equally evaluate it in terms of its flowering. Why judge a garden by the mud and not the lilies? Or by the earth rather than the roses? Is it that we are tempted towards this because mud and earth are "basic"? But there is no one phenomenon rather than another which can have our exclusive attention; and it is important to see both the mud and the roses. So the wedding between biology and cosmology reinforces the view of the significance of conscious life in the cosmos. Of course, the actual existence of other similar forms of life in the cosmos is speculation at the moment. But it cuts both ways. The myth that "humankind is made in the image of Brahman" (or God) may be made more not less plausible by the new view of the cosmos which we have in the XXth Century. But we are still left with the problem of particularity over and above this. (3) If nature has acquired its narrative dimension, from the Big Bang to human history and from primeval gases to conscious life, then we can come to tell that narrative in a way which will bridge the great gap. According to traditional Christian thinking, our role as humankind in cosmic salvation-history is crucial. Now this notion is reinforced by the *avatāra* belief: the faith that God is on earth in Christ. We shall return to the meaning of this theme later on; but for the moment let us just say that there is a vast deal to be said for the belief in incarnation. One of the most powerful arguments for our faith depends on the reflection of what it is like to be Creator. Let us be a little anthropomorphic for a moment and imagine ourselves about to bring the cosmos into being.

Divine Compassion and Creation

You could conjure up in your mind the swirls of atoms, the patterns of molecules, the growth of cells, the thunder of stars: and eventually you would see living creatures, and feel their consciousness, and in due course there would emerge humans, the creatures you would have endowed with your own consciousness, capacity for feeling and imagination. They would be in your image. It would be a wonderful ebullience to make such a cosmos. But could you bring yourself to make it, when you knew that rats would bleed to death in sewers, and birds fall suffering into the undergrowth, and women drown in seas, and men burn in fires? Could you create a world in which, inevitably, there would be suffering? Would it be enough that joys would outweigh pains, and happiness distress? It would be a partly callous thing, would it not, for a blissful God to bring into being swarms of suffering creatures?

But the Christian God is not a blissful God, or rather she is not a wholly blissful God. There is always the thought of the bodhisattva: that we cannot remain purely happy

205

knowing that other beings suffer. We cannot be happy till all are happy. That bodhisattva sentiment would itself cast a shadow on the light of bliss. It therefore figures that the Bodhisattva God would not create a cosmos, however glorious, in which creatures would inescapably have to suffer, unless she were willing herself to suffer: and that would mean entering this very cosmos. So theism already impels us towards that Christian vision of the suffering servant. Moreover there is no way of being human in the abstract. Each human is incurably particular, and lives in particular circumstances. So though it may in one regard be a "brute fact" that God reveals herself in Palestine, among the "elect" Jews, it is not a brute fact that the *avatāra* is particular.

So from this angle, there is a coherence about the Christian vision of creation, just because God is identical with Christ and Christ suffers in the particularities of human history. Further, as we interpret the Divine Being's nature, God is inner controller, and lives as it were beneath every consciousness: the silent witness of what flows through our minds and feeling. And so God feels our feelings, and lives through our sorrows and joys, and those too of every kind of living creature. So vicariously the Divine Being also lives through those who live. For both these reasons, then, if you can imagine yourself as Creator you would imagine yourself as willing to take on the sorrows of what you were about to make.

So the messages contained in the *Genesis* narratives have to be restated against the backcloth of modern cosmology and biology: but they still make sense – the continuity of Creation with human history and the central character of humankind.

(4) One may add too, in regard to this message of centrality, that rational conscious beings can enter into a dialogue with the creation. We can reflect nature's nature in our knowledge of it. We are the mirrors of nature and of the Divine Being. It is not that God is narcissistic; but in fact she reaches an even fuller destiny when there are other centers of consciousness that can revel in her glory. The

"dead" nature of atoms and stars also reaches a fuller destiny when she is perceived and felt and known by conscious beings. So consciousness is as it were the crown of nature, and able too to recognize, and find bliss in, the Divine Being.

But these reflections are a long way, of course, from the chapter and verse of *Genesis*. And we still need to comment on the *ex nihilo* aspect. The model which we here use is that of Ramanuja. The cosmos is the body of God. By "body" we mean that which is instrumental to the soul. Most bodies however are only very partially under the control of the conscious mind or soul. I can raise my finger; but have little effect upon my gall bladder or the way my kidneys work. The Divine Being, by contrast, has utter control over her body, that is over the cosmos. Thus the model does not limit the divine omnipotence. It also presents the cosmos as being most intimately involved with God. As we noted in the analysis of transcendence, effectively there is no difference between transcendence and immanence (at least in the sense in which God works in all things, is immanent therefore in the world, and is the inner essence of consciousness). In so far as we are parts of the cosmos, we are absolutely under the control of the Divine Being.

There are some questions arising from this picture about the scope, if any, of human freedom. But for the moment let us picture the relation of the divine body to the Divine Being as one of absolute dependence. This is the essential meaning of *ex nihilo*. The notion that God creates the world out of nothing is designed to signify that God's purposes are not limited or frustrated by the preexisting properties of matter. It is a doctrine meant to refute the Platonic idea that matter, preformed, clogs God's action somewhat. You cannot make absolutely anything of wood or stone, because of the clogging properties of wood and stone. So the picture which Ramanuja draws of the divine body – the cosmos – does the same job as the doctrine of *ex nihilo*.

The picture also, as we have mentioned, presents the relationship of the Divine Being and her creation as extremely intimate. This has important practical effects. It gives us a perpetual sense that God is working in and behind all things, continuously like a soul and intimately. So when we look around the world we can see it as glorious, as pulsating with the Divine Being. As immanent she is also the Mother of all things, the Tao.

Two aspects (Smart, 1983, pp. 162–72).
Literally of course you see the sun and the trees and the earth. But these objects which we perceive in our immediate environment can be looked on at another level as God's body. It is an analogy of course to see the cosmos as a body. More than that, we are involved here with a double level of description – the first level using the ordinary language of the world around us, the second level using the notion of Divine Being. So it is characteristic of religion to have a "two-level" description of things. The extra level, employing the concept of body of the Lord, does not contradict anything at the first level, including whatever may be concluded out of the physical and biological science. The ordinary or "lower" level description of the mosquito or the galaxy remains true (if it be true) whether or not we also see in the mosquito or the star the expression of the Divine Being.

This notion of double description indicates the lack of conflict, so far at least, between religion and science. Moreover not all the events in the world are of equal revelatory value, so that sometimes we want to use a second level description to supplement the first level one. Thus at the basic level we may be seeing in front of us a sunset. But the sunset, because of its beauty, may point, for us, to the Divine Being. If so, then it is a revelatory of the Divine Being, and again this second level statement does not conflict with any scientific accounts of the rainbow in terms of the refraction of light.

If there have been tensions between religion and science it is largely because of texts – texts which interpreted miraculously or using categorical divisions are in tension with the way modern science speaks. So the implicit gulf between humans and animals in the Bible led some pious people to resist that continuity implied in the Theory of

Evolution; while miracles also were for some people (as they saw it) the basis for faith. But the emergence of us rational creatures out of the primeval slime, ultimately, is miracle enough; and we do not need to be caught by the cultural and psychological traps which have set religion and science at each other's throats sometimes.

The two level description theory can be stated otherwise in terms of superimposition: that is the superimposing of religious concepts on what is given "naturally". The trees and the sun are seen not only as trees and sun but under the superimposed category of divine creation. Similarly we may see doing our duty as a kind of service of God. In this case we superimpose the concepts of worship and service upon the "ordinary" concept of doing one's duty. It is not a matter of seeing one thing as another, but of seeing one thing both as that thing and as another thing.

The Notion of the Cosmos as God's Body
  (Smart, 1966, pp. 112–29).

This concept of a body, by analogy, has a practical spiritual significance at several levels. (1) We are as part of God's body already sacramentally sharing in her life. (2) Since the Divine is working in all things then she is everywhere: we are forever in the presence of the Divine, so that whichever way we turn we find God. (3) This in turn means that churches, pilgrimages, sacred places, etc., are in essence no more where God is than is anywhere else. They may be of epistemological use, in guiding our perceptions of God; or they may have spiritual significance, as aids to increasing our awareness of the Divine. But since God is everywhere, no place is fuller of God's presence than any other. (The question of God's special presence in Christ by identity and thence in the Eucharist has to be dealt with separately.) (4) We can see in other faiths some of the same spiritual message – in Hinduism because, obviously, of Ramanuja's use of the analogy; in Taoism, for the Tao is the divine principle animating the cosmos; in many small-scale religions with an acute sense of the presence of Spirit in the things and forces around and within us. Because, too, of the notion that the Divine is present beneath or behind or within our consciousness, we see God more luminously in the consciousness of other humans in the way in which it manifests itself to us – through facial expressions and the *li* of everyday life. So we see the Divine luminously in other living beings, above all in human beings. So for us (as Christians) every other person contains Christ. We see the light of the Savior written in the goodness of others and in their joys and sorrows. What of their badness? That is there too, but every human has some goodness, and it is there that most livingly Christ is present to us in human form.

Of course, the badness of human life is not to be avoided in our thinking about Creation, nor the disorderly elements of the world – the earthquakes and tornadoes and fires and floods and other natural disasters. We cannot look on the world and avoid its *dukkha*. Is every good somehow tainted with evil? If the Divine controls the whole cosmos, she must be there in the earthquake and the storm and in the painful fire. She must be there too in the badness of humankind and in the predatory destruction wrought by animals and insects. Also, lurking in all this is the thought that after all we humans are not free, if we are parts of God's body wholly under her control and management.

Cosmic Order and the Problem of Evil
(Smart, 1964, pp. 152–80)

The Divine Being creates continuously a cosmos, and within it we have some freedom. How this is conceivable will occupy our thoughts a little later; but part of the answer is that we live in an orderly universe in which, because of this order, we can act as if God is not everywhere deep within the processes. She conceals herself from us through this order. Without it, moreover, everything would be quite indeterminate and equivalent to nothing. Further, the degree of order is high enough to permit, and even ensure, the evolution within the structures of the cosmos of intelligent, conscious living beings, taking after her.

As finite conscious beings we range around, and because of this can always be in conflict with the environment. Such

210

collisions can be fatal and painful: so in such an orderly world there has to be a certain amount of grief and suffering. God could we think intervene everywhere to save us from the consequences of our action: but if she did that consistently, order would collapse and we would slide back into nothingness again. It thus seems inescapable that there will be some suffering in a cosmos. As we have noted, though, the Christian idea of the Divine implies that she is willing to enter into the particularities of this world and to suffer a range of the consequences.

Even so: is the world worth it? Considering the Holocaust, the cruelties of animal life, the miseries of human cruelty and natural disaster, should God bring this world continuously into existence? And why does she not withdraw her support suddenly: there would then be no more disease and decay, no more weeping, no more torture? Is the joy worth the *dukkha*?

It is hard to make up the right sum. Can we just add up the good and bad points about the cosmos? In so far as the Christian faith is about our actions and reactions, it is for each of us to weigh whether life is worth living. And yet from the Christian angle of vision this cannot be a selfish calculation, whether I in particular find life pleasant: my calculation must go out to other people, and in a spirit of compassion. From this angle, and given that devotion to the Divine brings me close to the highest and most shining of all goods, it is impossible to see how the faithful person could reject life, could wish that he had never been born. Still, there are many who do not share this viewpoint: being ignorant of the Divine, or alienated, they go on suffering without the consolations of faith, and perhaps without much compassion for other living beings.

There is a paradox here. Why complain to God about the Creation because others suffer, if you have no compassion? And if you have compassion you will no doubt try to convey to others the message of your faith – namely that there is much splendor even in suffering, and it can draw you close to utter Glory? One merit of Existentialist approaches to the analysis of religion is that they stress the subjective, the autobiographical, angle of vision. From an autobiographical angle, do we complain about our lot? Job did, and from one point of view, quite reasonably: but from the relationship of I to Thou things proved different.

Yet not all living creatures can appreciate the subjective message of faith, and their sufferings remain. It is inevitable, as we have argued, that in an orderly cosmos with free range beings such as ourselves there is bound to be suffering. But how much? Has not God left us in a worse condition than we need have been?

We do not know quite how to calculate as to *how much* suffering is the least in a cosmos. Do the cancer cells stem from some very deep structure of living beings? Do the number of collisions signify some carelessness in God's design? If we try to think through alternative cosmoses we do not get much light. For instance, if God always intervened miraculously to save the sufferer the cosmos would crumble, as we have said. While if on the other hand we were ingeniously redesigned never to be cruel and the like, would we not end up as automata, our freedom essentially gone?

But the pathos and the agony remain, and we cannot help but think that maybe some force of Evil has been unleashed in the cosmos which perverts human beings and other living beings. In the past Christianity has made much of Satan. One reason may be that Jesus himself had experience – or thought he had experience – of the Evil One. Is the demonology of the New Testament something which we must simply demythologize, or does it hint at something real? It might seem from the phenomenology of religious experience that a sense of blackness often accompanies the experience of the Light, whether that Light flashes through the prism of the numinous Other or the bliss of the mystical, interior "vision". The compassion of the Buddha was integral to his insight, as if he saw the blackness of *dukkha* in the very moment that he had insight and perception of nirvana. So Christ is supposed to have seen Satan fall from heaven.

Yet as is well known, an omnipotent God cannot be exempted from any harm that the Devil does, for the latter

212

too is the creation of God. Does omnipotence, however, matter? It is, admittedly, a property traditionally ascribed to the Divine. There are those – many process theologians of today, and William James and others – who have felt comfortable with the idea of a finite God. In certain respects God has limited his power. For instance, creating a regular world involves a limitation on the actual practice of all-power. In that respect he leaves space in which his creatures may act freely. So we might conceive of angels as free agents too, one of whom, Satan, became chief architect of rebellion against God and leader of the forces of disruption and cruelty.

We shall later argue as to whether we really need in our *darśana* to treat the Devil as anything more than a metaphor. He enters nicely into narrative theology: but what is the status, after all, of those tales? His only real importance at the moment is whether he exempts God from the cruelties of nature: which patently he does not. Could the whole cosmos be messed up and distorted by some cosmic Evil One? That is on the edge of Gnosticism, for God and the Devil would be at least co-creators of the cosmos as we know it. To return to the question of self-limitation it does not destroy her residual omnipotence. As far as this cosmos goes, everything depends on God, and God is residually omnipotent. This seems to us an adequate account of the divine power. But whether in choosing this rather than some other cosmos the Divine Being was justified we do not know, for we cannot conceive other cosmoses in detail – ones at any rate that function according to a finite set of regularities, and still pursue life and bring forth consciousness. So although we cannot resolve the so-called problem of evil we can at least claim, as far as natural evil goes, that this may somehow be the best of all possible cosmoses.

But as far as free range evil goes, God indeed chose a terrible cosmos: that of Attila, Nero, Stalin and Hitler and many, many other cruel people. Could they not have been screened out by better genes? Did the human race have to exhibit such cruelty and viciousness? Are there any answers which we can give to these questions? The key issue here is as to whether the amount of evil in the world constitutes decisive counter-evidence against the existence and goodness of God. A.G.N. Flew was mistaken in thinking that religious statements such as that God is loving are not falsifiable (and hence not genuine factual assertions) in not admitting conclusive evidence to count against them (Flew and Macintyre, 1955). In our view, such statements are cognitive claims about reality, as pointless and irredeemable suffering can count decisively in refuting the claim that God is loving on two levels.

(1) In practice, it can eventually lead a believer to abandon his beliefs if he comes to see that the cumulative or total pattern of evidence is overwhelmingly negative against theism; the degree of evidence which precipitates such dissent would vary subjectively among believers and cannot be specified precisely in advance.

(2) It would also be falsified if there were no further levels of existence in the hereafter, provided by the Creator, in which human beings will have the opportunity for further spiritual growth and creative fulfillment of which they were deprived due to tragic evil and suffering in their earthly life; thus as pointed out by Hick, theism is also in principle verifiable eschatologically.

There are, we believe, two answers which put the Christian life in perspective, in the face of human evil. The first relates to our adopting an "autobiographical" or subjective angle of vision in relation to other human beings. We may recall that Christ enjoined us to love our enemies. This means loving those who are in principle our enemies, that is those whom we at least profess to regard as enemies because they are enemies of God: the enemies of morality and love. But to love someone is to treat that person in a way which involves seeing them as one of us, among other things. They are part of our group. That group, in the ultimate resort, is the human race (or living beings, beyond that — but let us here stick with the human race as the ultimate community). If we have a community loyalty ultimately then it is to humanity as a whole, both present, past, and future. So from an autobiographical angle of vision it is *we* who are cruel, and creative and all good things too.

This notion of *our* fault, as members of the human race, is the basis of the myth of original sin. Adam and Eve are pictorial prototypes of us all. Looked at externally it is nonsense to suppose that I should have defects due to the fault of an ancestor. I might inherit problems through my genes, but not sins handed down. It is however true that the structures and systems of human life because they are rooted in human choices and feelings and ideas stem from actual faults. In so far as we can change society we can have the vision of another world, and Eden, if only in the future. We can thus, autobiographically, acknowledge that our world is shot through with the consequences of alienations, hostilities and ignorance, with the effects of greed, hatred and delusion. And we can in this see even Hitler as our brother, and Stalin and those of us who bombed the "enemy" to hell during World War II: we are all sisters and brothers. So from this autobiographical or personalist angle of vision it is not for us to point a finger at others as though they were alien to us and to blame their existence upon the Divine Being. If I myself pointed a finger at God and complained that she had not made me good enough, I could rightly be upbraided for not attending to the practical matter of making myself better instead of moaning about my inadequacies.

But because we cannot fathom the nature of alternative cosmoses the origin of the evils which do in fact afflict us is inscrutable. This brings us to the second main point which can be made. Though it may be that this is the best of all possible cosmoses, we do not need this strong position in order (so to speak) to exempt God of blame for the sufferings of this cosmos. There might be more perfect worlds elsewhere. This fact does not mean that God would be wrong to make this cosmos: sufficient that this cosmos is good. That God makes angels does not make it wrong for her to make men. For her to make men does not imply that it is wrong also to make beetles.

There is perhaps something a little ludicrous about our

struggling hard by such arguments to exempt the Divine Creator from blame. We are of course only really concerned with the consistency of our thinking. For if we are fallen into contradiction then the *darśana* we present must fall into mist, dissolve away and so lose its compelling brightness.

This argumentation does not exactly touch the poignancy of loss. The horrors of life are not diminished by the observation that we need to look on the human community as us: that we need to take responsibility too for our sisters' crimes: that it is more important to do something about our viciousness than to complain about the Creator.

Our general position, then, is that the cosmos is the continuous creation of the transcendent Divine Being, and can be considered to be her body, thoroughly at her command. It is her body by analogy, since the cosmos does not appear to function like an organic body, and because the divine soul differs from the human. This analogy suggests a great intimacy between the cosmos and the Divine Being. The picture presented is the opposite of deism: the *Īśvara* is operative at every moment of the cosmic process, and there is no question of her having set the cosmos in motion but then abandoned it to its destiny. Rather every event in principle is caused and sustained by the Divine. So the *Īśvara* is within all things, and outside all things, and is thus both immanent and transcendent. She is also the "inner controller" or *antaryāmin* behind consciousness, and we shall describe this further.

Meanwhile we wish to draw back a little and see the creation against the background of divine transcendence. As we have argued previously the Lord is "beyond space", being without spatial attributes, and hidden so to speak behind the cosmos which functions as a kind of screen, in accordance with the divine characteristic as the Holy: not for mortal eyes literally to behold, though there are visions and intimations of God. The holiness of the Divine, and its character as being glorious and blissful, suggest that properly it is the focus of a religion of worship, as we express our recognition of the superb brilliance and wonder of That which lies beyond the cosmos. Also the Lord is personal, and this is part of our picture for several reasons, as follows.

(1) We picture the creation as a kind of fiat, an act of will. The Genesis myth suggests this. But we do not assume that this "Let there be light" is a once only event: it is the continuous command of the one Being. But its will-like character is important in reinforcing the dependence of the cosmos upon the Divine decision. So we picture the Creator as having will, and so as a person.

(2) The heart of the picture of Brahman as bringing the world about, according to the theistic strand in the Indian tradition, is that the Creator is the focus of *bhakti*. If the numinous has a more impersonal air in being *tremendum* it has a more personal feeling in the *fascinans*. The personalist picture of the Divine as Thou lies at the centre of Christian *bhakti*.

(3) The noblest of the aspects of the Creation is humankind, so far as we have experienced the cosmos. Humankind is conscious and rational, imaginative and able to exercise freedom of choice. The Source of the cosmos should not be inferior to the items in the cosmos, and so we see her as beyond (but positively, not negatively beyond) personal consciousness, rationality, imagination and freedom. She is thus a person or superperson.

Two Complementary Models of Creation

As we have seen, the creation of the galaxies and sentient beings causes the Trinity sorrow: for how could she create a cosmos with free beings unless she was willing to come down and be an *avatāra*, and so suffer among us? So though the casting forth of the cosmos was and is an effortless masterpiece, the suffering implied is a pain from which it would be easy to turn. As Aquinas says, however, love is of the nature to pour itself forth. It is effusive of itself. So from one point of view the Creation is like a dance, an exuberant pouring forth of energy. In doing so the Creator pours forth something different from herself – the material world. It is not spirit, though it has the motifs of the spirit woven into it, for the cosmos is composed in a most milky and mathematical fashion, all air and space and fantastic powers clinched by spidery forces, a web of equations and a ballet of observations. It is not that seemingly solid matter which our perceptions so much register, but more like a crisscrossing of unseen rainbows. Still, it is not spirit, however tenuously material it may be. But within the churning of the ethereal cosmic sea there stirred the yearnings for development buried deep in its fabric, and from the primeval forces there spun out the lines of evolution, culminating eventually in beings who could move about and see and smell and hear and touch the world about them. Something was in the making which albeit dimly resembled herself. In other words Love did not just cast forth the jewels of the cosmos, but also the beings who would from within the swamps of matter (swamps, however tenuous and beautiful) which set new bounds on freedom and insight. She created, then, a world in which persons could come forth, and in so doing she brought real joy into the cosmos, and the jewels of the cosmos did not just have to depend on the Divine Eye to be seen, but could bask, so to speak, in the admiration of the conscious beings who had grown up within it.

So we may think of the *Īśvara* as like a mother or father who delights in the babies that she or he has been responsible for. We love the babies and pray that they may prosper, and enjoy the wonders of this world, even if we know that there will be many sobs and anguish in their growing up in the cosmos.

It is sometimes thought, rather woodenly, that the Divine Being wishes to have creatures worship her. That makes it sound like flattery, and on the side of the Lord, vanity. But neither pride nor false modesty can characterize the Divine Being: it is only that Love knows the heat and glory of life and light, and for that reason can see how those who are destined (simply by being in the cosmos and not outside it) to be fragmentary consciousnesses cannot but admire and strain for the glory of the Divine, in so far as they come to know it. So we cannot say that the cosmos was invented in order that the Lord might be worshipped. If it is the chief end of humanity to worship God (as catechisms like to say) it is just in the sense that free beings who turn towards the light will feel impelled to adore it, and to see it as the Highest.

From one angle of vision, the creation is simply the exuberant self-expression of the Divine: the dance of the Lord. We can see how right from this angle Hindus are to picture the Divine as being King of the Dance. From another angle, the creation is Love pouring itself forth and giving birth to little lovers. And yet the cosmos might not have existed: it is a choice of the Lord, and as we know looking back at Christ, a choice which had pain in it, because God too would be destined to suffer in a cosmos. But the Lord had known that love and pain are often mates: and often tragedy is noble. Her world was not destined to be a place of lotuses alone, though many pleasurable and delightful things are to be discovered in this cosmos.

Beyond Anthropomorphism

We have here been indulging in a little anthropomorphism. But of course beyond the personal Divine lies that which is beyond descriptions. It is the side of God which like the other side of the moon we never see. For our interface lets us see only *sagunam* aspects. It is as having qualities that she is the personal Creator. Some have argued that ultimately this aspect of the Lord is unreal. The *Iśvara* shares in the illusory character of her cosmos. But we reject the picture of the cosmos as finally unreal or illusory. We do not deny that importantly we human beings suffer from delusion or *moha* or *avidyā*, ignorance. But the grounds for thinking of the cosmos as unreal, as expressed in Advaita Vedanta, are unsatisfactory.

The first reason has to do with the definition of true existence. It is often thought that which is not eternal (or permanent) lacks existence. This we reject, both on common sense grounds (the butterfly exists, though she be evanescent) and on philosophical grounds (no ontological merit attaches, so far as we can see, to permanence per se). The second reason has to do with mysticism, the contemplative life. For Shankara and his followers the highest experience was realization of one's ultimate identity with Brahman. But there are no special grounds in our view to prefer identity-mysticism to other forms of religious experience. And, in a way more importantly, the experience of identity does not imply identity with *nirguṇam* Brahman.

Two Languages, Again (Smart, 1966, pp.114–128).
Because the Divine is concealed behind the cosmos, it is of course quite possible for it to exist quite independently of any thoughts about God. As we have seen, the double-description or two-aspect account of truth which we here adopt (actually it should have many facets and aspects) helps to make sense of the relation between the language of transcendence and the language of science and of everyday discourse. In the language of transcendence we are involved in the relational exercise of talking about this-cosmos things *sub specie aeternitatis* and alternatively using this-cosmos language to speak about that which is Transcendent. But in the language of science and of everyday discourse we are just talking about what lies in this cosmos, considered by itself.

It is of course quite open to a person to eschew transcen-dence-discourse. Such eschewing may take several forms, but the two most prominent are as follows. One form is simply not to use religious language, but not from any articulated worldview. It is a kind of agnosticism, a shrug of the shoulder. The other form is to take a special epistemological, and with it metaphysical, stand. It is to say that all knowledge comes from science and everyday discourse. Indeed science becomes the norm for establishing what is and what is not true. This standpoint is *scientism*. There are of course some difficulties in such a view, but it can be held pretty coherently and honorably. It is a fairly frequent position among modern Westerners.

The difficulties stem from the nitty-gritty difficulties of agreement about the nature of science and scientific method. The way out of this may be by becoming something of a positivist about what counts as science — the positive or actual practices of the traditions known as physics, biology, chemistry, and so on. We have found an attitude, a few major branches of practice, experimental methods, the use of mathematics, and so on, which work very well; and without having to be too precise about what their common factors may be we can simply point to this industry and this tradition and say that that is science, and by extending the methods and tradition we shall learn more and more. Further, there is no other serious source of knowledge about the cosmos and about living beings. The methods we employ are admirably successful in probing the actual cosmos, and there is no point in speculating feebly about what lies "beyond" the cosmos. Science can have no access to that.

This kind of eschewing of the transcendent has a metaphysical edge. But it delimits us to the actual cosmos. The force of natural theology, such as it is, that it expresses stirrings in us about the cosmos itself. Why should it exist? There might have been nothing. More importantly, from our present perspective, there is nothing in a double-description or two-aspect theory which takes away any of the statements which we wish to make on the actual basis of science. It might contradict some of the metaphysical conclusions that some scientists may draw: but it can hardly subtract from any descriptive utterance or explanatory hypothesis, for it is of its nature a theory of *double* descriptions. The extra part of the description (what makes it a double-description theory) is something like this – that the moon declares the beauty of the Creator; that this world is a place of mystery; that God suffers with us in the cosmos; that the story of human salvation must stretch back beyond humanity into the recesses of evolution; that this cosmos is one which fosters consciousness and that consciousness can be directed towards the *Īśvara*. If we were Buddhists we would say something else, no doubt; that all life in this cosmos is replete with suffering; that our troubles are due to greed, hatred and delusion; that the true saint has mastered her passions; and so on. None of these utterances can be said to be in contradiction with science. It is just that they give a certain, and extra, picture of this cosmos. For neither set of extra statements would make sense without supposing an *aeternitas* beyond the cosmos, whether that be the *Īśvara* or nirvana.

Of course, there are certain effects of our advances of scientific knowledge on our *darśana-s*. Our worldviews are affected by changes in knowledge. The vast expansion of our cosmic horizons through the astronomical discoveries of this century assuredly change our feel of the cosmos. Similarly the whole revolution in biological thought in the last two hundred years has changed our perceptions about forms of non-human and human life. The invention of computers has given us new models to work with. These are not so much things which directly change our attitudes to religions, but indirectly they do. Because they present to us a novel cosmology, and much else besides, they take us farther from the world of Christian origins. We no longer can, without special psychological and epistemological damage, inhabit the world of the Bible as though after all it is *our* world.

Also science as a loosely knit series of enterprises in understanding the world, and technology as the application of scientific success, are important arrivals in the modern world which, so to say, alter the balance of power. Religion may remain important to us; but it has to live with these potent new forces, both for knowledge and for change. Inevitably science and technology combine to become a bit like a new religion, with powerful priests and experts to dispense the magic power of knowledge. This must affect attitudes to the old priests and yogins.

Moreover, it is important in the advance of knowledge that we should make room for criticism of received ideas. Already we have noted the effects of this upon religious authority.

For these various reasons there are powerful effects of the growth of modern science and technology upon traditional religions. But as such there is no conflict between religion and science save insofar as some people may feel wedded to a literalist interpretation of texts.

From our point of view, however, the exploration of the cosmos and within that of the world of living beings is a marvelous adventure of the human spirit. It is part of an ongoing dialogue between humankind and nature. It is the voyaging through the divine body, and seeing some of the vast wonders of divine creation. So knowledge is itself a pursuit of divine significance in which God's body becomes increasingly reflected in the consciousness of humans. Tensions between different authorities are merely human responses in a world of epistemological tribalism. If the truth be properly perceived, spiritual and scientific advances can go happily hand in hand, and the two-aspect account of truth is a way to present this complementarity.

Moreover, both religion and science, though for different reasons and in divergent ways, can adopt a critical stance. Science needs to do this of its own nature, though its success can produce arrogance in its practitioners (but the greatest scientists have a humility borne of a sense not only of the grandeur and mystery of the cosmos but also the waiting data ready to ambush hypotheses). Religion, which has traditionally often been dogmatic, and has frequently seemed conservative (out of the need to preserve traditions which embody visions), has passed out of its dogmatic phase, as we have argued in Part I. If we present a vision of the creative Trinity, it is only that: a vision. It cannot be represented as "established". It is at best a vision to which certain Christians can remain loyal. But that community is only a fragment of the world's community, and has no right dogmatically to force its vision on others. But it can be critical (not only of its own presentation but also) of the world. The vision provides a depth-understanding of happiness, of the environment, of the nature of human and other living beings. It is therefore critical of shallow interpretations of human happiness, of human nature and so on. It is from the Transcendent standpoint able to prophesy concerning "this world". It has a two-aspect Truth which it offers in criticism of one-aspect truth. But it does so in a visionary way, not claiming that its standpoint is capable of being proved, or unalterable, or the only vision. For in this single plural globe there are many visions on offer. But if our vision can be fruitful in spiritual life and in daily living, in political insight and human courage, then it has its justification, and can at least claim to be fecund. Obviously, the operations of science are somewhat different: but the spirit of the two enterprises is not so different that they are in conflict. So from this general point of view, science and religion can easily be two sides of a coin.

Problems Over the Miraculous (Smart, 1964 pp. 15–44; 1966, pp. 116–117).

It may of course be objected that religion implies miracles, and this is ill in accord with the spirit and structure of scientific knowledge. There are, however, various senses of the notion of a miracle. One concept is simply that of some revealing event, or of some providential event. This concept says nothing about its being caused in one way rather than another (not natural, but the intervention of God, for instance). This concept has to do with the *significance* rather than the *origin* of an event. But even that stronger sense of "miracle" in which it refers to a divinely caused exception to some natural law, with deep significance, does not by itself conflict with scientific method, for the following reasons. First, if an event actually occurs, it is unscientific to rule it out because it is anomalous. Second, if it is a single but unrepeated event it does not falsify some supposed scientific law, since this is refuted by some repeatable negative instance. It is destroyed, that is, by some mini-law. We do not simply shrug off a law because the litmus paper has we think turned red. If under the same conditions hereafter it keeps turning the standard and expected green, then we hold on to the law. In short: a single event does not refute a law. But it may happen.

The fact that a strange event occurs is not by itself ground for believing in divine intervention (as it is often misleadingly called). It might be a random exception to the law. It may be the result of a complex of causes we do not understand. It is only properly a miracle if it is regarded as having special significance. It is statues of the Virgin Mary which are noticed to be weeping. That seems significant. Healings are of course of profound significance to those healed: unless of course the healing is trivial – if a priest touches me on the hand and a slight scratch is observed to heal very quickly shortly thereafter it is doubtful whether we would think of this as a miracle. A miracle then is an important sign. We might think of such an event as having divine causation: but this does not mean that is has a different status from regular – that is law-controlled – events. They too are brought about by the continuous (and regular) activity of the Divine Being. The miracle represents a flutter of irregularity in the behavior of the divine body. Sometimes God acts irregularly. It is a variation in the pattern of God's continuous creation.

So from this standpoint there is no clash between science and religion from a metaphysical point of view. It may be that peasant women prone to believe in miracles may not have a scientific temperament. They may be epistemologically distant from the mainstream of modern thinking: but these are other issues, and we have in effect dealt with them in our delineation of the critical and visionary nature of both science and religion in their different ways. If the truth be told the peasant women are not modern in religion either: they do not glimpse the alternatives and they have a naive epistemology of worldviews (namely, whatever the Church or the priest says is true, and that's that).

We may notice at this point that there is an analogy between a religious worldview and a scientific theory. No scientific theory is simply falsified by counterevidence. Discrepant data can be fitted into an alternative model (Barbour, 1974). It is only when the cumulative evidence is against a model or theory that a paradigm shift occurs that alters scientists' perceptions and how they view the world (Kuhn, 1970). However, we do not wish to exaggerate the convergence because the way we falsify or verify religious claims is much more subjective or soft than is the case with science – for various reasons which in part stem from the nature of the differing enterprises.

Beyond Science: Reasons for Belief in the Creation
We began our account of creation with the narrative in *Genesis*. There are aspects of the account which need to be

explored further: above all, the idea on which Christians have tended to insist from the beginning, that there is no *necessity* about creation. God said "Let there be light", and behold there was light. She did not *have* to say "Let there be light". To that issue we shall return. We also need to make some comment on the way our social conception of the Trinity affects the doctrine of creation. But before getting to such points, let us underline our reasons for belief in God beyond the world.

We have stressed our loyalty to the age-old tradition, e.g. to the accounts of creation both in *Genesis* and in *John*. These by themselves help to impart part of the substance to our *darśana*. But we are opposed to an insistence that it is only by revelation that we know the nature of God. This idea, prominent in recent times in the writing of Barth, and sometimes evident in evangelical Protestant writings, and found too in a different form in the Ramanuja school of Indian philosophy or theology, rests on an error: namely the thought that because all knowledge of God is saving knowledge, and salvation is by grace (in faith), then all knowledge is founded on grace, not works. This seems a narrow and ultimately self-contradictory idea. Theorists of grace have difficulty with our "natural" knowledge of Jesus. Suppose we know nothing at all about the historical Jesus, beyond the empty fact that he existed, then how can he save us? No teachings, no fish, no disciples, no chasing of money-changers, no trial, no cross. . . . The fact is that even when we go far beyond historical fact and say that Jesus died for our sins, we still have in mind that he *died*. And he did not just choke to death at the age of eighty after eating a hard-to-digest dinner (like the Buddha). He died criminally and humbly upon the cross. But where do we get these facts from? From the tradition, from a natural reading of the texts. Maybe the eye of faith is needed for some things: but not for the notion that he was raised in Nazareth.

There are two opposite fallacies. One is to concentrate so heavily on faith that the man Jesus evaporates in a transcendental Christ. This is a kind of epistemological docetism, and to this Bultmann and Kierkegaard are more than a little prone. The opposite fault is to suppose that because faith demands historical certainty, we can affirm the historicity of scriptures on faith alone. This is the "fundamentalist" error. It is epistemological chauvinism.

The upshot of this discussion is simply that if in historical matters we have to rely on our "natural" powers, why not also in regard to the dependence of the cosmos upon God? Also, we may note that on our two-aspect theory my powers of critical evaluations of arguments and evidence are themselves a gift of God. They are also due to the operation of grace.

Now classically, as we know, the idea of natural theology – of our natural knowledge of God – has been conceived as centering upon the so-called proofs of God's existence.

Now in Part I we have alluded to the usefulness, within certain very close limits, of two forms of the proofs. There is a "suggestive natural theology". We do not here claim that there is anything approaching proof. We are dealing here with the margins of existence. We are also not dealing with a natural theology that exists in the abstract. Rather, we have in mind *reasons* for belief, and they may be intertwined. Thus we have a set of visions which can be classified as theistic, which involve a notion that the Lord is to be experienced (they range from versions of Judaism, Christianity and Islam to some forms of Hinduism and other religions of the East). These visions flesh the Lord out in history and experience, in narrative and ritual transactions. In our case we have our version of the Christian visionary viewpoint. Let us then stick to this version to illustrate its intertwining with some of the themes of natural theology. If we are asked for our reasons for belief, they range from highly speculative ones (our belief accounts for the existence of the cosmos) to more particular claims about the example of Jesus. The Christian myth gives us the thought that only a God willing to suffer should have produced this or any other cosmos, since free-range conscious beings would be bound themselves to suffer – excruciatingly in some cases, and in some degree at least in the case of others. It is not as if we need to separate reasons and put them all clearly

227

in one basket ("revelation") or another ("reason"). This is not true to the complexity of belief.

And so in contemplating the so-called proofs, let us not artificially separate them from other considerations. Nor should we think of them as consisting in some irrefragable rational edifice which has some kind of independent certainty.

It is by the way a rationalist illusion that reason can produce, in metaphysics, proofs. We have philosophers often of great subtlety and ability who use their reasoning power to arrive at conclusions which they think have some kind of necessity (because of the use of "reason"). But the history of philosophy is littered with theories which their authors once saw as irrefragably true and which we look at now merely as ruins from which we can quarry some fine insights. Rational "proofs" themselves have no more status than some other reasons, and do not affect our stance of soft non-relativism, which we sketched in Part I.

More: anything which might be established on the basis of the classical "proofs", whether Indian or Western, would by itself be of remarkably abstract quality – a Necessary Being, a First Unmoved Mover (or Unchanged Changer), a Designer. You might think that an intelligent Designer is not all that abstract: but that is probably because intelligent beings you know come with emotions, ears, hands, and a whole host of human appurtenances and characteristics. But a being who simply designs, a bare intelligence – what is that? It is because we connect the conclusion of the arguments with the "fleshed-out" Gods of revelation and myth that we think of the proofs as significant. But in the "fleshed-out" form the gods have the uncertainty that pertains to each worldview. So the rigid division between natural and revealed theology is hard to sustain. It itself is part of a worldview which we may not wish to accept. Still, the arguments do have some force, and that force happens to relate to questions about necessity, and these in turn relate to the issue of the contingency of the cosmos.

For the root perception upon which the various versions of the Cosmological Argument rest is that the cosmos might not have existed at all (Smart, 1964, pp. 81–95). Just as nothing in the world is necessary but the existence of each thing or the occurrence of each event depends in general on the existence or occurrence of others, so the cosmos' existence is not necessary. We therefore think that it depends upon some further entity.

We are treating the cosmos here as itself like a great big thing or a great big web of events. It is not just shorthand for "all events" or "all things". There might be objections to treating an open class as having the same property as its members, namely the possibility of not existing. But it does not seem meaningless to think that "all this" (as the Sanskrit has it: *sarvam idam*) might not have existed. There seems to be no necessity about *sarvam idam*. We can easily conceive that there might have been no cosmos. We can even in a sense imagine it, by pursuing certain patterns of meditation, as in Buddhism, where you wash away in thought all the entities and the space-time of the cosmos. And so it seems to make sense to ask: "Why is there this cosmos, rather than nothing?" But in this question we are necessarily going beyond the bounds of any possible science. For science deals with what goes on within the great web of events. It can trace their development, there interconnections, the logic underlying their evolution and manifestation. But how can science go beyond this cosmos? (We'll deal here summarily with the thought that black holes or whatever might give you entree into another cosmos side by side with ours, by simply saying that a cosmos side by side would really be an extension of our cosmos, or ours would be of it). Because we go beyond science and have no clear way of proving any one hypothesis about what transcends the cosmos, we might in a Kantian fashion abandon substantive claims about the Beyond. We are at the margins of experience. On the other hand the question does not easily go away once we have posed it. Anyway: we have a choice, and one path to take is that of affirming a Cosmos-Explaining Being.

It is of course immediately apparent that even if we explain the cosmos by such a Being, suitably interpreted through our elaboration of the idea of a Transcendent Being (wholly holy and non-spatial), the same question begins to pop up in relation to that Being.

In other words, if the cosmos exists because there is a Divine Being, then why does the Divine Being exist? We seem no better off, in climbing from one contingency to another. Or shall we say that it is in the nature of God to be necessary? Maybe the Ontological Argument works after all, as some writers have recently contended. We do not deny that we might well on religious grounds assign a kind of necessity to the Divine: if she exists, then she exists necessarily (just as we might say that if she exists at any one time, then she exists at all times, or eternally). But if She exists . . . After all, the total conceptual construction might not after all apply to anything. Anselm might be left harboring beautiful thoughts, but there might be no heaven to have them in. Moreover, in the fleshed-out picture of God there are many non-necessary aspects – she might not have been Christ, she might not have created the cosmos, and so on.

Now we might desire not to go beyond science, to reach the edge of the cosmos, so to speak, but to go no further. From a pragmatic angle, the cosmos itself would be the "necessary being": it is from here we would start. If we go further and postulate a Cosmos-Explaining Being then since that Being might not exist, might we not then go on and postulate a higher Being to explain the Cosmos-Explaining Being. Is this not an ascent on an infinite ladder? We would merely remark the following : Flesh out the CEB and you have an explanation of the existence of the cosmos that has more content than an empty affirmation that we can go no further than the cosmos itself or that we postulate a Being whose sole function is as a regulative Idea. The fleshed out Cosmos-Explaining Being gives focus to our view of the nature and origins of the cosmos. We can see it as having its center in the threefold operation of the Divine Being in nature and history.

So we would first of all assert that the question which expresses the heart and the anxiety of the classical Cosmological Argument, namely "Why is there a cosmos at all, rather than nothing?" is a valid one, and its persistence is one of the reasons for our espousing a Transcendental worldview.

The question also draws our attention to the contingency of the world, so that in contemplating the issue of why it exists we are acknowledging that there was no need for the creation. There might indeed have been nothing at all, but in our "fleshed out" view God chose that it should exist, and it does. This does not imply anything about the finiteness or otherwise of the cosmos in time. We do not have at this point to choose between rival theories in scientific cosmology. But as an either finite or everlasting expression of divine intentions the cosmos is contingent and as *Genesis* suggests is the consequence of a divine fiat. Given that entities exist and that no entity can bring itself into existence (which is absurd) there are then, two alternative ways of viewing the contingency of the cosmos: (1) it was created by an everlasting Transcendent Being which has absolute ontological independence or "factual necessity" (not "logical necessity" as its existence can be denied without self-contradiction); as such, Divine existence is self-existent, incorruptible and indestructible. (2) It is an everlasting causal sequence or process of temporally overlapping contingent entities which are conditioned, decaying and perishable. Whether or not this naturalistic view provides a coherent account or sufficient explanation for the intelligible structure of the cosmos is a subject of ongoing philosophic debate.

The Fiat Experience (Smart, 1958)

The sense of contingency is in part derived from the fiat in *Genesis*. It is found in the core myth of creation. But it has a significance beyond this. It implies that all the items of the world-process flow from the one divine Reality. They exist under God's continuous guidance and are expressions of his or her will. This sense of dependence has an experiential side to it, which integrates the spiritual life with the metaphysical kind of questioning which we have been exploring. The numinous experience when felt intensely leads to a sense not just of our unworthiness, but of power

flowing out of that which is experienced – as though all
power resides there. So there is as part of it the sense of
creatureliness – not only in the analysis given by Otto, but
also in the root perception of the sense of dependence found
in Schleiermacher's writings. We do not of course have to
rely on literary sources: there are in the very vibrations of
the numinous the intimation that behind the veil of the
cosmos lies its Source.

Often mystical experience emphasizes not so much the
dependence of the world as its evanescence and unreality.
We accept for instance the Buddhist account, which blends
both mystical contemplation and philosophical analysis of
reality, that everything in the cosmos is impermanent. If
permanence be a sign of reality, then the events of this world
are unreal. There is in this kind of attitude too the thought
that beyond the evanescent there lies the Permanent, beyond
the unreal there is the real: hence the famous words of the
Upanishad: Lead me from the unreal to the real. This
mystical sense of impermanence can go with the doctrine
of creation by an Other, of course. When the two are
combined there is a very vivid sense of the contingency of
the world. But the theistic attitude is to say that though real,
the cosmos and its processes, are not ultimate Reality. It
is this sense of the dependency of the cosmos which we wish
to affirm, and it is something well expressed through the
concept of a divine fiat. Our belief rests not just on scriptural
precedent therefore, but also on the phenomenology of
experience.

The Teleological Argument Revived

So far we have given a weak form of the Cosmological
Argument. In fact it is not so much an argument as a
question, but one which has profound existential meaning.
Of the classical arguments, however, the cosmological is only
one form. There are the ontological and teleological
"proofs". We do not, for various reasons which need not
be sketched here, accept the absolute validity of the
Ontological Argument. It has a limited use because it points
to the necessity with which God exists given that she exists.

232

But we think it absurd to suppose that it is irrational or confused to deny her existence. The uncertainties of worldviews, the doubtfulness of the rule of goodness in a cosmos in which there are evident cruelties and sufferings, and the fact that many wise people deny God are sufficient to sap the cogency of Anselm and Descartes (and Norman Malcolm) in the matter of this "proof". But the Teleological Argument has its own allure, in pointing to design and order in the world (Smart, 1964 pp. 96–104, 110–114). It rests on the thought that the world, as it turns out, is orderly enough to sustain life (when there was no need for such orderliness). It is itself a striking observation that we are in a cosmos which has enough stability in its processes to grow life, and beyond life, consciousness. We have a kind of ascending scale of organization: from the emptiness of space-time, through energy and matter, to organic life, which later by a complex and incredible process comes to find within itself consciousness. Such consciousness, remarkable enough in weasels and whales, shows higher degrees of intelligence with the arrival of human beings. They turn out to be formidable, with some of the organizational capacity of the ants and individual perceptions and thoughts of a higher order: which in combination make us into a highly powerful race, for we are at the same time one animal and many. We are in potentiality a single great leviathan circumscribing our beautiful earth, and capable of making the subtlest and most prized objects. In this "chain of being" we see the natural evolution of consciousness and with it ways in which, so to speak, nature reflects herself and understands herself.

Now we do not need to explain all this in any other way than through the natural sciences. We do not need to postulate a Lamarckian teleology. This may or may not exist in the evolutionary process, but it makes no difference, since we could as easily have a natural teleology as one which implied some supercosmic intelligence. Why should not purpose be one of the principles by which the cosmos organizes itself? Asa Gray noted that Darwinian theory requires the notions of purpose and teleological explanations as the adaptations produced by the process of natural selection are useful to living organisms and enable them to achieve goal-directed ends (telos). Our form of the argument is not, however, based on the adaptations to ends of particular living organisms (remarkable as these are) but on the highly complex order of the cosmos as a whole. This order has provided the necessary conditions for the evolutionary development of humans as self-conscious beings who are thus able to realize values: intellectual, moral, spiritual and the aesthetic appreciation of the beauty of nature, which as expressed in the Psalms, is filled with the majestic splendor of God (also see Romans 1:19–20). The argument thus raises the question as to how this teleological order and the overall direction to evolutionary process is to be accounted for. It is a remarkable and awe-inspiring thought – that this cosmos, which might not have existed, yet has that degree of order which is needed to sustain consciousness. With the arrival of that there came into view (so to speak) a whole range of new properties, of color, shape and so forth, which represents a revolution in nature herself. So there is existential force in the thought that the cosmos is orderly enough to sustain conscious life. In this it also grows within it something much more remarkable than the peacock's tail: a being capable of spiritual ambitions and the capacities to experience what is Transcendent. The human being (and her cousins perhaps in other galaxies) aspires to penetrate beyond the veil of the cosmos and to see the Spirit which she conceives as lying behind and within all things. It is not, then, absurd, though it is not mandatory either, to see the cosmos as the theater in which a Creator has brought about the conditions whereby a creature may reflect her own image, and strive towards her in love.

Neither the form in which we have presented the Cosmological Argument nor that in which we have expressed the Teleological provide anything more than soft reasons for going along with the doctrine of creation. But we do regard the Christian picture as very compelling to us. For it makes sense for the Divine Being to pour forth her power in love to create a world, and yet to recognize the suffering as well as the glory that will nestle there. So darkness also falls like a shadow across the face of transcendent Bliss.

The Unity of Nature and Emergent Characteristics

We have emphasized the novelty of consciousness and its products. We could underline this even more vigorously by pointing to the freedom and creative novelty of conscious creatures, especially in their cooperative ventures (to this we shall in any case come back). But we also perceive the cosmos to be unified, in the sense at least that we do not need divine interventions or other ad hoc hypotheses to explain the evolution of one form from another. But we do assert that there are emergent characteristics, such as conscious states, which come into being when an organism has achieved a certain degree of complexity. In its transactions with its environment the very complexity of things is a bar to that knowledge which a free ranging organism needs if it is to survive. The simplification of information coming inward is achieved by the arrangements of consciousness. Instead of an incredible buzz of electrons and what-nots I see a daffodil. Similarly there is a simplification of impulses and the creation of feelings. The deliverances of consciousness and feeling, though in one way simplified, are also very subtle. It is this remarkable range of new properties which emerges from the organism. But consciousness is rooted in material processes. Sometimes humans in a rather arrogant way have drawn a strong conceptual divide between humans and other beings. This attitude was fostered by elements in the mythic thinking of the Christian tradition. By contrast the Asian traditions and many smaller-scale cultures have a much more organic view of nature. The arrogance of Western mythicists has led too to the rejection by so-called fundamentalists of scientific approaches to the evolution of the human race. We ourselves repudiate this stance, and claim no more than that in our experience no other creature has a more highly developed consciousness, intelligence and spiritual capacity than the human being. But in fact there is a certain symmetry, already noticed and elaborated on by Sri Aurobindo, between the upward striving of the evolutionary process and the downward creativity and grace of God. We see Brahman from one point of viewing expanding outwards into her body, so to speak: creating the material cosmos, and beginning from the spiritual and spinning forth the subtleties of material processes, which in turn begin to strive back upwards by creating out of their own dynamism the centers of consciousness which reflect their Origin.

The Trinity and Creation

The emergence of consciousness brings about the novelty of a new kind of "substance" – conscious substance – in the cosmos. This enables us to see a certain schema in regard to the Trinity doctrine which is so central to our thinking. As we have argued the Transcendent is "beyond", but also omnipresent. In this sense, the Trinity is present everywhere where God is, and so the Trinity is all around us and within us. But if we are to think of the three Persons or centers of consciousness as specially connected with diverse aspects of reality, then we would sketch out a picture as follows. The Father is supremely creator and as such is present behind and within the whole cosmos. The natural world is the body of the Father. But within that material world Christ is present very particularly, as the individual Jesus. There is only one way to be embodied and that is as an individual – hence the scandal of particularity in the Christian faith. So Christ is present above all in Jesus of Nazareth. The Spirit thirdly comes especially into her own with the arrival of consciousness in the cosmos. She is the inner controller of conscious individuals, secretly enjoying the life of this world. Since as we have argued there are no persons other than social persons, the Spirit is also specially present in social bondings. So we can say: the Father is the inner controller or *antaryāmin* of the cosmos. The Spirit is the *antaryāmin* of conscious beings and above all humans, as the soul so to speak behind the soul. And Son is the inner controller of the personal identity of Jesus. This is the "three body Doctrine" of Christianity, and we shall return to this in the chapter on the Spirit.

236

In this schema, there is a certain logic. The material processes of the cosmos are, moreover, the veil which protects the creatures from the full glory and even wild force of the Divine Being. This veil is also the means whereby conscious beings gain their freedom. It has a salvific significance, in that without incarnation in bodies the living creatures could not learn their powers, and so gain their individual exercises of freedom. But such finitude means also the regularity which the Teleological Argument appeals to, and which can be in collision with, as well as a condition of, life. The Divine Being could see that the veil means suffering, so that she too has to penetrate through it, from the farther side, in order to live among her creatures. Incarnation is a moral necessity of creation, as we have already argued. But since social being is also part of being fully personal, this is something which could grow out of the social character of the Trinity. So it appears to us that the two stumbling blocks of the Christian faith are on the contrary necessities. The one is a moral necessity and the other is a metaphysical necessity. In brief, both the Incarnation and the Trinity doctrines flow logically out of monotheism.

The Question of Freedom (Smart, 1964)

The Christian worldview which we present emphasizes, through the analogy of the *śarīra* or body of God, the way in which the Divine is everywhere, present that is to us continuously through the power whereby he has created and maintains every part of the cosmos. Yet we have also underlined the notion that the cosmos as veil is the theater of freedom for creatures, and human beings in particular. But is that freedom illusory? How can God be omnipresent and all-sustaining and yet grant real freedom to her creatures? And how can it be that God guides history and yet leaves freedom to myriad human beings themselves to act in chaotic ways which when combined yield the drifting lineaments of history?

First, we must expound our concept of freedom, in relation to the laws of nature which permeate and surround us. From one perspective, we regard human actions and history itself as fundamentally open. Pragmatically there is a limitation on the degree to which human acts can be predicted, and we do not regard political or economic or any other social science as more than hypothetically predictive – that is predictions are sketches of certain trends, given that (this is the hypothetical part) some framework-disturbing event does not occur. Thus, the invention of the atomic bomb could not have been predicted a hundred years before the event, for the lack of the theoretical information and relevant conceptual apparatus. Because that could not be predicted a whole lot of other things, about intercontinental ballistic missiles, for instance, could not have been foreseen. However, given the nuclear bomb, and some other technological and scientific advances, one could predict that a race in nuclear armament would take place between the superpowers, that various smaller powers would develop the capability, etc. But even here, now within the nuclear framework, we may be caught out by new discoveries in physics. What if there is a discovery which reveals the possibility of making a weapon which will easily incapacitate anyone's nuclear weapons? That would destroy our present framework of prediction.

Sometimes there are revolutions in science, but similar things may be said on a smaller scale in regard to revolutions in music or the other arts. Could the evolution of French Impressionism be predicted from within the framework of prior academic art? There are also the human geniuses whose particular style could not be foreseen: the young Mozart, say (what if the particular genes had not entered into the particular cocktail that made Mozart?). Now in these cases, as with scientific discoveries, we perceive new ways of doing or thinking things. These cannot be predicted on the basis of current science and current knowledge, partly because they help to overturn that science and that (supposed) knowledge, and partly because if such discoveries could be predicted they would be already here. The predictor would be the genius and the innovator: but could he be predicted?

So it is reasonable to think that certain things cannot be

predicted – and this is not for lack of information but of the novel concepts and modes of operation which help to displace today's framework. So looked at at least from the human end there are a number of things which simply cannot be predicted, as a matter of principle. And we cannot have evidence of some metaphysical determinism below the level of prediction. It might at first be thought: We cannot predict new discoveries, but underlying events are a whole train of unseen causes which determine what the future is going to be. This metaphysical claim cannot have evidence for it. What lies beneath events which display radical novelty is inscrutable. So belief in determinism in the circumstances becomes an article of faith. It is one which we do not have to accept.

Now the picture which we have drawn has social significance in two directions. On the one hand it is clear that the creativity of an individual is itself a consequence of social belonging – the language and training and ideas handed on down and into him by society. Because his powers of thinking and imagination are in part dependent on these cultural factors it is clear that freedom is in a sense precipitated in him by society. This reinforces our view of the idea of the person as involving the social dimension. The second point about society leads in the other direction. The ideas and input of an individual or group in making something new spreads like a tide across society and across the human race: the telephone, the aeroplane, relativity theory, new musical styles – consider how these have rippled rapidly outward from their origins in a few human brains to affect virtually the whole world. The amplification of the new is today carried much more rapidly because of modern capitalism with its global scope and near-instant communications, sending tides of information outwards on the air waves. So if a crucial individual's insights cannot be predicted neither can human history at large. For instance, it was realization of the awesome power of the H-bomb which led Khruschev to offer the idea of peaceful coexistence – a concept not drawn from official Marxist thought. If the H-bomb could not be predicted, neither could the policies of Khruschev (or of anyone else). So we can say that from a human point of view, there are severe limitations on the predictive possibilities of the social sciences.

Now some might say: It is all very well to affirm the deep unpredictability of geniuses, but what has that to do with individual freedom? Moreover (it might be said) there has as yet been no mention of ethics, and yet one would think that the whole point of the discussion of freedom was to do with whether there is genuine freedom in moral choice. Let us take this second point first. There are changes and advances in moral insight: for instance, there is much more concern in Western societies about animal welfare than was the case a hundred years ago. There are sharp shifts in elements in worldviews which affect moral attitudes: consider here the work of Foucault on the "archeology of knowledge", regarding concepts such as insanity and the way the mentally ill are looked at now rather than two hundred years ago. There are, then, revolutions in worldviews too (the origins of religions especially testify to this). And so what applies in the case of science applies here also. As for the first point, individual freedom is rarely if ever a matter of isolated choice. For instance a person may give up smoking on the ground of higher prudence, and this is a sort of moral choice. But the decision is not unrelated to all kinds of social input: increased knowledge through research of the bad effects of smoking, public pressures, pleadings by the person's husband, and so on. So we do not need to think that because we are talking of individual freedom we are not also speaking of social influence.

Moreover, the openness of the future applies microscopically in the individual human being, in that each one of us is an incalculable congeries of millions of elements, with a learned cultural heritage of great complexity; and though we are forced (so to speak) to obey the larger laws, e.g. of gravity, it is unclear that we can apply the notion of laws fully to the individual. This is in part because from a conscious angle the individual is indeed a unitary object, to herself; and there is a single organizing center for our activities: but we are here looking at properties which have emerged from the vast complexities of the underlying material and biological organism. (We may also theorize that some behavioral changes might be tied to subatomic brain events, themselves exhibiting indeterminacy, for reasons canvassed by Heisenberg and Schrödinger.) We are, then, anomalous creatures, only partly constricted by the laws of our environment.

To give a more directly Christian interpretation of this outlook: we can see creativity in the sciences, in the arts, in everyday life, in the fashioning out of ourselves better people, as an activity which gives us some transcendence of our condition. It can especially be associated with the work of the Spirit, also our quiet *antaryāmin*. We can admire the changes we make, breaking loose from enslavement to earlier behavior patterns; and yet think "Not I, but the Spirit in me". A new feeling, a new perception, a new closeness to some companion – these changes seem to come like puffs of smoke into our brains and feelings from we know not where. They represent openness to the future. They are of the same kind as that openness to each other which bonds the Trinity together. So these unheralded acts of ours, great glories, can be ascribed too to the grace of the *Īśvara*.

For us, such freedom is enough. It also ties the idea of creativity in action to the social dimension and to our vision of the world. The Indians are right to stress the role of ignorance and delusion in circumscribing us. There has been too simplistic an emphasis upon sin as though this were just a matter of moral failing. There is much in the Gospel which is to do with seeing and hearing anew "Let him who has eyes see". Alienation is partly a matter of our moral attitudes, but it also has more widely to do with our total perception of the world. It can be a kind of worldview-dullness, the uncritical acceptance of a tedious and restrictive worldview. And that is at least part of what the Indians mean by *avidyā*. So from our point of view this very vision which we are trying here to present, a systematic vision of the object of the Christian faith, is a vital input into our social world, in that it helps to give people, we would hope a *darśana* which is liberating. It is intended to portray that light which can enlighten people and help them to see the Beyond in such a way that they can break out of some of the ideas and feelings that may hitherto have held them in bondage. From all this it follows that divine foreknowledge knows the future as possibility but not as actuality. In this we agree with Hartshorne (1948) that divine omniscience means that God knows everything that it is possible to know. The same position applies to divine omnipotence, according to which God can do everything that is possible to do (as argued by Aquinas), but not anything whatsoever (i.e., what is contradictory).

This, then, is our account of freedom. It is sufficient for us to make sense of our ongoing desire to change both ourselves and our world. It integrates moral and intellectual and artistic creativity. It thus does not too narrowly conceive of freedom as restricted to an area of human enterprise which we label "morality", as if there could be freedom when I choose to act this way rather than when the act is that conceived to have great moral significance, and yet I do not have freedom in thoughts and choices in other contexts. We should not compartmentalize the human being. But can we engage this sketch of freedom with the thought that the whole cosmos including ourselves is under the direct guidance and control of Brahman?

Providence Related to Freedom

The expanding cosmos exists as a dynamic process of events within the limitless extension and intensity of the Trinity's consciousness, by which it is continuously sustained. We have noted that this cosmos is a veil which in screening the Divine at the same time gives her creatures freedom to think and feel and act, without the overwhelming and dazzling presence of the Divine. From one angle, everything that happens in the divine body happens through the will of God: but there is a kenotic element here which needs to be underlined. God in letting creatures be, in front of the veil, assigns to them powers which involve the openness of history. It means that she has two kinds of effects upon the world, both of which can allow for this openness. First (from our point of view) there is the divine activity which is indirect: the Divine acts indirectly behind the waves, the storms, the sunshine, the mountains, the cities and the stars. There is not an event that does not contain within it the supporting presence of Brahman. But this indirect support acts on a regular basis. God kenotically has made a law-governed and regular universe. Second, more directly, God appears in human experience and history in ways that give humans more direct access to her. Thus there are the visions of saints and prophets. These experiences carry us beyond the veil. These experiences in their turn affect human history – they are important ingredients in the mixture which we call "history". Also we believe that in Christ God enters into history; and so there are the events which flow from him which have had a vital part in the shaping of world history.

There is nothing in the first sort of effect which under-mines human freedom. If there are irregular and novel events because of human actions then these are part of the ongoing fabric of the Divine body behaving in the ways in which in fact it behaves. God has left some unpredictability in the texture of her body's life. As the inner controller of human beings She is accessible, and at a deeper level our acts do participate in the divine process. We are ourselves part of the divine life, and the aim of our being, if we are Christians, is to progress until we share in deity, and become divinized.

Part of what happens in the spiritual life is the conversion of indirect divine activity into direct activity. So the Spirit works inwardly in us, and is concealed behind the veil of our consciousness. We may go blindly on – and often we do bad things from which we cannot in our blindness learn a lesson. But if we can lift the veil a little, it is by seeing our own acts as containing within and behind them the force of the Spirit. We can see God's guidance inside us if we have the eyes to see. Even our bad acts teach us a lesson, if we see them as foolish because we had not a deeper under-standing of the divine will for us. Once however we see the Spirit burning in the depths of our consciousness, and once we are aware of the divine hand guiding the events around us, we look with new eyes, and may perceive much more directly the power of God. This direct perception means that God more directly enters history through us. So while God is indirectly at work in all things, within the framework of her kenotic granting of freedom through the veil which shields us from her, she is always liable to "irrupt" more directly into the flow of events through the actions of God-inspired human beings. In this way we do not just deify ourselves, but we deify history also.

Threefold Kenosis

The Trinity in its activity in creation imposes on herself a threefold self-emptying. First, as *antaryāmin* of the cosmos as a whole God guides the forces of the world but by the very fact that she contracts to be regular, to provide a stable background for the free ranging conscious animals that she knows that the cosmos will grow, there are limitations on the ways she is willing to act (like removing the power of fire because someone is just going to be burnt). Second, she leaves freedom to conscious beings to learn from nature and struggle through to their own identities, and so does not dominate the individual from her position behind consciousness. Third, as Christ she is self-emptying in the way Jesus has abandoned omniscience and omnipresence and other divine attributes but really enters into the life of the conscious individual in that cosmos which veils the Father from him (and yet he becomes intimately aware of him).

There are many who feel that among monotheisms Christianity has the least intellectual appeal, because it relies on revelation to establish its central doctrine, the Trinity. According to classical and rather rigid conceptions of reasoning, the Monotheos or Prime Mover or First Cause, etc., can be proved, but the notion that it is also a Trinity is messily rooted in revelation. But if we look at creation from a moral perspective, the Christian view has a great deal of cogency. If we have a God who rules all, he secretly determines the lives of all humans, and we have a deterministic universe, in the style of Calvin or certain Muslim occasionalists. It seems to us that a Creator who wishes to have free creatures must involve herself in kenosis and make space for them in the fabric of the cosmos. But more than that: Who would create free creatures (the only creatures worth having) and invite them into an existence of suffering without being willing to bear their sufferings too? Morally, the Creator should become incarnate as an *avatāra* in her created world. And having so to speak split into two persons, God needs the perfected bond of love to bind together the divine life, and so we have the Trinity as a social entity. So in a way, as we have said, the Christian Trinitarian creator is entirely logical: and it is morally persuasive. It is in sharing the life of the divine society that creatures will attain to their greatest potential. But we too have to practice kenosis: some self-sacrifice for others is a necessary ingredient in the perfect life, towards which we strive.

Still, we should not be too negative in our thinking about the cosmos. The Divine Being may have to suffer to share life in her own cosmos: but also the cosmos is fun. It is, as we have noted, a dance, and the colors and beautiful music and food and water and wine of the world, and the roses and the hyacinths, even the dandelions, are there to be loved and enjoyed. The advent of consciousness spreads out before us, and before God who shares in our consciousness, the vast pleasures of color and form and scents and sounds and all the glories of this world. God saw that it was good, says *Genesis*; and the dark sense that death is in store for Christ could not blight his enjoyment of the wonders of this beautiful and stormy cosmos. And to further delight in this, the cosmos could grow artists to paint the persimmons in the snowtime, and the cypresses of the vinous South, and the spume on the breaking wave, and the wet pavements of Paris, and the smiling and dark faces of human beings. It could not only produce the mad and lovely song of the morning mockingbird and the lark on the moor, and the rush and gurgle of fat streams, but also grew musical composers who could weave entrancing tunes and strange harmonies. There are the joys of sex, and of eating, and washing the back of the throat with beer and running in the evening air. There are the joys of babies with early smiles, and the whispers of lovers, and tranquil old age, and sports and all sorts of glories. From within the consciousness that spreads the colors of the world before us the inner witness watches and enjoys. These pleasures are small foretastes of the bliss of the Spirit. And the divine being is not just committed to the sorrows of the world, which are real enough, but the many fine things which the cosmos brings forth. It is not surprising, for this reason, that Jesus was present at parties, enjoyed all sorts of company, and no doubt as a young man revelled in the blue of the hills and the glimpses of distant Lake Galilee. He could sense the terror of the storm, and the beauty of limpid waters where the fish swam in silver flocks, awaiting his keen eye. For all the wretchedness of the cross, a sad symbol of faith, there was much jollity among those around Jesus. He was able to taste the wine as well as the bitter vinegar.

Kenosis and Revelation

We must note that by standing off and giving his creatures freedom the Divine Being also draws a veil around them which precludes absolute clarity of revelation. A subsidiary part of the problem of evil is that human beings may be led astray and suffer because they cannot easily know the truth. Truth is something which has to be wrestled for, in a strenuous and long dialogue with nature, known as science; but it also needs to be struggled for as between different hints and diverse worldviews. It has to be struggled for even when there is religious knowledge by experience, since the interpretation of events is necessarily open to question. The Christian and the Buddhist may both voyage to the depth of their souls (so to speak), but each will find something different. The one will perceive the eternal life of the divine Trinity; the other an unspeakable nirvana. So the truth is not to be won easily. But reflection should surely show that having contained herself beyond the cosmos, God is hard to perceive (or nirvana is hard to come upon). We have then to reckon that revelation is in the eye of faith and partakes of the kenosis that the whole action of God partakes of in creating this world and in entering into it. Again, modern Christian faith as expressed by liberal Protestants has much to commend it, even if it be less fashionable now: for it (in perhaps too dry terms) points to the difficulties of faith. We should be more positive in tone, if abiding by the essential spirit of liberal Christianity, and see faith as itself a quest, a pilgrimage among the puzzlements of this world, a sincere journey towards the Truth. We can be more positive too because of the phenomenology of religion. We take a positive view of the varieties of religious experience and the varieties of religious expression. We do not of course hold that all faiths are absolutely benign, any more than we regard all kinds of Christianity to be benign. But we see other faiths than the main stream of Christianity as having much to say to those who may be gripped by the Christian picture and who tread the Christian Tao. The other religious movements are there to correct and chide us, and to complement the Christian message as we may understand it. God made faiths to keep us honest. But he was also bound to accept the possibility of diversity of claimed revelations and truths because of the kenotic nature of the creative act itself. So it is not surprising that he should have crept into the world into what was a very obscure part of the Roman empire; and should have lived not just eccentrically among the peripheral Jews, but peripherally to their perceptions of the center, in Galilee. It is outside the spirit of Christian faith in our view to imagine that we can have a dogmatic account of revelation which is somehow conspicuously evident. The theory that those who do not see the truth are misguided is more misguided than the misguided are supposed to be. But we recognize that this need to be a pilgrim in the long search for truth is an added burden imposed on the creaturely being. It is a part of the more general problem of evil and suffering: for it naturally allows others to propound rival doctrines, some of which may turn out to be cruel and destructive. But as we have said, it is all part of kenosis.

But the self-emptying of God means a greater fullness for those who are brought into being and sustained through nature. It gives them freedom and the possibilities of growth. It gives them pride and independence. It gives them the chance to explore varied alternatives in thought and action.

It also enhances nature itself. Because it veils God it has its own substance and reality. It is not a mirage, though it is a veil. But it is a painted veil with many beauties inscribed upon it. So the kenotic, and by implication somewhat chaotic, cosmos has its positive attributes. What God empties from herself she fills in to the created world.

The cosmos, then, is an open cosmos – open to freedom and creativity. It is a kind of divine gamble, for giving freedom is risking death. But we shall deal with the question of what lies beyond individual life in a different place.

8

Divine Embodiment

The Main Focus

The main focus of this chapter will be upon the human career
of Brahman: and in particular the human career of the
second "selfless spirit" of the Trinity. We wish here to present
a novel and dynamic approach to articulating the idea of
the embodiment of Christ. We shall do this by reference to
organic conceptions as we have developed them in the
previous chapter. We believe that our approach will help
to provide a way of thinking about what in the tradition
has been called the doctrine of the Incarnation which is both
intelligible and stated in terms which are contemporary.

Earlier in our typology of the differing strands of religious
language and experience, we drew attention to the
incarnation strand, in addition to the numinous and mystical
strands. We consider that the Hindu term *avatāra* or avatar
is appropriate to use: both because it is crosscultural and
because it expresses nicely the thought of the "descent of
the divine" into the human (or in principle other) form. It
is true that as the doctrine of avatars has been elaborated
in the Vaishnava tradition and beyond it may not have quite
that sense of "all or nothing" – the absolute commitment
of God to a particular enterprise – that we associate with
Christian teaching. But the diffuseness of Hindu ideas of
incarnation (so that we can even think of everyone possibly
as divine) is only a particular application of the concept of
avatāra: it is not intrinsic to it. It expresses, as we have said,
the idea of "descent" (Parrinder, 1976). This, of course, is
not to be taken literally. God is non-spatial, as we have
argued: the divine Being is so to speak everywhere, in that
she is omnipresent; but in herself she does not take literal
spatial predicates. But the notion of "coming down" into

human form (as far as space goes we could as easily say coming sideways or rising up into human form) signifies the kenotic character of divine incarnation. He descends from the perfect bliss of Trinitarian existence, from the heights of sublime love and the infinite shores of knowledge and love, with nothing given to him easily. So "descent" expresses a kind of valuational drop, and a shedding of the high glory of Trinitarian life. But we could as easily have spoken (as we have indicated) of Christ rising from the deep ocean of divine power.

Also in considering Jesus as an avatar of the Divine we wish to draw attention to congruences between Hindu thought, or some interpretations of it, and Christian faith. The notion of *avatāra* does not carry with it the conception of "enfleshment" which the concept incarnation bears. But in a way this is an advantage, for in modern English "flesh" bears a merely physical meaning, and fails to do justice to the idea of *sarx* which was so central to Paul's thinking, and which included spiritual dispositions as well as bodily impulses, etc.

Relations Between Physical Life and Divine Love

Out of his responsive love for his Father, Christ voluntarily consents to descend (or rise) to earthly life in order to save human beings from the destructive forces of sin and death which alienate them from God, from each other and from themselves. That this avatar may involve suffering is already appropriate, as we have seen, since a divine Being who creates finite creatures is bound to involve them in both joy and suffering: and the sufferings are something which he should in principle be willing to undergo. It is part of the very logic of creating a world like ours that the Creator should not draw back from solidarity with her creatures. But the chief concern that the Christian has with the earthly life of Christ is that it culminates in an act of self-sacrifice and a glorious resurrection, which not only expiate for the alienations of the human race, but also create the condition for the glorified participation in the divine life on the part of those who are one with Christ. It brings liberation both positively and negatively: negatively because death and sin are overcome; positively because there opens up the possibility of being united with Christ's cosmic body and entering so to speak into the very being of God (2nd Peter 1:4 NEB).

Previously we substituted for the outmoded idea of substance, which has a static and impersonal feel, the dynamic one of organic divine life. We believe that this enables us coherently to present a "high" or identity Christology – as opposed to those such as Hick who regard such a conception as philosophically unintelligible or contradictory. We must keep in mind too that the cosmos is made up of energy distributed in space, in waves and packages of vibrations: the whole system is vastly dynamic (and the old Aristotelian analysis in terms of substances of various kinds is not heuristically of any more value, though it does represent the schematization of perceptions presented to consciousness in simplified fashion). In limitless non-spatial extension of the three selfless spirits there is nothing which lies "outside" of the divine life. The cosmos is comprehended within the divine consciousness. Not only is the Lord omnipresent in the world of energy and flux but he is also there as a self behind the self of every human self-identity. We are swimming in the divine sea as fish in the ocean (for John of Damascus' aphorism that God is an infinite ocean of being we would substitute the one that God is an infinite ocean of energy). But (it may be asked) how does this modality of divine omnipresence differ from that of the particular embodiment of Christ? We can explain how the latter takes place as follows:

The Son as a divine energy undergoes voluntary self-limitation traditionally called *kenosis* in which he "contracts" his divine life form and consciousness from its limitless non-spatial extension to a specific location in space and time. He assumes the modality of a human life-form and consciousness through which he has his earthly career. Here we need, in terms of traditional formulae and piety, to consider the role of the notion of the virgin birth. If we wish to retain this doctrine of a miraculous intervention by the

Divine we would consider the following the most logical form: that Christ has his earthly origin in the implantation by creation *ex nihilo* of genetic material both female and male, in the womb of the Virgin. In this the fertilized egg is fused with the divine life and placed in its location through the vital energies of the Spirit. All this implies that the Son's divine life and consciousness is completely dependent in its modality of development and functioning upon the natural biological processes which govern human life. This interpretation of "fusion without confusion" was called the *communicatio idiomatum* by the Fathers of the Church. So during the period of fetal development and later in his babyhood and beyond, the Son is no longer conscious of his divine identity nor is he conscious of the cosmos, except in a limited individual way as one of the participants within the great fabric of the universe. If he attains to consciousness of his divine nature and destiny that is by the processes of intuition and experience befitting the modalities of human life. This interpretation of the Virgin Birth involves the thesis that all the human genetic material comes directly from the divine, and the Virgin is the host mother. We do not claim that this account is *de rigueur* for Christians: for we are no popes. It just seems a logical way to express the belief. This idea of original genetic material has the advantage of giving the fullest sense of identity between Jesus and the divine Trinity. It also, as it happens, expresses the androgynous and bisexual nature of the divine identities, while recognizing that the additional male chromosomes are present, which of course give the Son his male human life-form. Our view contrasts with the alternative view which holds that the female egg came from Mary's own body and to this was added male genetic material in a supernatural manner. It may be noted that whichever of these views we take there is a "miraculous" element. Neither view can be proved: both views are more in the character of inferences from the prior theological position on the Sonship of the human Christ Jesus. It may be noted in addition that Mary's position as Theotokos renders appropriate the kind of veneration traditionally accorded to her by the Catholic tradition (in its broadest sense).

Versus Adoptionism

The account which we have just given reinforces our central thesis that the embodied Lord is a single identity as a divine-human organism in which his divine life-form and his human life-form completely interpenetrate. Jesus' human consciousness is, as is his divine one, a selfless spirit, in which he is outgoing and selfless – his consciousness flowing back into close union with the Father and outward into union with his disciples and followers. Of course Jesus was also subject to human and cultural limitations: he had to realize his own identity as a human being through the mode of having normal impulses towards self-preservation and the like which are ego-oriented: but through this he achieved an outgoing capacity for the love of others and his Father which matched the selfless spirit of his divine life. As a person limited by the natural and cultural circumstances in which he found himself his awareness of his divine identity only reached him at the time (in our view) of his baptism when he through the illumination of the Spirit is given an insight into how he has a special destiny as the son of the heavenly Father. It is this divine status which justifies his prerogatives, e.g. for forgiving people their sins against the divine Being. On our view, he could be aware of who he is without having more than human knowledge and abilities. But he needs the help and guidance of the Spirit. At his resurrection he regains his divine form: but into that form (looking at it from the human angle) there is imprinted his crucifixion and the vicissitudes and joys of his life.

We would hold too that such an imprinting is of the essence of the processes of the divine life from the beginning. In the divine nature is the willingness to be a particular human being and to suffer what happened to Jesus. This may remind us about something important in particularity. We often and rightly muse upon the so-called "scandal of particularity": that God is identified with a particular person in a very particular swathe of human history. But you cannot be an individual without being an individual in that place and that time. You cannot be a universal creature. You cannot suffer as a collectivity alone: but you always suffer as a particular human being, maybe joined into a collective, but still as an individual. If the Lord in contemplating the creative process wished to undergo the joys and sorrows of the world he was conjuring up out of nothing, he had to enter into that world as some person who was particular. So we might better call the "scandal of particularity" the scandal of avatar-hood. But as we have seen, though there are of course intellectual and emotional problems about having a God who is also human, there are reasons to think that a creator who did not identify with her creatures would have an ethical and existential problem.

As we shall see, our "high Christology" alone makes possible the fulfillment of the following three conditions: (1) the efficacy of the atonement; (2) the subsequent worship of the Son; and (3) the real presence of Christ in the community and in particular in the Eucharist, and its healing power. Now of course there may well be those who freely reject the assumption that there is need of an atonement: and there are those who prefer to tread another path than the worship of Christ and so on. But we consider that the three conditions are marks of Christian faith: mainstream Christians have for the most part adopted these traits, of faith in salvation through the atoning work of Christ, the worship of Christ and attendance at the Eucharist.

Our presentation does also show that we mean by the avatarhood of Christ more than some transformation of a god such as we encounter so frequently in the Graeco-Roman literature of the times. That high Christology involves such a transformation is a caricature which Paul Tillich asserted in his *Systematic Theology* (1957). We are not here asserting that the divine life-form turns into something else while no longer retaining its divinity, but only that it alters its modality of functioning. We assume that the human dimension of Jesus' life is fully human. And retroactively, so to speak, we are saying that the divine life-form was always faced with its human destiny which was always imprinted upon it. If that involved a perception of suffering, then indeed that is a shadow contained within the divine bliss: a tear in the eye of eternity.

Jesus and Other Important Cultural Figures

We do not — because we emphasize the human character of Jesus' life — wish to deny that he fell into various phenomenological categories: in certain respects he was a rabbi, a shaman, a prophet, a guru, a bodhisattva and so on (though he transcended these categories also). But we do wish in our doctrinal exposition to leave room for his uniqueness as Savior. Again we do not wish to be dogmatic: we are delineating a vision here, and presenting a picture which human beings, as free agents, may or may not take up. But the vision is of a person whose saving work is central to his life, and does not make much sense save in the context of seeing ways in which his role differs from that of other famous and holy and profoundly impressive world figures. They too on our view have their role ultimately in a world history which according to our vision helps to bring about an ideal rapprochement of the human and divine, who are mutually alienated. But meanwhile, before we depict that history, let us attend to ways in which our doctrine gives a particular place to Christ in the unfolding of human life.

For us, as Christians, Jesus suffers through his self-sacrifice and then comes to reign in glory of which a taste is found in the resurrection experiences of his followers. Through his death and victory he displays a particular pattern crucial for the realization of human destiny. As we have said, he is involved in a type of "going beyond" roles which we have called *category transcendence* (Smart, 1979, pp. 205–210). This is a concept which is rooted in the historical evidence and helps indeed to explain how it was that many people misunderstood what he was aiming to do: for instance his projection of messiahhood was very different from a more classical Jewish understanding of the role and mission of the Anointed One. But more importantly still from our perspective, it serves to bring out the mysterious power and peculiar intensity and originality of his teachings.

Compared with the classical Hindu accounts of the avatars of Vishnu, Jesus' humanly embodied divinity makes him distinct. The fact that in the Hindu tradition there is no clear dividing line between the human and the divine, as witness not just the multiplicity of avatars, e.g. Krishna and Rama; but also the tendency to treat gurus and other holy people as divine, means that avatarhood is not an intense and unique divine commitment. It also ties in with the doctrine of rebirth or reincarnation where different bodies (or different individuals) provide a temporary manifestation of the same identity. There is an issue about the historicity of the avatars. There are those who see in the various avatars mythic creations of the human religious imagination which are also highly useful to humanity in embodying various ideals – the virtues and other qualities prescribed in dharma. They are at the same time concrete embodiments of the ultimate which have pragmatic spiritual value in leading people onward to the Supreme. Thus there is a tendency to look on the avatars in a somewhat docetic manner: as mere manifestations of the divine suitable for not yet at the highest stage of spiritual growth. This attitude is reflected especially in the "modern Hindu ideology", the neo-Vedanta with its ascending levels of reality and truth, eventuating in attainment of the realization of identity with the One, with Brahman-Atman. Although the idea of the unreality of the cosmos is on the whole played down by influential modern exponents of Hindu Neo-Vedanta, there is, even so, a powerful suggestion of the ultimate unreality of the foci of piety at the mythic level.

It is quite understandable that modern Hindu teachers should see Jesus through the lens of Hindu concepts. Because yogic knowledge plays a central role in many Hindu systems of belief and practice, it is natural to see Jesus as a yogi, who had a perfect consciousness of his identity with Brahman. His statements are then interpreted in a Hindu manner, to claim identity with the Father. His transcendence of joy and sorrow can even be seen as a supreme equanimity operating even during his crucifixion. These are, we repeat, quite plausible accounts from a Hindu angle. But they conflict with some fundamental motifs that we have stressed, such as the real humanity and suffering of Christ, his *bhakti* relation to the Father, and his full humanity.

Christ's physical embodiment also differs from the

Mahayana Buddhist concept of a multiplicity of bodhisattvas and of the idea of the transformation-body of the Buddha in the so-called Three-Body (or Three-Aspect) doctrine of the later Yogacara. In this notion, which has some rather superficial resemblances to the Trinity idea, the Buddhas manifest themselves as celestial beings, like the great Buddha Amitabha. These Buddhas are accessible to humanity in visions and in meditation, and they play a vital mythic role in the more florid and delightful forms of Mahayana piety, notably in the Pure Land School. They are real enough to the eye of the faithful beholder: though if you take the "two-level" theory of truth in Nāgārjuna and elsewhere, then they too fade into vacuity when we have the higher (or deeper) knowledge of the universal emptiness of everything (also accessible to experience, through meditation). As for the earthly Buddhas, they are transformations, through which the doctrine gets preached and exemplified. Here too there is a touch of docetism. In any case, the general Buddhist position is not to start with a divine Being who may or may not be fully incarnated on earth: but rather with a sense of ultimacy, which is accessible primarily to meditative practice, and which points to the moon of illumination or enlightenment. So the fundamental basis of Buddhism is different, even if the Pure Land variety verges on theism. Many Buddhists, among them distinguished modern scholars such as Edward Conze and D.T. Suzuki, regard celestial Buddhas and bodhisattvas essentially as objects of meditation. It is argued by some too that this fact of the virtually fictional character of such great beings is an advantage, for Buddhism does not, like Christianity, have to depend on the nitty-gritty of history. It is a tribute to human imagination that it can come up with such powerful symbols. Or else – for those influenced by C.G. Jung – it is a sign of the deep nature of the symbols that they well up from the human unconscious, and help in the process of integration.

Now we do not wish here to argue directly against Buddhism which with Hinduism has so much to offer the modern Christian. But we do need merely to restate a difference of assumptions. Certainly the bodhisattva ideal is a much more fictional being than the historical myth of Christ. This is partly because of a different attitude to history. It is also because Buddhism has a semi-idealistic view of the world which leads it to think of the state of our consciousness as central and so the criterion of worth of an idea is its capacity to transform consciousness. But we in starting from the Trinity have a somewhat different vision, though in certain ethical and pious respects one which can converge with Buddhist outlooks.

We may note that the self-sacrificial compassion of the Bodhisattva has a strong likeness to the selfless love of Christ. There are also close resemblances between the idea of Avalokiteśvara's transferring his merit to the otherwise unworthy faithful to assist them on the path to paradise and medieval conceptions of the treasury of merit available through the Church and Christ to the faithful. We may be reminded thus of the themes which recur in religious and ethical experience across cultures. But though in a certain way we can look on Christ as a Bodhisattva, in another way we cannot: for the total Mahayana Buddhist framework is so different that in context the ideals of following the Bodhisattva path and imitating Christ have very different flavors. As these concepts are embedded within wider, and very divergent, doctrinal schemes, their meanings differ substantially.

But of course if we look upon avatars and bodhisattvas in the Hindu and Buddhist traditions just as symbols – if they be figments (profound figments) of the religious imagination – then importantly they do not represent alternatives to the historical Christ. It may be that they can function as magnets and aids in drawing people upwards on the spiritual path. If we can look on them as we do the Jataka stories, as edifying tales, rather than reports of divine or transcendental actualities, then maybe we can simply add them to our equipment for hacking our way through the jungle of this world. As fictions, the Bodhisattvas and the Hindu avatars may be inspiring. Certainly it seems that devotion to Bodhisattvas has helped to improve the human condition. But the Hindu avatars keep sliding back into historical reality. Was not Krishna really there, beside the Jumna at Brindaban?

Christ as Guru and Shaman

Another embodiment which does not quite fit the figure of Christ is that of the holy teacher, the guru. It is true that Jesus was in his own way a guru. His teachings were less systematic than some Hindu gurus – resembling those of Ramakrishna, perhaps: earthly, parabolic, flashing with light and darkness. He spoke, like a guru, as one with authority. But unlike most gurus in the Hindu tradition, who speak directly to disciples and who pass on their teachings to pupils who may take up the line of succession in the teaching, Christ is conceived in the Christian tradition as much more than the Teacher: because his energy is transmitted sacramentally through his special presence at the Eucharist. Moreover, in his life he transcended teaching because much of his message lay in action (there are reminiscences here, by the way, of Zen), and it was his life, death and resurrection that counted ultimately for much more than his sermons and parables (though one cannot in practice make the division between the two sides of his legacy). With the relative lack of distinction between the divine and the human in the Hindu tradition, there is a tendency to see the gurus themselves as divine. This gives them some kind of absolute authority (which in our eyes constitutes a problem in today's epistemology: who has the right to dogmatize, and do we not have to be critical of our mentors?).

In our phenomenology of religious experience a key place is held by the shaman. He exhibits at least the foretaste both of prophetism and mysticism. So in a sense he holds in his religious experience the potential of the two major lines of spiritual experience in human history. There is another dimension in which he has a link to the life of Jesus, namely the healing power that comes from the depth-psychological dismemberment which he undergoes on behalf of his community. This "death and rising again" involves vicarious suffering upon behalf of others, and ecstatic visions of the life beyond. Jesus' self-sacrifice on the cross can be seen as an outward enactment of what the shaman undergoes inwardly. Now there is reversal here: for Jesus' outward life, death and resurrection is re-enacted inwardly by the Christian, through the sacraments and in other ways. So in a way, the faithful Christian is being asked to tread the path of the shaman in following Christ. Of course we no longer live in a pure shamanic world: the shaman had knowledge of fertility and the hunting grounds: she knew the leaping of the fish and the teeming of the deer, the flocking of the birds and the multiplication of berries. We now live in a very different world. But as the old fertility rites and chthonic myths were adapted to the new conditions prevalent when the Roman Empire had its hey-day, and the mystery-religions flourished, so shamanic motifs recur in the modern world in depth psychology: and it is easy to see ways in which the path of integration may lie through the reformulation, in a Christian context, of the shamanic quest. But to the characteristics of a shaman were added so many other things, in the case of Jesus, that we can see category-transcendence at work once again. But we can see shamanic motifs for all that: how he overcame the powers of darkness in his wrestling with Satan, whom he saw fall from heaven; and his healing practices remind us of how the visionary healer is not an unimportant type in the history of religions.

Jesus as Prophet, Mystic, etc.

Out of the shamanic visionary heritage there stems the *nabī*, the prophet: and in so many ways Jesus corresponded to the great figures of the Hebrew Bible, as well as to the numinous figure of John the Baptist, farouche, calling for repentance, wild, critical of "this world" from the standpoint of the desert. Jesus had that affinity with the wilderness which is itself a symbol of the frightening other shore where God resides. It was a place from which to come to critique the life of the city, the world of agriculture, the whole enterprise of settle human life. By adding to vision the communal demands of ethics we have the quintessential prophet: and Jesus in some degree fulfilled that role too. But he saw himself as more, we guess.

Of the mystical contemplative side of Jesus' life we know little. As we noted, there are modern Hindus who love to see him as a yogi, united with Brahman in inner experience. There is not much in the New Testament about the contemplative life, though we can divine from other sources that the Jewish world of Jesus' day saw some definite experiments in contemplative mysticism (e.g. among the Essenes and the Therapeutae of Alexandria). We think that Merkava mysticism, so-called, was more in the shamanic mode, with its themes of vision and ascent. But the mystical life fairly early became such an important strand in Christian life that it would be natural to project the contemplative life back on Jesus. But if he was a yogi he was a somewhat maverick one: and his ultimate experience seems to be of communion with the Father, and not of course the blissful emptiness or non-dual unification found in much of Eastern mysticism.

It would seem too that though he is here and there called Rabbi in the texts, his concern was not primarily to expound the Torah (though he did that). As it turned out he was to change the course of the history of the religion out of which he came. A new and vigorous form of Judaism developed to which was given, ultimately, the name Christianity, and through its crossfertilization with classical civilization it became a very powerful intellectual and spiritual force from way beyond the bounds of the old Jewish tradition. It helped by its emergence to define Judaism itself, where a different version of the myth of the Suffering Servant was predominant.

In these various roles Jesus could more generally be said to fulfill the role of the holy person (Smart, 1958). The holy persons exhibit such characteristics as mysteriousness, purity, other-worldliness and moral power. Even here there were surprises: he did not stick to the ritual purity that was expected by his co-religionists, and consorted with unclean and ungodly people, such as taxcollectors and prostitutes. He liked parties and seems to have been a cheerful as well as a mysterious companion.

261

So far we have looked on Jesus somewhat phenomenologically. We have tried to place him in the map which we drew of some of the main kinds of religious experience and kinds of persons embodying them. Our survey of some particular types, from avatars to yogis, and from Bodhisattvas to prophets, indicates ways in which Jesus exhibits in his own person so many crucial characteristics in the history of religions. It is an interesting state of affairs: but it may indicate how it is that he has symbolically had so many divergent kinds of appeals. It also helps us to understand how different parts of his role-complex are taken up in differing movements within later Christianity.

Transcending the Concepts of His Time (Smart, 1979)

Now we shall proceed to the important discussion of the ways in which Jesus transcended the varied concepts and roles of his time. This idea of category-transcendence helps to explain the nature of Jesus' mission to the world, and from it too we can see why he attracted both initial support and incomprehension as his brief public career developed. The Gospel narratives already indicate that there are fundamental ambiguities in his life, actions and words, making him an elusive and paradoxical character. We believe that our idea of category-transcendence illuminates how these ambiguities came about. The Gospels present us with the many faces of Christ: (Smart, 1979, pp. 201–217) and yet none of the pen portraits is entirely adequate to characterizing his career. Some of the titles and epithets ascribed to him overlap with our prior phenomenological discussion, but our exposition here is directed to the immediate historical circumstances and the understanding of the ideas likely to be present during his time. At various times he is pictured in the Gospels as prophet, holy man, rabbi, preacher, itinerant healer and exorcist, the Son of Man, Messiah, beloved Son (of the heavenly Father) and suffering servant. Jesus exemplifies aspects of all these, and yet creatively transcends the conventional meaning associated with these important categories. The result was that people were often baffled by his words and personality.

262

There was a mysterious and forceful quality about him which accounted both for people's loyalty towards him and their misunderstanding about his teachings and the meaning of his actions. This ultimately brought about the alienation of a large coalition of enemies.

It is important to note here the relevant concepts, like others in the religious and social field, have ritual and behavioral aspects, in that given the classifications implied, appropriate behavior may be generated. These classifications often have a strong emotional charge. Those individuals who belong somehow to betwixt and between categories, whether politically, religiously, ethnically, socially or sexually are often regarded both as powerful and as dangerous. They can often be treated with hostility. In the case of Jesus, we argue that Jesus transcended the relevant categories, and so transcended the rules and ritual concepts of his historical period in which he lived. This brought him into that dangerous betwixt and between territory through which both the divine and the threat may be perceived. He thus exhibited a dangerous ambiguity, which helps, as we have said, to explain how it was that his contemporaries in some degree turned against him, and even his disciples displayed a marked lack of comprehension of the ultimate meaning of his career.

Jesus, like John the baptizer, was hailed as a prophet (significantly, as contemporary "othodoxy" held that prophecy had ceased with Daniel in the first part of the 3rd century B.C.E.). Like John and the older *nabī* Jesus was a charismatic figure filled with the power of the spirit of God and he criticized social injustice. However, unlike these other figures, Jesus was not simply someone who transmitted the words of God. By claiming authority beyond this, e.g. to forgive sins, Jesus transcended the role of prophet, and in this way was regarded by many as blasphemous. He was also accused of operating on behalf of the Evil One. So though in some respects he was a prophetic figure he was disconcerting in his apparent claim to originate somehow in his own person divine teaching and powers.

He also preached and taught in synagogues and outdoors to small gatherings. Though he was accorded the title of

263

Rabbi this may have been more in recognition of his charismatic authority than in virtue of any formal training as an interpreter of the Torah. He was critical indeed of such people (scribes). His interpretation of the tradition was fresh, and he used stories drawn from everyday life and from nature in order to impart a fresh vision of life to people, and a new picture of the nature of God. There was it seems little systematic exposition in his teaching such as would have characterized scribal work, but instead he presented parables and comparisons which had the power to arouse his hearers. Often they seem to have been designed to shake folk out of their performed categories so that the freshness of his vision could break through. This vision had above all to do with God's loving will, but it was connected to a radical appraisal of the state of social life in his time.

Jesus' dangerous ambiguity is brought out perhaps most strikingly in regard to his relations with the Pharisees. As modern scholarship has shown there were in many close affinities between some of his attitudes and the teaching of the Pharisees. He can plausibly be seen as a Pharisee of the "liberal" school of Hillel, as opposed to the more conservative school of Shammai. The latter opposed proselytism, among other things. It is a view of Jesus' position which has found favor with some Orthodox Jewish scholars in recent times, notably by Harvey Falk in his recent (1985) study. Falk sees Jesus as a pious orthodox Jew of the time whose chief critique was directed at the conservative wing. Falk's work deserves consideration in part because he indicates how by concentrating on one aspect of Jesus' life and teaching (or on one of the "faces of Christ") it is possible for Orthodox Jews to see Jesus as a faithful follower of the Torah and so in a very positive light. For the liberal Jewish view we may cite the parallel treatment by Gregory Vermes in *Jesus the Jew* (1974). There seems to be little doubt that Jesus respected the Torah in its essential substance and indeed saw himself as fulfilling it. In form if not necessarily in detail Jesus shared certain themes with the Pharisees such as belief in eschatology, angels and the resurrection of the dead. Such themes were of course carried over into Christianity. If Jesus criticized the Pharisees often rather sharply this can be accounted for by his affinity to them. Stalin criticized Trotsky more vehemently than he criticized Mussolini, and there are greater bitternesses between Social Democrats and Labour than between either and their Conservative opponents. Often the strongest critique is reserved for one's "alienated brothers and sisters". It may also of course have been the case that the Gospels exaggerated Jesus' critique of the Pharisees, partly in order to differentiate out the new sect from its Jewish counterparts. For we must remember that only gradually did Christianity crystallize into a genuinely separate religion: in the early days, when things were much more fluid, the Jesus faith operated as a new religious movement within the Jewish ambience, but with an open and growing presence in the Gentile world.

From the Pharisees' point of view and later that of Judaism as it formed itself during the Rabbinic era, there were incompatibilities between his message and that of the tradition they sought to maintain and form. Jesus' attitude to the tradition was ambivalent. Despite his claim that he was fulfilling the law in detail he seems to have rejected parts of it as interpreted by his contemporaries among the Pharisees: e.g. dietary laws. He did not take to a rigid view of the oral Torah (and we may note that other groups ranging from the orthodox Sadducees to the non-orthodox Samaritans did not accept the oral Torah). He attacked the Pharisees for replacing the word of God with the traditions of men, rendering it null and void: and in this he quoted the prophet Isaiah (29:13). His emphasis on God's universal and boundless love and mercy towards bad folk such as taxgatherers and prostitutes, because of their sincerity and lack of pride, squared ill with the more exclusive aspects of Pharisaic observance. His revolutionary notion that such sinners would enter the Kingdom before the proud virtuous conformists set him at a distance from the others. His message could not be held within a legal framework: but this did not mean that Jesus was not proud of his Jewish heritage and aware of the importance of the law in preserving it. (But he came from Galilee, itself an ambiguous region for the orthodox.)

As Guenther Bornkamm points out, for Jesus the Torah and its complex casuistry were not the sole and authoritative mediating framework of human beings' right relationship to the Divine. People are close to God through receiving his grace and forgiveness, as a number of parables, notably that of the Prodigal Son, clearly indicate (Bornkamm, 1974). There is here, by the way, no tension between the Jesus of the Gospels and Paul. This point is well brought out by Joachim Jeremias in his *The Central Conception of the New Testament* (1963); at the center is the fatherly rule of God, and in ethics the Golden Rule as the essence of the law. Jesus' attitudes could seem two-faced. While respecting the Law he also infringed it – e.g. healing on the Sabbath; and he was indifferent to barriers between human beings even if given ritual sanction – so he could have easy relations with people of all types, even outcasts. So some at least of his contemporaries could see his actions as dangerously antinomian. So both Pharisees and the followers of the Baptizer could point critically to many things – he enjoyed wedding feasts and parties, the conversation of women, the company of taxgatherers and other kinds of "sinners". He was no less threatening to the Sadducees. The tradition of his prophesying the destruction of the Temple is testimony to this, and his action in clearing out the Temple courtyard of moneychangers, etc., had ominous implications.

Another group of his time was the Zealots. S.G.F. Brandon's 1967 attempt to characterize Jesus as close to the Zealots is not convincing. At least ideologically he was not with them. Though it is true that he may have shared some of the emotional intensity of the Zealots and may like them have deplored the sad state of the Jewish people, he did not, it seems, believe in armed resistance, and his famous remark about rendering unto Caesar the things that are Caesar's could be seen as his acquiescence in the Roman rule of Palestine. But his messianic status, ascribed to him by himself and his followers (it seems) could arouse expectations, according to the conventional understanding of the concept of the "Anointed One", of a violent upheaval against Rome. It is not surprising if one or two of his disciples were themselves Zealots.

As for the Essenes and the ascetic Qumran community, Jesus did not endorse their teaching about an apocalyptic ending to the present age. Nor did he limit entry into the kingdom to a minority of selected pious folk. But there were some formal overlaps of ritual themes – for instance in the case of the proto-Christians these occurred within an entirely distinctive web of meanings. Jesus' role, for instance, differs from that of the Teacher of Righteousness of the Qumran group.

This brings us to the important and emotively laden topic of the titles of Jesus. We shall argue that they well illustrate our concept of Jesus' category-transcendence.

The Titles of Jesus

We have to relate these to the central message of Jesus' teaching about the kingship and reign of God. The breaking into human life and history of the divine wondrous royal power had both a future and a present aspect: the new age of the kingship of God was already dawning in the middle of Jesus' career (Luke 17:20–21), but it would later be consummated in its fullness at the end of time. It seems that Jesus rejected speculation about dates and times, and this is consistent with the interpretation that his view of eschatology was one in which process is important: the future age is continuously in the process of realizing itself. Though he may have used some of the language of John the Baptizer, he rejected the strict and more literal interpretation of John, that the new era was about to come about in the literally near future (though there was a sense of course in which the kingdom was nigh, for it began with Jesus' own career and death, together with the subsequent glorious events of the resurrection and the coming of the Spirit). He also did not go along with common messianic hopes in a political restoration of Israel free from Roman domination (in other words he rejected the Zealot program). This indicated that some scholars, notably Albert Schweitzer and

Norman Perrin, have been wrong in thinking of Jesus' preaching as eschatological in a straightforward and literal manner, and thus that Jesus was just wrong about his predictions of an imminent end to the present order. We consider also therefore that Schweitzer was wrong in holding that Jesus taught just an "interim ethics" in the Beatitudes. Rather for Jesus, the Heavenly Father's universal, holy, loving will is everywhere normative and at all times: and it receives its key expression in the embodied life of Jesus himself (Bornkamm, 1977). This love demands in reciprocity the holiness and uprightness of character expressed in the Beatitudes.

Although the coming of the kingdom is referred to in the Gospels within a temporal framework, it has so to speak a "spatial" side to it, as brought out by the metaphor of "entering" the kingdom. It is as it were a realm, or a territory: and the metaphor here can be explained by seeing the dynamic power of the kingdom in the immanence of the divine life of the Trinity. This unifying power of love draws men and women into a new community in which they are related to one another as it were in a family, as sons and daughters of the loving heavenly Father. Jesus' teachings on becoming fit for the kingdom involve the love and forgiveness of one's enemies, and such an attitude shows that one is indeed an offspring of the Father. This is also expressed in his prayer: "Your kingdom come, your will be done, on earth as it is in heaven." This means that the social life style of the divine reality is to be experienced in the new community. So the kingdom to be entered is the life of participation in the divine life. It is at hand, this kingdom, because Christ is the one who bridges earthly and heavenly life, and through the events in and beyond his earthly embodiment.

We turn now to the question of the crucial titles applied to Jesus, "Son of Man" and "Messiah". He failed to fit current meanings attached to these terms. The idea of the Son of Man referred to an idealized man who concentrated in himself divine power, and who would appear at the end of history and judge the wicked and rule over the upright (as in Daniel, 1:13 ff.). Jesus utilized this mysterious title for himself, it seems; but it is clear, given his teachings about the kingdom sketched above, that he did not understand the title in the normal apocalyptic way. Nor likewise did he understand himself as the Messiah or deliverer in the political sense, that is that as "son of David" he would actually restore the kingdom of Israel. He was not so to say a Zionist of his times. Rather in our view his creative achievement was that he brought about a new constellation of ideas in which these concepts of Messiah and Son of Man underwent a radical change. He effected a fusion of the notions of the Son of Man, as being a representative and concentrated form of humanity, with that of the Suffering Servant drawn from Isaiah, which many of course interpreted to refer to Israel, but which now pointed to an individual. So thus was effected an identification of idealized humanity with his own person and with his suffering to come. He in this way used old categories but with a new meaning (Smart, 1979, pp. 210–212).

We do not by the way need to suppose that he had as clear a view of what he meant as later Christians might have, seeing events in retrospect. His understanding was doubtless in large measure intuitive, and shot through with powerful images the implications of which he did not fully comprehend, for they lay in the future. But his apprehension in experience of the divine fatherly love and of the power of the spirit working within him gave him the necessary materials to interpret his life in a novel and creative way according to the categories of his times, yet developing these in ways which transcended their older meanings.

All this sheds light on the problem of the "messianic secret", as it comes out in Mark's Gospel. From our perspective, we would argue that it was not the case that Jesus wanted his messiahship to be kept a secret not to be whispered abroad: as though he were literally a Messiah and he did not yet want his followers to let the cat out of the bag. Rather it was that they had to see that he played (in terms of the concepts available then) a transmessianic role in his work as the deliverer. We see that he perceived himself as a king, but in a new key, in the description of his entering into Jerusalem on an ass, in conscious fulfillment of the prophecy of Zechariah (9:9). This indicates that he felt himself to be a royal messiah who would establish a universal kingdom: but it was to be a novel sort of kingdom "not of this world". It was transworldly because he would give those who followed him participation in the heavenly life of the Divine. So in his life and acts Jesus succeeded in transforming current understandings of the meaning of the messiahship. He worked out a new creative synthesis which brought together various images, both of the king and messiah and of the Son of Man and suffering servant.

All this imparted to the faith which had its trajectory from out of his life a dynamic universalism and a revolutionary reinterpretation of the Jewish tradition and its key concepts. His kingship is well symbolized in the crown of thorns. It is paradoxical. Victory was achieved through the path of defeat. The overcoming of the forces of oppression, of sin, death and ignorance, was accomplished not by triumphalism, but by a man riding on an ass who would end up dying a criminal's death.

Though Jesus' followers after his death continued for the most part to continue to practice Jewish ritual in a pious and orthodox way, it was not long before it came to be seen that the whole system of the temple cult was rendered obsolete, since Christ himself could be seen as both priest and victim. But note here an analogous phenomenon: these concepts of priest and victim are thus given entirely new meaning, but based in a sense on the old.

Finally we may note that in the concept of the kingdom Jesus goes beyond the confining of this idea to the restoration of Israel itself. The new order in principle embraces the whole of humanity, in which people receive new identities by sharing in the divine life. So he transcends ethnicity. The face of Jesus as messiah is particular in being Jewish, but his gaze is universal and as the Church came to see it he looks to all human beings to draw them into his boundless love.

We may note that category-transcendence means that from

a Christian perspective it does not matter that Jesus did not fulfill all of the traditional conceptions concerning the Messiah. It also means that we should not be content simply to settle down with an external understanding of Christian doctrine. Nor should we conclude that because Jesus imparted novelty and a fresh dynamic to his Jewish heritage we can criticize Jews who do not see it this way, but cling to the developments of mainstream Judaism. The very fact that Jesus transcended both in his teaching and in his own person the categories of his time meant that he was necessarily somewhat opaque to his contemporaries. But the creative power of his new synthesis imparted a numinous, mysterious quality to the words and life of Jesus. In so far as he transcended the conceptions of his contemporaries we may think of him as "transmessianic" and "transprophetic", etc. He is not alone among leaders in being "beyond" the thoughts of their time: but it helps us to understand one dimension at least of the so-called "messianic secret".

The Atonement (Smart, 1958, 1960)

In this section we move on to a consideration of the logic of the avatar strand: here we explore the reasons interwoven in a whole web of religious concepts, including holiness, purity, sin, guilt, sacrifice, expiation and grace. These are central ideas in a number of major religions. They also have a use in "ordinary" life, that is in interpersonal transactions. In order to understand the idea of Jesus' work as suffering servant we need to think through the logic of sacrifice.

Most basically a sacrifice is an act, which is a concrete symbolic gesture in which human beings offer something of value to the Divine Being, in order to maintain or to restore a right relationship between themselves and God. In the Hebrew Bible sacrifices are not something which God needs, but they are a means which he graciously provides for maintaining or re-opening benign communication. This keeps lines open between himself and his people. There are a number of differing types of sacrifice in the Old Testament, and we shall concentrate upon those which are specifically aimed at overcoming alienation.

Such alienation is brought out by the fact that when confronted with the numinous purity of the divine love and uprightness (moral holiness) human beings can scarcely consider themselves to be other than unholy. That is: the sense of sin is the obverse of the perception of supreme holiness. This feeling is greatly strengthened when they come to see that moral defects are an offense against God, and that they are full of evil, immoral, and therefore alienating tendencies. When a person feels his sinfulness he feels it is imperative that he should do something about it. She ought to make up for her sins.

Let us flesh this out with an everyday example. When we offend or wrong someone, say a friend, then we feel that we need to perform an act which is an appropriate gesture which will make things right again between us. It will restore friendly relations, assuming it is recognized in the spirit in which it is meant, by the other party. The gesture is an outward expression of our inner feelings of sorrow and contrition for what we have done, and of the desire to "make up for" our wrong and so amend the broken relationship. Words are often thought not to be enough: they are "too easy", and humans have a considerable gift at insincerity. A concrete gesture, then, is needed. Thus to make amends means to right a wrong and adjust a personal situation which has gone amiss or astray. The same conditions apply in the religious case, although here a specific type of gesture and terminology apply. The sinful state of human beings and the acts which flow from this have the negative effect of alienating or separating them from their Source. This disrupts the flow of lifegiving communication and power which emanates from the Divine, upon whom the deepest welfare of humans depends. In the Hebrew Bible people's sins are conceived as pollution and infection which defile and corrupt, and later as personal guilt which deserves punishment.

This brings us to the important concept of expiation which we must spend some time on. It is of the same root as the Latin *pius*. *Piare* means to purify with sacred rites. The words connect up with the various concepts of God's holiness and purity and with the two senses of sin mentioned above. Expiation is the act or gesture through which humans seek to make amends for their sinful or impure acts. Specifically it refers to the means by which atonement (at-one-ment) between God and humans is effected. This brings us to our three principles:

(1) Humans' sin needs expiating;

(2) Sin is expiated by sacrifice: people's sins need to be purified, cleansed, washed away, wiped out or covered by a concrete gesture. This brings us to our third principle.

(3) Repentance and expiation go together. Without a gesture which concretely expresses one's sorrow and contrition and a sincere desire for renewed communion with God, repentance is just cheap. This is where the necessity for concreteness in the gesture is vital. Such a gesture can be of a number of kinds – ritual offerings, penance, fasting, prayer, performing spiritual and physical acts of mercy, etc. Though the sacrifices of the heart are broken and contrite spirit, as Isaiah declares, this means that such attitudes must accompany the outward gesture. The inner and the outer go together: this is the nature of true *li*.

Ritual offering or sacrifice involves the idea of giving up something of value. It must, that is, be of value to the person or group who makes the sacrifice or on whose behalf the sacrifice is performed. The sacrifice typically may include the physical destruction of something, as in the killing of animals in the Jewish Temple sacrifices. Here the gesture has strong symbolic value in that blood, which was perceived as the life-principle, was poured out as an offering. It is also a purifying substance which washes away sins. The shedding of blood signifies the costliness and seriousness of the offenses committed. The sacrificer also has to have the requisite inner attitude, as we have stressed: and in response God will be pleased; and friendly communication will be reestablished. In the ancient Jewish sacrifice of the "sin-offering" people guilty of certain sins would lay their hands on an unblemished sacrificial animal. This would effect an identification of themselves with the animal, making it their representative but not as Raymond Firth (1974) well emphasizes, their substitute: their sins are not transferred to it. The animal was then killed and its blood was poured on the altar by a priest. The sacrifice was not undertaken to appease God's wrath but to deal with sin and to reestablish lines of communication with the Divine. These ideas of blood sacrifice came to be transcended in the Christian tradition in the sense that Jesus' death was seen by analogy with such a sacrifice. By a certain irony the whole system within the ongoing Jewish tradition was also transcended, since on the one hand the destruction of the Temple meant their literal cessation; and on the other hand the meaning of such sacrifices was kept alive in paper and ink (so to speak) in the commentarial literature. If anything the Christian Church was more literal in its understanding of sacrifice (the blood of Jesus). But really Jesus' death though modeled as a sacrifice was not strictly one in the old sense. He was not killed by a priest and his blood poured out on an altar. But is was a meaningful transcendence of the older conception to see his death as sacrificial. The Eucharist with its transformation of wine into the blood of Christ has also of course been looked on, again by analogy, as a form of sacrifice.

Avatar and Atonement

We now come to the"logic" of the divine embodiment – at least as seen in the context of atonement and salvation. Why did God "send" an avatar? Given the immense gulf fixed between the supreme majesty of the Divine and the sinfulness and unholiness of humankind, none of the previous sacrifices is effective in restoring an unbroken unity between God and humanity. Human beings need the light of and vision of the One to give them the hope of liberating themselves from the welter of sin and mess in which they characteristically discover themselves. Can they of their own efforts rise above their confused struggle? Even in the case of Theravada Buddhism where the prescription of self-help is given in some detail by the Buddha men and women yet need the Buddha himself to pierce downwards from heaven to lighten their lives. For the Christian who sees the Light as itself the Source of all being the gulf between the Transcendent and herself yawns even more vastly than the distance which separates the Theravadin quester from nirvana. We are mired in our own defects, which show up the more starkly because we have before us the vision of the Light. Both from an empirical and from a spiritual point of view human beings are embroiled in defective motivation to achieve perfection on their own. Original sin, as we thus understand it, as a condition or ontological state, is an inevitable and universal characteristic of the human race (see chapter 9). But it should not simply be viewed as a moral condition. It is perceived by contrast with the holiness of the Brahman: but such holiness, though it includes moral attributes (so far as they can meaningfully be extrapolated and applied to God), is more than moral perfection. It has the light, the purity, the fascination of the numinous. It draws the aspiring faithful to it. It presents a new glory beyond the glories of the world. It beckons us to adoration and to action. It is there, and to it we reach out. It is the Everest of the spiritual life. But we can never climb up of our own accord and grasp it. It has to come to us.

But this leads to the following dilemma (and upon this dilemma rests the paradox of Christ's both-human-and-divine nature). On the one hand humans feels the need to expiate their sins, to cleanse themselves from the mire of confusions and bad choices that are part of the very fabric of everyday life. On the other hand, no concrete gesture by humans is adequate to the task: only the Holy can impart holiness. It cannot be gotten by magic; it cannot be extorted by merely human effort. It cannot be found in holy water, or pilgrimages, or self-abnegation; or by tantric means, or by worldly success. It cannot be grasped by the proud outreach of magnificent humanity. Only the Holy can create holiness. Only God has the inherent power to save. This is the essence of all monotheism: nothing divine outside the Divine, save by reflection of the divine Light. The source of all utter goodness must lie in God. We may then put our paradox thus: only God can save: only humanity can expiate. Only the God-human can achieve both together.

This is part of the central logic of Christology and why the Christian tradition on the whole found itself compelled to reject docetism as weakening the humanity of God and unitarianism as abolishing the Divinity of Jesus.

Of course a further step is needed. What is Jesus, the God-human, to us? First, he stands as a kind of representative of the human race as a whole. He concentrates in his own person the identity of human kind as a whole. But second the Christian binds himself to Christ, through the sacramental participation by baptism and the liturgy in the life of Christ himself. The goodness of salvation seeps deep down the branches and tendrils of the vine to invigorate the life of every Christian.

By becoming holy human beings will resemble God more. They can in principle become deified: thus the gap between humans and the focus of worship is diminished and overcome. But this is not something which humans can achieve on their own. Though they need to express contrition for their condition, and so expiate their sin, only God can save. So we can say concisely: only humans can expiate, and only God can save. The double act is achieved by the God-human who as the ideal representative of the human race sacrifices himself, and establishes full communication between the Divine and the human race.

In addition to the qualities which we mentioned earlier as belonging to the holy person (mysteriousness, purity, other-worldliness and moral power) Jesus as a candidate for divinity must exhibit two other qualities, namely sinlessness (a limiting case of purity) and the power to save. By the first we mean that he was able to reflect his Father's holy will through love, moral goodness and a sense of justice. We do not wish to imply that Jesus lacked all human weakness; but rather we affirm that in the crucial matter of his teaching and leadership his purity of character and depth or insight gave him the creative power to institute new ideas and challenging teachings. His power to save flows from his divine identity, but from the human perspective it is seen in the direct manner in which he gave himself in self-sacrifice to liberate people from their spiritual alienation.

Although as we have argued there is logic in the notion of the Incarnation from a different perspective, in that the Creator should be willing to experience the sufferings that are the inevitable accompaniment of the sunlit joys of the world, the primary logic of the Jesus avatar is the doctrine of salvation as herein explicated. We should notice that so many diverse sides of the Christian life intersect here: the sacramental sharing in the saving work and life of Christ; Jesus as perceived to be moral exemplar; the experience of devotion which implies the Otherness of God, and of mystical communion which implies togetherness. These and other motifs are woven together in this powerful vision of Christ's death as a kind of sacrifice. It transcended older concepts of sacrifice and it went beyond most interpretations of Jewish life. But it made a lot of sense in the Hellenistic world and beyond. It saw Jesus, category-transcendence in a new light. It deified humanity but remained realistic about sin and confusion. It promised a new vision of monotheism, since Christ's divinity as perceived on earth through the doctrine of salvation was the heavenly first step to the full formation of the idea of God as a social Trinity, whose agapeistic life could be imitated and shared on earth in the growing community. For all these reasons, the new vision was a potent synthesis and it reaches down to us today as explaining how we may reach towards the Light of Brahman through its avatar Christ. Incidentally, because Jesus is here seen as the representative of the human race as a whole he cannot as avatar be multiplied on earth (what we say about life in other worlds has to be found later). Our doctrine of the logic of the avatar strand implies a rejection in effect of the many incarnations of the Hindu tradition. But we do not of course reject the reality of the *bhakti* mode of religion, which lies at the heart of Christianity too, as we seek in warm devotion to echo the divine Love. Nor do we reject the impulses lying behind Hindu avatar religion, to see reflected in earthly life the restorative power of the Divine. If we look to Jesus as saviour it is in part because of the unique example of the Jewish tradition out of which he came. For those times the powerful drive to monotheism was an essential move if the human race was to share in the truth. It may be that the synthetic convergent drive of Hinduism in more recent times is something important for our times. The unity of humanity and the unity of God meet in the unity of the God-human.

Atonement and the Images of Christ

We can now relate these points to our previous discussions in this chapter of Jesus' roles. Through his fusion of the images of the Son of Man and the suffering servant he functions as the ideal representative of the human race. The suffering servant is no longer the people of Israel but the single individual who yet reaches out to humanity at large. As Son of Man he concentrates in himself the ideal essence of the human race. Jesus' act of expiation on the Cross is thus a communal gesture in which he voluntarily accepts responsibility for the sins and infirmities of the human race, considered as a group who have a sense of solidarity. Jesus' own intimate experience of his loving Father may have given him a strong sense of how in another sense God is responsible for human sin. For though up to a point human participation in evil is voluntary it is also something which emerges out of the haze of feeling and the clouds of ignorance surrounding the first human evolutionary stages. Our school is the cosmos and the cosmos conceals God. It hides as well as displaying the Light. So in the first stages of human history, beyond the earliest ken however of historians, human beings set the pattern of mess which they handed on to their successors. Even now the moral sensitivity of the human race is not so great. And so in part what we call original sin is simply a consequence of creation and of the pattern of the cosmos into which we as human beings have been projected. This being so then however much God may have striven to create free beings she still has some responsibility for the moral unholiness of the human race. So it is not unjust for Jesus himself in his death as a representative of both human and divine dimensions of existence to accept responsibility for human alienation.

His self-sacrifice fulfills the idea of the Jewish expiatory sacrifice as follows: by analogy with the unblemished and innocent animal. Early Christian literature therefore represented him as being spotless or sinless. Of course he was as a human being plunged into the confusions of this world. But he could be seen as sinless in that his actions were singularly appropriate to his moral and historical circumstances (here we draw on one sense of "perfection" as being "complete appropriateness of characteristics to relevant circumstances" – the perfect fit). The analogy with expiatory sacrifice also implies a crucial distinction which we shall be returning to later: that his death was on behalf of others but not in place of them.

From the Christian perspective the sacrifice of Jesus is superior to prior sacrificial practices and ideals in the framework of Judaism. First it is a voluntary act of expiation. It is neither a case of the scapegoat nor of some sacrifice demanded by (and expressive of) God's numinous wrath. The bloodiness of such a rite may be an impressive way of saluting the power of God, but the disappearance of blood sacrifices, though not of the idea of sacrifice, may be deemed to be an improvement in the sensibility of the human race. There is no question of the scapegoat meaning, because it is God himself who voluntarily suffers humiliation and death. This willingness to die is permanently imprinted in the consciousness of the Trinity. Second, the sacrifice is looked on by Christians as perfect and complete in being effective for all human beings. Its healing and spiritual power is seen to be available down the ages through the sacrament of the Eucharist. Christ is viewed too as both priest and victim: so once again there is no question of this not being a voluntary act. To some of course when viewing the matter externally and without true inwardness of comprehension, it looks like human sacrifice. But there is a world of difference between the killing of a human captured and restrained for the purpose and the free stepping towards death which Jesus had a premonition of when he set out on his last journey to Jerusalem. There is a heroism about Jesus' death which also found its parallel in many of the martyrs whose blood has irrigated the seeds of spiritual life in the history of the Christian communities through history.

In short, on our view there can only be one adequate sacrifice and that is by the death of the God-human. As we have said more than once it is most natural that Brahman should seek entrance to the created world, to undergo it sorrows as well as some of its joys. Nothing less than a violent death would no doubt fully convey to the divine consciousness the penalty of those who live dangerously in his beautiful but tragic cosmos. It so happens that within the framework of the phenomenology of sacrifice and in the particular historical circumstances of his chosen instrument the Jewish people, his death could be marked as fully atoning for the mess and evil of human life. The differing motifs of the divine avatar here work together and provide not only a powerful theme of life in the Christian community but also a haunting symbol which has seemed to illuminate life for so many Christians.

As Juergen Moltmann (1981) stresses, the other members of the Trinity also suffer in the atonement. The pains of the Son and his death deprive the Father of his joys of fatherhood. The Spirit as the bond of love feels the desolation of the Cross. The willingness to enter the world that God has created already presages suffering in the divine mind.

Atonement and Alternatives

We can see from the above account that the idea of expiation creates a difficulty for a unitarian faith. It is not then surprising that in Islam it is repeatedly stated that God is merciful. This is something which its adherents have to take on faith, since there is not the same concrete gesture that is there in the case of the Christian faith. This brings us to an important critique made for instance by Walter Kaufmann in his introduction to his translation of *I and Thou* by Martin Buber (Kaufmann, 1970, p. 37). He says that people need only to turn to God in repentance and faith and they will be forgiven. So Christ died in vain, as there is no need for such a sacrifice. But this critique is based on a number of notions which we might wish to take exception to. First, we must emphasize that the atonement transforms the human relation to God and not God's attitude to humans, for this is always one of reconciling and forgiving love. It is not a case Christ's sacrifice, or any sacrifice, changing the attitude of God from one of vengeful wrath to that of forgiveness, by some kind of appeasement. Second, our analysis of the idea of sacrifice was meant to demonstrate that acts of expiation and repentance inevitably go together. Can you show repentance of some dreadful deed without reaching out for some concrete way of making up for it? Given the gravity of sin and the great gap which yawns between the Holy and the unholiness of human life, none of the human gestures of expiation, save one, is sufficient to create the situation of atonement. We see the sacrifice of Christ as opening up the chance for all humans to become adopted sons of God, and in this there lies the true possibility of a holy-making process. Thirdly, and most importantly, Kaufmann, Hick and others seem to overlook the fact that without expiation there would only be a kind of easy forgiveness. This point is expressed in an enhanced manner by Reinhold Niebuhr who argues that given the uprightness and holiness of the Divine Being, the forgiveness of sin without expiation would mean that God condones our errors and evils, and this would be to trivialize both the depth of God's love and humanity's evil acts. Christ's death preserves the sense both of God's justice and of her love: we shall return to this point shortly. In turn the faithful Christian is united by the sacraments to Christ's death and so is willing in principle to make similar expiatory sacrifices and to suffer for others. In this he or she does not directly deal with sin, but taps into the atoning achievement of Christ's self-sacrifice. The notion of Atonement thus brings out the depth and seriousness of the divine drama. Kaufmann bypassed these points. We do not demand of course that these points should be perspicuous from the angle of the Jewish tradition. But we need to make them as plain as possible, for without an understanding of the doctrine, and myth, of the Atonement there can be no true appreciation of the nature and career of Christ. In all this we emphasize the suffering as well as the joy of God.

It is as if there is a dialectic within the divine Being. Being full of love and joy it desires to create. Love spills forth from it, and the creative power of God brings about the brief joys of birds, the purring of cats, the stealthy pleasures of the jaguar and the fox. It brings about a wondrous coloured world and the amazing talents of the human race. It spins forth galaxies. But in doing all this the creative power sees the death and suffering that finite life comprises. Who could doubt that it is better for it to exist than for it to stay there unrealised in the smug depths of nothingness? Even the sad suicide who can glimpse the light from above might not wish oblivion on the whole world. It is not for men to crush the juices out of the living world. But this creative urge of the divine Love, in perceiving suffering, has to accept it. God has to be willing to suffer too. And this pain and death is imprinted for ever and from always upon the divine Consciousness. so from the very beginning the joy of God was modified. The love had this shadow upon it. So perfect love called forth creation: creation called forth God's self-sacrifice: the sacrifice called forth suffering in God from always: so perfect love was always flecked with pain. Maybe that is how perfect love has to be: namely imperfect. And perfect joy has to have its shadow: it too in its perfection has its imperfection.

From all this it is clear that we absolutely reject the Neo-platonic and Scholastic idea that God is impassible and so cannot suffer. If God cannot suffer then she cannot truly love. In our view, the divine Consciousness is such that it does not "break" under suffering. It can absorb suffering without becoming disintegrated. There are noble humans who have this power too, but not absolutely. You can meet people who have suffered persecution in prison camps for instance, but emerge from their trials without bitterness. They remain integrated human beings, with a kind of noble calm. They do not deny the pain of the past but they are not poisoned by it. But there are others whose spirits become embittered, who seek for vengeance, who cannot cope with the joys of life which are always hidden by remembered shadows. Such a disintegration does not happen, we believe, in the divine consciousness. The passionate intensity of God's feeling-awareness enables the Trinity to experience the joys and sorrows of all their creatures. The Trinity lurks at the depth of every consciousness, both bright and dim. The suffering of humans is transfigured, moreover, in the divine awareness, for God sees that ultimately all human beings will be healed and eternally brought together within the divine life, by being incorporated into the Son. All of humanity will be funnelled through the life of the ideal human being, the Son of Man.

So the doctrine of the Atonement, as we have expounded it, reveals the boundless grace and mercy of Brahman as well as his love and saving justice. God opposes evil everywhere but is always seeking reconciliation. In these ways we have brought order to some of the hints and conceptions of Christian and Jewish scriptures.

Other Galaxies, Other Rational Persons

An issue has become more urgent today, in the light of the immense advances in scientific cosmology in the last sixty years or more. It is the question of life in other galaxies. It seems to us statistically probable that there will be rational persons elsewhere in the cosmos. It should not surprise us, given the rich proliferation of galaxies and the billions of stars which we see scattered in the sky and which lie too beyond our vision, but not beyond the subtle probings by which modern science can look outwards from out of our blue planet. If life arises naturally where the conditions favor it, such as places where there are reasonable temperature and water, then since it is likely that somewhere or other planets like ours are to be found, we might well conclude that there are other evolutions, other "humans" – persons at least as much made in the image of God as we are. If so, then what does this say about the uniqueness of Christ? Our opinion is that the Supreme Ultimate would descend to these other places too, to draw more self-conscious beings into the divine life and love. This may weaken our insistence on the uniqueness of Christ on our own planet. It might point to a cosmic scene rather like that depicted by the many avatars of Vishnu in the Hindu tradition. Maybe: but we think of each world as drawing towards a unity, and matching the monotheism of our tradition we see a unitary world in which the spirit of one Saviour would rule. If other galaxies and the places of life are ever locked theoretically from us, as may be, then there would be no interference of one Christ-field with another. These are interesting and in their own way important speculations.

The Atonement and the Substitution

The interpretation of Christ's atoning work which we have depicted is essentially a new way to present what is often seen as the "classic" view of the atonement. This view, brought out by Gustav Aulen in his own classic work *Christus Victor* (1931), sees the sacrificial death of Christ as a dramatic cosmic victory over the forces of sin and death. Jesus' expiatory death liberates human beings from the destructive forces which enslave and entangle them. This way of understanding Christ's work is clearly expressed in the New Testament and was the prevailing view of the early Eastern Fathers such as Irenaeus and Gregory of Nyssa (not to mention Origen). Though the New Testament writers and the Fathers thought of the destructive forces as supernatural and demonic, being "out there" under the leadership of Satan, we understand them to be the destructive powers within humans. They are truly demonic in that they derive from structures which can disintegrate the being and the human quality of people who willingly succumb to these dark powers. In our next chapter concerning the Holy Spirit, creativity and the daily life struggle we shall provide a phenomenological analysis of these powers. They reflect the structure of human existence, both individually and collectively.

In our presentation we have placed Christ's work as sacrificial victim within the context of Jewish sacrifices of the period and within the perspective of the Temple cult. Though we recognize that these ideas belonged, from the

Christian angle of vision, to the "Old Covenant", it is essential that we see Christ as operating within, and transcending, the historical and religious milieu which he occupied.

But we need carefully to distinguish our view from the "penal-substitution" theory of the Atonement. This view was presented both by Luther and Calvin and is the official position of most conservative-evangelical protestant organizations. It is usually espoused by so-called fundamentalist groups. On this view Christ's death is seen as a substitute for the punishment which the human race deserves. Thus, Calvin held that divine justice demands the death of the sinner, but Christ pays this penalty: the results of this are transferred or credited (so to speak) to our account. This is often called "vicarious atonement", since Christ suffers as a substitute, that is vicariously, for us. Of course the word "vicarious" could also imply something else, namely that Christ suffers for the benefit of others, and this would fit the meaning of atonement as we have presented it. However to avoid ambiguity we have not used the term. The key passage in Isaiah 53, 4-5, would fit either meaning, but the "substitution" sense is not supported by the New Testament, as we shall see. Supporters of this view fasten on the Greek term *hilasterion* which Paul uses in a key passage in Romans 3:25, which is understood by proponents of the interpretation as "propitiation" rather than "expiation" (which we find, by the way, in the New English Bible). The terms "propitiation" and "expiation" are definitely not interchangeable. To propitiate means to appease or conciliate another's anger and its application here leads to a perversion of the meaning of the atonement. On the substitutionary view Christ's death appeases God's anger and in effect purchases his favor.

The key passage (3:21–26) is as follows:

> But now, quite independently of law, God's justice has been brought to light. The Law and the prophets both bear witness to it: it is God's way of righting wrong, effective through faith in Christ for all who have such faith

– all, without distinction. For all alike have sinned, and are deprived of the divine splendor, and all are justified by God's free grace alone, through his act of liberation in the person of Christ Jesus. For God designed him to be the means of expiating sin by his sacrificial death, effective through faith. God meant by this to demonstrate his justice, because in his forbearance he had overlooked the sins of the past – to demonstrate his justice now in the present, showing that he is both himself just and justifies any man who puts his faith in Jesus.

In verse 25, Paul says that God the Father designed or put forth Christ publically as a *hilasterion*. *Hilasterion* is the word used in the Greek translation of the Old Testament (the septuagint) for the "mercy seat" in the Holy of holies with the Tabernacle or desert tent sanctuary and later in the Temple of Solomon (Leviticus 16:2, 11–17; Exodus 25:17; Kings 6). The mercy seat was a gold altar which was sprinkled with the blood of animals by Jewish priests on the day of Atonement (Yom Kippur) as a sacrifice to purify the sins of their people. C.H. Dodd's analysis (1931) has shown that in Biblical Greek the word is used to express (1) God's mercy and forgiveness and (2) the ritual purification (expiation) of sins which defile human beings and render them unfit for communion with the divine Being. Thus under the New Covenant, Christ, through his self-sacrifice, is both the agent of expiation (by his blood) and the locus where God's mercy and forgiveness become manifest for all humankind to see.

Verses 23 and 25 illustrate the need for expiation to uphold God's uprightness in forgiving sins. Given that the previous sacrifices were not sufficient to wipe out humans' sins and put them right with himself, God patiently tolerated this state of affairs without condoning it until the time (*kairos*) he set things right through his Son's sacrifice.

Further, Vincent Taylor's careful survey *The Atonement in New Testament Teaching* (1954) came to the conclusion that there is no sound basis for this interpretation in New Testament teaching, and not in particular in Paul's teaching.

We think, with John Macquarrie (Macquarrie, 1977) that the account is less than Christian, and involves a peculiar and outdated view of God's nature. With its juridical view it gives a distorted picture of divine justice, and often has the negative effect of alienating people. We think it is dangerous for Christians to ascribe punitive attitudes to God or they themselves will find endorsement for their own punitive actions. But though we oppose the tone and substance of this view we would be unchristian to assume that those who hold it necessarily fall into this unloving trap. Anyway it is useful for us to list some of our objections to the view, and we here take up some points which we made earlier.

(1) Christ's sacrificial death as the ideal representative of the human race was on behalf of others, for the benefit or welfare of human beings, not in place of them.

(2) His crucifixion was a sacrifice for the purification of sins in order to restore or create communication between God and humanity. Human beings' sins are not transferred to Christ. So to say that "Christ died for our sins" means that he died as a gift for our liberation and healing. The "for" does not mean somehow "in place of".

(3) Also, as we noted before in the "Old Covenant" sacrifices are not something God needs or demands, but rather they are seen as the means which he freely provides for re-establishing communion. We should note here that the whole point of the story of Abraham and the potential sacrifice of his son Isaac is the ram in the thicket.

(4) Lastly, the atonement does not change God's character or attitude, that is from anger to forgiveness. Rather, it expresses his suffering love.

Atonement and Satisfaction

Closely related to the theory of penal substitution is the "satisfaction theory" of St Anselm. This is the primary basis for Roman Catholic atonement doctrine. On this view, humanity's sinful disobedience casts a stain on God's honor. It is an injury of infinite proportions because of the infinite character of God's honor. To make up for this infinite offence there is needed a sacrifice of infinite merit. In so far as the theory is expressed in archaic medieval and feudal categories it is likely to seem outmoded. It implies something about God's attitudes which is open to objections which we have already cited, bears little relation to the Old Testament conceptions of purification of sin, nor to the notion of liberation of humanity and the healing of our condition of confusion and sin. But in so far as it implies that a divine sacrifice is needed (to be of infinite merit) it has an advantage over the penal-substitution theory. We must stress again and again that the understanding of Jesus' death is also the understanding of the death of God. This is the event which for us lights up the whole attitude of the Trinity and the nature of divine Love.

The Moral Influence Theory

Lastly there is the theory first propounded by Peter Abelard. On this view, Christ's death on the cross reveals God's self-sacrificing love which moves people to respond with repentance, gratitude, faith and love. Hence the atonement brings out people's need for divine forgiveness as well as the ever-present reality of God's loving disposition towards us. This view was espoused by Hasting Rashdall and other liberal Protestants, and is currently held by John Hick and by process theologians such as John Cobb and David Griffin. It fits in with Hick's version of adoptionism (Hick, 1973). Now of course we do not deny that part of the meaning of the cross is the nature of God's self-giving love. The moral lessons to be learnt here are most important, if we want to follow in the way of the Trinity. But by itself it does not seem an adequate theory. We have to connect up Christ's death with the Eucharist and the sense of power flowing into and through the community. But the moral theory seems to render the atonement as we have understood it superfluous. It is not of the essence of the faith. For God's moral self-sacrifice is not necessary as a means of inspiring a sense of wrongdoing and the desire to respond to the divine love. That already is there: Hick remarks that the fact that God participates in the sufferings of his creatures renders the Incarnation unnecessary. Moreover, if Jesus is just a mere exemplar then he can be put aside other exemplars – Socrates, the Buddha, Confucius and various others – hundreds or thousands of them if needed for inspiration. Now we do not think that it is wrong to be wide-ranging in choosing our models. Far from it: we are deeply committed to crosscultural faith and with it crosscultural ethics for the world community. Our ancestors and heroes should indeed range over all lands and times, if possible. But relying merely on moral example seems to destroy the very logic of the worship of God in Christ which has been of course a central and distinguishing characteristic of the Christian heritage. This is what we have tried to do in our exposition of the divinity of Christ. But without the need for reconciling atonement the divinity of Christ fades, and with the fading of Christ's divinity, there begins to disappear the Christian religion.

God himself needs to perform the act of opening up the lines of communication between humanity and the divine Trinity. And Christ's expiatory sacrifice is effective only because it is the divine-human flesh which underwent torture and humiliation on behalf of the human race. God is a *philanthropos*, lover of human beings in the deepest way.

The moral influence theory, moreover, fails to bring out the costliness of the reconciliation which the Lord brings about. It is only a suffering God who would feel confidence in the love which she expresses through creation.

Religions and the Avatāra

We shall focus in this section on the vital question of the implications for our vision of the divine embodiment for the presence of God and salvation in other religions. We shall give special attention to some views expressed on this topic by John Hick (Hick, 1982). He states that we ought to reject the traditional doctrine of divine embodiment because of the unacceptable implications it has. He states that it would follow from the doctrine of the incarnation that those who are not Christians are outside the sphere of *mokṣa* since the Christian way of liberation has been provided and appointed by God himself in person: it is this Christian claim which provides the substance and the imperative to try to convert all humankind to faith in Christ as each person's Lord and Savior. He thinks that this idea conflicts, however, with Jesus' own teaching that the Lord is the loving heavenly Father of all human beings; and that it would not be fair to have narrowly restricted the possibility of salvation to certain historical periods.

But we think that these inferences are wrongly drawn. Hick's conclusions are mistaken. We shall answer these objections and other points which Hick has raised. We do so by presenting our position as follows.

First, we do, with Hick, indeed reject the unkind over-confident conservative Protestant kind of view which holds that there is no salvation outside of explicit and conscious faith in Christ. Not only is such a position in conflict with God's nature as *agapē* and so is morally intolerable. We hold that furthermore it is empirically falsified. Our phenomenological typology of religious experience and of the ways of life bases upon the varieties of experience make it abundantly clear that we cannot exclude knowledge of the Divine in other faiths: and if there is knowledge there is implicitly liberation or salvation. The other world religions have apprehension of differing facets of the Trinity. Thus, firstly, the *bhakti* and prophetic traditions which focus on a Theos are related to the common divine I of the Trinity. How can we think of their forms of worship as not being acceptable to the *Īśvara*? All of these traditions one way or another have a notion, and an experience, of divine grace. As Reinhold Niebuhr pointed out, the creative consequences of an encounter with the true God are "the humility and charity of true repentance and the absence of pride and pretension". It is indeed a fact that many worshipers manifest these and other Christlike virtues even if they do not "belong" to the Christian tradition. Further even the non-theistic systems such as the Theravada have a knowledge of the Transcendent, for in our view they are in contact with an aspect of the infinity of the divine life, internally or externally apprehended. Such systems incorporate as central to the quest for liberation the aim of knowing the infinite. They derive from the pursuit of liberation lofty ethical and spiritual values that theists can embrace. (Huw Parri Owen, 1985, p. 143). Christians can learn from these examples. It is obvious that Theravada Buddhism nourishes in some people a peace, serenity and compassion that are deeper and more loving than the qualities found in the life of many Christians.

We draw from all this the conclusion that the transforming and saving power of divine grace is operative widely in other faiths. It is true that the atmosphere of such religions may be very different: thus in the Theravada there is no sense of being alienated from a personal Lord and holy God: and the theory is propounded that one can attain a kind of self-salvation. But such theoretical and theological judgments, though at variance with the vision which we here present, are not the only vital features of such non-theistic religions. Looked at more widely such religions can be seen to produce fruits which are signals of the transcendental contact which, on our view, is contact with the Trinity herself.

Though we accept Hick's judgment about salvation in other faiths, we do not endorse his objection that to sacrifice exclusivity about liberation is to sacrifice the substance of the identity claim concerning Christ. It is not an either/or situation. Christianity should, as vision and way of life, be an all-inclusive faith, containing the variety of types of religious experience and practical religion. The distinguishing features are not in this, but rather as follows.

Christians gain a sacramental mode of the knowledge of God through the embodiment of the divine: they have a sacramental life based on this through the new relationship metaphorically spoken of as being adopted children (Schmemann, 1973). The symbol of this is the Eucharist by which the faithful are incorporated into Christ's identity and into his cosmic body. Thus Christ's embodiment represents a special opportunity for those who call them-selves Christians, but it does not represent some kind of darkening disaster for those who do not call themselves Christians. The light that shines through the Eucharist does not blot out other lights. Moreover, while Christ's act of expiation for human sin is sufficient to purify the life of the whole of the human race it does not at all follow that those who experience the "eucharistic opportunity" and experience the Savior are automatically freed from their mired condition. What they find is new life and liberation from the guilt and state of their past errors and moral failures. Now is the time when the difficult climb of spiritual growth begins: and many Christians make little progress indeed. They do not go far in the transformation into the likeness of Christ, who as a selfless Spirit is completely self-giving and open to all. In the likeness of this divine outwardness the Christian surely is not called on to make belittling comments about the spiritual force of other traditions.

So it is, then, that many do not go far in the growing towards a truly divine likeness. Their awareness of being adopted into the life of the Three-in-One is dim and ineffectual. So while the process of being changed into divine likeness is distinctively sacramental in the Christian life (and is connected, obviously, with the historical Jesus) it is not automatic: it does not guarantee easier spiritual growth. This obvious fact about the Christian life means, again quite obviously, that the non-Theist and the non-Christian may in fact be closer to the divine reality than many who style themselves followers of Christ. It is also of course in this connection wise to remember that there are many Christianities and Buddhisms, and this is so in all dimensions: there are varieties of the faith not just from the point of view of the interpretation of doctrine or myth, but from the angle of ethics and experience. These diverse spiritualities occur within the fabric of the institutions of Christianity (or Buddhism, etc.). And so it is that there is a grave danger in neglecting the quality of life and thought in dealing with the mutual relations of religions. There are many Christians who have a distorted, anthropomorphic, pride-filled view of the faith. They are not the only ones who "write off" other faiths: but they represent a form of anti-world-religions attitude which we can well do without.

We shall now move on to the issue of fairness mentioned above. This of course is directly related to the scandal of particularity implicit in the Christian view of the divine embodiment. The scandal lies in the givenness that the Supreme Ultimate has acted in history and in particular through one person. (Or rather has acted most vitally through one person, because that person is identical with the Lord: there are of course millions through whom God has shown herself in history, since all history displays God's actions.) There is – it will be felt, quite naturally – a certain arbitrariness in the way God has acted through a "chosen" people and through a special person. But as we have pointed out before, action of this sort in history must be particular, or it would not be history, and so arbitrariness, where it exists, is not itself arbitrary, but inevitable. Thus wherever the divine embodiment occurred there would have been a scandal. (We could have thought: "How odd of God to choose Hindus": Smart, 1960). But we can see in retrospect that since in our view God is inherently personal as a Trinity of divine identities, the personal modality of revelation is understandable. Moreover, the Jewish background to Jesus' life was natural (to put it no more strongly) because of the positive view of history in that culture and belief in a loving God who is qualitatively distinct from the cosmos. Also, the attendant cluster of ideas in the Jewish religion – of sacrifice, sin, guilt, holiness, purity, reconciliation, and so on, provided an important conceptual framework within which to interpret Christ's earthly life and career. From the Christian perspective, the history of Israel provides the build-up for the full disclosure of the divine life: the experience and ethical insights of the prophetic tradition are vital ingredients in the resulting picture of God's saving activity. This view, by the way, does not imply that Brahman's self-disclosure was clear to all. We do not consider that any revelation can be transparent, and if many of the Jewish tradition went on to form a parallel form of religion to the Christian, that is natural: moreover later Jewish testimony is a witness to – among other things – another way of interpreting the virtues which God favors. Despite the nobilities of Buddhism, had Christ moved East, the revelatory doctrine would not have included certain accents, such as the importance of the historical process, and the idea of atonement, which are vital in the unfolding of God's message, as we see it.

If Hick considers this situation to be unfair, our reply is that he is inconsistent. He does not consider that all symbols or ikons mediate the divine Reality equally. Given that human religious consciousness evolves, as do other powers of insight, and given that we are at an epistemological distance from the divine Reality, the opportunities for a fully developed relationship to the Transcendent are necessarily limited. Human history must be uneven in its qualities of revelation. Not everyone comes into the world with equal access to any sacrament. Any idea of God has to be in some measure culture-bound. There are many resting places of course for the pilgrims on life's way, but there are also tracts of desert. Hick is asking for a kind of "justice" which is unimaginable.

Given the need to protect the autonomy of human and other creatures, the revelation must happen progressively and must conceal itself somewhat. It must show its face with ambiguity and gentleness, peeping as it were from behind the cloth of the ordinary. This is exactly what happens in the Christ avatar: the divine Lord appears incognito. Hick makes it seem as if it is patently obvious that Jesus reveals God's nature: but that is not at all clear to the majority of people living today; and this opaqueness has always been there. Does not such unclarity seem unjust? But it reserves to us freedom.

Rebirth and the Future Life

We can now go to the heart of the matter. We unequivocally state our conviction that there will be universal salvation ultimately: this is the *apokatastasis panton*. We agree with Hick that there are other levels of existence beyond death in which spiritual growth can take place. Hick develops this notion, which was put forth by the Eastern Church thinkers such as Origen and Gregory of Nyssa, in his masterly work *Death and Eternal Life* (1976). We reject the idea of a static and unchangingly eternal heaven and an eternal or

294

everlasting hell where there continued unredeemed suffering. Out of such pain no good could come (and the thought that anyone might take satisfaction in such a state, by contemplating it from the heights of sainthood or from the Creator's own throne, appears to us to be unChristian, to say the very least: inhuman, indeed, and undivine). Such a hell would frustrate God's overwhelming love. The denial of Christ is not an unpardonable sin, as certain conservative religionists seem to believe. There is no, however horrible, unpardonable sin in any case, because God is unsparing love. Purgatory yes: hell, no. Or as some argue there may be a hell, but it is empty.

On the other hand we are not convinced by the doctrine of rebirth in this world. It is attractive, but it has two problems attached. One is that it does not at all easily square with modern genetics. One would have to postulate some metaphysical force which homes a "soul" (or individual – on the Buddhist view) on to its biologically appropriate parents. There is no "third genetic force" of karma, so far as we can see. That is, we do not discover the genes of father and mother and some third force at work. Also there is the problem of how we can conceive of being reborn as animals, insects or ghosts. Second, though it seems in a way to deal with suffering and moral evil, the appearance is somewhat deceptive. If the cosmos depends upon God then karma becomes her means of punishing or rewarding people: so why not go straight to the divine will? Moreover, as some Indian metaphysicians have argued, karma as a moral force must have behind it a discriminating intelligence (namely God): and again, if so, then why postulate it as an intermediate force?

But the principle of rebirth is a good one in so far as it points to different levels and conditions of life. This idea enables us to deal with certain deep problems. First, it allows us to account somehow for the future of people whose levels of knowledge of the divine Reality differ so greatly, partly because of the vicissitudes of history and of the particularity of divine self-revelation. It is relevant too to the problem that so many people have suffered tragically in ways that have made it impossible for them to grow spiritually here on earth, either because of natural or moral cause. We suppose that there may be opportunities for happiness beyond death, and in the light of the divine Love.

The doctrine of many levels of existence (of "many mansions") also provides a vision of purgatorial purification for those who have been especially wicked in this life. Of course we have all been bad (and good) to a greater or lesser extent. But we substitute for the picture of total alienation in hell another one in which the *Īśvara*'s gracious love comes down to meet with and purify the selves of even the cruelest human being. Even Hitler and Stalin will feel the outpouring of the Lord's love.

Salvation and Social Trinitarianism

Universal *mokṣa* will on our view have as its focus the social Trinity. The liberated self will be assimilated to the loving relations of the divine Brahman. All will be adopted children of Christ, and will live within his organic body. To them the divine will be all in all. They will so to speak be enfolded in the glimmering light and wondrous music of the divine Love. Hick is not happy with such an account, for he complains (regarding the Trinity doctrine) that non-Christians do not possess full knowledge of the ultimate, even though in salvation they have turned from self-centered existence to Other-centered, i.e. Reality-centered, life. But such an unease is not justified for several reasons. First, we do not wish to put all accounts of Reality, compatible or otherwise, on a par. Second, many non-Christians are much closer to the Divine, in our view, than many Christians: our vision or *darśana* of reality has no implications on this front, beyond the modest one that the Christian has a greater opportunity of plucking the fruits from the Tree of Life. Third, we consider, for reasons advanced elsewhere, that the life of the Social Trinity can fulfill both non-personal and personal aspirations among adherents of other faiths.

In brief, if the divine is a Social Trinity then it is a Social Trinity which lies at the center of the world's religions. We of course admit that we do not have proof of this: this is merely our vision, to the articulation of which this book is devoted. But it is naive to suppose that all traditions and subtraditions have an equally valid (or invalid) version of the nature of the one Reality. It is our confessional obligation if we do hold to the Christian vision of Reality to testify to it, and to depict its shining glories for others. If they do not see this Reality, then so be it. Either we have a distinctively Christian (or Buddhist or whatever) vision or we give our faith away. It follows from our general position, however, that each faith must see hidden messages of its own Focus in all other faiths: the Buddha is hidden in the Christian life, as Christ is there, mostly unseen, in the path of the Buddha. The Social Trinity loves all living beings and all human beings in their striving for spiritual fulfillment. There is no need to confuse epistemological preference for any kind of exclusiveness.

On our view it is part of the divine plan that humankind has worked out its visions in a number of great religious traditions and powerful subtraditions, not to mention those lesser faiths which have sprung up within and outside of the ambit of the great civilizational blocs which have played so notable a part in human history. The plural character of the religions helps them to criticize and correct each other: to keep each other honest. Moreover it is only by looking in many different mirrors that the Christian faith can begin to see clearly her own physiognomy. The Christian can see not only new things in these other traditions, but can also come to a clearer understanding of the phenomenology of that cluster of subtraditions which she calls her own. Some of the values of the Christian tradition are embodied more perfectly in other traditions. Given the ugliness, fanaticism, confusion, racism and anti-Semitism which has blackened Christianity as an historical phenomenon, is it at all surprising that many people are alienated from it? As Christians we should therefore rejoice if the Holy Spirit in history has created other avenues of grace and other channels of salvation.

Christ and Mission

On our vision, faith in Christ, fruitfully pursued and nurtured in goodness, drives us inevitably on the upward path, and we would hope that God will sooner, rather than later, fold us to her bosom. Because of our universalism we do not see Christ's work as sending some to hell: we do not see this life as finally determining the way we shall find to reach the ultimate paradise. We hold that through the sustenance of the Christian sacraments we shall gain the strength and divine energy to move upwards. We do not, as we have just noted, deny that there is grace and divinity in other worldviews and in other patterns of life. Does this knock out justification for missionary endeavor?

The really only good motive for trying to convert another person or culture to your own is that you are sure that you have something excellent to confer on others – something which can be a gift and not a prideful imposition on other humans. We are all searchers for the truth which will make us free and fulfilled. The very act of searching leads us to see the plural character of human civilization. It leads us to perceive great alternative views, alternative, that is, to those of our own tradition. We cannot be objectively sure of doctrines, but we can be sure of the power of our own experiences and the fruits which faith can generate in us. So it is as imparting experience and goodness that we can offer ourselves and our faith as a gift to other beings.

It is this kind of gift which is the true content of mission. There is not contradiction, of course, between our eirenical and global view of the religions of humankind and the desire and need to testify to our own vision as a gift. But it does not mean that the Christian pearl has to displace that Buddhist diamond. There is no need for mission to destroy other cultural and religious traditions. So we see mission as gift and as presence: it does not deny that those among whom we are present necessarily lack power. They too have their channels to the Transcendent.

All this follows Christ, who plunged into a human world: it is in that multiple world that we swim also.

Reflecting finally on our treatment of creation, Christology and doctrine of God, we may characterize our position as being: universalist, social-Trinitarian panentheism.

9
Spirit and Psyche

The Trinity and Human Psychology.
In this chapter, we will focus on the presence and creative activity of the Holy Spirit as *antaryāmin* or Inner Controller within the lives of human beings and other living beings. As we have seen, the Trinity may be conceived of as having three bodies – the physical cosmos (the Father's created body), the Divine-Human organic body of Jesus (the Son), and individual human and other beings (the embodiment of the Holy Spirit). Vladimir Lossky brings out the point that individual persons are the modality of the Spirit's expression in a special way, in terms of revelation – the Heavenly Father is manifested in the face of the embodied Son, who in turn is revealed to people through the illumination of the Spirit. The Spirit, however, is not unveiled through another divine selfless spirit, but in the transformed lives and creativity of men and women (Lossky, 1957, pp. 160, 192–3). Much of the subject matter in this chapter comes under the framework of the Psychology of Religion; methodologically, we think that it is appropriate to cover this topic here, as it is the dynamic power of the Spirit which enables human beings to grow and mature spiritually and to realize their creative potentialities through freedom. Here, we will draw upon valuable insights concerning human nature and our existential situation from Christian theologians such as Paul Tillich, and Nikolai Berdyaev; as well as psychologists such as Maslow, Fromm, Jung, and Lowen; we will also draw upon the work of anthropologist Montague. Our discussion will focus on important topics such as the nature of humankind, the creative and destructive forces in human life, the human quest for maturity, salvation and healing, creativity,

freedom, values and the meaning of life. We hope that our presentation will bring out the real practical value of the Trinity doctrine for human existence.

We think that our systematic theology is one of the very few to pay attention to questions of healing and health, and to suggest approaches towards such societal problems as addiction, dependency and recovery. After all, nearly a third of the Gospels is devoted to healing. Moreover the meaning of the sacramental life of the Church relates to wholeness. We shall begin by presenting our view of human nature in order to bring out the needs human beings have for the salvation effected by Jesus and the Holy Spirit.

Genesis and Human Goodness

Our view of human nature derives from our interpretation of the existential import of the symbolic creation-myth in *Genesis*. We think that this pictorial creation-narrative expresses some important truths about life and human nature; these truths are presented by means of symbols and motifs derived from ancient Near Eastern culture and mythology. The sacred story tells that human beings are created in the image of the Divine Being, and that humanity's original nature is originally and essentially good. Further, it is only subsequently that humans become alienated from their Creator, themselves and one another by becoming narcissistic or egoistical and thereby hostile, defensive and disordered creatures in need of salvation. Here, we will develop our view of human goodness in terms of our Christian *darśana*. As expressed previously in chapter 7, we see the creation of self-conscious human beings through a process of emergent evolution as proceeding from the self-giving love (*agapé*) of the Trinity which desires them to share in the joy and bliss of the Divine Life forever. As the Trinity has created men and women as a reflection of its own androgynous nature and social life for communion with herself, it follows that men and women will realize spiritual wholeness and find fulfillment through loving interpersonal relationships and with God, within a harmonious universal community. The divine embodiment of the Son to liberate

301

us from our estrangement, the Holy Spirit's descent at Pentecost and the formation of the new community of *agapé* were the beginning of the realization of this desire. Within this context, men and women receive the divine energies (grace) and gifts (charisms) of the Spirit and can strive to fulfill their exhalted destiny of being co-creators with God by realizing their creative potential through spiritual freedom. Through creativity, humans bring into being new values and realities which enrich their lives and the Divine Life itself. As embodied self-conscious personal life or the life of the spirit, with the capacity for reason, creative imagination and novel action (freedom), humanity can transcend the limits of physical nature and produce culture and civilization. Being created in the image of God means that human beings are each unique, and possess unlimited worth and dignity in the eyes of the Creator who loves them with an unimaginable intensity; thus in our view, persons are children of God and centers of intrinsic value whom we should treat with reverential loving care and affirm their own sacredness. Also, as embodied spirits with psyche, humans are religious animals who are thus able to experience and respond to the Transcendent. We will now look at the biological evidence for human goodness.

Human Goodness – Biology
Biologically, human beings share the same innate urge to grow as plants and animals do. The urge to grow and attain completion is the basic need of all life. In *The New Biology* (1988), Augrous and Stanciu point out that the essential quality of living things is the capacity for self-directive activity and self-regulation. The protoplasm of our planet is restless. Every living thing seeks to attain its telos or end state of development through the full actualization of its potentialities. We view the Holy Spirit as the elan vital behind the creative process of emergent evolution and growth in all living things. At the level of human existence at which the capacity for self-awareness arises as an emergent property of the psyche, the basic life urge to attain fullness of life manifests itself in a distinctive way – (1) it operates

both physiologically and within the psyche towards maintaining the vital balance of health through the process of homoestasis (internal self-regulation) and (2) it operates psychologically and spiritually within the psyche in the dynamic process of individuation towards conscious self-realization or spiritual wholeness (internal self-directive activity). This brings us to an important point − (3) the human physical body grows relatively automatically through an exchange of energy with the environment as by assimilating foodstuffs and it undergoes changes but does not evolve, and eventually decays; by contrast there is no set limit to the evolution and expansion of human consciousness through spiritual growth. This expansion takes place by the ongoing emotional assimilation and cognitive integration of novel experiences, especially those associated with the fulfillment of our human needs − experiences that enrich a person's consciousness and inner life and enhance the quality of one's existence. Spiritual growth involves continuity and development, experiment-ation and integrative cohesion; at this level, the life urge manifests itself in a creative tension that continuously impels human beings towards new levels of consciousness and creative achievements, each of which still leaves one restless and seeking further enrichment and satisfaction. In this way the Spirit inspires humans to seek ultimate fulfillment for their spiritual need or deficiency in the inexhaustible riches of the Divine Life. This is brought out by St Augustine's words that our hearts are restless until they find rest in God. As we shall see, the process of psycho-spiritual growth is very difficult as it involves an ongoing conscious struggle with life-thwarting forces within one's self and our overall environment which can frustrate our deepest aspirations for becoming complete. We shall devote a considerable portion of this chapter to this process of self-actualization. As regards the nature of the human psyche, we view it as complex-unity of conscious and unconscious non-physical life energies interacting with the physical organism (we analyze the deep structures of the psyche later also). Together with Karl Popper (1977; Smart 1964), we think that there are sound philosophic arguments for rejecting physiological-materialist views of mind. Recently, John Eccles has presented arguments which indicate that the conscious psyche interacts and communicates with the material liaison brain through an act of intention at the supplementary motor area. Also, as a dynamic self-directing organizing center of conscious experience, the psyche possesses the distinctive quality of life most fully. Concerning the origins of the non-physical psyche, Eccles argues that the experienced uniqueness of each human self cannot be attributed to environmental differences nor to its brain built by the genetic instructions of one's genome and the infinitely improbable genetic lottery from which a person's genome was derived (10 followed by 10,000 zeros). Eccles concludes that the only explanation is that "each soul is a Divine creation which is 'attached' to the growing foetus at some time between conception and birth" (Eccles 1984 p. 43). Eccles' arguments merit serious attention. In our view, an alternative account of the psyche's origin might be given in terms of the process of emergent evolution through continuous creation by the Trinity as presented in our work; here, since matter itself is created by Divine volitional consciousness, it is spirit-bearing and we see consciousness as an emergent property arising at complex levels of matter under the Spirit's influence – in either case consciousness comes into the cosmos trailing clouds of glory. We now look at the evidence derived from psychology in support of human goodness.

Human Goodness: Psychological Views

Our view that human nature is essentially good and life-affirming was assessed long ago by Meng-tzu (Mencius) and is supported by a psychological analysis of our human needs; each of our human needs is a manifestation of the underlying life urge towards self-actualization – the process of becoming more fully developed and complete. Our needs are inherent urges or drives which must be satisfied if we are to develop and maintain adequate physical, emotional and mental health. These urges arise whenever there is a deficiency in the human organism which must be replenished or fulfilled in order to satisfy the requirements of health in soma and psyche. These urges create tensions which organize our perceptions, memory, thoughts and motivate us into taking action to search and obtain what we require to supply what we lack and satisfy our wants and desires. Next we shall focus on describing these needs and draw upon these works of Montague, Fromm and Maslow. Here, we can distinguish between organic drives or physiological needs and character-rooted passions which are generated by our existential needs which are psychological and spiritual (Fromm 1973). Organic drives include the basic urge towards self-preservation and sex or conjugation aimed at biological reproduction in order to enable the social group to survive. However an individual can survive in mental health without sexual intercourse. Other physical needs include adequate nutrition, sleep, exercise, shelter, clothing and affectionate bodily contact and warmth through touching and embracing fellow humans and animals which is also vital for emotional health (need-love). In addition to these, humans have a number of psycho-spiritual needs that are uniquely human and not found in other animals, and their functioning interrelations constitute the innate nature of humankind. All of these needs are good, and drive us towards what is good and being good. Noted anthropologist Ashley Montague has gathered considerable evidence from studies of culture and child psychology to show that human nature is life-affirming. Montague points out that human beings are born with an innate need for love, to respond to love, to express love to others, to be good and to be cooperative: that there is a spontaneous creative drive of the human organism toward maturation in terms of social cooperation. Thus, it is not the case that children are born egotistical and anti-social according to the Freudian view of "primary narcissism" (Montague 1966). The first and most important human need is for (1) self-esteem – an inner fundamental conviction that I am lovable (possess intrinsic value or goodness) and worthwhile (I possess the competence to adequately handle the daily challenges of life) (Briggs 1975); this positive self-image and these feelings of self-respect and self-confidence are the basis of emotional health. Self-esteem enables us to see the goodness in others and enrich their lives out of our own abundance of loving-goodness within ourselves. A child's self-esteem is derived primarily from the nurturing love and affection from its parents. All of our other needs contribute to and reinforce our self-esteem. (2) The need to overcome our separateness and achieve productive loving-interpersonal relationships with other persons on the basis of mutual care, respect, responsibility and understanding (Fromm 1956). Without right self-love we cannot love others and without first receiving love from a significant person who confirms and validates our worth, we cannot love or nurture ourselves. Thus, Jesus' teaching on loving ourselves and our fellow humans as children of our Heavenly Abba is the fundamental spiritual law of human existence, without which fulfillment is impossible. Our communion with others in a creative togetherness and belonging which supplies our need for (3) rootedness – that we are an integral part of the world and this relates to (4) the need for security, a safe environment in which life can flourish; this includes an emotionally secure family setting to raise healthy children and a community that is not ravaged by poverty, violent crime and massive social unrest. Next is (5) the striving to attain a sense of personal identity, to be acknowledged as a unique individual. This goal can optimally be achieved by one's own creative accomplishments in the art of living or by identifying oneself with another person or social group – then however, the sense of identity is derived from belonging to someone rather than being someone. A strong sense of identity develops in the process of individuation as a person grows in self-knowledge through relationships involving creative mutual struggle in terms of the effect others have on one's emotions and self-image. An important mark of a mature sense of identity is the establishment of clearly defined ego-boundaries, psychologically differentiated from others and overcoming one's emotional dependence upon one's parents to achieve independence. This leads to (6) self-direction and functional autonomy – having the power or capacity of healthy self-assertion and inner freedom to strive to fulfill one's needs in the quest for self-development. This involves a dedication to reality as it is, accepting responsibility for actions and effects on others and becoming a productive human being who can influence others positively; this links up with (7) the need for transcendence, to rise above our animal nature to be creative utilizing our capacity for imaginative vision, intuitive insight, heightened self-awareness and life-affirming passion in a process of self-expression. Later in this chapter we will focus on the nature of creativity in the spiritual life. This links up with (8) the need for accomplishment and recognition – achieving our creative potential, overcoming obstacles, doing productive work, nurturing and caring for others, contributing to the betterment of society and receiving recognition and appreciation for our efforts (without which we stagnate). All this contributes to our sense of personal dignity and worth. (9) There is the need for a frame of orientation and an object of devotion or ultimate concern in order to make sense out of the world and human existence. Our religions or worldviews aim to provide this in the form of a stable and consistent way of perceiving the world; our need for an object of devotion or ultimate love (Augustine, Tillich) leads to (10) the need for an existential meaning in life, in order to strive to persist in one's own being in the face of suffering, tragedy and death. Earlier, we noted that a need arises when there is a defect like a hole that needs to be filled in. In this context Victor Frankl (1969) speaks of an "existential vacuum" or void, an inner emptiness that is experienced when a person finds life meaningless and without purpose. This state leads to apathy and despair. Humans need to dedicate themselves to serving something (ideals or values or a cause) or someone other than one's self (loved ones, a community, the Buddha or God, etc.). They thus transcend a state in which they are primarily concerned with themselves, and find meaning through encountering other human beings in creative mutuality and love which literally fills our psyche full with nourishing life energy. By living for others we increase the value of our life and enrich and expand our own consciousness and ego-boundaries which become more all-inclusive. This brings out the significance of Jesus' saying "Whoever seeks to save his life will lose it; and whoever loses it will save it and live (Luke 17:33). Lastly, there is a need for (11) the courage to be (Tillich 1951) – to be one's own authentic self – true to our own values, convictions and capacity for independent thinking and forming our own judgments and expressing ourself; courage to affirm one's own being through volitional consciousness in the face of ontological anxiety which arises from threats to which human existence as such is subject – suffering and death. Here Tillich notes that the ability to bear the loneliness of being an individual is a decisive mark of emotional maturity and the prerequisite for mature productive loving fusion with another which preserves the integrity of each (Fromm 1956) which is the courage to be as part of a social group, without giving up one's unique selfhood in total conformity. The fulfillment of these human needs is absolutely necessary if we are to function sanely and realize our potentialities. As we shall see, a person can be motivated by affective passions of love or hate in the effort to achieve these. This analysis makes it clear that Freud's view that there are two equally basic inherent urgent impulses in humans – a life urge, and death urge is untenable (Freud held that the death urge manifests itself outwardly as destructiveness and inwardly as self-destruction through psychophysical pathology, masochism and suicide).

All the evidence presented above is against this and it is contradicted by the biological law of self-preservation and the basic urge of life to grow. Further, if our nature was inherently destructive, we could never trust our needs and impulses – constant repression of these forces would be required which would itself be self-destructive in time. While it is true that there are varying degrees of self-destructive impulses in most people (though, often hidden in the subconscious levels of the psyche) these are not fundamental in human nature; rather these feelings result from the existential frustration of life-affirming feelings in the struggle for fulfillment. The goodness of human nature is further brought out by Abraham Maslow who states that humans have spiritual needs to seek truth, beauty, justice, goodness, order and unity in their lives. Maslow has discovered a common core of traits that self-actualizing people possess – they are realistically oriented, more accepting of themselves and others and tolerant, are more spontaneous in their relationships, are problem-centered rather than self-centered, have a need for privacy and detachment, have an autonomy and independence from cultural influences, a freshness in their appreciation of people and things, have a capacity for transcendence and profound mystical and ecstatic peak experiences, a deep identification with humanity, more profound intimate interpersonal relationships; have a humorous and democratic character-structure; have a wealth of creativeness; resist conformity to their culture and have a capacity to creatively resolve moral dichotomies and dilemmas, and have fresh vision (Maslow 1968). This is undoubtedly an inspiring view of a healthy and fully functioning human being! Next we will give an account of the destructive forces in human life which thwart the drive towards happiness and wholeness.

Human Destructiveness

To many of our readers, our view of human goodness is naive and flatly contradicted by the seemingly overwhelming evidence of human destructiveness. Indeed, both Montague and Fromm who are non-theistic humanists, have devoted considerable attention to account for the origins of human destructiveness. Looking back upon the 20th century from here in the early 1990's, we see that it has been a chronicle of unimaginable cruelty, and destructiveness. To reflect upon the horrors of Nazism and the holocaust, Stalin's reign of terror and the Gulag, to the killing fields of Cambodia of Pol Pot, the enslavement, dehumanization and torture of millions under tyrannical communist and fascist regimes and the specter of international terrorism and nationalistic fanaticism and violent social upheaval, can drive a person to despair. How can anyone believe in the innate goodness of humankind or that we are created in the image of a loving

God? We will attempt a threefold analysis in terms of (1) negative social conditions harmful to human needs; (2) the destructive forces in the subconscious of the psyche; and (3) human sinfulness: intentionally hurting others. Montague believes that human beings especially during the first six years of life are conditioned to become egocentric, fearful, hostile and disordered creatures through a lack of nurturing love and other deprivations. This hostility that develops is a reactive-aggressive response and is an expression of frustration at not having one's physical and emotional needs adequately met. It has become evident that the damage done to children and their self-image by emotionally sick and dysfunctional parents is far more devastating and widespread than previously imagined. It is estimated that over 90% of all families in the USA are emotionally impaired in varying degrees of severity, operating according to poisonous rules of pedagogy and harmful patterns of emotional reactions (often unconsciously acted out) passed on from generation on down (Bradshaw 1988). These include destructive discipline, threatening encounters, unrealistic standards to match up to, excessive competition and continual comparisons with others and parent's explosive rages, physical and emotional abuse, all of which serve to humiliate a child and fill him with the toxic feeling of shame and unrealistic guilt. The effects are tragic often resulting in crippling inferiority complexes; further, the child is forced to repress his hurt feelings from being traumatized, in order to cope, adopting a rigid defensive posture and muscular armouring (more on this later) so as not to feel the intense pain. Now it is a basic principle of psychoanalytic theory that a person retains the qualities and traits of their previous stages of development in the psyche which form layers of the personality. (Lowen 1976) such as babyhood, childhood and adolescence. The childlike aspect has the qualities of fertile imagination, spontaneity and trusting receptivity which when combined with adult realism yields high levels of creativity. When a person was shamed when she was young, she carries an abandoned and wounded child-self within that needs to be retrieved from the unconscious and healed. Hence a number of recent books in psychology emphasizing the need to heal the inner child within oneself. It is fascinating to consider the application of Jesus' teaching concerning the need to become childlike in the sense indicated above in order to receive the new life of the Kingdom, and the Divine Christchild within. Also any unresolved conflicts with one's parents and unhealed emotional wounds and unmet childhood needs will serve to sabotage and undermine one's relationships with the opposite sex and the creation of a healthy family: for instance a man who reacts dysfunctionally to his wife's own anger which he unconsciously associates with his mother's rage and hysteria in childhood. The unhealthy family situation is often a microcosm of the sickness in society with its widespread addictive behavior to alcohol, drugs, especially cocaine, sexual addiction and the thriving on the negative excitement of violence. There is also the problem of codependency – being emotionally dependent upon someone who is an addict or emotionally dysfunctional (often in order to fulfill the need to be needed); add to this the serious problem of sexual molestation by parents, and the outlook for society in millions of emotionally crippled and mentally sick people is grim. It is interesting to note here in addition to Alcoholics Anonymous there are now adult children programs for various forms of addiction which also employ the 12-step program for dependency and recovery which calls for the reliance upon God as a Higher Power to help the person affirm oneself daily as worthy to abstain from addictive behavior (here with alcohol and drugs the only cure is total abstinence). Many Christian churches are now working with dependency counselors to assist members of their congregations who need help and who call upon divine grace and loving communion with God (most programs utilize meditation techniques and contemplative prayer to help bring harmony and balance). One hopeful sign is this cooperative effort between medicine, depth-psychotherapy and religion to heal a person in all the dimensions of their being. (see Morton Kelsey, *Psychology, Medicine and Christian Healing*, 1988.) On top of all this in many parts of the world, cities and communities are ravaged by poverty, economic destitution, homelessness, unemployment, widespread crime and gang-violence, over-crowding, pollution, scarcity of money to fund local government programs to help the needy, racism and ethnic divisions, the spread of disease. All these combine to create a climate of fear and insecurity, wariness and suspicion which is life-thwarting and inimicable to the fulfillment of our human needs whether we be in Cairo, Bombay, New York or Jakarta. This combined with overbearing stress and strain of the daily struggle to work and make ends meet, often results in outburst of rage, senseless violence and destruction. This causes loving persons to become egocentric and defensive to protect themselves against the rival egoisms, hostility and ruthless competitiveness of fellow humans – the quest for a "minimal self" geared to psychic survival becomes widespread (Lasch 1984) in a mad society. In light of all this it is clear that social conditioning contributes to narcissism and hostile aggression and greed. We will now criticize the view that hostile aggression is innate from a biological and cultural perspective.

Fromm (1973) together with Montague (1976) marshalled evidence to show that the views of Konrad Lorenz (1966) on innate human aggression were mistaken. Here we need to distinguish between aggression in the sense of (1) a dynamic energetic forwardness to achieve wants, which is a probably healthy form of self-assertion characteristic of an individuated personality, and (2) hostile aggression, which is behavior directed toward causing or threatening to cause physical and mental-emotional injury and harm to other living beings. Lorenz held that as a result of the evolutionary process and their animal ancestors, humans are innately aggressive (2nd sense) and have a blood-lust to kill. Lorenz maintained that aggression is continually generated in the brain and accumulates to the point where pressure is too great and must be released. This is why according to him, violence, destructiveness and war are inevitable. Lorenz's views gained great popularity with the educated general public as it provided consolation in the form of a simple and fatalistic explanation for the widespread cruelty in human history. A more recent account of the myth of the beast within is P. Maclean's "triune brain" theory – humans possess three functionally distinct brains at war with each other – the reptilian (base instincts), paleomammalian (complex emotions) and the youngest neo-mammalian (intellect); this is literally a house divided against itself (schizophysiology) with humans wreaking havoc with hostile reptile behavior. This view is critiqued by Klama (1988).

However, animal aggressiveness is not sadistic and cruel as it is in human animals. Rather, it serves to protect their vital interests or biological needs. Even predators, such as wolves, typically attack just to attain food. Further, neuro-physiological evidence shows that hostile aggression does not accumulate in the brain, but is mobilized when there is a threat, in which case there is also the impulse to take flight. Lorenz' view is not supported sociologically, for if it were true, we would expect to find similar levels of aggressiveness everywhere and in various cultures and societies; but this is precisely what we don't find – examples are peaceful groups such as the Pueblo Indians in the USA and the pygmies in the rain-forests of Africa. Even in our closest genetically related primate families of chimpanzees and baboons there is remarkable cooperation and peacefulness in their social groups – recall Montague's point earlier that humans are born with a need to mature through social cooperation. This brings us to an important point, namely that there is now very strong evidence that Darwin's account of the mechanics of evolution in terms of the struggle and "survival of the fittist" is profoundly mistaken – *cooperation* between all protoplasm (cells) plant life and animals, is the means of survival in nature. This evidence is presented in great detail in *The New Biology* (1988) by Augrous and Stanciu. We think that this is a book which deserves to be read by all thinking people. It reveals the beauty and harmony of the Divine Wisdom in nature and stimulates humans to be ecologically-minded to preserve and save our blue and green planet. Also, it serves as a necessary rebuttal to the extreme Neo-Darwinian view of sociobiologist Richard Dawkins

(1976) and his "selfish gene" theory – he holds that human organisms are merely the means through which selfish DNA molecules seek to reproduce themselves to survive for the sake of survival. Thus human persons exist for the benefit of genes rather than the other way around and humans are selfish. We think that this is a very bad way to view our fellow humans and that this position is riddled with absurdities, especially the sociobiologist account of the nature of culture, ethics and altruism (Peacocke 1986, Lewontin 1984). All the views we have been considering – innate hostility, destructiveness, egotism – are dangerous because they can easily become self-fulfilling prophecies, and encourage unwholesome attitudes towards people who can become expendable say for the sake of a ruthless ideology, or result in cynicism and moral despair.

We now come to an important point made by Fromm (1973) which adds greatly to our understanding of human aggression, namely that there is a reactive defensive aggressiveness biologically programmed within the human brain, which may be activated when there is a threat to an individual's vital interests. However, in humans this reaction is far more extensive than in animals for a variety of reasons. Unlike animals (1) humans can anticipate and react aggressively to threats in the future by launching a preemptive strike. (2) Humans are subject to suggestion as through propaganda, and perceptions which can lead them to react aggressively whether or not the perceived threat is real or not. This is related to (3) the problem of unconscious projections whereby humans attribute their inferior qualities on to others who are seen as a threat to the security of their ideal self-image. And (4) humans have far more vital interests than just biological needs, such as values, ideals and institutions which are of passionate concern and with which they identify themselves. An attack on these is viewed as an attack on themselves. This evidence leads Fromm to criticize B.F.Skinner's behaviorist view according to which human nature is completely malleable and that aggressiveness is simply a learned trait and that circumstances alone make people that way through operant conditioning (Watson).

Behaviorism also fails to account for the unconscious depths of the psyche (which on that theory does not even exist) and human spirituality. Even this, however, does not account for what Fromm sees as the most serious problem of all, namely, that humans are the only primates that kill members of their own species without any biological or social purpose and feel satisfaction in doing so. Moreover humans can be sadistic and cruel, and torture other humans. The widespread use of torture by oppressive political regimes and their secret police is appalling. Fromm calls this non-biological malignancy narcissistic personality; it is this form of malevolence which constitutes the most serious threat to the continued existence of the human species. This malignancy manifests it self in (1) sadism – the passion for absolute control over another living being and (2) necrophilia – the passion to destroy life and a love for everything that is dead, lifeless or purely mechanical. Fromm thinks this evil character type is a result of individuals seriously failing to fulfill their existential needs due to harmful social conditions especially a lack of nurturing love. Fromm contends that people can also become evil gradually over a period of time as a result of their free choices which lead to a failure in the art of living (Fromm, 1964).

Fromm's other contribution is his account of human passions; earlier we noted that our existential human needs within the psyche generate passions or energy-charged impulses whose function it is to satisfy those needs. Fromm has observed that in order to satisfy a particular need, such as the need to affect others, a person can be motivated by the passions of love or hate in their relationships with another – this shows that love and hate are not simply opposites – hate is a frozen love, while apathy is the opposite of love. Fromm distinguishes between life-affirming passions which further well-being and spiritual growth – mature love, tenderness, sharing and the striving for the ideals of justice, truth, solidarity and creativity; and the irrational passions which are life-thwarting and destructive – hate, greed, envy, violence, cruelty and fanaticism. Both these types of passions are present in varying degrees in every person and these conflicting emotions make the process of spiritual growth most difficult. Our passions arise from the attempt to make sense of our life and experience it with the optimum of intensity and spiritual strength that we are capable of under the given life-circumstances. These life-affirming passions are the source of our cultural creativity and the motivating powers that make life worth living. Fromm's remedy for destructiveness is for humans to identify with life-furthering passions and renounce greed, share and create a perfect utopian society which he calls "humanistic communitarian socialism" which he says is the answer to our need for salvation – psychic health and well-being.

We find Fromm's view of salvation unsatisfactory and rather naive. Experience shows that more often than not, human reason and our will power (the intensity of conscious intentionality) are ineffectual in directing our irrational passions or in coping with the powerful diabolical forces within the subconscious dimension of the psyche. Further the attempt to transform our own settled attitudes and habitual patterns of emotional responses and thought patterns (especially compulsions) by self-effort paradoxically makes a person more frustrated. As Christian theists, we believe it is by the transforming power of divine grace that we can be liberated from our existential conflicts, compulsions and disordered passions. Before proceeding we should briefly mention Maslow's similar view that when our needs are denied, frustrated, twisted or warped, that humans become neurotic and destructive. This is an important insight that when our creative potentialities are pent up, thwarted and dammed up within the unconscious, they degenerate into life-negating powers, leading to destructiveness, morbidity and despair.

We will now turn to C.G. Jung's analytical depth-psychology in order to gain further insight into our human condition and our need for divine salvation.

Depth-Psychology: Jung and Deep Structures
We feel that Jung's analysis of the dynamics and deep structures of the psyche are filled with a number of insights

316

some of which we will delineate here. We should mention however that we ourselves are not Jungians and do not wish to follow those who have turned Jung's psychology into a religion similar to Neo-Vedanta where all religions are more or less culturally relative symbolic systems which aim to liberate the ego to function as a medium for the Divine Self (a union of opposites) to realize itself in the realm of space and time, a type of mystical Hegelianism. Nevertheless, some of these Jungians such as Edward Edinger (1973) reveal insight into the processes within the process of individuation towards spiritual wholeness or self-realization. Edinger believes that Jesus was a person of astonishing psychological insight, and his life and teachings are a paradigm for achieving wholeness through sacramental Christianity (see also John Sanford, *The Kingdom Within*, 1987).

Jung's model of the psyche also provides a framework for understanding inner religious experience, mental illness and healing. Together, with Jung we can view the psyche in terms of levels – (1) the ego, the unifying center within the perceptual field of consciousness; the ego has a relatively high degree of continuity and identity. At birth, the ego or focal self begins to emerge out of a matrix consisting of a vast reservoir of psychic energy which makes up the subconscious dimensions or levels of the psyche which contains symbolic patterns and processes of which we are unaware of. Here there is (2) the personal unconscious – this realm consists of energies in the form of personal memories, and repressed experiences, thoughts, feelings and desires, many of which are distressing or unacceptable to one's conscious orientation and ego-image. Although Jung came to reject Freud's "psychoanalytic atheism" (see Küng 1979), with its psychological or "hard" determinism in terms of biological instincts (sex and aggression) and unconscious forces (neurosis and traumatic experiences from early childhood), his work built upon Freud's pioneering discoveries in this realm. Then there is (3) the archetypal psyche, also somewhat misleadingly called the "collective unconscious" which is a common inheritance of psychic functioning, based in evolution. Archetypes are latent or potential patterns of psychic energy, which when activated, structure our experience and perception and our patterns of emotional responses and behavior. At the level of conscious activity, archetypes manifest themselves in common or typical forms in symbols, imagery, themes, and figures that are found in the mythology and religions of the world. When human beings undergo dramatic life experiences such as spiritual death and rebirth, encountering the numinosity of the Holy, or rites of passage, and healings, the archetypal psyche depicts or expresses these in universal patterns of symbolism. Jung's notion of these inherent patterns of functioning within the matrix self was a brilliant suggestion. He also regarded this dimension as the medium from which divine inspiration and creativity wells up from within. Also of value from the standpoint of our theology is Jung's idea of the androgynous or bisexual nature of the psyche. This indicates that humans are created in the image of the androgynous selfless spirits of the Social Trinity (see chapter 6), the feminine spiritual qualities constitute a sub-self in the male, the anima, while the masculine spiritual qualities constellate in the animus in the female (these seem to be the psychic counterpart to the sets of male *and* female chromosomes the member of either sex carries as part of their biological inheritance). No less a thinker than Berdyaev arrived at the same view independently. He thought that the human being is not only a sexual but a bisexual being, combining the masculine and the feminine principle in herself in different proportions. He believed that it is only the union of the two principles that constitutes a complete human being (Berdyaev 1948). We are ready now to analyze the conflicts within these levels. The horrific discoveries made by Freud of the irrational and destructive passions, compulsions and obsessional fixations which exist in the personal unconscious, constitute a serious moral and psychological problem. In varying degrees, everyone can be driven by hidden forces of which she is unaware. In this sense, sin is enslavement to what we do not know about ourselves which causes us and others harm. Jung saw that the contents of the personal unconscious can form together in clusters

associated around a particular theme; these bundles of
feeling-toned or emotionally charged ideas or complexes can
have a disintegrating effect on the personality – they are
centers of energy which act like a vortex or whirlpool,
drawing needed energy from other dimensions of the psyche,
in particular from the conscious identity center, the ego. This
can lead to the possession of a person's consciousness by
partial elements within the psyche which are enslaving and
potentially destructive. This brings us to Jung's notion of
the shadow or dark side of the personality. The shadow is
also an archetype which develops through a person's
individual experiences; here the archtypal form acts like a
magnetic nucleus around which complexes form. Thus the
latent archetypal patterns interpenetrate with the personal
unconscious. The shadow constitutes the inferior and
consciously rejected qualities in an individual's personality
which in this case constellate around this archetype. The
shadow is that part of the psyche that is infantile, sick, and
neurotic as well as vulnerable and defensive. Jung has
pointed out that the shadow is a vital part of one's wholeness
and humanity and it must be consciously acknowledged and
accepted as one's self. However, ego-inflation and a lack
of humility prevent this. Most often, people are filled with
self-hate against their inferior inner self and deal with these
inferior qualities through the following defense mechanism
(1) they repress them, and in this leads to inner conflict and
imbalance, eventually leading to emotional outbursts of rage
and violence; or, which is the obverse side to this (2) they
project these negative and inferior qualities onto others; this
makes interpersonal relationships difficult, and when this
is done collectively as onto and entire group of people, as
the Nazis did with the Jews, the results are catastrophic.
The Nazis sought to kill off what they hated in themselves
by finding a scapegoat which is a sinister and insidious evil.
The shadow contains powerful energies and when these are
creatively assimilated by the ego, serve to enrich one's
consciousness and provide greater stability within the
personality; energy that was also used to maintain the
repression against the pressure from within can now be

utilized more effectively. Jung's picture of complexes and the shadow enable us to give a coherent account of the phenomenon of demonic possession, which is a prominent theme in a number of healings in the Gospel records in which Jesus liberates people from evil or foul spirits. These dark powers not only split people's minds, they destroy their bodies at the same time. In the New Testament writings, these destructive forces are often thought of as supernatural beings such as Satan and his legion. In his book *People of the Lie* (1983), which focuses on the reality of evil in human life, psychiatrist M. Scott Peck has affirmed the ontological existence of Satan who has been a liar from the beginning and who possesses individuals and drives towards violences and existential self-destruction.

Peck bases his position on his many years of clinical experience and his participation in exorcisms. However, from our perspective, the enslavement of an individual's consciousness can be interpreted differently and more constructively in terms of possession by destructive emotional complexes, the shadow, or other archetypal forces within the unconscious levels of the psyche. These powers are truly dangerous in that they have varying degrees of autonomy and are centers of energy; they can manifest themselves through dreams, visions, images, fantasies, voices, sick feelings as well as emotional outbursts. As noted above, by drawing away psychic energy from the unifying center of a person's consciousness, these partial elements can split the personality into fragments and enslave them. As Paul Tillich has emphasized, being split is a demonic state which is opposed to wholeness or being integral. The problem with the supernaturalistic explanation that Peck espouses is that it leads to a type of Manichean Dualism between God and the Devil. It also seriously undermines personal responsibility in that people can try to escape their freedom and responsibility by ascribing their own evil thoughts and sinful acts to the influence of Satan or as viewing other people as satanic. Further, with such demonic alien beings, there is no way to creatively transform them; from our view, the energies from a person's complexes can be transformed and integrated by the power of divine grace. Jung maintained that while the psycho-analytic process can enable people to become conscious of the dark powers within the unconscious, this is not, in and of itself, sufficient to deliver them from these enslaving powers and compulsions. The disintegrative capacity of these psychic energies is often so great that without the "other help" of divine grace we cannot cope with them alone: from this, we can see that health is wholeness and sickness is disintegration. We shall expand upon this further a bit later.

This brings us to the important function that symbols play in the wholeness-making process of individuation (Edinger, 1973). Symbols are the spontaneous expression of processes occurring in the psyche below the level of consciousness. Symbols convey the existential meaning of these processes so that they can be consciously apprehended. Further, symbols transform raw psychic energy and channel it upwards from the subconscious levels in a form that can be cognitively and affectively assimilated by one's consciousness. Symbols are also a vital medium whereby the divine energies of the Holy Spirit are transmitted to persons. Here, Jung stressed the necessity for the "symbolic life" for spiritual development and healing and cure of the soul. Highly significant from the standpoint of our own theology – Jung regarded the symbolic practices of sacramental Catholic Christianity as the best therapeutic religious system ever provided to human beings for their ultimate transformation (see Kelsey 1988 and Schaer 1949). Through liturgical worship, sacraments and contemplative prayer, the transforming power of the Trinity is channeled to people in these symbolic processes; this shows that religious symbols participate in the power and living meaning of the Reality to which they point (Tillich) and communicate divine wisdom to us.

In vital religious experiences and in dreams, symbols play an important role in healing whereby the conflict between creative and destructive tendencies and energies is overcome in an integrative synthesis of which the symbol is a unifying factor – the word for symbol in Greek derives from *sumballein* which means to unify or "throw together". During individuation crises of psycho-spiritual death and rebirth, the numinous creative Energy of God is often manifested through sacred symbols of completeness or totality such as a cross or crucifix or mandalas (diagrams with circular and concentric shapes as those in Eastern religions). In these symbols of wholeness, the unifying power of Divine Love absorbs and transforms destructive energies into life-enriching energies. In his psychology, Jung has brought out the need humans have for healing and divine help as well as illustrating the many ways in which the Spirit effects this. Next, we turn to the sinfulness and evil which also necessitates our need for salvation.

Human Sinfulness and the Need for Salvation

In our discussion of human destructiveness we delineated the many ways in which human sinfulness manifests itself and the effects of negative social conditions in frustrating humans' need to be good; here, we will focus briefly on an analysis of sin both individually and collectively from our theological perspective. First, we need to distinguish sin as a disordered condition from which the compulsive tendency to commit particular sins derives. Sin is primarily an orientation of character or personality expressed in a set of emotional attitudes which reflect a person's way of viewing others and habitually acting and responding towards them. In our view (following *Genesis*), narcissism or egoism is the chief error from which all the other deadly sins follow. Narcissism is an unhealthy and excessive absorption in one's own concerns and ambitions together with a preoccupation with defending one's idealized ego-image against others who are perceived to pose a threat to it and one's psychological security. Narcissism can lead to (1) self-isolation and a neurotic withdrawal from others and life into constricted defensive posture (the "minimal self", Lasch 1984) which often results in becoming schizoid or even schizophrenic; and (2) ego-inflation in which a person seeks security in the form of psychological power over others through various means as delineated by Reinhold Niebuhr. It is this latter form which is condemned as the First Deadly Sin in Christianity. Traditionally this ego-inflation (puffed up, distended beyond proper limits or blown up, see Edinger 1973) is called "pride" which in our view can be misleading, since normal pride is part of self-esteem – a healthy self-confidence and positive satisfaction in one's achievements and attainments in the struggle for maturity. What is really meant is an overweaning pride or an arrogance concerning one's stature, abilities, and achievements over and against others (self-aggrandizement and exaggerated sense of self-importance); a more useful rendering for self-absorption in this sense is the Greek word *hubris* as utilized by Tillich in his *Systematic Theology* (1957), which brings out nicely the theological sense – hubris is a self-elevation of the human to the sphere of the Divine – (the same sense as Augustine intends to convey in the Latin *superbia*). *Hubris* is a sin in its total form – it begins with unbelief: a turning away from acknowledging God's Reality or in disbelief (or refusing to believe in God's loving-goodness like Ivan Karamazov in Dostoyevsky's masterpiece of world literature) then turning towards one's self which one views as the center of the world and ultimate concern; from here one then strives with unlimited desire to suck in the whole of everything in reality to satisfy an insatiable craving. We shall look at this from the Buddhist vantage point a bit later. Note that earlier we referred to the Spirit's influence on humans' restless desire for fulfillment which can only be satisfied in the abundance of God's inexhaustible and endless Life (aseity); being finite and deficient, humans seek abundance and thereby fall into the perennial temptation to seek unlimited abundance within the realm of finitude which is inherently impossible. Our reasoning appears to be somewhat circular. However, we simply point to the fact that human nature is not neutral – either humans are created by God for God or they are not and are alternatively the result of various other forces. We are not attempting a "proof", only a phenomenological description. This rebellion against God not only leads to disintegration of the personality by disordered passions of hatred, fear and cupidity but also to materialism and the pathological ego-centric megalomania of political dictators and the cult of personality they seek to create for themselves amongst those they enslave. Our 20th century alas has had far too many of them; here, we should note that religious fanatics, who are often fundamentalists who want to set up a theocracy, suffer equally from this hostile egoism.

Karl Menninger sums up these aspects of sin as defiant withdrawal, supererogation, and self-absorption (Menninger, 1973). This illustrates that egoism is not simply a result of social conditioning but is expressive of an act of will or conscious intentionality (May, 1969) in which an individual intentionally acts to hurt or harm another person. This stems from one's inner negativity and a contemptuous disregard for the welfare of others. Earlier, in our discussion of human needs, we referred to the need to transcend one's self in willing service to a life-affirming ideal or the welfare of others and God's loving Will. Scott Peck distinguishes between willingness to serve based upon humility and willfulness based on an arrogant unsubmitted will seeking to dominate others and protect a self-image of perfection or superiority over them (Peck 1983). Here psychiatrist Lowen points out that the inflated egoist is also cut off from his feelings and sensitivities (as much as the schizoid neurotic) because of his defensiveness expressed in the rigidity of his conscious attitudes and muscular armoring and tension in his body (Lowen, 1985). Egoism leads to the other deadly sins which harm one's self and others – (2) hostility, hatred, rage and violence. It can inflate (3) lusts – any compulsive disordered passions and desires but here used especially for forms of sexual behavior which debase, corrupt, distort, or destroy the personalities of the participants; (4) greed – aggressive overacquisition, avarice, selfishness and hoarding, (5) gluttony, here we can include the insatiable desires and appetites for alcohol, and drugs such as crack cocaine and even valium; this is sin as addiction. (6) Then there is envy, coveting, and jealousy which is often expressed by insidious gossip and hostile resentment toward another's happiness, attainments and achievements: this may arise from inferiority complexes, and (7) laziness (traditionally called "sloth") in two senses. First, there is (a) a sin of omission – callous indifference and unwillingness to care, tend to, and respond with sensitivity to the needs of others; here, it is interesting to note that in his portrayal of the Last Judgement, Jesus does not condemn people for acts of wrongdoing but for refusing to respond to the needs of our fellow humans and leaving good things undone (as restoring good relations and reconciliation). Second, there is (b) resistance or refusal to face reality and to make the painful effort to grow up and become a mature adult; as we shall see, Scott Peck (1977) regards this the fundamental sin.

In contrast to this attitude of sin, humility is the chief Christian virtue or excellence of character. Humility is a courageous acceptance of one's limitations and theologically it is the recognition for one's spiritual need for divine grace, emotional healing and forgiveness expressed in Matthew 5:3. Here the familiar rendering of "beggars for the spirit" – namely "poor in spirit", is effectively captured by the New English Bible (1970) and by J.B. Phillips (1975) as "Happy are those who know their need for God". Edinger states that Jesus' teachings in the Beatitudes and elsewhere are in divine praise of a non-inflated ego (Edinger 1973) which is necessary for spiritual health. Humility expresses itself in life-enhancing qualities of gentleness and patience, that is, meekness (literally means "tamed" by discipline) and a loving concern for the well-being of others.

Next we will look at sin on the level of collective irresponsibility and what we see as another source or ego-inflation. In our view, much of our stupidities and cruelties in our relationships with other people, stem from fear and our sense of inferiority and insecurity. All persons have some feelings of inferiority about themselves with regard to various talents, capacities, deficiencies or defects especially in comparison with others. These feelings are further aggravated in the often ruthless competitiveness of modern society. Such feelings of inferiority can occur in persons with good self-esteem (one's lovableness and competency to handle life's challenges) as one's sense of worthiness is not dependent upon any particular talent, function or quality of one's self. This normal sense of inferiority can serve a positive function in helping people develop their own unique talents and creative life-style. Here, a person seeks to overcome her feelings of inferiority and weaknesses in areas of her being by striving to excel in one area of concentration whereby she compensates for defects or deficiencies in others; in this way, people are motivated to develop their own creative potentials.

On the other hand, this sense of inferiority and vulnerability results in ego-inflation through overcompensation whereby humans seek to achieve psychological invulnerability in the form of willful power over other. Reinhold Niebuhr points out that this ego-inflation is often expressed in pretentious claims to possessing either more powers and abilities, knowledge, virtue or special favors from the Divine Being in opposition to others who are seen as threats to one's mental security. Niebuhr notes further that when this arrogance is manifested on a collective level in the form of ethnic, racial, religious, or political groups and nations, the results are impersonal, irresponsible, and immoral pressure groups which seek to assert themselves over and against others in hypocritical self-righteousness. This *groupism* typically leads to political violence and oppression. In this way many of our basic human needs – self-esteem, security, recognition, effectiveness, accomplishment, etc., become twisted and distorted in these unhealthy and destructive attempts at fulfilling them. Thus, the fundamental drive towards self-realization is distorted into the will to power, superiority and domination as emphasized by Nietzsche, among others. This notion of sin as collective irresponsibility expresses our view of the meaning of Original Sin. The Churches' traditional explication of this doctrine in terms of inherited guilt and depravity has struck many persons of intellectual integrity and moral sensitivity as being irrational, morally perverse and psychologically harmful (such as Ashley Montague, 1976). We agree, and will critique this in Barth's Neo-Calvinist theology in a moment. In light of our detailed analysis presented thus far in this chapter, we conclude that Original Sin is the humanly created disordered social environments and present world-order which thwarts our human needs and warps and disfigures our humanity and essential goodness – in short, it is the mess that we all grow up in.

In line with our cross-cultural approach, we shall take a Buddhist look at ego-centricity.

The Buddhist Analysis.

Further insight into this ego-inflation is derived from the Buddhist psychological analysis of human personality. From a Buddhist perspective, egocentricity distorts an individual's consciousness and warps the emotional and evaluational ordering processes by which a person views himself and others. This leads to the repression and projection we covered earlier, egoism expresses itself in the three poisons of greed (*lobha*), hatred (*dosa*) and delusion (*moha*). Delusion is seen in the fact that people willfully deceive themselves in order to justify to themselves the claim that their attitudes and actions are not unethical or immoral, when in fact they are. This self-deception is carried out by re-thinking a situation in terms of the way one wants to view it. Egoism results in a disintegrated and unstable personality, filled with mistrust and anxiety, and leads to psychic illness.

Sin and Atonement: A Critique of the Conservative Protestant View

We are now in a position to know how the atonement of Jesus and the work of the Holy Spirit function to deliver human beings from the dark powers within them and their sins which alienate them on all levels. Before discussing this, however, we must critique an alternative theological view of human nature that is prevalent in types of Protestantism. We reject the Calvinist doctrine that humankind is totally depraved and inherently sinful as expressed in the work of Karl Barth. There are serious objections to this view that render it untenable. As we have seen, the biological and psychological evidence is against this, and it is tied to an outdated view of Original Sin as an inherited corruption or guilt that is transmitted through generations as a result of the Fall. This notion leads to the view that all that comes from human nature is evil; this degrades humankind below the level of personal responsibility as one is convicted not because of any particular sins which one freely commits but simply because one is human. Also Barth's view blurs the marked differences between rival political systems, i.e. the open society and totalitarian systems and ignores the relative rights and wrongs of social morality. Berdyaev rejects this theological degradation of humankind; for him, the human being is the icon of God, in whom the image of God may be distorted by sin but never completely destroyed. Culture and civilization ought in Barth's view to be related to our moral and spiritual nature. Can one really (as Barth did) listen to Mozart and believe in total depravity? And we might add, to Chopin?

Jesus and Salvation

The human being's existential frustration and conflicts drive him to seek liberation from this condition. In non-theistic religions this is through identity with the Ultimate or a transcendent state of existence, i.e. nirvana; in theistic religions this is through reconciliation and communion with God. In both cases, it is the Spirit who inspires people to search for salvation. In the Christian tradition, the human alienation from God arises from our sins. The awareness of the destructive and sinful tendencies within one's self fill a person with guilt which needs expiation or purification; this guilt can express itself through a shattering awareness of the gulf between what one is and what one ought to be in relation to the numinous purity of God. When humans come to realize that all their attempts to expiate their sins are inadequate, they are driven to despair, or self-hatred and disgust. As we noted earlier, all the attempts to transform one's habitual attitudes and responses that make up one's character traits, only make a person more absorbed in himself and frustrated, especially with regard to changing his thoughts and passions. This leads us to the logic of the Incarnation that we discussed in the last chapter – Christ as divine and human both saves and expiates. Here a key role of the Spirit is to enable human beings to participate in the salvific effects of the Atonement.

Jesus' expiatory self-sacrifice on behalf of humankind has a number of healing and therapeutic effects which can be seen in the light of our analysis of humankind's existential condition. (1) Jesus' act of expiation liberates human beings from the guilt of their sins and moral failure by revealing God's forgiving love which bears our sins while always seeking reconciliation. This brings a purification of toxic emotions and a catharsis and purgation of repressed destructive energies and complexes in the unconscious; (2) it also liberates us from self-hate, despair, and excessive concern and anxiety over our own status and self-image. Through the divine embodiment, we are given the awareness that God loves and accepts us as we are, even when we are unacceptable to ourselves. This is Paul Tillich's fine contemporary restatement of St Paul's teaching of justification by faith. This has profound transforming effects – through self-acceptance, a person can courageously accept her limitations including their dark side, and love herself as the image of God. In this way, she can forgive and accept others as they are and be more tolerant and compassionate towards them; this in turn opens up possibilities for fulfilling interpersonal loving relationships through which people can grow in self-knowledge. (3) This experience of God's self-giving love (*agapé*) is the answer to our sense of inferiority and insecurity and the need to seek psychological security through power and egocentricity. Jesus Christ's self-emptying (kenosis) reveals the divine power of passionate self-giving love through human powerlessness. By participating in Christ's divine identity through the Eucharist, a Christian ontologically shares in the joy and sorrow of God; there is nothing greater for him or her to lose. In this way, a Christian gains security – a peace or spiritual poise and stability at the center of her being in the midst of suffering and adversity in life; we call this an "exalted humbleness". This gives a person a sense of self-worth that does not depend upon specific achievements or worldly success, power, or status as measured by society; this frees the person from inferiority complexes. In Jesus' ethics, weakness, suffering, spiritual poverty and outward worldly failure are accorded a special dignity. (4) Through the Spirit's power the Divine Son becomes the living center of one's personality and reconciles the conflicting powers within the unconscious through an inner psychic re-orientation and transmutation of destructive energies; this brings harmony and balance. (5) Lastly, the Trinity's love, in all of these effects, melts our egocentricity thereby overcoming our alienation on various levels. Rigidity and uptightness are replaced by gracefulness and spontaneity in communion with the Spirit. We shall now look at some of the ways in which the Spirit helps people grow within the sacramental life of the Church.

The Spirit and Growth.

The Spirit's activity in enabling human beings to participate in the liberating salvific effects of Jesus' expiatory self-sacrifice constitutes the beginning of the process of spiritual growth within the Christian life; this entry into the Christian Way can take place through a sudden dramatic conversion experience or gradually over a period of time through an intellectual and spiritual quest in which people come to embrace Jesus as their Lord and Savior. Also, for many people who are born into the Christian community, the Spirit works to help them as unique individuals consciously to appropriate the salvation effected by Jesus, and this often takes place through an extended process whereby they seek to understand themselves and their own tradition better. In each of these ways, we can distinguish between two aspects of salvation – (1) there is the experience of liberation whereby people are delivered from the immediate threat of existential destruction owing to intra-psychic conflicts including the guilt of moral failure (this can also include dramatic physical healing) and (2) the process of ultimate transformation of spiritual growth and maturation whereby Christians are gradually recreated into the likeness of Christ through the holiness-making activity of the Holy Spirit within the Church. This brings us to an important point, namely, that the experience of liberation (or justification) does not in and of itself constitute salvation in any final sense; the experience of new life in Christ (regeneration) does not bring about a complete transformation of a person's consciousness, character or behavior, or bring intellectual or emotional maturity. The self-righteousness, intolerance, willful ignorance, and other uncharitable attitudes and destructive passions which many Christians manifest constitute sufficient empirical evidence that this is so. At this point it will be useful to focus briefly upon the concept of grace and distinguish between two senses or applications of it with regard to these aspects of Christian experience. Grace is the free and spontaneous gift of the Trinity's lovingkindness towards human beings. This boundless lovingcare is especially manifested in the Heavenly Father's gift of his only Son to save us through his expiatory self-sacrifice. In relationship to the atonement, grace refers to (1) God's unmerited favor expressed in the forgiveness of sins freely offered to all through Christ; in this context, grace is closely related to St Paul's concept of justification – God's merciful acceptance of sinners as being just or in a right relationship with herself through faith in Jesus as their divine savior; this forgiveness and new life becomes existentially actualized in a person when received in faith (trusting acceptance). As we noted earlier, a person experiences a purification of emotions, guilt, and healing, which brings revitalization and integration. (Thus, justification is not merely a forensic acquital, but serves to effect regeneration by the Holy Spirit.) God's generous help and assistance is also manifested in (2) the gift of the Holy Spirit's sanctifying and strengthening power; here the Holy Spirit not only transforms people, but also infuses the creativity and vital power of the Divine Life itself (the divine energies), especially through the sacraments. Thus, grace refers to the Trinity's loving influence upon human beings. From this perspective, justification, regeneration and sanctification, can all be viewed as phases in a unitary process. We will now develop the concept of salvation by focusing on the nature of spiritual growth.

Attaining Wholeness.

In our section on human goodness we pointed out that the urge to grow operates in humans toward self-realization in the wholeness-making process; this brings us to the literal meaning of salvation – to make whole (from Greek – *soterion* and Latin *salus*). The concepts of wholeness, health and healing, and holiness are intimately related in meaning and etymological origin; wholeness means to be in sound condition in the sense of completeness and integration, while health is a sound condition in which the various parts of the body and powers within the psyche function together efficiently in harmonious co-ordination. Healing is to restore to health from an unwholesome condition, while holiness is spiritual wholeness; as such, holiness is a condition characterized by a purity of consciousness and emotions and moral goodness. From this perspective, we can see that illness and mental sickness are destructive and disruptive powers which impair the vital functioning of either a portion or the whole of a living organism's being. Thus, illness as an organic or functional disorder is opposed to health as a vital balance and integration or dynamic wholeness (Meninger, 1963).

Further, physical and psychic illness results in a malfunctioning and distortion of consciousness (Sanford, 1977); whereas health involves an attitude of openness to life and to the development of the full range of ones' potentialities, nuerosis (emotional disturbance resulting from trauma or unconscious complexes) has a constricting and crippling effect which limits a person's growth and capacity to productively relate to life and others. The two aspects of salvation can be expressed in terms of the healing of an unsound condition and the ongoing wholeness-making process. Growth as the never-ending drive towards completion through the actualization of vital potentialities involves a continuous conflict between life-affirming forces (health) and life-thwarting forces (sickness). At the physiological level this is manifest in the anabolic and catabolic processes and in the conflict between antibodies and disease, while at the level of the psyche this is seen in the opposition between creative and destructive passions and energies. At both of these levels, healing of various illnesses and conflicts occur, as long as the life-process itself continues. Thus, while a person can experience liberation from the threat of psychic illness through divine grace, such healing is always limited and partial given the limitations of human finitude. Further, as Tillich has noted, the human psyche is a continuous battleground for divine and demonic forces (Tillich, 1963). Thus, salvation as the quest for wholeness is part of the daily struggle to be well and more fully human.

Earlier in this chapter, we referred to spiritual growth as involving the expansion of consciousness through a process of self-transcendence towards the Transcendent which is seen as the ultimate goal of human existence. At this point, we must emphasize the intimate relationship between spiritual and psychological growth. There can be no progress in spiritual development without progress in achieving emotional maturity and stability, the important marks of which are: (1) self-knowledge, which involves three inter-related aspects (Lowen 1985) – [a] being in touch with one's bodily self by sensing and experiencing one's feelings in their full intensity (self-awareness), which is dependent upon [b] having the inner capacity and freedom to express them fully (self-expression) and [c] being in conscious command and flexible control of their expression (self-possession); here, hypersensitivity and emotional instability is a mark of immaturity and often indicative of inferiority feelings and defensiveness; (2) the ability to establish and maintain productive loving relationships with others. The degree to which a person can create nurturing relationships that promote the growth of others as separate persons is a measure of the growth that she has achieved in herself. Further, it is only through such meaningful I-You relation-ships which involve creative mutual struggle that a person can grow in self-awareness by the effects that the other has on one's feelings, emotions and self-image. Also (3) it is important to take responsibility for one's actions, obligations, and the overall task of becoming an effective and worthwhile human being, all of which requires discipline and diligence. We should also foster (4) a sense of humour, a capacity for enjoyment and being able to laugh at the absurdities of life and the incongruities within one's self. Further, as we will see, the quest to attain intellectual integrity and sexual maturity and health, is also necessary for, and inseparable from, spiritual development. The inter-relationship between spiritual and psychological growth is also seen in the necessity of integrating the conscious and unconscious levels of the psyche in order to achieve spiritual wholeness. Becoming conscious of the processes and contents of the unconscious is needed in order to attain depth in self-knowledge. Dream analysis and the technique of active imagination provide insight into this dimension as do the various types of meditation and contemplative prayer that are found in the world's religions. Further, far from uprooting and eradicating religious feelings and beliefs, the psychoanalytic process can actually serve to foster the development of forms of religious experience and expression that are consonant with emotional maturity and mental health. Psychiatrists Louis Linn and Leo Schwarz (1958) point out that

> Emotional growth by way of psychoanalysis can actually result in an upsurge of religious feeling where none was consciously present before. It can result further in the replacement of the distorted religious expressions that accompany mental disturbance with forms of religious experience that are at once deeply satisfying and consistent with emotional maturity. In short, Freud's own technique, applied with apparent clinical success, has resulted in case after case, not in the disillusion of religious feelings, but rather in its augmentation and stabilization.

Spiritual Growth in the Church
The process of growth in the Christian life begins with the sacrament of baptism and being received into the New Community. Here we must emphasize the following points: (1) growth in the Christian life is continuous with whatever level of psycho-spiritual development a person has attained

at the time they become Christians: As we noted previously, the Spirit as *antaryāmin* is active in all human beings, driving them towards self-actualization or growth even though they may not be conscious of her Identity; this illustrates that divine grace perfects what is in human nature by bringing potentialities to creative fulfillment. (2) This process has a specific goal – deification or theosis by being transformed into the divine likeness of Jesus and this involves a progressive ontological participation in the Divine Life; this is expressed in St Irenaeus saying "In his unbounded love, God became what we are, that He might make us what he is." (3) Christian spiritual growth and salvation is communitarian in which personal integration takes place in a specific liturgical and sacramental context; it is not an individual path of salvation nor can it be reduced to a pragmatic symbolic system for attaining liberation as in some forms of Eastern religions. We can now look at some of the ways that life in the Church helps to provide for the important human needs that Fromm has delineated.

Participation in the fellowship of *agapé* in the New Community helps to overcome the loneliness and alienation that human beings experience. The need for interpersonal union is met spiritually through relationships of mutual support and loving concern which also foster human growth; in this context, members seek to respond with warm feeling and sensitivity to the needs of one another. Social life in the church also offers people opportunities to help people in the community which their particular church serves; this includes caring for the poor and needy. Such unselfish devotion to the welfare of human needs contributes to a person's self-worth by being productive and affecting others positively. Further, the Christian *darśana* as we have set forth here offers a unifying vision and focus of devotion which enables human beings to affirm life meaningfully in the face of absurdity, suffering, and tragedy.

Next, we will look at the role of the sacraments and the life of worship and prayer in promotion healing and spiritual growth. In our view, the church may be considered as an institutional communicator of divine power to human beings through the sacraments, which as Augustine held, are special visible means of channeling invisible divine grace. It is primarily through the sacraments and liturgy that the transforming power of the Holy Spirit is infused into human beings. Here, the Eastern Orthodox view of the church as a sacramental therapeutic organism is of real value and has a specifically Social-Trinitarian framework. Bishop Kallistos (formerly Timothy) Ware points out the church is (1) an earthly image of the unity-in-plurality in love of the Trinity; (2) the Mystical Body of Christ in whose Divine Organism Christians share; and (3) the locus of an ongoing Pentecost, in which the gifts and dynamic energies of the Spirit are imparted (Ware, 1976). With regard to the last point, the Spirit expresses herself in two complementary ways – (1) firstly, through communal bonding, she unifies people of different ethnic and social backgrounds in love and works to transform them into the divine likeness. St Paul lists the common gifts or fruits of the Spirit which express Christ-like virtues or excellences of character – love, joy, peace, patience, kindness, goodness, trustfulness, gentleness, and self-control (Galatians 5:22); through this holiness-making process, Christians grow in knowledge of God (see Colossians 3:10). Here we can bring out the importance of these virtuous attitudes and holiness for health. Christian virtues provide spiritual strength and unity to personality; they make for the emotional stability and self-control needed to accept and adequately cope with life's problems and frustrations. This is why in Greek philosophy virtue was looked upon as a vital power or potency. In addition to reconstructing our attitudes, the Spirit works to heal and transform our sick patterns of emotional reactions, which is vital for psychological and physical well-being. Holiness then, is a life-affirming condition of spiritual wholeness and moral integrity. Whereas God inherently possesses this quality in absolute perfection and numinous purity, human beings can to some degree manifest this holiness in themselves through the sanctifying grace of the Spirit. And (2) secondly the Spirit bestows the special gifts or charismata upon Christians as unique individuals to exercise these talents in serving the church and the community. Here human holiness is expressed in a life dedicated or consecrated to creatively serving God and helping others; thus, at this level, holiness also refers to the quality of being set apart or sacred through intimate contact with God. St Paul discusses these gifts in I Corinthians 12:4–11 which include healing, prophecy, miracles, discernment, wisdom and speaking in tongues; while in Chapter 13 he lists the higher gifts of faith, hope and love/ *agapé* which are given to all and the most excellent is *agapé*. In our view too much emphasis is placed on speaking in tongues in some Protestant denominations as a criterion of the presence of the Spirit in a person's life (Baptism by the Spirit). The value of the phenomena is rather questionable and is certainly on a lower level than the personal qualities such as love that the Spirit manifests herself through.

The Spirit and the Sacraments

Now we will focus on the Spirit's activity in the Sacraments. In accordance with our Anglo-Catholic and Orthodox traditions, we list the number of sacraments at seven; this is in contrast with various Protestant denominations which have reduced the number of sacraments to those of Baptism and the Eucharist. The sacrament of Baptism, while it occurs only once, is very significant as it is the means by which a person is initiated into the agapeistic life of the church. Baptism, like marriage and holy orders, is a rite of passage which marks an important transition stage in a person's life and signals a change in their status. Here, through the regenerating power of the Spirit, a person receives a new identity as an adopted child of God by participating spiritually in the death and resurrection of the Divine Son. The once and for all character of Baptism indicates that a person has begun a new life and a process of spiritual growth in which the demonic powers of sin, sickness and death have lost their power to keep her from ultimately reaching fulfillment eschatologically. In Baptism, Christ as it were, becomes embryonically implanted by the Spirit who is also sealed or imprinted on the person's identity through the

Sacrament of Charismation or Confirmation by being anointed with oil. As a person grows in the Christian life, he begins to realize his own unique wholeness in union with Jesus whose spiritual wholeness progressively unfolds and is manifest in his life; this is the meaning of realizing the mature or full stature of Christ.

In our first chapter, we noted that since the earliest times, the Eucharist has been the central act of Christian worship and expresses the continuing living presence of the Risen Lord in the midst of the faithful. Together with the early church, we view the nature of the Eucharist in a very real physical sense – by partaking of the elements, Christians partake of the Body and Blood of Jesus who becomes present in the bread and wine in a manner similar to that of his embodiment, i.e. the same healing power that flowed through Jesus' human body is now communicated in this sacrament. The life-giving and healing power of the Eucharist was emphasized by the Eastern Fathers such as Bishop Ignatius of Antioch who referred to as "the medicine of immortality". The sacred meal or love feast unifies the members of the church together with one another in solidarity in union with Christ. The Spirit is operative here in the mass or Liturgy whereby she descends upon the elements and consecrates them and transforms them into the Body and Blood of Jesus. Marriage, the sacrament of love, is also a gift of the Holy Spirit.

Marriage is blessed by Jesus and overcomes human alienation through spiritual and physical closeness and communion. The companionship of married life serves to promote growth and healing through mutual acceptance, loving care and mutual support. Through commitment, friendship (*philia*), pleasure and intimacy, marriage is ideally the most fulfilling type of relationship that men and women can share. Marriage also provides the context for experiencing the Trinity through the ecstasy of erotic love. In the passionate fusion of sexual intercourse and orgasm, a couple can existentially participate in the intensity and joy of the Communal Bond of the Holy Spirit, through whom the Father and the Son fuse themselves in the eternal process of love which is the essence of the Divine Life; also, this mutual self-giving of lover and beloved may procreatively bring into being a co-beloved who is an image of the Holy Spirit; in this way, family life also reflects the we-community of the Trinity. This connection between erotic love and the Social Trinity shows that *eros* (passionate desire for interpersonal union inspired by the beauty or sexual attractiveness of another), need not be opposed to *agapé* (reverential lovingcare given to nurture a person's spiritual growth), but can serve as the modality of its expression. Within the context of a monagamous relationship involving genuine mutual caring, respect and responsibility, the biologically based drive of sexual energy (*epythemia*) can be transfigured and imbued with spiritual value and meaning. We also recognize that relationships of this quality (which respect the sanctity of a person) are possible outside of and prior to the consecration of marriage, and represent a real achievement in the art of living. With regard to the issue of divorce, we think it is cruel to force people with irreconciliable differences to remain married and live in hypocrisy by not permitting them to divorce or threatening to exclude them from the sacraments if they do; both of our Anglican and Orthodox traditions recognize the tragic necessity for divorce when all possible attempts at reconciliation have failed.

In the sacrament of holy orders or priestly ministry ordained men and women receive special charismas from the Spirit. In addition to administration of the Sacraments, and inspired preaching and teaching, the Spirit is especially manifest in the ministry through the healing, pastoral counselling and spiritual direction which priests carry out. There are a number of ways in which priests are involved in healing – in the sacrament of holy unction or anointing of the sick, the grace and healing power is communicated to the sick through prayer by laying on of hands, and anointing with holy water or oil; in cases where the sick person is terminally ill, the Spirit imparts peace and spiritual strength to accept death and the start of the next level of existence in the eschaton; laying of hands is also used in many other instances. Intercessory prayer for people is also an important aspect of pastoral work. In his book *Healing* (1975), Francis MacNutt discusses prayer offered for the healing of spiritual sickness caused by sin and guilt, physical illness, emotional wounds and hurts including those in the form of painful memories from the past, and also prayer for deliverance as from possession from demonic forces or complexes in the unconscious. Through spiritual direction and counselling, the Spirit imparts the gift of discernment to enable the priest to guide, help and console people with problems and crises in their lives (especially involving interpersonal relations) and in assisting them to make progress in their prayer life and grow spiritually. Together with the shaman, priests are wounded healers and it is only through having undergone spiritual and emotional crises in their own lives and getting sick, that they are able to function effectively as healers. This is closely related to the minister's activity in the work of reconciliation and the sacrament of penance or confession. Repentance is a very important aspect of the Christian life as a person's sins cause spiritual sickness and disrupt their fellowship with God. Confession along with daily repentance are needed to keep oneself open to the transforming power of the Spirit. Confession is therapeutic in that it releases repressed anxiety, guilt and anger which creates psychic disequilibrium. Jung stressed the importance of confession: "There appears to be a conscience in mankind which severely punishes the man who does not somehow and at sometime at whatever cost to himself, cease to defend and assert himself, and instead confess himself to be fallible and human" (Jung, 1933, p. 39). Confession and forgiveness are closely related to the Eucharist which also purifies persons from their sins. We will now look at how other religious practices in the Christian life promote healing and growth.

Worship and Human Transformation

Thus far, we have seen that the sacraments are visible means of conveying divine power and grace to Christians. Here, we will focus on the importance of the activity of worship as a transforming experience. The institutionalized rituals of the Mass and Liturgy both express the awe-inspiring power and holiness of God and evoke sacral sentiments in the worshipper. Worship expresses a person's adoration, praise and faithful devotion towards the Divine which is seen as the Most Real of all realities and the Ultimate Value. Sacramental worship involves liturgical celebration and provides the primary context in which the vision of the Trinity is apprehended. We can illustrate these points with reference to the Eastern Orthodox Liturgy. The liturgy symbolically presents and reenacts the key events in the life of Christ as the drama of humankind's salvation and enables people to participate in the power and meaning of these events. The majestic splendor of God is conveyed through the beauty and richness of sacred artistic forms (such as icons) and ritual actions. In this sacramental vision, sensuous and material forms are appropriate mediums for communicating the Holy as the divine embodiment of the Son effected the sanctification of the matter of the cosmos. In the beauty of colors and forms, the vibrating sounds of chanting and singing, the fragrance of incense, the performance of bodily gestures, and partaking of the bread and wine in the Eucharist, a Christian can both worship and experience God through all the five senses. Religious experience in worship has transforming effects by illuminating a person's consciousness and purifying and sanctifying their emotions.

This liturgical worship provides the "symbolic life" that is necessary for spiritual health and growth. As we noted earlier, religious symbols convey divine power and meaning and have the healing effect of unifying conflicting tendencies in the psyche. In the liturgy Christians experience many of the same dramatic symbolic patterns that appear in their dreams and visions. In this ritual activity, the divine energies flow into a person through both the outer and inner worlds of experience which begin to form a unified continuum; thus, in the symbolic life, the Spirit functions to progressively integrate the conscious and unconscious dimensions of the psyche in the process of self-transcendence. Here, not only are the numinous and contemplative strands of religious

341

experience fused together, but also the pan-en-henic as the whole cosmos is seen as transfigured by divinizing energies of the Trinity. All of this brings out the importance of tradition as the ongoing life of the Spirit in the church throughout history. Participation in the richness of the symbolic life of Christian tradition not only enables one to share in the cultural creations and accumulated wisdom and values of the past, but also gives one a deep sense of human history; this adds breath to consciousness and contributes to a person's sense of meaning in the present.

The transforming power of worship is also effected in the inspired preaching of the Gospel, through which the dynamic power of the Spirit is expressed and is transferred to the listener. Here, through the medium of the Scriptures, the Spirit often brings people to experience Jesus as their Savior in conversion experience. In prophetic preaching in the church, the Spirit shakes Christians out of the complacency of their current status quo and self-image thereby challenging them to further moral and spiritual growth. The Spirit also moves Christians to get actively involved in helping people in need through the performance of spiritual and corporeal works of mercy, and in working to create a more just society by striving to eliminate oppression, discrimination, intolerance and other social ills that degrade and dehumanize people. By inspiring sincere worship and prayer, the Spirit urges Christians to become more honest with themselves and their Creator by setting aside their hypocrisies and self-deceptions of daily living; by doing this, they can rededicate themselves to becoming more worthy and responsible disciples of Christ.

Creative Effects of Christian Faith

Christian faith is an attitude of trustfulness or reliable assurance in the reality, goodness, and lovingkindness of the Trinity as revealed in the divine embodiment of Jesus and cognitively apprehended through the grace of the Spirit. This trustfulness is characterized by an openness and receptivity to God's loving Will together with the desire to express this in one's life and actions. Thus, faith includes three components – belief (assent) and trust based on experiential knowledge; (without knowledge, trust and belief are groundless – Owen, 1985, p. 3). Faith has the effect of integrating personality by focusing a person's psycho-physical life energies upon God as the object of ultimate concern. As Tillich points out, mature faith unifies volitional commitment, emotional participation and intellectual assent together in an act of self-affirmation (Tillich, 1957). Further, faith has a biological dimension as expressed in the trusting acceptance of one's body and sexuality and receptivity to the Spirit's vitalizing energies which permeate these (Lowen, 1973). This physical basis of faith is necessary for emotional health and a sound spirituality (we will develop this further a bit later). Faithful devotion to serving God also has the therapeutic effect of promoting a disciplined way of life that is purposefully oriented towards realizing one's potentialities through self-giving love, productive work and creativity; this productive character orientation is the antidote for laziness as well as the dissipation of one's energies through aimless activity or wasteful self-indulgence (both of which are irresponsible). Beyond this, faith in God provides hope and courage which are connected to the doctrine of divine providence, which expresses God's foresight, inner guidance and sustaining care in relation to her creatures. From a Christian perspective, providence is most clearly evidenced in the Heavenly Father's gift of his Son to be our Savior. The Christian attitude of hope is the confident expectation that our desire for fulfillment will be realized eschatologically in the agapistic life of the Trinity. Earlier we noted that by being ontologically united with Christ in the Eucharist, Christians share in the joy and sorrow of God and this enables them to courageously affirm life in face of suffering and tragedy. Hope gives a person the confidence that no matter what suffering they may have to endure due to the tragic necessity inherent in nature and biology and history, these contingent events (which do not, as such, reflect Providence) cannot prevent God's sustaining care from enabling them from growing spiritually. Divine Providence then, is the sovereignty of the Trinity's passionate self-giving love which cannot be thwarted by the forces of evil and destruction but works creatively in spite of these in the spiritual life of Christians through their faith, hope, and love. Thus, in this Christian perspective, suffering endured with grace can purify a person's consciousness and emotions. Further, this identity with Jesus can give a Christian the courage to risk and sacrifice his life for the welfare of others as well as undergoing martyrdom as the ultimate act of worship and self-determination.

Contemplative Prayer and Growth in the Christian Life

The practice of contemplative prayer in Christianity is highly developed in the Roman Catholic and Eastern Orthodox traditions (Leech, 1980). Prayer is making contact with God and we can distinguish between two main types — (1) first there is the personal dramatic type of prayer which is expressed in petitions, confession, intercession, praise and thanksgiving; here, God is addressed personally as You; and (2) contemplative prayer, which is more reflective, less discursive and generally occurs within a disciplined routine involving periods of silence. By this practice, a person seeks to enter into intimate communion with God within the still center of her being; here, the Divine Light of the Trinity is cognitively apprehended in an interior unifying vision through a kind of "love-gnosis" (Lossky, 1957, p. 207, 215–16). Silence, stillness and solitude provide the context needed for self-discovery and making progress in developing one's capacity to pray. This ability to experience solitude and loneliness is also an important mark of emotional maturity and the courage to be. Contemplative prayer involves the symbolic and intuitive-wholistic hemisphere of the brain and the cultivation of "feminine" spiritual qualities such as creative receptivity, patience, listening and nurturing sensitivity. Jung's theory of the androgynous nature of the psyche (which reflects divine selfless spirits of the Trinity) shows the need for men to cultivate their inner femininity (anima) and feelings; this indicates that male machismo is not conducive to wholeness. The processes that take place in contemplative prayer are similar to those that take place in depth-psychology. In both cases, a person begins a journey and exploration into the depth of the unconscious at the center of which is the Divine Reality (Thompson, 1982).

The continuous mental recitation of the Jesus prayer with breathing in and out, as we discussed earlier, helps to unify the scattered energies of the mind and bring stability and balance. This type of prayer also helps to cleanse a person's consciousness of distortions caused by unconscious complexes. Contemplative prayer has the additional therapeutic effect of bringing up repressed anger, resentment and memories of past emotional hurts which can then be healed by divine grace; this contributes to growth in self-knowledge which is co-relative with experiencing God more fully. Next, we will focus on some of the problems encountered in the process of spiritual growth.

Emotional Maturity and the Spirit

Earlier in this chapter, we pointed out that there could be no progress in spiritual growth without progress towards achieving emotional maturity, intellectual integrity, and sexual health; here, we will develop these points further. The quest to become the mature persons that God intended us to be is a continuous day to day struggle. In order to make progress towards this end, human beings must be willing to undergo considerable inner suffering by experiencing anxiety, loneliness, insecurity and also conflict, separation and loss in their interpersonal relationships; this entails the willingness to renounce secure patterns of existence by taking risks and embracing new responsibilities and challenges in order to realize their creative potentialities. Moreover, people have to wrestle continually with destructive passions in themselves and cope with difficult problems and situations at each stage of the life process. This stressful and taxing struggle requires such courage and commitment that many people do not want to make the effort and prefer to remain at less mature and spiritually impoverished levels of personal development. This last point is emphasized by M. Scott Peck in his book on the psychology of love and spiritual growth – *The Road Less Travelled* (1978). Peck states that human beings have an almost inherent tendency to resist growing spiritually and to refuse to co-operate with God's nurturing grace and love which is available to help them in this painful process.

Peck calls this spiritual inertia "laziness", which in traditional Christian theology is called the vice of sloth; this lethargy manifests itself in a lack of concern, sensitivity and responsiveness to the needs of others and an obdurate refusal to grow up. However, the sense of security and reduced anxiety that is obtained by remaining at less responsible stages of emotional development has detrimental effects and leads to neurosis, which is always a substitute for legitimate suffering, i.e., that which is connected with growth; here, a person's pent-up and unrealized creative potentialities degenerate into a psychic cancer of negativity resulting in emotional sickness and destructiveness. All of this is related to the Christian life as follows. Often Christians utilize their religious beliefs, attitudes and practices to shield and protect themselves from confronting the difficult and painful problems connected with personal growth and even experiencing the fullness of life. In this case, Christian spirituality has the pathological effect of preserving emotional immaturity, instead of helping people towards integration and wholeness and a more responsible existence. Some of the common ways in which this neurotic spirituality manifests itself are as follows.

Pseudo-Innocence

Many Christians identify themselves with an idealized self-image or persona of spiritual goodness or virtue. The formation of this image is often influenced by the ethical teachings and exemplary models of piety and saintliness of the particular denomination to which a Christian may belong. While these can provide inspiration, they can also stifle a person from developing their own individuality and expressing their own authentic feelings when they uncritically identify themselves with these models of belief and piety; this artificial persona separates a person from their true self and leads to self-deception and hypocrisy. This self-image of goodness provides psychological security outwardly against others who are seen to be less virtuous and inwardly against the darkness in oneself which is repressed and projected onto others. Rollo May refers to this immature spiritual orientation as "pseudo-innocence" (May, 1974). However, mature spirituality is based on real life experience and is incompatible with naivete in any form or childhood innocence. As we noted earlier, growth in self-knowledge requires that a person confront and consciously accept their shadow or dark side of themselves which exists within the unconscious. This involves recognizing the potential for evil and destructiveness in oneself. Here, the Spirit will try to stimulate a Christian to let go of immature self-images and patterns of behavior by arousing anxiety within the unconscious through psychic energies in the form of voices, visions, thoughts, feelings and also dramatic images and symbols in dreams. The Spirit's use of anxiety as an urge to growth reflects the inexorably demanding character of God's agapistic love which aims at a creature's fullest development. Continued resistance to God's nurturing grace (blasphemy against the Spirit) typically results in serious emotional sickness which can involve psychotic symptoms (Boisen, 1955, Sanford, 1977). However, if a Christian can see the spiritual meaning of such an individuation crisis, healing and a creative transformation of the personality can take place. Jung emphasizes that during this time, it is vital for a person to have the help of an experienced spiritual guide or else they may become disintegrated by the fear and panic evoked by the numinous power and strangeness of the unconscious material which spontaneously and involuntarily wells up into consciousness from within. It is important to note as John Sanford (1977) points out, that such numinous and often seemingly threatening psychic automatisms are actually creative forces in disguise. This problem of pseudo-innocence is closely related to problems concerning human sexuality which we will turn to next.

Sexual and Spiritual Liberation
Another and even more serious form of pathological Christian spirituality results from the failure to achieve sexual

347

maturity and health (Leech, 1977). The integration of one's spirituality and sexuality is absolutely essential for attaining personal wholeness. As is well known, the Christian tradition contains teachings about human sexuality that are negative, distorted and psychologically untenable. The substance of many of these views is a disparagement of sensuality, sexuality and the body which are seen as real obstacles to attaining holiness and spiritual perfection. The teachings of St Augustine in particular, have had a widespread negative effect; Augustine (influenced by Manicheanism) regarded sexual intercourse in marriage as sinful (i.e., "lustful") unless it was for the purposes of procreation in his work *Marriage and Concupiscence*; this position was also endorsed by Aquinas, Luther and Calvin and was expressed in Pope Paul's encyclical *Humanae Vitae* of 1968 which rejected artificial methods of contraception. This irrational position has received widespread criticism from Catholics, including laypeople, priests and psychiatrists. This view fails to recognize that sexual intercourse is not simply for procreation but for the expression of self-giving love (*agapé*) between two persons. It is also, in our view, cruel to insist that couples engage in intercourse with the fear of conception and having unwanted children; it places anxiety and strain on both partners and leads to emotional distress. It also suppresses the natural expression of healthy sexual feelings and passions.

Another injurious teaching is that masturbation or auto-eroticism is a sin and is harmful (as stated in the recent Pocket Catholic Dictionary, 1985). Here too, the medical and psychiatric evidence is completely against this. Rather, it is a normal and rational way of relieving psycho-sexual tension. The use of ascetical techniques often employed in contemplative spiritual practice to subdue bodily passions, has also had unwholesome effects. The tradition also contains negative views regarding women who are still denied the right to be ordained in the Catholic and Orthodox traditions. These warped and suppressive views about sex and the body have been most harmful and the source of numerous broken lives through serious emotional illness, neurotic guilt, repression, confusion and fear. By contrast, mature spirituality is the creative expression of the integral unity of a person's psycho-physical life energies in states of being and activity in relation to the Transcendent. The false separation of religion and sex leads to a schizoid condition in which a person is out of touch with his or her feelings and insensitive to his or her body and sexuality; this leads to detachment and the avoidance of close personal relationships involving touching, physical contact and warmth and sensual pleasure which are vital for emotional health. Beyond this, it can lead to demonic splits and repression in the unconscious; this can manifest itself through overcompensation in obsessive and compulsive ritual practices or in frustration which leads to hostility and violent outburst; here, the criticisms of these conditions by humanistic psychology must be taken account of. Such "angelic" or disembodied spirituality often represents the attempt of Christians to avoid coming to terms with their sexuality and feelings. However, religious piety or intellectual activity cannot serve as a substitute for emotional and sexual maturity. Earlier, we referred to the work of Dr. Alexander Lowen who held that faith has a biological basis in the trusting receptivity to the Spirit's creativity which permeate one's bodily nature, passions and sexuality. The integration of one's spirituality and sexuality provides a strong sense of identity and of being grounded firmly in reality and meaningfully related with all life (Lowen, 1973).

In these harmonious states of being, people can truly manifest the gracefulness and spontaneity of the Spirit in their lives; also, as we will see, being open to one's intense feelings and passions is necessary for creativity. Here, Lowen's psychiatric work (which follows that of his teacher Wilhelm Reich) is valuable as it shows that the repression of feelings, as in the schizoid condition described above, is reflected in the muscular tensions and rigidities in a person's body ("muscular armor"); here, sexual love culminating in full orgasm has the therapeutic effect of loosening these crippling inhibitions. Also, as Lowen points out, masturbation provides the opportunity to fully encounter and confidently accept one's bodily self (Lowen, 1965). Thus, the betrayal of the body in much of traditional Christianity leads to illness; here, the Spirit will also function through anxiety to urge Christians to honestly confront their fears and insecurities about their sexuality so that they can be healed. It is important that people be knowledgeable and informed as regards the latest findings in human sexuality, such as the recently confirmed discovery of the G-Spot and vaginal orgasm in women in order to help one another to find sexual fulfillment (Ladas, Whipple, Perry, 1982). Lastly, we think that our Social-Trinitarian theology has the wholesome practical effect of bringing out the sacredness of erotic love, i.e., the ecstasy of making love can be the means whereby enlightened Christians can intensely experience and share in the joy of the Communal Bond of the Holy Spirit; this is Christian *tantra*.

The Problem of Dogmatism

Another unstable form of Christian spirituality results from the failure to achieve an intellectually mature and responsible religious orientation which combines critical reflection together with existential commitment. This viewpoint is expressed in our principle of "external softness and confessional certitude" which forms the epistemological basis of our modern Christian theology (see Part I on methodology). In this context, critical reflection involves the conscientious use of both theory and praxis to analyze the veridicality and soundness of Christian beliefs and doctrines. This critical outlook requires honest self-criticism and a courageous dedication to the pursuit of truth by subjecting one's beliefs to the most rigorous scrutiny and examination. However, this mature religious orientation involves a willingness to live with a large measure of doubt, and uncertainty about the finality and particular formulations of one's beliefs (Tillich). As we have expressed it, faith is primarily trustfulness and commitment based upon religious experience which constitutes its cognitive content. However, this experience is necessarily partial and limited by the entire cultural and psychological mediums through which it is apprehended, as are the propositions and formulations with which it is expressed. Thus, faith is certainly compatible with having serious doubts about the adequacy of the interpretations and doctrines which delineate it. Further, this mature religious attitude involves the recognition that neither the Bible, the teachings of the Pope nor the doctrines of a particular Church, are inherently infallible or not subject to criticism and revision. This entails that all authority is in a vital sense adopted, that is, the authority of the Bible or the Pope depends upon an act of acceptance through commitment on the part of the individual who acknowledges them as such. Here, we adhere to the standard Anglican position on biblical revelation – to qualify as revelatory or authoritative, a belief or doctrine must satisfy the dictates of reason and conscience and be confirmed by personal life experience in harmony with community testimony. For us, this requires analyzing and testing these beliefs and various theological positions in using the criteria of truth in religion which we set forth in our last chapter.

However, some Christians are unable to cope with doubt and uncertainty and seek psychological security by repressing their doubt in the unconscious, rather than responsibly confronting it; this often takes the form of embracing the religious and moral "certainty" offered by fundamentalist groups which regard the literal text of the Bible or of some other document as infallible or inerrant. However, as this view is contradicted by the data of modern science (i.e., cosmology and evolution) and historical scholarship and textual criticism of the Bible, it is unsound and requires an abdication of intellectual responsibility to adhere to it. This separation of intellectual integrity from the emotional and volitional dimensions of faith (Tillich) results in a distorted religious consciousness. The repressed doubt leads to dangerous splits in the personality which cause instability and conflict. Typically, this manifests itself in uncharitable attitudes and behavior such as self-righteousness and hostility and intolerance towards others who reject such views and who are seen as threats to one's security. Doubt which is repressed and hidden behind a self-deceptive mask of triumphant faith and certainty (i.e. by overcompensation) can lead to dangerous fanaticism. Thus, emotional commitment and ultimate concern without critical reflection easily lead to rigid narrow-minded dogmatism and fanaticism on the part of fundamentalist religious groups or quasi-religious groups, such as Marxist or Fascist "true believers". Finally, we should point out, intellectually unsound forms of Christian belief are reflected in distorted views of God, who is pictured in terms of the worst in human emotions such as jealousy, hate and vengeance. As Berdyaev accurately points out, these exoteric and revolting conceptions of God (which are warped psychological projections) have had the negative effect of driving many people of insight and sensitivity away from Christianity towards atheism, which they affirm on humanistic grounds (Berdyaev, 1948). Together, with Berdyaev, we think that the vision of the Divine Reality as Social Trinitarian Love is the best answer to this problem. Next we will look at the creative life in the Spirit.

Freedom, Creativity and the Christian Life

In this last section, we shall focus on freedom and creativity in the Christian life; here, we shall draw together material from our previous discussion. By enabling human beings to share in the redemption effected by Jesus, the Holy Spirit sets them free to become all that they can become through a life of self-giving love and creativity. In this chapter, we have seen ways in which the Spirit works to heal and transform people. The Spirit always operates in ways which respect a person's freedom. We think that the conflict between St Augustine and Pelagius over the role that human free will plays in salvation is in some respects misleading, as both positions contain an element of truth and both are reflected in the concept of the *antaryāmin*. Here, our cross-cultural perspective is especially helpful as regards this topic. In Hindu theism, followers of Ramanuja's theology (Vaishnavism) divided into two different schools over the question of grace and free will in salvation. The one held to the cat-offspring method doctrine according to which God brings people to salvation as a cat transports her young: here, the kitten is passive, and is taken from point A to point B by the scruff of its neck. The other held to the monkey-offspring method in which God leads people to salvation as a mother monkey carries her young: here, the little one needs to make some effort himself, clinging to the hip of his mother to get from A to B. We think that these two views are complementary and reflect the two aspects of salvation: in the initial act of being saved or healed by Jesus (liberation) a person may be quite passive (even here, she must at least have the desire or will to be saved, even though she cannot liberate herself by her own efforts); while in the process of transformation, the Spirit requires the active co-operation and efforts on the part of the Christians to help them grow. Thus, we see the relation between human beings and the Spirit as constituted by a genuine synergy involving grace and free will, while recognizing that the divine energies of the Spirit are indispensable for salvation.

This brings us to the distinctive quality of Christian freedom and life in communion with the Spirit. In this context, freedom is not simply the capacity to act without external or internal constraint, but a state of being in harmony with the movements of the Spirit within oneself. Through a trusting receptivity to the Spirit's transforming power and creative energies that permeate one's life, freedom is experienced as graceful spontaneity. Here, a person can truly be themselves and can naturally and un self-consciously act in harmony with God's loving Will in their lives. This spiritual freedom also gives Christian ethics a distinctive flavor. "Ethos" primarily refers to a lifestyle rather than to a set of norms or principles to guide behavior. The Christian ethos is midway between two diametrically opposed positions: the first is that of legalism or "heteronomy" (Tillich) in which an individual's behavior is determined by restraints imposed from without. The primary example of this is seen in Orthodox Judaism, which follows an extensive legal code that prescribes precise norms (precepts) of religious piety and ethical behavior; the meticulous observance of these divinely inspired laws is necessary to attain holiness and remain in a right relationship with the Creator. This view is also seen in conservative Protestant denominations that are influenced by Calvin, who held that Old Testament laws (excluding Jewish ceremonial laws) as the ten commandments were to regulate Christian life; he also regarded New Testament ethical teachings (as the Sermon on the Mount) as rules which prescribe proper behavior and serve as a standard to measure progress in sanctification. This heteronomous structure is also typified by the extensive system of natural law ethics and casuistry in the monarchical Roman Catholic tradition. However, the spiritual freedom of the Gospel is different from the ethics of and the outward observance of laws, which cannot transform so effectively, we believe, a person's character traits. Moreover, this position is ultimately problematic as the imposition of restraints provokes rebellion and hostility, especially when these are life-thwarting and stifle individual self-expression; this typically results in demonic splits in the psyche in which resentment and doubts about these laws are repressed in the unconscious. Heteronomy, then, spiritually enslaves people.

The opposite position to this is antinomianism or autonomy (Tillich) in which an individual's behavior is governed by his own criteria and norms of what is ethical; people who reject the legalism or supressive teachings of their religious tradition or socially established morality, are often led to this type of rebellious independence. Some Christians, in affirming the freedom of the Gospel, have made the mistaken inference that because faith alone is sufficient for salvation, a person is not obligated to observe generally accepted principles of ethical conduct: historically, this can be seen in St Paul's conflict with the Church at Corinth and Luther's with elements of the radical Reformation (see his essay *The Freedom of a Christian*); this type of spiritual anarchy is often used as a pretext for engaging in libertine self-indulgence, but this leads to a new enslavement to desires and egocentricity. This immoral selfishness is characteristic of secular Western "possessive individualism" in which people exercise their freedom as "self-rule" (see Moltmann, 1981, ch. 1) in the form of power over and against others with whom they compete with in a capitalist society; also, this arbitrary freedom can be expressed in irrational and capricious acts.

In contrast to these, an authentic Christian ethic is life in the Spirit, or what Tillich calls "theonomy". As we noted above, through a harmony of wills, the Spirit enables Christians to fulfill spontaneously the law of self-giving love (*agapé*) which is internalized within a person's being. As God's love seeks a person's deepest welfare and fulfillment, receptivity to the divine Will in no way constrains their freedom. Unlike freedom as self-rule, this spiritual freedom unites people together in a communion of love and friendship in the church (called "sobornost" in Eastern Orthodox theology). Thus, the Spirit's power liberates people to realize their own unique potential through creativity, which is our next topic.

Realizing Our Creativity

In his brilliant work *The Destiny of Man* (1931), Nikolai Berdyaev argued that the authentic Christian life is a creative life. According to Berdyaev, Jesus referred to humankind's creative vocation in his parable of the talents; these talents are divine gifts and creative potential which are given to human beings. Here, men and women receive the high calling to fulfill their exalted destiny by being co-creators with God; Berdyaev calls this life the ethic of the Holy Spirit. This brings us to the nature of creativity. Creativity is the act or process of bringing something new into being; it also refers to the ability that people can have for producing novel ideas, insights, solutions to problems, mechanical inventions, artistic forms or objects, among others. This creativity is manifest in all areas of human cultural activity as in the arts and sciences, law, philosophy, religion and ethics, and sports. Creativity involves the actualization of potentialities in both the biological and spiritual dimensions of human life. As such, creativity is life-affirming in sustaining and bringing forth new vital physical and spiritual life energies in the process of growth. This shows that agapistic love or giving one's best self for another's good is always creative.

Agapé is valuing and caring for other persons by actively seeking their welfare and spiritual growth as unique individuals. The highest form of creativity is the mutual self-giving of sexual love when it produces a new living being that reflects the image of God.

Modern psychological experiments and studies have disclosed a number of important factors which in varying degrees together are necessary for creativity, and these include (1) the capacity for novel insight as seen in the richness of ideas and originality of thought (divergent thinking). While intelligence in the form of analytic reasoning (convergent thinking) is also involved here, creative people have developed powers of intuition upon which they often rely; they also are receptive to the non-rational powers in the unconscious which are a source of inspiration and wisdom; closely related to this is (2) the capacity for imagination and vision. Imaginative fertility is a vital source of creativity by envisioning new images, symbolic forms and new possibilities for human existence, and it was through imagination that God created the cosmos (3) Passion or intensity of feeling and a heightened sense of consciousness in the encounter with the object of creation is also necessary. This point is stressed by Berdyaev and more recently by Rollo May (May, 1975). Here, being highly intelligent or possessing inborn talents is not sufficient for attaining the highest levels of creativity and realization of potentialities unless there is a willingness to commit passionately one's whole being to the creative process; for example, a talented painter or musician must spend years of diligent work to perfect her techniques. This involves the courage and willingness to make sacrifices, endure anxiety and stress and suffer intense feelings such as frustration or anger. How often have people failed to develop their potentialities because of laziness, fear of failure, or of over-exertion! However, Jesus warns that failure to develop one's talents and return them with profit will result in their being taken away; as we saw earlier, pent-up creative potentialities turn into a destructive psychic cancer of negativity.

Further, as Berdyaev states, these divine gifts are not to

be passively awaited upon and received, but must be freely taken by man and performed actively and responsibly as tasks. This brings us to the fact that highly creative people experience greater internal conflict within their personality and in the unconscious between the life-affirming forces and diabolical forces of chaos and disorder, especially compulsions (Leonard, 1989); this often results in periods of mental and emotional imbalance or even madness (as in the case of Van Gogh). However, with their more profound level of self-awareness, creative people are both madder and saner than the average person. Also, as creativity is an expression of the whole person, highly creative people typically have powerful and robust sexual passions or animal spirits which need to be affirmed (Lowen, 1965). (4) Lastly, creativity requires freedom, which is indispensable for individual self-expression and spiritual growth; a free and open democratic liberal society provides the best context for creativity to flourish in. In the Christian life, the grace of the Holy Spirit is operative in each of these dimensions of human creativity. The Eastern Orthodox philosopher Boris Vysheslavtsev points out that the Spirit stimulates the imagination and inspires persons by introducing images of beauty into the realm of the unconscious; this arouses the desire and the will to embody these in the physical reality of space and time through creativity; also, through the process of sublimation, the Spirit can transfigure both sexual energy and that of dark strivings and powers in the unconscious and channel these into the activity of creation (see his *The Ethics of Transfigured Eros*, 1931). Communion with the Spirit allows Christians to experience creativity as self-justifying fulfillment; this actualization of their creative potentialities fills a person with Joy which is a state of being and not just a momentary "peak experience". Through the ecstasy of creativity, human beings bring into existence new values and realities which enrich their own lives and the Divine Life itself. In relation to creativity, values are conscious states of being and activity that enrich life and actualize humans' potentialities (such as loving relationships and productive work). Here, value also refers to the worth that created realities have both instrumentally in terms of utility and intrinsically as objects of human and Divine consciousness, such as beauty. This brings us to the question of the meaning of life.

The Meaning of Life

In this context, meaning is not used in a linguistic sense as referring to significance that is communicated in symbols; here, meaning is used in an existential sense to refer to a state in which a person can affirm life creatively and strive to continue to persist in their being. Meaning in life depends upon the maintenance of values that make life worth the effort and struggle of living; this question of the quality of conscious existence brings us to the reality of suffering in life and spiritual growth. As Berdyaev points out, there is suffering that crushes and demeans people such as the ravages of disease, famine, poverty, unemployment or political oppression and slave labor from which people must be liberated if they are to attain fulfillment; here, in much of the world, the majority of human beings must concern themselves with day-to-day survival, and so they have no opportunity for creative self-realization and fulfillment as in the Western liberal democracies. There is also suffering that can purify a person's emotions and enables them to become a more truly humane being through an increase in sympathy, pity and a lessening of cruelty (Berdyaev, 1931). This suffering is more generally connected with the painful process of spiritual growth and personal tragedy owing to loss of loved ones or illness in one's life. Here, suffering with the companionship of Christ and borne gracefully (patiently and without prolonged resentment) will enable a person to affirm life and grow spiritually. Berdyaev is right when he says that the ultimate value and act of creativity in the Christian life is the disinterested love of the Trinity for her own sake and loving all human beings as the image of the Divine Reality; for by this, a person can experience meaning and joy even in the midst of suffering. She can also experience eternity in the present.

10
Love and Behavior

Criteria in Ethics and Politics

In addressing ethical and political matters we do not wish
to pontificate on matters which can be illuminated by human
judgment in the natural course of things. There are ambiguities in life which make it unrewarding to lay down a close
program which is purportedly "Christian". We have no body
of law, as does the Jew or the Muslim or to some degree
the Hindu which will serve as the basis for a detailed
description of what it is to be a Jew or a Muslim or a Hindu
in particular circumstances. But it does not follow that there
are no principles guiding us, but these principles enshrine
values drawn from the doctrinal, narrative, experiential and
ritual dimensions of the faith. Not only that, because we
are writing this in the context of world history, and of world
religions and worldviews, we need to consider inspirations
drawn from the relevant dimension of other traditions. We
shall use these principles as criteria of the Christian life. They
are values which the individual or group has to ponder in
working out its own liberation and its own program of
behavior, both ethical and political.

The Trinity Doctrine and Ethics

Since the Trinity doctrine is the central teaching of the faith,
it is itself a criterion of how to judge attitudes and behavior.
The heart of the social Trinity is mutual love: this is how
and why it is that God is love. Consequently loving attitudes
towards other human beings constitute the essence of
Christian ethics, and politics. Each member of the Trinity
is open towards the others, and this lack of barrier between
the members can be mirrored here on earth, as we open
ourselves up to other living beings. Indeed, love can be said

to extend to the whole cosmos and not just to living beings and humans in particular. The attitudes we find in some small scale religions of reverence towards the forces in animal life and in the environment (sacred streams, mountains, thunderstorms and so on) can be a useful reminder of the kind of love the Christian should exercise towards the whole of creation. But it is of course in interpersonal relationships that the central application of the value of *agapé* is exercised.

The Christian therefore should be concerned with overcoming barriers between persons. This can occur at various levels. At the political level, it means that the Christian should not take with ultimate seriousness group identity: not even Church identity, insofar as it militates against open friendliness towards other humans. The Christian therefore is not the ultimate patriot: nationalism has to be tempered by the thought that we are each a citizen of heaven and of humanity as a whole. Such final loyalty overrides the demands of any lesser group. Yet we may be called on to fight for our country. It is up to individuals to decide whether such a fight constitutes a just war, which for us implies that in the long run it reduces violence. The Christian may not be a pacifist, but she does have to believe in the minimization of violence, because it issues in harm to other human beings, and love implies that we strive for the welfare of all so far as it is possible. Moreover, not only should violence towards other groups be minimized, but the Christians should not feel hatred towards others, even the most monstrous of people, such as Hitler.

Because the central theology is an "other-help" kind – that is we need, in Christianity, to turn to God's grace for liberation – there is a tendency in Christianity to neglect self-training, in the hope that improvements in character will come if not naturally then at least supernaturally. This neglect of practicality can be dangerous. We have a duty to improve our characters, for character is what lies behind behavior. We need to cultivate good dispositions, and here we can learn from other traditions. Noticeably we may wish to employ methods of yoga, especially those forms of meditation in Buddhism which generate compassion (like

360

suffusing the beings of the different quarters of the universe, in imagination, with benevolence and compassion). It was also the genius of Gandhi to see that right attitudes are important to political action. If the revolutionary hates some of his fellow-humans, then woe betide the State after the revolution is successful. Much of the problem of the modern world arises from the way in which one order is displaced by another in the name of revolutionary hope, but the new order brings as many ills with it as the old order generated, often, because the new order is not founded on real benevolence. So benevolent and loving attitudes even towards rivals and enemies are as important in politics as on the personal front.

Often hatred and violence breed themselves in the reactions to them. Hatred is not overcome by hatred, but multiplied by it. So though punitive actions often seem to be satisfyingly justified by the moral wrongs committed by the enemy, they tend to be counter-productive. Thus politically the Marshall Plan and MacArthur's rule in Japan were wise after WWII. They seduced, by good treatment, the Germans and Japanese to the camp of the Western victors, rather than causing the alienation of Versailles (against which Keynes so eloquently wrote) which was a major cause of the rise and of the motivation of hate-filled Hitler.

The Buddhist diagnosis of our ills as due to the threefold combination of greed, hatred and confusion is well taken. In some ways it gives a more practical idea of human troubles than the notion of sin. It deals with the main patterns of the seven deadly sins. These it may be recalled are : Envy, lust, gluttony and avarice, which are forms of greed; hatred, which is hatred; and sloth and pride, which involve distortions of values (decay in one case, self-centeredness in the other) which stem from confusion as to how things really are. The selflessness of the Christian lies at the midpoint between pride and slothful depression. To love our neighbors as ourselves we have in a way to love ourselves, but at this midpoint which is born out of a sense of participating in the Eternal. It is lack of confidence which leads to paranoia, and fear; and paranoia and fear easily breed hatred. This self-destruction is cured by the sacramental life in which the Christian participates in the Divine. It is cured by the vision of the lovely Light which lights every person.

This has economic meaning too. Though poverty can generate nobility in those who in spite of it rise to a fine human dignity, we do not wish poverty on others (and chosen poverty is not the real thing, for it represents directly an ideal). The lack of means and comparison with others generates insecurity, and hatred. The better distribution of wealth is a means of ensuring human dignity and providing the matrix for more equal personal relationships. From this point of view what is most important is an adequate or more than adequate standard of living for all people, so that they have an easy way of expressing their human dignity.

In our last chapter, we stated that agapistic love is giving one's best self for another person's good by actively seeking their welfare and nurturing their spiritual growth as a unique individual. This self-giving love is based upon an *act of will* and an attitude of respect for the dignity and intrinsic worth of another person; this means valuing and treating another human being as a *person* – as a living being with self-consciousness, whose feelings matter and is worthy of our personal attention and concern. As such, *agapé* is a capacity for caring for persons by responsibly relating to them with sensitivity based on empathetic understanding and knowledge. Also, *agapé* is both unconditional and universal in its range of application, as it is given to a person because they are a person.

We began by trying to show how the central Christian attitude flows from the nature of the Trinity, which is internally bonded together with love which is of the essence of the Divine life. Not only in the political and economic spheres but also in the personal such love becomes the most important criterion of judging issues. We shall return to this in our further discussion of *agapé*. Meanwhile let us dwell on the meaning of some other aspects of Christian doctrine.

The Omnipresent Creator, Outside and Within, and Ethics
As we have pointed out only a fine metaphorical line divides
transcendence and immanence. As Creator the Divine is
present throughout the whole creative process. She is
omnipresent in all the texture of what we perceive. The world
around us is full of God, and this reinforces the point made
earlier, that we should love the world. This need not be
sentimental. When we are sitting in the sun, surrounded by
bougainvillea, and honeysuckle, and the garden grass, and
can glimpse the blue ocean in the hazy distance, and listen
to the chatter of bright birds, it is easy enough to love the
cosmos and see the imprint of the Trinity's divine love upon
it all. We can understand the exuberance and artistry of the
Creator. But in the rain in a side street in a more squalid
section of Glasgow, and seeing some of the human flotsam
of the slum, it is not so easy to remember that God is there
equally. But ours is a suffering God who accepts the pain and
misery too. The Christian loves even the bad side of the
cosmos, and even the bad people (or "bad" people) in it. So
the doctrine of creation reinforces the love of human beings,
because they are part of a creation. But more: the Divine is
also present as *antaryāmin*, and has a character as inner
controller which is stamped with the historical avatar. So the
figures of the Trinity combine to remind us that every human
being displays Christ and has the potentiality to become
deified, truly Christ-like, in her behavior.

The external creator, present to us everywhere is, also the
numinous focus of worship and devotion. So the reaction of
the Christian to this presence is to use every moment, in
theory, as giving the opportunity to worship. All behavior
thus becomes in principle an act of worship. Hence the tag
laborare est orare. This implies that the *bhakta* who models
her behavior on worship throughout her life has an attitude
of humility before the One she serves. This is why pride is
the fount of the deadly sins: it represents confusion about our
true status. The humility of the worshipper is also reflected
in the humility of the Divine itself in becoming instantiated
in the flesh of Christ. In Christ the Brahman suffers here on
earth, and though Jesus spoke with self-confidence and

THE VISION OF LOVE

authority, he also was the Suffering Servant willing to undergo humiliation on behalf of his beloved creatures who were also his friends and among whom he moved and lived. So a central accompaniment of *love* is *humility*.

Unfortunately, this has often been taken in Christian history in a heterobiographical manner. That is, it is a virtue commended by the powerful in the Church to the rest, to the faithful. We must remember that all these Christian virtues are to be seen in an autobiographical way: humility is to be my or our attitude. Insofar as the idea of the *imitatio Christi* has application, it primarily indicates that we should be willing to act and feel in ways which do not stand on status and pride.

We have noted that moral action can have a ritual significance in flowing from the doctrine of the omnipresence of God as numinous creator of the universe. We shall come back to these matters when we turn to the effect of the ritual dimension of Christian ethics. But we need to look further at the doctrinal dimension. So far we have considered the love flowing from the Trinity, and the humility from recognition of the creator and from following the example of Christ.

But there is another aspect of creation we need to note: creativity. We have insisted that the creation is something which involves changes in God: it means that we are co-workers, as being in the image of the Divine, in the ongoing fashioning and meaning of the cosmos. We have already adverted to the way creativity is nourished (we hope) by life in the Spirit and by the sacramental life of the community. From a moral point of view, creativity implies that we should use our imagination in the Christian life, seeing new approaches to human relations and relations with the cosmos. While we may remain wedded to some of the major traditional values of the Church, we also need not be frozen into obedience to interpretations of the Christian life as handed down. The Church has often been terribly timid and sometimes reactionary about moral change. The Roman Catholic Church has taken a very backward-looking view of contraception. The criterion we need to employ is: Which view enhances love, and reduces suffering? Love is itself an adventure, and is not served by the mechanical application of past rules.

But how do we combine humility with adventurousness? It is essential that our following Christ in humility is not governed by the false humility of self-depreciation. In that middle way we need self-confidence. And through the Christian life we can have it very easily, because through the sacramental life we participate in the eternal Light and in divine Life. We have everything, and we shine with heaven. So what can threaten us?

Christology and Christian Ethics
Another element in the doctrinal dimension, and lying of course at the heart of mainstream belief, is the doctrine of the Incarnation. The Christian community has for long been exercised to preserve its crucial balance: Jesus is both God and a human being. The important consequences for the Christian life are: first, that the spiritual world is incarnated in the ordinary world – our attitudes then can never be purely other-worldly; second, that humanity is the vehicle of the Lord. The first consequence is like the Mahayana equation that *saṃsāra* is nirvana. The second consequence reminds us that the Christian faith is not so distant from the *advaitin* motif in modern Hinduism – the Christian life involves progressive deification (and this process may continue after death – but dwelling on this point may take us too far in an "otherworldly" direction).

But concretely what do these things mean? They mean first that as far as others go we must combine concern for spiritual and material welfare indissolubly. The vision of the good life is also the vision of healthy and good food. Consequently Christian ethics involves its politics, a concern for creating a good society, founded on the ideals of happiness and justice. The incarnation combines the divine and the human in one: and so the good society must combine spiritual welfare and material welfare, and this will become a criterion for political action. In our opinion, spiritual welfare must be exercised freely and from within. Totalitarian and authoritarian systems cannot provide the milieu for human welfare, even if humans can triumph despite the oppressions of such systems. We admire the cohesion and international character of Roman Catholicism, but we do not feel that its older authoritarian monarchism was a satisfactory mold for spreading the ideal of the free acceptance of the Divine Life. Nor are we sympathetic to those evangelical Christians who wish to censor and restrict education – for they too are not giving complete freedom to the questing of the human spirit.

In seeking deification, we humans must grow in imitation of the forgiving and loving nature of the Divine Being: and so there can be no place in our evangelization of cruel threats to sinners, and we must always strive to love those whom we struggle against in the name of human welfare and justice. In fact, evangelization consists in presenting a vision. It is like displaying a painting: it is not for us to complain about those who do not think it wonderful, but strive only to arouse in others the inspiration which has helped us along the path of life.

The Question of Evil Supernatural Powers

Nevertheless, we have to rid ourselves of too sentimental a view of ourselves, our fellow humans and the cosmos at large. A motif that is to be found in St Paul, and recurrently in the teachings of the Church, is the idea that the world is ruled by evil supernatural powers (and beyond that by the Devil). This is a mythological way of thinking of the forces which exist beyond any individual to darken and corrupt human beings. They are inevitably there, in the sense that society is a continuing framework which imposes constraints on individuals and transmits evils of earlier generations. Thus anti-Semitism of earlier generations was a "given" in the Vienna of Hitler's youth; the long previous reaches of history are present in the Indian scandal of untouchability; the Battle of Blood River is there in the application of apartheid; the cruelties of Tsardom and the inhumanity of ideological abstractions are there in Stalin's ruthless collectivization campaign; the arrogances of British history are present in the schools today; the corrupt interplay between Church and State are there in the quietness of Orthodoxy in Romania; and so on.

Though built in to such institutional and socially transmitted evils are wrong impulses deriving from human nature (the tendency to groupism, for instance, and feelings of hatred for those who arouse insecurity) much of the problem comes from lack of vision, from spiritual ignorance, *avidyā*. The creativity of the Holy Spirit is the dispersal of such ignorance. So there are two forces in history, in a sense: the forces of ignorance and those of vision.

This situation is inevitable. It springs from the nature of a creation, for the Lord in giving us freedom lets down the world as a screen between the Light "there" and the lights here. Between the transcendent and the impulses in ourselves lies the visible world. In giving us independence God gives us the reality of alienation. We have to claw our way onwards, using the light within to change our world. If Paul and others thought of the world as controlled by evil angels, this was a (from our point of view) somewhat primitive way of expressing this fact of alienation, which we are faced with overcoming. The struggle against such alienation and ignorance should inspire sadness and compassion in those who, we feel, obstruct the bright and upward path. It is not a matter of turning towards them in hatred and envy.

The Mythic Dimension and Ethics: The Imitation of Christ
In the tradition one way of conceiving of right behavior has been through the idea of imitating Christ. Because of the concept-transcendence inherent in his mission, it is hard to delineate the Christ we ought to imitate: pinning it down to some formula itself helps to create the kind of concept which Jesus broke out from and reached beyond. And how literally should we take it? He was not (it seems) married: but so what?

Time and again the Gospels stress how Christ looked beneath the rules to the attitudes and intentions. We can, then, begin to answer what the imitation of Christ consists in, by considering what the right attitudes are. We would assert that the most vital of these is a blend of humility and poise. This was the style of Jesus. Though he spoke with authority he was willing to die on the Cross, to wash the disciples' feet, and live with all kinds of human beings. Indeed his consorting with taxpayers and prostitutes – with national traitors and defiled creatures – not to mention with outsiders like the Samaritans bears witness to his lack of arrogance; and yet at the same time he often spoke with authority. So we, rooted in heaven and in Christ, can be given the poise to speak and feel what we truly feel, and to criticize the powers of the world, and yet without pride. Needless to say these attitudes have to be suffused with love, since Jesus participates in the loving life of the Trinity.

Because the Christian faith hands on a tradition, and part of that tradition is the Biblical narrative, there are rich and various ways in which we can take to heart, and apply to ourselves, the great narratives therein contained: we are children of the Exodus, we have been there by the waters of Babylon, we have been in the whale's belly and danced at the wedding in Cana of Galilee. But though this tradition has much to offer, it also from an ethical angle carries with it a demon: the thought that we can simply derive our ethics from some formulae in the Bible. It is easy for the Churches to adopt such a position, for instance, over divorce and other sexual arrangements, even though the conditions and insight of society have manifestly changed (for instance, because of contraception in modern times). It seems to us that as Christians we need to dig below the regulations of earlier societies to see what the underlying principles are which ought to govern our mores. Our Christian vision of the perfect marriage is a monogamous one: we hope that partners can ripen in love through the vicissitudes of life, into old age. But it in no way follows that we should be in the business of forcing non-Christians to accept this point of view, or to condemn any couple who find that without the supports of a wider community and without the mutuality that successful marriage requires and which is hard to reach, they prefer to get divorced. All we can do, as we need to repeat again, is to present what seems to us a fine vision and hope that we can realize it and impart it to others. The Christian tradition has a fine record in upholding the sanctity of persons and the nobility of marriage: but it has a bad record in often trying to force this ideal on others and it has often had a timid and foolish view of the joys and modes of sexuality. A certain grim asceticism (which misses the point of giving things up) has often pervaded the faith. From our perspective we can sum up the true pattern of mores as being controlled by the vision of Christ which points to underlying attitudes, and so we must not mechanically transmit rules from the Bible or anywhere else. So for us the imitation of Christ is above all imitating his humanity, poise and desire to dig beneath the surface of human behavior.

This means that we conceive Christian ethics in a profoundly different way from that through which Jewish orthodoxy conceives the Law. We do not want here to deny the importance of the path which Judaism came to take as it formed itself during the early Christian centuries. But the fall of Jerusalem in 70 C.E. was a point of choice. Two paths opened up, profoundly different. One path was hedged by the Torah. The other path was devoid of a Torah – save the somewhat fragmentary inheritance of parts of it such as the Ten Commandments. Eventually, the Christian faith was effectively to shed any absolute agreement about what, as rules, should be followed. This was inherent in its turning away from a Torah (and rejecting a Shari'a). Christians struggled to adopt rules which seemed to correspond to the major attitudinal motifs of the New Testament, and today it cannot be said that in the wider world of ecumenical Christianity there is agreement on pacifism, homosexuality, divorce, masturbation, capital punishment, abortion, revolution, capitalism or any other major topic of ethical and political concern. Perhaps this is a sadness, such division. But it is surely to be expected, once Christians had turned away from a Torah. Christian ethics is as much a matter of search as is the Christian life itself: searching for God, searching for the Good.

By sticking with the rules of the Torah, Judaism was able to invent by a miracle of ingenuity means of adapting the commandments to the changing circumstances of ordinary life. It is a major human option, from within the theistic stream of Abrahamic religions. The major alternative is the creation of an idea of right and wrong which is governed by higher order attitudinal principles – loving God and my neighbor. That was not absent from the Torah, of course, but it summed it up in quite a different way from the Christian mode. In the latter right and wrong emerge ultimately from a calculus of love. What is right and wrong become ultimately a matter of individual judgment rather than community decision, though the community is always there administering the sacraments through which the Incarnation is extended.

Other Aspects of the Imitation of Christ
The Gospels incorporate a substantial number of healing miracles, and this has given the Christian tradition an impetus to do much for healing – the creation of various organizations, forerunners of modern hospitals, for the tending of the sick and dying. There is also a strong emphasis in Jesus' teaching on sustenance of the poor. It seems inescapable that the Christian is concerned in both politics and social action with the less privileged in society. This is the foundation of modern Christian socialism and social democracy. It is the basis of such movements as Christian Aid. Wherever Christianity becomes too entangled in the ideology of the rich and healthy and powerful, there is cause for criticism. While we do not seek here to prescribe a political stance necessary for all true Christians, we do aver that the criteria of social policy relate to effectiveness in raising the material levels of the poor, providing community action to help the sick (particularly the sick and poor), and giving people at the same time a free milieu to work out their own lives and destinies. The Christian community has to speak out where these things are not to be found.

The Ritual Dimension and Christian Ethics
In so far as we have already written on the life flowing from the sacraments we have importantly dealt with this aspect

of Christian ethics. For the sacraments are at the heart of the ritual dimension of the faith. But there are aspects of the ritual dimension which have a general character, and it is worth seeing how it should affect action. Here we can learn from the rightful Confucian emphasis upon *li* in life. First, there is a ritual accompaniment to the omnipresence of God, namely the practice of the presence of God, which is a vital part of Christian prayer. It is the practice of reminding ourselves as continuously as possible of God's being with us in the world around us at all times, and being within us and our neighbors. We have to practise prayer in such a way that it becomes second nature to relate the Divine in all existence, and to see Christ and the Spirit in the visage and the heart of all those whom we come to meet and work and play with in the round of life. Christ is there in the mailman and in the old woman, in the cab driver and the bank official, in the cop and the bureaucrat, in the black person and the white, in the drunk and the sober, in the whole parade of humanity which daily passes before our eyes: just as the Father is there in mother earth, in the rain and the air, in the blue and the green, in the storm and the calm, in the rock and the brick, in the stream and the plaster, in the concrete and the rubber, in everything. We swim in God: in her we have our very being. In here we draw breath, and draw too sustenance from the Spirit within. In so being turned to the Creator and Sustainer and Destroyer of this world in continuous *bhakti*, we can lose our self-centeredness, replacing our ego with the Pneuma, our self with Christ. That is the meaning of prayer, that we come to serve Christ and the other members of the Trinity, without however losing our sparkle and joy and spontaneity.

To this *bhakti* activity of praying continuously to the God who is around us we can add the techniques of yoga: to calm our interior, to cause the waves of wrath and envy and the other deadly sins to diminish and fade before the bright Sun of divinity. We can conceive this calming effect as unveiling the Light within, for through the practice of the *brahmavihāras* we can remove the egotism and passions which obscure the presence of the inner controller. As egotism diminishes so the Spirit appears: this is how we imitate the *anattā-pneuma* character of the persons of the beloved Trinity.

Eschatology, Ritual and Politics

The practice of the presence of the Divine and the Christian yoga of stilling our passions are important ways to act to help towards a sense of conforming with the Light which creates the world and illuminates every person. That inner quest reminds us too that in the last resort we cannot learn goodness externally, but must rely on conscience. But these attitudes can be conceived and practiced in a static and timeless way. They are indeed constant factors in human life under the Christ-vision. But in addition, the Christian has a sense of history and directionality. "Thy kingdom come", says Jesus' own chief prayer which he taught to his disciples. What is this kingdom? It has of course been an inspiration to many a millennial movement.

Every age no doubt has a glimpse of hope. For us, the most important thing in today's world is the vision of a planet earth populated by human beings who live in peace with one another – a universal Scandinavia, a world-wide coexistence in peace of all the nations and ethnicities of the globe. We can in principle banish war. Many of the present trends point that way, despite the perils of a nuclear holocaust. We need international cooperation economically and to limit the dangers of atomic terrorism. We are getting bound together more closely by the communications satellites and airlines that crisscross our skies. So we can envision universal human peace, before we take off on the next phase of human history, rising towards the colonization of our cosmic neighbors. But that peace must not be the grim peace of totalitarian rule, and the enforcement of conformity through the computer and the truncheon. We must maintain openness, and the dignity of individual human beings. This will itself requires a struggle. But in that peaceful and open society humans will be free to practise their visions.

Now this is not necessarily the kingdom of heaven on earth. Though the vision of world peace and a world order is an old dream, it is not more than the next step on the way. Maybe ultimately the earth will be transformed, but the sufferings of humanity will not go away, even in Scandinavia. So we do not identify the Kingdom with a particular order: but there is no doubt that universal peace at least in the external sense will be a grand blessing, and an immeasurably important step along humankind's upward way. So we conceive talk of the Kingdom as being the expression of a regulative idea: the Divine reveals himself not merely from behind and within the cosmos but also out of the future. It is as if the future itself is a veil through which we discern the smoky lineaments of the Lord of Lords. There he is in the thunder and lightning of the order which lies beyond us in the future. So while we do not wish to be precise about the shape of the Kingdom, we can yet be more precise about hope for the next stage. We can look then to a greater life for our children, if we be spared the deathly tragedy of a nuclear war.

So from an ethical point of view we can treat Christian eschatology as regulative, drawing us onward towards the foundation of the Kingdom upon earth. In the ritual mode, this remains at the heart of the Christian life through the affirmation "Thy kingdom come" in the Lord's Prayer. It is a reminder therefore that Christian ritual itself is designed to foster hope, and hope in its collective aspect signifies the faith that we can and ultimately will make a better world.

Love and Political Violence

The fact that the Christian is implicated in trying to help the Kingdom to arrive on earth means a political involvement that sooner or later brings up the problem of pacifism. The problem arises because there are two strands in Christian thinking through the ages – the one the pacifist strand and the other the strand of the possibility of the just war (and by implication therefore the just revolution). The non-violent motif has been immensely important, and had its apogee in modern times in the thought and life of Mahatma Gandhi, perhaps the greatest Christian of this century (despite being a Hindu) But while we respect the pacifist strand, we do not subscribe to it literally. We take its two truths seriously. One truth is that we need peaceful motives. The inner side of action is supremely important, and you cannot achieve true non-violence (as Gandhi stressed) while hating your enemies. We consider that also *violence* needs to be controlled by the right motives. Secondly, the truth that we need to eliminate violence is an ideal about which we may feel that it is not possible to achieve. Nevertheless we can live up to the ideal by always seeking to minimize violence. So we can adopt this as a utilitarian principle: "Always seek to achieve the minimum of violence". This implies a non-violent attitude, seeking to reduce the physical and spiritual harm which we inflict on one another.

There are of course questions of the definition of violence – whether for instance we should count so-called "institutional violence". Our opinion is that institutional violence has its expression sooner or later in actual violence, so that it is not necessary to count it separately. It may be that a society is very unjust, and as people become aware of the depth of injustice they may protest, and this will provoke police action, i.e. violence in the literal sense. While we respect the reasons why the concept of institutional violence is invoked, we do not go along with it since it tends to justify real violence on the grounds that it is just a response to institutional violence. It tends to take too favorable a view of violent action. We do not rule out just revolution, but it is best if it takes the form of *li* – the uses of "secular" ritual acts, such as protests. If such are repressed with actual violence it may be necessary in the long run to institute a guerrilla war, but this in turn ought from a Christian angle to be suffused with the spirit of loving enemies and not using indiscriminate violence to achieve its ends. Unfortunately it is easier to inculcate hatred in order to stiffen morale, and so often such revolutionary struggles feed off hatreds which then find their expression in the revolutionary regime once it is established. This of course helps to create new injustices.

Similarly police training through most or all of the world does not stress the minimization of violence and often police actions take the form of police riots in which hatred and cruelty have freer reign because in theory they are on the side of "law and order" and morality in general. It is a sad fact but the justification of violent action by ethical principles and ideological goals conceived as noble brings with it increased violence because now it is licensed. Righteousness is a fuel of cruelty. So the Christian in our view does not justify the violence she may be forced to use, but always should regret it and seek to diminish it.

Agape and Li

The ritual side of religion has its wider secular counterpart in the use of various gestures and speech-acts which give expression to various things – e.g. reverence for other people. Good manners and the use of sincerely-meant forms of greeting and the like are a way of expressing our respect for others. The Confucian emphasis on *li* should be echoed by the Christian in which secular and spiritual forms of *li* smoothly integrate with one another. If with regard to the cosmos and our immediate placement in it we should practice the presence of God, then in regard to other people we should cultivate the image of Christ, and so have reverent love. This expresses itself in not only good manners but those deeper and more spontaneous forms of *li* which express the warmth of our relationship to other human beings.

In the early Church this *agapé* was the basis for the treatment of all groups as belonging to the One Group, the sons of God. There was to be neither Jew nor Greek, nor woman nor man, nor "us" and "them". This is the basis for saying that our ultimate community is the human race, and the Christian community should aim at being a kind of reflection of that ultimate group. In a way it may seem odd that such universalism should have spread from out of a people much concerned with their own sacred identity over against Gentiles. This exclusiveness, however, was greatly modified by the idea that the Lord gave all sorts of differing groups equal justice and equal status, only that the Jews had a special task and destiny. The Christian community is the new Israel, of course, and has a sense too of being chosen: but in both cases the peoples are called to witness to their vision and "be a light to lighten other people". They are to be a beacon to the human race through living out their vision. But in the last resort it is wrong for Christians to divide up the race into us and the others, as though we are saved and they are not, or as though we have a different status ultimately from other human beings. Christian universalism abolishes pretensions to being the insiders. It is true that Christians are those who share a vision or rather a set of visions having family resemblance. But though this may give them opportunities which others have less access to, this does not form the basis for any deep divide between the group known as Christians and "outsiders". This is so for various reasons. First, Jesus' parables show that orthodoxy however conceived is no passport to rectitude or the true love of the Divine (consider the parable of the Good Samaritan). Second, who is saved and who is not is a question only the Ultimate can answer definitively. Moreover we believe that in the last resort all will rest preciously in the bosom of the Divine. Third, we are instructed to love all human beings, not just some of them. Fourth, the global interdependence of all humans is becoming increasingly obvious in today's world. Fifth, ethics is no respecter of persons and we have overall the same obligations to all other human beings: ethics does not discriminate by skin-color, or ethnicity, or gender.

If there is a point of view in our vision on the special role of Christians it is the simile of the salt. We are supposed to be the salt that enhances the human race's taste. We are the chili in the curry.

The Experiential Dimension and Ethics: Humility and Self-Confidence Again

The heart of the theistic faiths is the numinous experience of the awe-inspiring Other. This sense of the *tremendum* ought to make our hair stand on end: the Divine is powerful in its creative power. Before we therefore feel like Isaiah and Peter: unworthy. We feel puny and impure before the thunder of the Holy. The Spirit which lies behind the vast energies of the cosmos must be mighty indeed. And as we look at our vast universe and see the "starry skies above" it gives us a sense of humility. Who are we? Mere ants in the face of the All-Powerful. But in the Christian vision this sense of awe need not and should not crush us. For also Christ became human and through that fact we can daily, hourly, share in his divinity. We are in our own way divine: the puny divine, but divine nonetheless. And so we can combine also from out of the Christian experience the senses of humility and self-confidence which enable us to work our way through this world without arrogance or faltering, if we have faith.

But the Christian faith, through much of its main stream, has also valued highly the mystical path, the search within, and this culminates in a different kind of experience from the numinous. It yields a sense of intimate communion with the Light. It reinforces our sense of deification. Now it happens that in the practice of Christian yoga through the ages a lot of emphasis has been put upon mortification of the flesh. Bodily and mental self-control are vital ingredients – it has been held – in the search for this Light within. So it has been common to combine the inner quest with celibate and typically monastic or conventual life. In turning inwards we have in a way to be turning from the world. So prudentially it has turned out that there has been sponsoring of ascetic practices in the Christian tradition. But this has in some degree been modified by the insistence on the real character of the Incarnation. Christ as an avatar was really human: and sacramentally this world is to be prized for that. It is true that there has also been the motif, to which we referred earlier, of the domination of the cosmos by evil supernatural powers. But, as we saw, God in order to give us independence and a freedom in our search has had to create a kind of anti-god. The world beguiles us, but we are often enough reminded by it of the need to see the Light which gleams through it, to fix our eyes both on the here and the Beyond. Because this world offers its joys and sorrows in a poignant counterpoint, we need to live our spiritual life in and through the world. Nothing human can be foreign to us. So a world-rejecting asceticism is not

Christian. In our vision the training of the ascetic life is a means to an end only. We often need severe self-control if we are to make progress in yoga, so the search within is liable to generate in us a need for discipline.

But it should go without saying that such self-discipline should be voluntary. Maybe we put ourselves under a spiritual master, or under the supreme Master: but this is our choice. We choose a guru, perhaps, and become obedient, but the authority resides ultimately in ourselves. So there is a sense in which Christian yoga is like Theravadin yoga: it is a "self-help" kind of path. However, the Christian tradition has also emphasized, partly because of the importance of the *bhakti* mode of religion, the experience, and the doctrine, of grace. If we make progress in treading the yogic path to being united with Christ it is through the Trinity's exercise of grace towards us, and many Christians have reported their sense of grace in living encounters with God. Such grace can be thought of as a personalized version of spontaneity in the Buddhist tradition. The Buddhist does not look on the path as unfolding mechanically, but rather there are leaps through which the aspirant gains deeper insight and peace. The cultivation of such spontaneity is, of course, a major motif in Zen or Ch'an Buddhism. It is a spontaneity which perceived as coming from the Divine is counted inspiration: but not in that modern secular sense in which inspiration has lost all sense of its relationship to the Spirit. At any rate, the ideas of spontaneity and grace are two sides of a fused creativity. So the Christian life of contemplation is not something which is rigidly controlled by rules, for which reason the Orthodox wisely encourage in the monasteries the idiorhythmic mode in which each practitioner has some freedom in the way in which he or she adapts her or his rhythms to the wider life of the community.

In all of this we regard the "giving up" implied by the ascetic life as having no virtue in itself, but merely as a means towards a goal, for those who feel called towards a contemplative life in monastic community. The Christian should see his work and his play as patterns of response to the present Other, the numinous One.

Puritanism is not as usually seen a very attractive aspect of the Christian ethos, because its spirit is typically not utilitarian in the way we have just argued. The giving up of pleasures only makes sense if their indulgence does some harm or gets in the way of some higher goal or happiness. We consider it to be one of those areas of Christian practice where we need to attend to the *autobiographical* nature of the faith. It may be that I shall feel the call to asceticism, because I purpose to voyage into my soul in an intense way, and to uncover clearly the Light of Christ within. But that in no way entitles me to lay self-denial upon others as an outer burden. I can be here exemplar but not dictator. It is true that sometimes the community as a whole may have some rule (for instance, fasting in Lent) which it desires to lay upon its voluntary members: and there can be no harm in this, if indeed it is seen for what it is – a rule of a voluntary association.

Being "Born Again" and the Christian Life

Another experience on which much attention has been focussed in recent years, especially in the United States, is the experience of being existentially turned to the faith, being "born again". We consider this to be important; and we consider it a fine thing if human beings have felt a quickening of their life. But it has dangers, if it accompanies an inappropriately rigid interpretation of the faith. It is often unfortunate that such an experience is hooked on to a literalistic interpretation of the Bible, and to a generally conservative religious outlook. We consider that this type of Christianity is not good for the sense of world community. It neglects modern thinking and a lot of pioneering scholarship. It is not self-critical. It tends towards an intolerant view of others' religious options. It cannot be enough stressed that, in our opinion, the epistemological criteria of belief are ineluctably soft, that the best we can have is loyalty to a vision, and that it is unwise to run down other faiths and other positions. Now we do here criticize the fundamentalist Christian mode, and this itself should by our own criteria be unwise. Well, we only speak because of the *mode* of holding a conservative faith: we do not criticize the fervent *bhakti* of Christian evangelicalism nor the zeal of evangelicals in trying to form communities. We do object, however, to the aspects of intolerance often found among fundamentalists. Our vision dances before our eyes: it sometimes shimmers and grows faint. But it comes dancing back, and the light then shines from it: we do not believe in static visions, rigidly defined.

We interpret the authoritarian nature of a lot of fundamentalism in the Christian tradition and its analogues elsewhere as similar to some hierarchical and obedient forms of the faith, such as belief in the ultimate authority of the Papacy. We see all these things as expressions of a sense of insecurity. People want their faith, often, to be a certainty. They seek sure guidance. But they cannot have it. And because you cannot have that outer certainty, your certitude is something you have to nurture quietly in your heart. Your faith has to be your responsibility. You have then to be gentle in propounding it. If you are born again, you do not need to shout. There is a gentle and outward-looking mission for the Christian, because in this rich human world there are many faiths, and no hard message will drive them away. We have to be gentle because the demand of Christian ethics, the light of epistemology, is to be tolerant. It is also necessary for the Christian to consider whether and how much she can learn from those beyond her own tradition and assumptions. It seems to us therefore that the true meaning of being born again is that we acquire certitude and a quiet confidence in the Light. It does not entitle us to embark upon crusades.

The Institutional Dimension and the Christian Ethic

Because of the sacramental life of the Church, it has a priesthood, and this has typically meant a certain organizational hierarchy. Because of the mystical tradition, it has a monastic order. But these marks of the Church are not universal, and we have a variety of experiments in organization through the various branches of Protestantism. In modern times we come to something of a federal structure in the Ecumenical Movement and the World Council of Churches. This we regard as appropriate to the present realizations of the nature of religious truth. It is our understanding of the soft epistemology of religion that we should have an open texture to one another, who have different formulations and practices of religion. Ultimately there maybe a powerful federal system of religions in which a World Council of Religions commands the adherence of mainstream varieties of faith across the human race. But the actual federal character of the WCC can stand for the idea that we do not need "organic" unity in order to work and testify together. This federalism is a way to organize openness between groups, while allowing pluralism of behavior, and that fulfills our ethical requirements as expressed above.

However, the Christian churches have at various times united religious and political authority, especially under the principle of *cuius regio eius religio*. Whatever we may reflect about the way this worked in Byzantium or Sweden, it is not in our view an appropriate thing to happen today, and it is to be regretted that there are established churches (and Marxist parties) left in the world. It is not in our view at all appropriate to modern societies that any set of substantive beliefs should be imposed upon citizens. Though the Church of England was an established church it did at least pioneer a degree of internal freedom unusual among Christian denominations. It is this heritage of plurality in unity which we favor in world Christianity; but we deplore any system which requires citizens to subscribe to beliefs or suffer bad consequences to their careers or lives.

An important ethical principle is enshrined, of course, in the international character of the Church. This implies that there is a higher obligation than national loyalty. It is a bridge to the idea of world citizenship.

Though the Anglican Church had the merit of pluralism, we feel that the way the Orthodox Church came to be organized has many merits. While we do not think that liturgy necessarily should be unchanging, it should have an obvious continuity with the past; but such conservatism need not and indeed ought not to be found in modern times in the doctrinal, mythic and ethical dimensions. The emphasis on ritual orthopraxy in Orthodoxy is correct, and it is backed by the institution of priesthood. The monastic system exists as a voluntary alternative for those who have the calling. By reserving celibacy for the monks and having married priests the Church preserves a reasonable balance. At the same time it favours lay theologians, and so does not set up its hierarchy as laying down the laws of belief and interpretation. Thus in theory at any rate it makes space for criticism within the Church. It may be that at the present time Orthodox thought is not fully flourishing (with some exceptions such as Fr. Staniloae): but it contains within itself some of the apparatus both for preserving the spiritual and sacramental tradition and incorporating lively, critical and modern interpretations of the faith. But it must be said that it is among liberal Protestants that some of the most radical rethinking of the faith has actually occurred. So we here try and combine some of the best organizational values in the attitudes we commend today for the Christian. To the radical Reformation we owe the destruction of establishment, and the fine example set by the U.S. constitution owes something both to the religious radicals and the rationalists of the Enlightenment; to Anglicanism we owe a sense of internal pluralism; to Orthodoxy we owe the thought of a differentiated Church in which there is conservatism of practice and the potentiality for radical rethinking of doctrine and myth; to liberal Protestantism we owe the greatest degree of intellectual self-criticism any religion with the possible exception of Buddhism has hitherto undergone. If Catholicism is in our view too hierarchically conceived we also acknowledge that it has shown the capacity for revolutionary change since Vatican II.

But rather than giving good and bad marks to the various Churches we have to think how we can exploit the riches of the Christian heritage as found in the ecclesiastical institutions. What role does a federal Christianity have to play in the modern world? How does this role gear into the values of Christian ethics and politics?

We do not pretend that only the following reflections are correct. It is part of our position that we ought to debate things, ponder them, provide constructive criticism. There can be no single "party line" which all Christians should recognize. There is bound to be room for difference of opinion. Nevertheless, in striking for the Kingdom, we have to sketch it. We have to picture it so that we can guide our actions towards a new order of human life.

A Sketch of the Human Future and Our Way of Striving For It

We take it as axiomatic that we have to look upon humanity as a whole and that national loyalties are secondary to human loyalties, of which transnational Church loyalties are a foretaste. The leadership of the Christian faith should therefore be visibly multi-ethnic. Though Christian churches cannot easily follow the Unification example, it is a nice thing about that community that it encourages and indeed virtually enforces cross-national and often cross-racial marriages. Anyway, it is an obvious Christian duty to foster transethnic harmony. Christians therefore should oppose forms of discrimination of all kinds. But though this is elementary, few seem to realize the corollary: that all political action and political values need to be conceived on a global basis. As we have stressed more than once, humanity is our group of ultimate concern. But in the modern world for the first time humanity is gelling into a single unit: there is nearly a single world economy. This means that we have to be worried not just about justice in one country, but justice in the whole system. Manifestly there is a severe division between rich and poor on a global basis. The Swedes or New Zealanders cannot sit back and say that they have solved the problem of poverty because they have fine welfare systems. For there remains poverty in Bourkina Faso and Tanzania, in India and Guatemala. Now it is naive to suppose that it is because the rich countries are rich the poor are poor. But it is true that the poor remain poor in part because of properties of the global system. So the Christian has to think and act on a world basis in moving towards dealing with the problem of the maldistribution of the world's wealth. Of course the question of relative economic prosperity is by no means the only vital political issue. The problem of how to retain liberty and individuals' rights is equally important. A solution to the world's food problems which took away all freedoms would not be worth having. We have to solve our differing problems together. But here we are working in a world which is rapidly evolving into an economic system the like of which we have not experienced before in human history. It is one in which a few score major transnational companies dominate the world, plus a few major governments, such as the Soviet and Chinese, which themselves virtually constitute national companies on a vast scale (USSR Inc., and China, Inc.). For the most part the transnationals are gradually leaving behind their national roots. They can exist well by having moveable headquarters. They can therefore constitute the basis of a new imperialism without an empire. The question of how we can adapt and modify the new global economy, in order better to distribute human wealth, in order to diminish poverty, is thus an important one, and it is a new question. We do not profess to know what is "the" Christian solution to the problem of economic inequality in the world, but we do emphasize that it is a world problem, not a national one: therefore national politics is on the whole irrelevant to it. This implies that the older position occupied by different national parties is also irrelevant. One of the testimonies therefore of the Christian is to the transnational character of human problems.

The Church as Having Its Roots in Heaven and Prophecy
Apart from the human properties of the Christian Church (that ideal community which is somehow in some degree incarnated in empirical churches), we must not forget that because the shape and purpose of the institution are determined by the self-manifestation of the Divine in its midst it has its roots in heaven. It is guardian of the Light. It has to show that Light in its sacramental life. Consequently the Christian's values belong both to this world and the other

world: she has her cynosure in heaven. The roots of the Church lie in the heavenly light.

It is the vision of the Good that forms the source of a critical stance. It is the basis of prophecy. The Christian – as we have emphasized a number of times – has the obligation to criticize the shallownesses, cruelties and ignorance of the world, from the perspective of the deeper values which the Trinity manifests to her.

We cannot here lay down in detail what the Christian's prophetic testimony should be. But we can at least suggest two aspects of this: what may be called the "deeper happiness" principle and the bodhisattva principle.

By the first we mean that while we agree that utilitarian tests of morality are in order in particular in the political sphere, the happinesses which we seek to maximize must be judged worthily. We should not trivialize happiness. We should strive to create institutions which will provide for happiness, but at a deep and serious, not a trivial, level. For us the vision of the Trinity is cause of the deepest satisfaction and while we cannot impose this goal upon others, we can at least point to the satisfactions of the Eternal and of a sacramental living out of love. Very often the superficially attractive things which in a consumer world we may gain bring no great happiness: what counts is the "seeing the world in depth" and experiencing that depth.

By the bodhisattva principle we mean the constant observance of that truth contained in the myth of the bodhisattva, namely that there can be no final happiness for any one of us while other living beings still suffer. Even for those who have attained the world's greatest well-being cannot conceal from themselves the sadness and pain which also exist in the world. We cannot luxuriate in some earthly heaven with joy unalloyed if we see over the fence those who exist in misery and want. This is why even in heaven there is not pure joy, save the joy of knowing that "in the end" all suffering is alleviated and all sadness washed away. There is a patch of darkness at the heart of the eternal Light.

So as Christians we have to be bodhisattvas, to take the vow to help others, putting off our own ultimate satisfaction.

We also need to be Jeremiahs, or critics of this world: to speak from the Light into the shallows of human existence, so far as it is given to us to do so.

In Conclusion on Christian Ethics

We have here presented something of what we see as the spirit of Christian ethics from the perspective of the other dimensions of the Christian life. We do not here pretend to have worked out a casuistry. For the most part we have confined ourselves to exhibiting the attitudes which lie behind *Christian action*. Thus we have stressed love as reflecting the Trinity, self-confident humility as reflecting the Incarnation, hope as reflecting Christian eschatology, selflessness as springing from Christian ritual, the desire for creativity as coming from being "born again", human brotherhood as coming from the transnational aspirations of the Church, and so on. In underlining these right attitudes we are following the main motif of Christ's teaching. We are critical of hanging on to older Church ethical traditions where they may conflict with the attitudinal demands of the faith. Thus though the spirit of the just war is a good one, limiting the evils which war brings, its spirit has to go beyond the letter of the theory when we contemplate nuclear warfare.

Because often the Church drags its heels in moral reform, because it (rightly) feels it has to hand on a tradition, its actions often look timid. Often Christians are indeed timid in making changes in their moral recommendations. It is obvious, for instance, that modern methods of contraception, and the abandonment of older conceptions of family property, alter our whole perspective about sex. But the Churches while in some cases allowing artificial means of contraception have come somewhat reluctantly to that position. We do not consider that we should be other than outspoken and confident in speaking to our real beliefs. The Church should be in the vanguard of moral reform, not dragging along behind: and this means that we need to encourage open debate and flexibility of response to a changing world.

But we are committed to a deep individualism. We are through the Christian doctrine of creation wedded to the vision of every person as made in the divine image; and through the Incarnation narrative devoted to the thought that every person reflects the image of Christ. Through our faith in the Spirit we see the Divine as within every person. So reverent love towards all other human beings issues in a transfigured individualism – every person has as it were a halo. To this we respond ritually in courteous and loving symbolic behaviour, and in our experience of the presence of God we see other living beings as shining with a specially intimate beam of the Light of the Spirit. What we make out as our duty should flow from these visionary attitudes. Loving God and loving our neighbor are indissolubly bonded. It is in principle a simple ethic to understand. It is less easy to follow, although easier when the grace of the Trinity flows into you.

11

Patterns of World History

Preliminaries

It is part of our whole vision that we have to see Christ in the context of world history. We affirm that the Trinity is evident in the whole of world history — that is, the divine Spirit works in various cultures and civilizations, and not just in the story of the Jews and Christians. She is there to illuminate people and to correct the vision of Christians. But before we come to describe in outline what we can discern of the Spirit's work in world history, we need to think in more depth about the way in which the Divine operates in history. There is a cluster of problems to consider — whether we should look on the course of history in a deterministic way, the scope of laws in history, the relation of the individual to the structures he acts within, the question of how "salvation-history" occurs, the nature of providence, etc.

No Separate Salvation-History

Let us begin by repudiating the idea of any cleft between sacred and secular history. All history involves the action of the Spirit, and it is quite artificial to think of some special corner of the historical process which is uniquely the scene of the saving work of the *Iśvara*. In this we agree with the judgment of Gustavo Gutierrez (Gutierrez, 1973), and this accent of so-called liberation theology is entirely correct. It is true that we can see events simply as historical and human, without going on to ascribe to them sacred or divine meaning. But this second act of interpretation, divining the divine in the human, does not mean that we have invented some parallel history.

The Christian vision centers on Christ, of course: and

there are special meanings in the Jewish life as it flowed from the dim past towards the foundation of the Church. But it is illusory to think that these form some sort of line in human history which is "salvation-history", as though God were not there among the Chinese or the Oceanians, and did not whisper anything to the Kenyans and the Winnebago, before the Whites arrived. Rather, as we shall see, God may be more apparent in some events than in others, and more expressive of herself. But this does not imply that she is wholly absent anywhere. How could she be? We have already seen that God is omnipresent in the cosmos; and she has to be doubly so in human history – both as Creator and as *antaryāmin*. And trebly so in the human shape of Christ. So what we need to be able to do as Christian visionaries is to discern, as best we can, the patterns of divine activity, especially in the various religions. But here again we do not wish to make some kind of sharp division between religion and other aspects of human life. The economic, political, aesthetic, religious and other sides of life are fused together in practice. Nevertheless we put special emphasis upon religion because religions (and to some degree ideologies or secular worldviews) shape civilizations. We follow Christopher Dawson (Dawson, 1950) in seeing spiritual values as deeper determinants of whole cultures which we need to understand: religions are the keys to civilizations. This is not to deny the importance of various economic and material factors: but we have a more Hegelian than a Marxist view of the historical process. We need to fuse the ideal and the material perspectives.

Moreover, as we have had occasion more than once to observe, actual worldviews bring together differing elements, drawn both from the spiritual and "secular" environment (for instance, Buddhist nationalism in Sri Lanka, Christian patriotism in the United States, Marxist Catholicism as among some liberation theologians, and so on). Once again we cannot disentangle in experience different sides of life which we label religious and secular; but we can of course make the distinction for purposes of analysis.

So we do not wish to draw lines: but we do wish to

discover a responsible vision of world history which will enable us to perceive something of the work of the Spirit in human events. Because human beings have freedom, and even groups can be said to have a "life of their own", a kind of group freedom from necessity, there appear to be problems about how we look upon the results flowing from such freedom: are they to be seen just as human events, or should we also discern the divine in them? Should we simply see the divine in every event, since God is omnipresent in the universe and therefore in human occurrences which happen within and as part of the cosmos? First, we need to consider how it is that we are not determinists, theological or otherwise.

Patterns of History

We take a position which is midway between historicism and anti-historicism. We are impressed by Popper's considerable critique of the deterministic elements in Hegel and Marx. It seems obvious to us, as we noted before, that the future is in some degree unpredictable, because of the creativity of humans, e.g. in making new discoveries in science, which themselves may impinge very powerfully upon human history (e.g. the H-bomb). But this does not preclude shrewd projections of the future, nor good explanations of how things happened in the past. We need not follow Tolstoy into a view of history as an accidental flux, nor follow others into determinism, whether theological or otherwise. So we reject the Calvinist account of predestination (though we recognize its motivation – to affirm the divine grace in action and to ascribe salvation to the Lord alone). Part of our conception of divine kenosis is that he withdraws a little, and hides himself from us in the cloth of the cosmos, and leaves us a little space to exercise our freedom.

It is doubtless because of the felt need to ascribe every good thing to God that some Muslims and Calvinists have seen salvation in a deterministic way. What they challenge us to do is to explain how it is that there is both freedom and divine action in the same events. How does grace operate in relation to the free creativity of some of the things we do and think? We imagine the situation to ourselves in the following way: As conscious beings we respond to the preceding state of affairs in a special way, through revisions and conclusions which flow from a complex of unconscious (and quasi-conscious) and conscious forces. The immediate cosmos as we perceive it feeds into our choices, which result from the play of feelings, experiences and so on. Where a free or novel choice or conclusion or creative act occurs, there is something not uniquely determined by what went before, but something analogous to the emergent characteristic arising in the evolutionary process. Among the forces playing on us, by the way, is the *antaryāmin*, for the Spirit hidden within us is present to us as the light of consciousness. It is God specially present because our consciousness renders the world more "transparent" to her. It is like a window onto the heavenly Light. So all this play of forces on us occurs, but the outcome is open, and it is wrong just to think of these forces as just like the various planets exercising pulls on each other, so that the position of the various bodies can be determined exactly in advance by the use of Newtonian mechanics. Once a person makes her choice she can see it as the outcome of all that came before and that is heavily determined by the Divine Creator: moreover the creativity of the choice is Creator-like, and so we discern the Lord in that very act. So from this angle the actor says "Not I, but Christ in me" or "Thanks to the grace of the Lord".

For if a person does something noble and creative, she will think of how she came to her choice by the magnetism of duty or the charm of novelty, and these themselves are divine features which we can see shining in the world. In them we see the hand of Brahman and the glimmering of the Great Ultimate. They are signs of the *Īśvara* from within the cosmos that she has exuded. So from all these points of view we can see that grace and human freedom fuse together. They are not antithetical. But it is misleading to speak of determinism. The Spirit, including the human spirit, blows where it wants, like the wind.

But if we do not wish to speak of determinism, this does not prevent us from thinking of patterns or structures of historical process. Before, however, we turn to this, let us briefly consider whether we can think of groups as having similar freedom to that of the individual. If so, can groups escape necessity, plunging into good and evil?

The Relative Autonomy of Groups and Institutions
That groups and institutions possess a degree of radical unpredictability is clear since novelties not only occur within a social context but affect that context. Einstein and Fermi were members of that ongoing institution (or set of overlapping institutions) known as "modern physics". Their original thinking and research imparted a creativity to that "institution". Conversely they would never have been able to exercise their individual creativity without reference to and drawing on the resources of the group. So from this perspective we can assign to groups also a degree of openness, because of the role played in them by unpredictable individuals.

The fact too that individuals are shaped by the social milieu in which they are embedded gives the group a strong role in fostering or inhibiting the desirable characteristics of love, integration, openness and so on which the good moral life, and the Christian (and world) spiritual life as well, demands. It is particularly in the sphere of *moha* or *avidyā* or nescient confusion that groups play a vital role: how can a poor boy raised in East Los Angeles or the darker parts of Brooklyn see a vision of the wondrous opportunities of life, of the spiritual dreams of great men and women, of the joys of the material creation? For him heaven may only be glimpsed in "crack" or heroin. And there the portals of heaven only open up on a greasy path that slides them into purgatory. So we in combatting ignorance and greed and hatred (all of which are properties of groups as well as of individuals) need, in the ethical and political life, to combat our social evils, both at home and in the wider world.

That is why, whatever we think of the particular measures

advocated by reforming socialists, we cannot struggle against, but must applaud, the motives of spiritual liberation animating socialist thinking. We may of course often find that refraining from some kinds of interference in the market turns out to be productive for all: but it is wrong for us not to recognize that our quarrels here are about means not about ends. (The notion however that by a stifling collectivism human beings can be liberated calls in question the power-hungry motives that may animate some of the Left, just as we note the greed that often inspires those of the Right.) But, as we say, the question of means has to be distinguished from that of ends. The ends should surely be the nurture of individuals within wider social structures which themselves avoid the greed, hatred and delusion which may also characterize the individual. This is a perspective which might be named "Buddhist social policy", since we are using the Buddhist formula here in an analogical mode to apply to groups.

The fact that a certain autonomy applies to groups means that we can think of patterns of action and development in the historical process. Our earlier reference to "Position Theory" is an example of the kind of view which can be used in explicating such patterns. Thus two cultures which have contact have only a restricted number of positions which they can occupy. Hindus faced with Western power and education had various places to take up, and did so. Their new synthesis showed a genius in dealing with the varied aspects of the challenge, in the form of the "New Hindu Ideology", the neo-Vedantin spiritual humanism of Vivekananda and others. It happened in Gandhi the new position had a special advocate who hitched it in a most particular and original manner to political action, while being in alliance with Nehru, a very different sort of politician. This Gandhian mode in Indian nationalism was unpredictable too, a creative way of fashioning a new political position as a result of his experiences in South Africa. So we ascribe a certain originality and even "accidentality" to modern Indian history. (Incidentally, another curb on prediction is the fact that relatively

independent causal sequences collide: under some circumstances we call such events coincidences, but they also are
"accidents" – so Indian independence movements came to
be affected by the outbreak of World War II, which came
about because of relatively insulated consequences of the
Treaty of Versailles, Western economic conditions and so
forth.)

From our perspective the benign and creative aspects of
group phenomena exhibit the work of the Spirit in history.
So the Church (or churches) too have creative aspects which
are vital in ongoing historical development. In so far as the
Church is merely buffeted by outside forces and is the mere
creature of other-generated fashion, it has no effect upon
the world. But it is supposed to – called to – have an
influence upon human affairs. So we in presenting this vision
wish to indicate a way of seeing and acting out our destiny
in this life. The Church and the Spirit are not there simply
to nurture individual spiritual growth from amidst the
thickets of darkness which so often surround us. They are
present also to nurture social changes which will diminish
confusion, greed and hatred. But alas, often this is not how
it works out. In trying to preserve the traditions, Church
leaders often shut off free enquiry (consider how Catholic
modernism was treated), and stimulate hatred (consider anti-
Semitism among Christian groups). Often it is thought to
be enough to restrain greed. Anyway, the Church has a
destiny which it must have a vision of.

It is because of the relatively autonomous way in which
wider institutional forces develop that early Christians
thought of the world as dominated by evil "principalities
and powers". There was thought that Christians should be
loyal to the properly ordained institutions of the State, etc.,
because these were perceived as having benign qualities,
restraining some of the dangerous forces at work in the
world. Whether this way of looking at political power is
justified at any given time requires judgment. The liberation
theologians are right in saying that it is necessary for
Christians to strive against those autonomous social and
economic forces which grind down the poor and inflict

violent injustice upon the lower classes in a given society, or more broadly in world society.

Religion and Culture

It is useful at this point to pause to think through the way we see the relationship of Christian institutions, and Christ as embodied in those, and the surrounding culture. The term "culture" of course has various senses. It sometimes has an educational sense, as of cultivating and nurturing some good things in human nature. It sometimes means the artistic and intellectual products of a society. Much important Christian-theological discussion has gone on in regard to sub-themes of this meaning – religion and literature, the role of religion in art, etc. But we wish to use the word in the third, more anthropological way: each society embodies values and products which constitute its culture. Culture is the whole way of life of a people; as such, it consists of all the ideas, objects and particular ways of doing things that are created by a group of people. Culture is comprised of a complex whole that includes language, beliefs about life, morals, values, customs and traditions, social organizations and law, inventions and technical processes, arts and artifacts; it also consists of all of the learned ways of thinking, feeling, acting and all other capacities and habits that human beings acquire by being a member of society (this classic definition of culture and delineation of its characteristics was set forth by Sir Edward Bennet Tylor in his work *Primitive Culture*). Here, civilization refers to advanced and highly developed cultures. An understanding of cultures is important for our topic as religious experience is apprehended through the medium of its forms, which in turn is influenced by geography, climate and economic circumstances (for example, ancient nomadic and agricultural societies).

Now it is part of our general attitude that we need to be critical of the culture out of which we come, and in principle of all cultures (but only insofar as we assimilate them and recognize them as part of "our" world or human history). We agree with those who see corruption in cultures: they are, as we have seen, bearers of hatred, delusion and greed.

But we do not for that reason advocate sectarian withdrawal. We need a midpoint between sectarianism and establishmentarianism. The latter leads to smug identification with a culture, and the former with the smug imagination that we can avoid unholiness by withdrawing. The seeds of ignorance and evil are of course buried in each one of us. We recognize that cultures are part of the inescapable fabric of human creativity and spiritual development. So we hold to a middle or "synthetist" position as H.R. Niebuhr called it: the Trinity is ultimately in command of cultural processes and is engaged in the creative ways in which cultures operate.

This by the way throws light on the creative role which tradition can play in life, and in the life of Christ. Our preoccupation has been very much how we can evolve a critical traditionalism. Now let us consider the way the ritual and sacramental glories of our faith are transmitted to us. They are modes of behavior which have been handed down to us: they represent ways in which the Church in a fairly early period came to work out the reenactment of the Lord's Supper. With modifications those early patterns have been reproduced down to the present day. All this is a manifestation of traditionalism. There have been resistances to changing the format of the Liturgy. You might comment, with a sniff of superiority: "Merely medieval". Well, it is true that what we have goes back to medieval and pre-medieval times. But from the standpoint of today's culture this traditionalism injects something new from outside. The ancient too can have a novel and creative impact in the meeting of cultures. So we as Christians wish to refresh ourselves by a kind of time travel: the rituals transport us to the time of the Cross and the Resurrection. So it was also with the Renaissance – the interplay of late medieval culture (then the "up-to-date" state of Western Europe) and the classical civilization unlocked again by the events of the 15th century. The crossing and interplay of cultures can occur both across time and space. So we see traditionalism in the Church itself as constituting a kind of critical challenge to modern society. This does not of course have the implication that we back political conservatism. On the contrary, as liberation theologians have emphasized, the voice of the New Testament has some unnerving accents, and among them there is heard the cry of the poor and the sick.

We have then to look to the spiritual life as it flows out of Christ and is transmitted to us through the sacraments as part of our cultural condition but also as a challenge to aspects of our culture.

Since the world is divided chiefly into nations, we can consider cultures to be national cultures, such as Italian, Thai or Colombian. But nations exist in wider groupings, so that we can talk of European, Southeast Asian and Latin American cultures. There are even broader groupings which some use, like "the West" (meaning, Europe, America, Australasia, etc.). The fluidity of the notion of a culture arises from the messiness of the modern situation. It is part of British culture that there are supermarkets, for instance: but these were first an American invention and are gradually becoming part of universal human culture. As we converge into a world history, so national and regional cultures become subcultures of the one world culture. We have not quite reached this stage but we are getting close to it. But roughly we are now in a situation where we participate in a loosely organized plural world culture, and it is in this context that we have to view the work both of the Church and of the Holy Spirit. Our view is that though there is for us central meaning in the sacramental Light which the Church at least dimly conveys, the Spirit is working creatively everywhere, not only in fashioning the originality and beneficence of the world's cultures, but also in the religious traditions of humankind. We attach especial importance to the latter in that they were matrices of civilizations and cultures. They have been at a deep level the shaping influence on so many groups and nations.

Rejections of Arrogance

Somewhat under the influence of Barth, Brunner and Kraemer, A. van Leeuwen has, in his *Christianity in World History* (van Leeuwen, 1964), sketched another view of the relation between Christ and for him all religions are human creations (following Barth and Kraemer), above which stands the God of the Old Testament and Christ. Somehow, though, Western religion, or rather the Christian faith and to some extent its surrounding culture, have stood under the influence as well as the judgment of God, and so the West, even its secularism and materialism, have a different, eschatologically oriented, set of values from the great religions of the East. The latter are stagnant, buried in cyclical time, and subject to oriental despotism. Western mission combined with secular values and technology functions to break down the "ontocratic" structure of Eastern cultures. He sees this as the expression of the Divine Will.

This seems to us an imperialist response to other cultures. It neglects the elementary fact that the Barthian manoeuver of putting Christ beyond religion can be undertaken (and has for long been undertaken) by exponents of other faiths: the Eastern image of the finger pointing at the moon means that religions point to Emptiness and Brahman and Dharma, and the Transcendent element which they lead us to in a sense stands above the doctrines, myths, institutions and so on which make up the religions. Moreover, van Leeuwen's view of Eastern civilizations is simplistic, and the histories of China and India, to go no further, are full of creative novelty, and even (on occasion) eschatology. Barth and van Leeuwen, for all their wide erudition, fail to feel that what is sauce for the goose is sauce for the gander: we could equally well have *Sangha Dogmatics*. It is true that Barth's theology helped him and others to stand up to the Nazis in a dark time. But so did some liberals, and the principles of liberal Protestantism should have been more powerful to deal with the mindless chauvinism of the Hitlerians than a theology which is deeply non-rational and liable to religious and cultural chauvinism.

We do not deny that Christianity has been an element in the birth of modern liberalism, science and other movements which have been and are creative in human history. To that extent, we are proud of our tradition. But one of the features that should bring greatest pride to us is the evolution of the modern study of religions, which is multicultural, empathetic, seeking for the truth of things and based on no one religious tradition. It is a noble fruit of human intellectual history, and it is one which impels us towards a view of world history which finds chauvinism hard to stomach. When mingled with the Christian faith it surely has to reject the type of modern arrogance expressed in Barthian missiology.

There is an implicit chauvinism too in much of the "secular theology" which was fashionable twenty years ago. The secular city of Harvey Cox implied, for instance, that modern mission would be in effect by Western secular values eroding popular Hinduism and other religions. Though Cox has gone beyond his *The Secular City* (1965), its implications are still worth pondering, for the secular aspect of his program is after all a reflection of Westerners' views, of the irrationality and backwardness of other (or all) religions, and the need to spread the secular gospel. We have got some cold feelings in our feet, however, since that secularist movement within Christianity and outside, because of the turbulences of the late sixties and the growth, among other things, of environmentalism, and the failure of many of the Third World imitations of Western culture. We ourselves, however, remain, of course, enthusiastic about some features of the modern world – its freedoms, its powers to assist in human sickness, its scientific creativity and so forth. But we take with deep seriousness the spiritual values of the great cultures, and we do not respect visions of Christianity which leave out these riches, both secular and religious.

Forces and Patterns in History

There has of course been much discussion of the notion of "laws" in history, and it is obvious enough that we cannot really think in these terms, if that is we are trying to assimilate history to physics or even to meteorology. This is not because there are not structural factors (for instance the effects of industrialization on various societies) or patterns (consider the various responses which happen within Position Theory). Especially in retrospect we are able inductively to discover patterns of change on a crosscultural basis. This produces a kind of phenomenology or typology of historical changes. Such results are tantalizing and lead some thinkers on the elusive task of finding laws of history, and making history a science. But because of human creativity and historical accidentality that hope is vain. Because of human consciousness we have to take seriously too the play of conscious and other forces which flows into a decision or thought: ideas and feelings become forces operative within and beyond the level of consciousness, both collectively and individually. For instance, though it is hard to measure, a "climate of opinion" can be politically important, and it is something which has arisen in a very complex way through various conscious forces at work. We sometimes in retrospect think that the outcome was somehow inevitable: but that is a misjudgment in that the play of such forces could have been modified by other conscious interventions, and the lack of these is not predictable because of the possibilities of human novelty. What we may look back on is a kind of positivistic necessity: given what happened, the outcome was inevitable. But none of this enables us to speak of laws of history. But we can discern patterns. These are patterns of choice of outcome as in Position Theory and tendencies (e.g. towards the breakdown of premodern monarchies in the age of industrialization and nationalism, etc.). This is what Maritain refers to as "typological laws" (Maritain, 1957), though we prefer not to use the term "laws" at all.

So we can see individual human acts and thoughts, etc., which are accessible to history as biography, in the context of particular socio-historical situations, and against the background of drifts and trends making up patterns within the welter of human history. In the case of religion the patterns emerge in the phenomenology which we have sketched, but individual and group experiences themselves occur within the configurations of various cultures and times. The delineating of how a culture is at a certain point is a kind of biographical exercise: the life of a culture is under scrutiny at a given period. So we have individuals partly shaped by their cultural groups which themselves are subject to patterns of historical change. In saying this we are roughly speaking following the account of Herbert Butterfield (1949). But he wanted, as we do, to go further to a third level, and see how the patterns of history and the events of biography might display the hand of God.

Because the forces at work in history are in part determined by the shape of different cultures (e.g. not all cultures react in the same way to the introduction of banking) we can see some patterns of response within the context of culture-formation, and this is an important activity of groups. Our pluralist approach to world history reinforces our evaluation of such diversity, and in this we follow Heerman Dooyewerd (Dooyewerd, 1960) in seeing this diversity both within and outside societies as multiplying the opportunities of human experience.

In some measure the question of where to discern the Spirit in human history is the same topic as the question of what are the criteria of religious (and worldview) truth. But in the next Chapter we shall discuss these in relation to the question of worldviews: here we shall merely consider the criteria of what we discern as the divine activity in history from the perspective of our *darśana*. There is, too, the converse picture of the course of human events: the emergence of evil. What is good and what is evil? And how does evil relate to the question of God's Providence?

The Spirit in Human History

We regard all cases where human activity displays consciousness of the Transcendent through religious and other experience, every case of the manifestation of love, every kind of creativity in thought and art as being signs of the Trinity in action in human affairs. We therefore have no difficulty in thinking of Shankara, the Buddha, Muhammad, Shembe and many others as showing forth experience of the Ultimate, as well as originality of thinking. We have no problem in seeing something of the hand of the Divine at work in creative political acts, even where the actors may also have been involved in crimes (for all human events display a mixture of good and evil − even the noblest acts

401

of self-giving can be touched slightly by pride). We think of those who have formed or slowly helped to form religious civilizations as showing the influence of the Spirit. Wit and new wisdom are signs of divine creativity. By the same token we regard art and music and the other creative arts as showing the signs of the Spirit, even where they may have something rude or "unchristian" about them. An exhibition of Aztec art can inspire in us a wonder at the way a divine breath blew through a civilization, even if we may think of human sacrifice with great repugnance.

And now we have a retrospective duty to follow Toynbee to interpret and enter into all of human history. Our ultimate family is the human family, and so we have to respect the myths and annals of that family. This does not mean that we need to go back to any part of it: we do not need to restore some of the evils of the past; but it does mean that we should assimilate their lives into the fabric of our memory. Confucius and the Buddha as well as Moses and Muhammad are part of our ancestry. Now in an important sense, at the third level of Butterfield, history becomes myth. We tell it to ourselves selectively to emphasize whoever are our value-laden heroes and poets and politicians – for Americans, American history does emphasize Washington and Lincoln and Henry James and Sousa, Martin Luther King, John Kennedy, George Gershwin and Hemingway. British history speaks of William the Conqueror and Good Queen Bess, Cromwell and Churchill, Shakespeare, Dickens, Elgar and Benjamin Britten. When we begin to see ourselves as members of humanity as a whole we shall surely reach out for an account of world history which highlights its most meaningful figures.

Indeed, there is in such myth-making a form of meditation to be conducted, beyond the forms of yoga and self-awareness; there is the training of the human memory to look back on its flow of history, that is its flow of human events, so that we assimilate all these people to ourselves. Just as in loving our enemies we seek to see them so far as we can as "us" not an alienated "them", so that we mourn the enemy dead as we mourn our own, so in the dialogue with the past which is this third level of historical reflection, we encounter human beings as belonging to "our group", that is, the human race. We do not in this need to like Hermann Goering or Attila, but we need to see them as human beings. We do not approve their evil and benighted acts, but still, they were motivated by human thoughts, and the spark of light was not utterly absent from them. In pursuing the search for light, we are looking for marks of the Spirit. There are many such marks in human history, and we do well to treasure them. In a way, the pursuit of historical memory, seemingly a human compulsion, is a mode not only of honoring the dead but of giving them renewed life. We are following the Trinity which "remembers" every human and conscious life, with its goods and evils, pains and joys. History at this level by entering a dialogue does in a way call forth the spirits of our ancestors and nourishes them in the thoughts and feelings of the present. In all this we may see Christ at the center; but we do not for that reason neglect the rest of the circle.

Evil in History

We have already remarked that the very act of creation and the coming into being of free-ranging animals like ourselves implies evil. It is inevitable in that our condition is necessarily somewhat ignorant, and it is easy for us to forget that confusion, hatred and greed are the other side of the coins of divine gnosis, love and self-restraint (the beginning of giving ourselves to others). But how could we have been born omniscient, with all the wisdom that comes from living? Or completely unselfish, without having gone through the process of growing and integration? Or without hatred as we learn to live in groups? So the evils of the world are predictable, and yet we are free beings, and we have access to the Light. We can nourish our love at the source of Love. So it is not possible for us to shrug off our individual or collective defects and say "They cannot and could not be helped". We have remorse for what stupidities and cruelties we have committed. Moreover, if our view of the "third level of history" is correct and in this we adopt the human past and see all of humanity as "us", we can regret all human folly and evil the way in which we may regret the sins of our ancestors, such as the Scots or the Bulgarians, with whom we may be identified. So the fact that there is an inevitability of folly should not mean that we do not in some sense take responsibility. It is in this that, according to our *darśana*, we encounter the atoning work of Christ.

Another way of seeing the evil of the world is in some of the structures of human life. For instance, there is a certain autonomy, as we have argued earlier, to institutions, and though this may have a creative side it also may move willy-nilly into evil. There are of course many unintended consequences of social actions. It is doubtful whether the early pioneers of nuclear weapons could foresee that the superpowers now align thousands of weapons and rockets at one another, more than enough to destroy the whole of the human race. Another case of autonomous collisions of forces is where a natural disaster befalls. Humans settle in San Francisco, and one day the San Andreas fault explodes.

The perspective of our vision remains autobiographical. We cannot see the arms race or the earthquake as things desired by the Lord. If he had withdrawn his sustaining power of course he could have abolished them, but could he leave a hole in the cosmos thereby? Our cosmos is a system of connections: *pratītyasamutpāda* prevails and we are caught in the jewel-net of Indra. The *Īśvara* has chosen this system: he sees it as giving freedom, but its disorderly aspects give him grief. From our autobiographical point of view we have to deal, or try to deal, with the nuclear arms race and to heal the wounds of catastrophe. Had we a clear solution to the so-called "problem of evil" someone else no doubt would already have found it: but there remains an enigmatic surd as we look at the world, and it sometimes makes us angry. But this response is not constructive or loving. Our vision is meant to nurture these attitudes. But at least, as we have often emphasized, our Lord is one who is willing to plunge into suffering and to experience both the joys and pains of the cosmos which he creates.

Eschatology and History

There is one last topic we need to discuss before we enter into our account of the religious history of the world from a Christian perspective. That topic is the last things. How do we interpret the eschatological aspect of the Christian *darśana*? One point about the idea of the "last things" is that somehow the future conceals the Brahman, as does the present material veil. It is notable that there is this future orientation to the idea of divine self-revelation at the core of the Gospels. The Light not only is, but will be. Now this is already consonant with our interpretation of history. Our "third level" perspective is forever widening. We can see more of human history and crosscultural richness than ever before in previous times. We see the past as "our" past, as we begin to see ourselves as being part of the group of ultimate concern, namely the human race. So as history moves forward we have, from an autobiographical perspective, a better view of it, as well as a better knowledge of the past in a purely technical way. The wake when seen from the stern of the ship widens as it goes, and we have a better vision of it. Revelation increases then as we go. We reject the view that the nearer we were to Jesus the more we knew of Christian truth. This is a trap for those who in reforming the Church wish to go back to a New Testament ethos.

This sets the scene for the thought that in principle we can have clearer vision as we progress through human history. The idea of last things is then a regulative idea which draws us ever onwards, in the hope of more and more perfect understanding of the divine Truth.

We interpret the Biblical imagery of catastrophe and light in the "last things" as indicating the numinous character of the Lord's final self-revelation. It will be more than we can bear. But as to the details, these are not to be taken literally, and we humans can know no resting place, so far as we can see it, in our restless striving towards the Kingdom. We hope amid backsliding and chaos to found a wondrously just and creative system of human society on this earth. Such a hope is useful as a Utopian ideal, regulatively thought. It has often refreshed human ideals. We are given a new dynamism with our picture of heaven on earth. Without it we would fade into sloth, that depressing lack of hope which is, interestingly, one of the seven deadly sins (but is it a sin to be depressed? It shows that even what we have little control over can be a case of self-inflicted alienation).

The ambiguity of our numinous utopia is interesting. It invites us to think of the end. What will the human race ultimately be remembered for once the last embers of the planet have burned out and the last space-voyagers have died out? Yet it is an end which has its own life, as we shall have when we have passed through the veil of death.

Finally we may reflect that though the concept of human progress has often been too naively presented, it is this which we hope and strive for. We can think, looking back on human history, that the spirit's work is becoming more conspicuous, as our knowledge of life increases, and as our understanding of the nature of *darśanas* becomes clearer. So with the fading of certainties that were ill based we acquire a better way of thinking about the vision which draws us onwards in human history and prepares the way for the next and vital stage of human history. We should not forget that the genius of modern technology, often arising from the evils of war and the pressures of ideological rivalry, have brought the world together and helped us towards an appreciation of the main lineaments of our common heritage, the pluralistic cultural history of humanity.

In some ways our accent on the universal character of human history echoes the views of Pannenberg, though our approach starts from a somewhat different place. It is through the avenue of religious studies that we have come to this place, and not primarily the traditions of European theological scholarship. Our "vision of hope" matches that of Moltmann's theology of hope, too. But our *darśana* has emphasized more the spiritual side of human history: to that we now turn.

The South Asian Experiment
If we step back from the ideological and civilizational areas of the modern world and look at some of their major

components, especially in the non-Western world, it is clear that the old Asian loosely knit bloc, ranging from India to Japan, is the remains of three or four overlapping Asian civilizations. The first of these is South Asia, including India, Nepal, Sri Lanka, which has produced the Hindu and Buddhist cultures primarily, with other smaller religions – Jainism, Sikhism and so on. The second is China, Korea and Japan. The third is South-East Asia, which in part blends both Indian and Chinese motifs. The fourth is the trans-Himalayan cultures of Tibet and the Mongolias. All these are bound together by Buddhist influence. So first it is useful for us to sketch what appears to us to be the meaning of Indian religious history.

The first thing to be remarked is that India south of the Himalayas has been the world's greatest laboratory of kinds of religion. It has seen the greatest and most original development of devotional motifs; it has experimented in a wide and perceptive way in the development of inner-directed mysticism and in particular yoga techniques. It has also and in connection with these produced various theologies and myths which can be a rich mine of insight. Our perspective is to see these modes of thinking and feeling and acting as valid but not necessarily true alternatives, and ones which in presenting a challenge to the Christian faith act as a deep and ongoing critique of features of the faith which require it to rethink some of its accumulated tradition.

In a way the complexity of Indian culture, by giving freedoms to various alternative kinds of spirituality, allows each to develop in an intense way. This can, for instance, be said of yoga techniques, both Hindu and Buddhist. There can be little doubt that despite the examples of Hesychasm and Ch'an Buddhism (for example) which indicate special ways in which the contemplative life has developed in Europe and China, it is in India above all that technical virtuosity has had its greatest demonstration in the spiritual life. The procedures for clearing away the extraneous and for concentrating the mind as a preparation for one or other of the forms of mystical insight and communion are refined and clearly laid forth. They are the accumulations of

THE VISION OF LOVE

centuries of practice. The respect accorded to the yogi has
made this rich understanding of such techniques a possibility
in Indian society. As recent developments in Indian forms
of Christian spirituality have made plain there is a rich mine
of methods here for the Christian seeker to make use of.

The fact that the yoga tradition uses techniques might
seem to some commentators to be unfortunate, for after all
God appears to us through her spontaneous grace. It is on
the basis of this thought that Staal finds theistic mysticism
unexaminable from an experimental angle. But this is of
course a thought which is sloppy and ill-conceived, for
various reasons. Does it, first, imply that we should not work
at our own self-improvement? Do we simply let our characters or potencies drift along hoping for transformation from
Above? Second, the powers of doing yoga are themselves
powers arising out of created history and should be used,
like other gifts, as heavenly. Third, if the Divine lies at the
depths of each person's soul then should we not make use
of means to try to find her by clearing away the super-
ficialities of everyday consciousness? Such a clearing away
is at least partially effected by yoga techniques. Fourth, as
Indian mystics, and especially too Chinese and Japanese ones
in the tradition of Ch'an attest, spontaneity and not human
"effort" is part of the experience of the seeker: it is perhaps
this which is the existential reality underlying doctrines of
grace in this context. It is unwise to bend our judgments
to merely doctrinal proprieties as we see them, and if there
is to be room for the concept of grace it must be rooted in
the living life of the seeker.

So we see the Indian development of yoga as one of the
vast resources for global religion and for the Christian faith
in particular. It injects a certain professionalism into spiritual
practice, which is a sign that we mean business in this form
of life. But also important in this connection is a Buddhist
form of the path of meditation, since it tends towards a
minimalist position in interpretation of the transcendental
state. In the Theravada, nirvana is not seen as a Brahman-
like basis of existence, nor is it either in the Mahayana
emptiness schools. Moreover, early Buddhism did not

concentrate upon the notion of a Creator, and indeed had an ironic attitude towards the pretensions of Brahma. The fact the Buddhism could set forth on its long civilizational history with assumptions so different from those of Semitic culture and its offspring such as Christianity and Islam is a telling fact. From our perspective Buddhism serves as the clearest great alternative to the Western theistic traditions, and within Indian culture too it served as a dialectical alternative to the Hindu complex. It has several features which indicate its critical function within Indian civilization.

First, it adopted a conventionalist account of language. It rejected the idea of an "original language", Sanskrit, which was molded into everlasting sacred scriptures. It always took a somewhat pragmatic stance about scriptures. This rejection of a guarantee of truth in words is an important criticism of all literalist and inerrantist viewpoints. Second, Buddhism started with a critique of the very idea of a substance. It thus distinguished itself from virtually all Hindu theological and philosophical systems. Its picture of the fluidity and impermanence of the world is not only in accord with modern science but also provides a much better model than substantialist accounts, including Aristotelian metaphysics. Third, it provides a stance which is on the whole against ritual: or at least takes a pragmatic view of the effectiveness of rituals. It is a critic therefore of tendencies (which are evident both in Indian and Western religious traditions) to treat rituals as mechanically effective. If the Christian tradition has a use for the ritual concept of the sacrament, this is governed by the notion that the sacrament is a personal transaction between God and the individual or group. It is like personal gesture, such as shaking hands. This personalistic mode of treating rituals is, however, not important for much of Buddhism because of its lack of an active conception of a creator God who is omnipresent (even if later Mahayana piety verges on this belief). Fourth, in the Buddha it has a marvelous example of the analytic teacher. It was perhaps necessary that the incarnation of the one God, in the Christian context, should have taught and lived mysteriously: he had to transcend the categories which provided him with a conceptual take-off point in history. There is in Jesus' non-analytic and imaginative style something for all. But the community soon discovered that it needed analysis as well: there had to be some fusion of Christian spirituality and Greek philosophy. The Buddha starts as the greatest analytic teacher in world history. He appealed to reasoning as well as inspiration, and he fused cerebral thinking and the practical pursuit of peace and insight. In this he exhibited a more general feeling, evident in the Upanishads and in Jainism also, that what we centrally lack is understanding, gnosis, existential knowledge of the way things really are. Original Ignorance rather than Original Sin is our bane. This is a good complement to the Christian preoccupation with sin.

Yet for all the difference of assumptions found in Buddhism compared with Christianity and with much of Hinduism, it is interesting how the evolution of the tradition led to strongly pietistic forms, such as Pure Land, and a convergence towards theism. If such near-theism could arise out of non-theistic tradition, it heralds a relatively easy living together of the monotheisms and mainstream Buddhism in our global city. But we do not here wish to stress the resemblances of Buddhism and the Christian tradition: rather we see Buddhism as providing a corrective in various respects to over-emphases or possible weaknesses in the Christian tradition. But to some degree we have strayed from our theme: the Buddhist critique of the Hindu side of Indian civilization. Some more words on this topic are in order.

Not only by its attention to a realistic account of language, its critique of substance, distrust of priest-managed ritual, its strongly analytic character, has Buddhism leveled challenges to mainstream Hinduism: but at the ethical and social level it has posed an alternative. Its rejection of the *varna* or sacred class system is not head-on, but it is real; its strong and systematic emphasis on compassion and its evolution of the Bodhisattva ideal is a perspicuous way of exhibiting some prime values latent in the Indian tradition. Its attempt to form a sangha built upon open principles; and its relative moderation between extremes in the earlier (and later) forms of Indian life both are important strands in Indian social thinking. Its taking up of the theme of non-injury gives it a means of checking the cruelties of political life. In various ways it provided a pervasive good sense and transmitted this benign attitude to other cultures in its successful missionary endeavors beyond India.

We have already touched on the Buddhist counterpoise to Christian values. In the dialectic of religious history it is vital for Christians to give heed to the implicit critique by Buddhism. The Buddhist emphasis upon what cannot be articulated in the Transcendent must be a corrective to the too easy anthropomorphism of the Biblical tradition. It reinforces the negative path of Dionysius the Areopagite (whose position in some degree could be endorsed in rather different language by the Madhyamika Buddhist). The difference in assumptions between the faiths is a warning about the softness of our reasons for holding a position. Its good sense about language should lead us to pause in our claims on behalf of any scriptures. Its non-violence should lead to soul-searching about the violence of much of the Christian tradition. Its analytic approach to its accounts of the inner life not only holds up a model to Christians: but also reinforces modern attempts to see part at least of the Christian message in existentialist terms. There is much to learn from Buddhist psychology as well as from its more particular techniques of self-training.

It was also within the Indian framework already that Buddhism thought out its idea of *upāya*. This famous doctrine of the need to adapt the message to the psychological and cultural condition of the receiver of the message helped to give Buddhism flexibility in its missionary outreach. It is a doctrine which in its emphasis on "skill in means" or as we might say sensitivity should reinforce the need for dialogical encounter between peoples and cultures. It suggests too that the way a faith is expressed will be liable to vary considerably, not just over time but between one area of the world and another. It thus is a principle which suggests federalism in the expression of religion: the allowing of the existence of various ways of practice and kinds of belief but within an overall sense of unity. (This is a virtue of the Ecumenical Movement in Christianity, that it does not impose a credal or ritual straightjacket upon the diverse branches of the Christian heritage.) Buddhism has gone forward much more conscious of the *upāya* principle than has any other faith advanced with its analogue to "skill in means."

In taking up the ideal of non-injury, Buddhism shows its indebtedness to a prior tradition which found alternative expression in Jainism. Jainism for a long period was highly influential in India. But if now its numbers are small, it represents an important type: a religion devoted to a core of heroic austerities. The picture of the Jaina saint provided by some of the great statues, such as that at Sravana Belgola in South India, of the holy person who has stood so long in an upright, naked posture that the creepers are already beginning to wind up his legs, is stunning. This indifference is tremendous; and the bodily control amazing. It is a hard and stupendous asceticism. It is part of the genius of India that every possibility is taken to its logical conclusion. With its minute concern not to take even invisible forms of life Jainism places such austerities within a caring context. It is this strand in India which serves as a warning to humans about cruelties to other forms of living beings. It is a warning of special concern to us today, not just because cruelty to animals has been somewhat technologized in the West; but also because we now (in the West) realize our affinity to other creatures, through the theory of evolution. No longer can that cold line be drawn between living beings and humans. The soul cannot be exclusively placed in the human being. We have to reflect that the growls of lions, the bites of mosquitoes, the play of panthers, the wriggling of bacteria are all part of our heritage and ancestry. We should respect life as we might respect our ancestors. In this respect, the Jains for intuitive and other reasons (connected with karma doctrine) have led the way, by extreme example.

Hindu Themes in the South Asian Experiment
Gradually out of a complex Indianness there has emerged that system we know as Hinduism – a modernly conceived

federation of cults. At the doctrinal level we have made use of the Ramanuja type of Vedanta as a good way of expressing the divine creative omnipresence. It is indeed one of the glories of Indian experimentation with ideas that despite the great conservativeness of the mechanisms of passing on and developing the tradition such divergent Hindu theologies have emerged. Not only are the varied forms of Vedanta in mutual conflict; but they in turn are in contradiction with some or all of the other so-called darśana-s. The forms are enriching to our imagination. If we have here stressed the centrality of the Viśiṣṭādvaita school, it is not for want of respect for the other Vedanta schools: the remarkable intellectual achievements of Advaita Vedanta have been built upon in modern times by Vivekananda in creating a Neo-Vedanta which has been vital for the Indian national struggle and represents an important and enduring statement of the major Hindu point of view in today's world.

Indeed the elaboration of Advaita categories to establish the thesis of the fundamental unity of all religions represents a very powerful challenge to the Christian view which we here espouse (and to Buddhist, Muslim and other more determinate spiritual darśana-s). It seems to us that we are treading one of the middle paths between two powerful alternatives: the unificationist thesis of the neo-Hindu ideology based on the Advaita, and the humanist rejection of religions in favor of a new scientistic outlook on the world. The Hindu synthesis has a fine claim to be rooted in tradition, and yet it makes sense of the plurality of religions. It provides a fine platform both for the secular State and for the unity of religious mankind. If we were not gripped by the Christian vision we too would be neo-Hindus, for this is the best way of following what Hick has called the "Copernican revolution". So the Hindu framework has much to offer us by way of materials for convincing worldviews.

But the very richness and chaos of the other dimensions of the Hindu tradition are also signs of India's experimental working out of the major themes of religion. We have already noted how at the experiential level we have the intense development both of fervent bhakti and of cool and effective yoga. The mass of Indian mythology leaves one amazed, and at the same time uneasy. For the many forms of God refracted through these stories can mean that often human beings' intense *bhakti* is directed towards somewhat inferior objects. But that doubtless is a common matter: not only among the gurus who have done well in attracting fervid followings, but in the many lesser gods of the pantheon. Yet the Hindu tradition can teach us how theism can be refracted – how many faces of the Divine Being can be mythically presented, and yet the sense of unity behind the many ideas which humans have projected upon the one Reality can be held onto in the life of devotion.

Part of the mythic framework concerns the avatars: here Hinduism has had a different perspective from the Christian. There are many who find the Christian doctrine too obscure, as if God should have plunged into this world but once. We on the contrary see this not only as a sign of divine commitment, but also as sufficient in the work of sacramentally giving humans power to overcome their ignorance and alienation.

On the whole, the Hindu emphasis, in the diagnosis of our ills, is upon ignorance. We are influenced by this and think that it is good as a counterbalance to what has become a too one-sided stress upon the defect of the will which has brought us to our present state. But the Indian tradition has pioneered the thought that it is a kind of spiritual confusion which possesses us. And this in many ways is the truth: how often do we think, looking back, how foolish we were – we should have known better. As Wilde says youth is wasted on the young, precisely because we need to grow in wisdom, and many of the bad and stupid things we once did could have been eliminated, and suffering spared, if we had only known then what we know now.

India as laboratory has continued, with the influence of the West and of the British. One of the great signs of the working of the spirit in that tradition has been the life of Gandhi, who managed to produce such a creative synthesis between traditional Indian themes, both Hindu and Jaina, and Christian values. He is the greatest Christian of this century, as well as the greatest Hindu.

India Goes East

One of India's major contributions to history is the way its ideas and practices spread well beyond it, and to virtually all of Asia through Buddhism. It left a profound imprint on South East Asia, which has incorporated Indian, Chinese and indigenous values into a fruitful and delicate synthesis. It is one of the modern evils that various group impulses got out of control and have destroyed great areas of Indo-Chinese culture. Thus, nationalism felt impelled to take a Marxist form in the former French colonies. That Marxism was solidified into an extra rigidity by the greed of the French in fighting on for their Empire, and the hatred of the Americans, in continuing the colonial war. The rigid Marxism of North Vietnam masked chauvinist ambitions, while in Cambodia (Kampuchea) the anticolonial mentality was taken over by Khieu Sampan's ideology and Pol Pot's regime, with tragic consequences. Nevertheless there remain imprints of that traditional synthesis in South East Asia, and it is of course the major center for Theravada Buddhism, with Sri Lanka. For us this tradition touches on the pure divine life, though it does not incorporate the conception of a Creator or of a primary object of worship. But it is a clean critic of the anthropomorphism and over-confidence of so much theism in the past, whether in India or in the West.

But even more striking, in its march of influence, was the way in which Indian Buddhism percolated into China via Central Asia. In doing so it made that faith a major component of Chinese civilization, and from there it helped to shape both Korean and Japanese culture. It became an ingredient in a new kind of synthesis in Chinese civilization, to which we now turn.

Chinese Expressions of the Spirit

Two major forces strike us as we look at the Chinese experience. One is the continued emphasis upon Confucian ritual and performative practice. No other culture has given greater importance in the general sense to the ritual dimension of religion, allowing it to permeate through daily life, without however falling victim to ritualistic entanglement. The Chinese concept of *li* is nicely balanced, between ritual and good manners. Other cultures have sometimes become too thoroughly preoccupied by the ancient formulae and the sacred demands of a sacred law which can get in the way of expressive cultural flowering. This did not happen in China. Second, the Chinese experience involved the unification of a vast culture in a manner which gave centrality to scholarly and literary accomplishments. The civil service examinations of classical China were essentially literary, and often the ambition of such functionaries was to retire into artistic and poetic endeavor as a sign of their true breeding and avocation. In our view, the modern world and especially the West has reached a similar set of values but in a lopsided way. We prize music and the arts, and the amount of space in our papers and weeklies to the arts is impressive. But they exist somehow as a spiritual exercise on their own, encouraging sensitivity, but not in an integrated framework. We admire many attempts in modern times to bring depth to our concept of well-being through the arts: but we consider that this depth has to be seen in a wider way, as a sign, for instance, of that creativity which we share by analogy with the Creator. But apart from these two sides of classical China, we see the general religious synthesis as reflecting something important in the questing of the Spirit.

It emerged for various reasons, including importantly political ones, that the three great religions of China (as they are often regarded) came to form a single ideological and practical system. They managed to assign to the three main traditions of China interlocking relevances. They thereby exhibited a pattern of mutual toleration very different from the assumptions usually operative in the West. Now admittedly some of this was in the political interest of the imperial regime: but nevertheless it set a pattern for Korean and Japanese practice too where frequently people count themselves as belonging to more than one religion or denomination. China also was a main force in thinking through a kind of ecumenical Buddhism which harmonised the practices and teachings of the various schools.

Vital too was the mood of philosophical Taoism which left its panenhenic stamp on Chinese life, religion and feeling. It was in part out of this that one of the most creative achievements of Chinese spirituality arose, namely Ch'an Buddhism. Here was a kind of practice which can teach us much in penetrating beyond words to direct experience: the nature-oriented character of much Ch'an and Zen is relevant to the practice of the presence of the Divine Being in a very different context.

Chinese and Japanese religiosity went to extremes in a sense, for as well as the contemplative and non-personal character of the Ch'an or Zen quest there is the pietism of the Pure Land: and in Japan we approach teachings, for instance those of Shinran, so reminiscent of those of Ramanuja and Christian Reformation theism that it is hard not to think of them as alternative wellings up of the same Spirit.

Japanese religious pluralism has since World War II been given new freedoms; and we can see a congruence between it and the democratic values which were imposed by MacArthur after the catastrophe of defeat. Despite the horrors of the war, the more recent period has been fruitful, for there is the beginning of the formation of a "Pacific mind" in which the diverse cultures across the Pacific Ocean are participating in a dialogue between Buddhism, Christian and Jewish values, and democratic institutions – which may in combination become relevant to the situation of the smaller cultures of the South Pacific, which have an interest in a pluralistic political stance.

Peoples of the South
Those peoples of the South, the Polynesians, Melanesians, Australian Aboriginals and others have suffered grievously from the incursions of the Whites. There are aspects of their creativity we are only now beginning to rediscover, such as

417

the bold voyages of the Polynesians, breathtaking in their skill and courage, and the remarkable knowledge of their environment displayed by the Aborigines. Their predicament is like that of nearly all small-scale peoples in the world – how to preserve something of their traditions while undergoing domination by others and economic upheavals. It can be hoped that a new synthesis of cultures, White and non-White, can be worked out in the Pacific, and in ways which will blend with the East-West pluralism of the mutual relationship between American and Asian values, as pioneered above all in California.

Some similar problems have faced the Native American and the pre-Columbian peoples of Central and South America. Already these of course had pioneered great and original civilizations, which we are now only beginning to rediscover. Mostly the relations between the conquerors and the native peoples have been deplorable, and though the Church did much to protect the Indians, it was also part of that arrogant and triumphalist European and particularly Hispanic culture which earlier vicissitudes in Europe had bred. Now with a renewed feel for the possibilities, despite the poverty, of Latin American culture we may find ourselves at a new creative point in the evolution of the Americas. Already Latin values are making a deeper impact upon the North, and it would be nice to think of a new spirit and optimism in contrast to mutual suspicions between North and South which have been born out of America's imperialist mode. But the whole story of the Americas, as seen in the large variety of cultures, exhibits part of that world-wide experimentation in living which the small-scale societies especially have tried out. From this large experience in human culture the Spirit has played with differing modes of ease in community. If often there have been group conflicts, this is the other side of group security. From this groupist mentality the human race needs to free itself.

In Black Africa we can see some modern effects of the underlying diversity, namely the large number of new independent churches and other religious movements which exuberantly display a vitality in the reinterpretation of

Christianity, often expressing it in ways which distinguish it sharply from missionary Christianity. This will lead us to a richer view of the possibilities of the Christian tradition. It also will help to integrate certain powerful themes from classical African religions into the interpretation of the faith: themes such as healing, reverence for ancestors, the role of dance in human spiritual self-expression, harmony with the environment, and shamanism. These themes exist, as we have more than once seen, elsewhere, and in the coming world civilization they will no doubt take on a somewhat different from traditional form, but they will remain vital elements in our *darśana*. The dead and rising god who lovingly restores humans to health is reflected in the figure of the shaman: but at another level the shaman's work is replicated in the depth psychologist. As we have seen, the work of Jung is significant here (but not definitive, for knowledge progresses) because he shows ways in which the symbols of traditional religions have a new life and meaning in today's world. Likewise, African experience of harmony with nature, in that the spirits lurk in and behind everything around us – the pools in the stream, the long grass, the mountains, the animal herds – will translate into a new appreciation of the natural at a time when it is being so greatly transformed and often robbed by the work of humans. Reverence for ancestors will translate into a new world recognition of the great persons of the past, heroes and saints of the whole race. But also from within Africa will arise new wells of creativity in which a distinctively African contribution to culture will, we hope, emerge. It is true that the modern world is phasing out many beautiful experiments in living: the nomadic life with its floating satisfactions and camaraderie is bound to crumble because of frontiers and bureaucracies (also Gypsy life in Europe and elsewhere). The can and the refrigerator will displace hunting and gathering. The murmuring nights under the stars, and the pulses of traditional music, will be submerged in other sounds. And it is in Africa too that one of the last major clashes between races will work itself out, as fear and groupism stir hatreds, which will demand the highest human love to combat. We may also recall that Africa has nurtured an ancient and distinctive form of Christianity, namely Ethiopian, which has also been for many African-descended people in the Western hemisphere a shining goal and focus of eschatological expectation. What such aspirations point to is the discovery of authenticity in black culture and the need to nurture identity after the terrible uprooting experience of slavery and its aftermath.

Race and Suffering – Slavery and the Holocaust

Although humans can be creative in adversity and sometimes because of it, it is well to remind ourselves of the terrible cruelties and tragedies of the African slave trade. It is not the only slave trade in world history, but it was the most traumatic; and by and large it was conducted at the instigation of Western European powers who claimed to belong to a Christian civilization. If later it was abolished in part because of the vigorous views of Protestant Christians, working to influence the British Parliament and through it the Royal Navy, then queen of the oceans, it is nevertheless a sad commentary on the moral force of actual Christianity that it should have reconciled the African slave trade with Christian practice and belief. Part of the cause of this was demonic groupism in one of its most widescale and far-reaching forms: racial prejudice. It was easy to think of Africans as inferior because on the whole their technology and style of life was not "advanced" (it corresponded to earlier stages in civilization, as the Europeans saw it). The "savage" was less than fully human. A variety of feelings, including of course greed, went into the attitudes fostering slavery. And such notions are still by no means dead in the West (or even in India and China against the blacks). So while Europe was fashioning great splendors of the human spirit it was also arrogantly considering that blacks could be bought and sold for work in the plantations and great houses of the transatlantic world. Beneath that yoke, and in between the scourges and early deaths, heroic spirituality could develop: and Africans made a vital contribution to Brazilian, Caribbean and North American cultures. But that cannot of course justify the viciousness of the system, created from within the bosom of "Christian" civilization. If blacks themselves, and Arabs, were a factor too in the trade, this underlines the pervasive grip of groupism.

The other vast disaster connected with the West was of course the Holocaust, which was conceived and executed as a planned attempt to exterminate a whole population as defined racially (Nazi atrocities against Gypsies, Slavs and others were also racially motivated, and these crimes against humanity also need emphasizing): and because the definition of the race is in part through religion, it poses some questions about the mutual treatment of religions. The magnitude of the disaster coupled with this factor has created a whole theological literature both Jewish and Christian seeking to interpret the history of those terrible events.

One of the sources of anti-Semitism is a fallacious epistemology. It was thought by many Christians in various forms that the meaning of the Old Testament was plain. It was therefore deliberately that Jews persisted in their rejection of Christian interpretations of the scriptures. And so they were seen not only as wrong, but as morally wrong. This provided part of the general excuse to limit the rights of Jews. Our soft epistemology points in a differing direction, for it involves by the same token a soft hermeneutics. Thus, it is appropriate to say that two great books underlie Western civilization, one known as the Old Testament and the other as the Hebrew Bible. From one point of view the answer as to how it is that two streams of religion have issued forth from the one matrix is that this is perfectly normal, given the softness of the epistemology and hermeneutics of religion.

We may note that such softness is demanded of other ideological stances in relation to the Jews in modern times. The growth of European nationalism meant that Jews were put in an ambiguous position. The terrible irony was that they joined Europe's glittering civilization in time to be viewed with suspicion by those who were gripped by the new-found spirit of linguistic and cultural nationalism. The nationalist ideal eventually drove the Jews (or rather, a wing of Jewish culture) towards Zionism and the creation of a Jewish State. Likewise secularism could look at traditional Judaism with a certain contempt. Elements of all three Christian, nationalist, and secularist attitudes entered into the Nazi virulence against the Jews, even though Nazism turned its back both on Christianity and on the rationalism flowing from the Enlightenment. Of all the forces at work, though, in the 19th an 20th centuries it was nationalism – Russian, Polish, Czech, German, French, and so on – which fueled the hatred of Jews. But Christianity was not notably successful at combatting nationalist hatred in this or other connections. It is thus a mark of shame that the Christian worldview's true testimony towards the Jews was undertaken by only a heroic minority.

It is worth mentioning that the days of Hitler are a witness to the interconnectedness of sin. The greed, hatred and delusion displayed by the Allies at Versailles were a powerful ingredient in German disillusion with the Weimar experiment and a powerful stimulus to those hypernationalist forces to which Hitler gave such articulate expression. World War II was the second act in a single German war, and the peace of Versailles ensured many of the bitternesses to come. We cannot blame Clemenceau or Lloyd George for the Holocaust: but they contributed to its causation. There is a Buddhist moral here.

The early Church maintained both a Jewish and a non-Jewish version of the faith. This may be a sign to us that both the Jewish and the Christian traditions have something vital that the Spirit wishes to tell us. The Holocaust is a terrible condemnation of the negative ways in which the Christian community has treated its brothers and sisters. If there is a practical message it lies in the eschewing of two things: dogmatism and groupism, both very prevalent within the Christian outreach. On the whole Judaism, despite its tight knit community life running through much of the fabric of its history, has not been groupist. It has been particular, but not arrogant. If the idea of being a chosen people sounds arrogant, that is mostly a semantic issue: for Jews have been chosen for much suffering, and they maintained their tradition without, on the whole, wishing to crush or enslave others. They have had a benign religious nationalism.

The Torah and the Presence of God

The Jewish continuance of a detailed Law has had maybe its absurdities; but it has also been a means whereby the Jew is continuously reminded of his obligations to the Brahman. The Lord is forever reminding her or him of the relationship through regulations to be observed – in bathing, in eating and drinking, in domestic and external living, in love and marriage and so on. As we have noted, the practise of the presence of God is important, and for the Christian, as opposed to the Jew or the Muslim, it is carried on without much benefit of law and regulations. It can easily disappear: to this extent the Jewish and Muslim means are more effective, when obeyed. For the Jew, the Torah is an aspiration to God-oriented existence, from within a group that suffers and has joy together. It becomes a transnational freemasonry testifying to the one God, knowledge of whom was pioneered through early Israelite history. The Islamic Law is a way of extending this notion, e.g. through frequent daily prayers, to the whole of the human race. The aspiration is important and in itself good; but it is based on a more rigid epistemology than the world in actuality warrants. The more mysterious and esoteric Sufis can make use, however, of the Law as a daily reminder of God while being somewhat open to the spiritual quests of other and parallel religions. We are, however, already trespassing on the borders of the question of the world-historical meaning of the religions of Abraham. Before we meet that, let us look briefly at the Iranian and Graeco-Roman heritages.

Western Asia

Of the various great religions which emerged in Western Asia (Babylonian, Assyrian, Egyptian and so on) the one which came to have the most universal impact was that of Zoroaster in its varying forms. Some crucial ideas from it entered into the body both of Judaism and of Christianity, and through them into that of Islam. The eschatology of the Pharisees was deeply marked by Persian influences, and it helped to impart to Christianity that drive towards the future which still marks it. Zoroastrianism gave the history of the world dramatic shape: the savior who comes will prepare the way for the final triumph over evil and the resurrection of the dead. This picture has drawn Westerners onwards in their quest for ultimate revelation fused with the concept of a return to paradise. From this there springs our vision of a regulative kingdom of God when social evils will have been put right and humans live together under the Iśvara in creative harmony. Zoroastrianism also had a marked effect on Mahayana Buddhism, helping to shape the conception of the Buddha Amitabha and the Pure Land which he creates for the benefit of unworthy beings who call upon him. It is a link between two eschatologies, as Iran also is a link between two sets of civilizations. Zoroastrian prophetism helped to reinforce the ethical monotheism of ethics and ritual in the Jewish religion. The numinous faith of one Lord was linked with the moral intuitions of seers.

Graeco-Roman Civilization

The brilliant and plural culture pioneered in Greece and fused together with Roman organizational qualities helped to generate a dialectic in human history which has been profoundly important for world civilization. The fact that Judaism existed within the borders of the Empire and before that in the post-Alexander Hellenistic culture of the Eastern Mediterranean meant that it could spread cellularly throughout much of the empire, and so provide the milieu for the transmission of the early Christian faith itself. It was the synthesis between Greek, Roman and Jewish-Christian motifs that really gave rise to Christianity as we know it in the Catholic West and Orthodox East. Probably the two most significant movements in the ancient world were Neoplatonism (possibly influenced from India) and Stoicism. In some degree the Jewish ethic and that of early Christians more so (because relatively disengaged from the Law) were to Romans reminiscent of Stoic values: and Neoplatonism came to be an important vehicle for conveying Christian theology and mystical ideals in the imperial culture. Greek philosophy also contained that critical strand which helped later to supply a questioning dynamism from within Christian civilization at the time of the Renaissance and beyond. So Classical rationalism and Christian synthesis came to be a heady combination which sparked the achievements of the West in the 12th century and later of the Renaissance.

The Meaning of Islam

The Eastern synthesis between Christianity and Hellenistic civilization yielded Byzantine Orthodoxy. One of its creative achievements was the Liturgy, which, because of the conservatism of the tradition, remains with us today. It also successfully proselytized to the north, the culmination of which was the conversion of Russia. However, it had at its fringes new forces ready to be given dynamism: above all, Muhammad as Prophet of God released the energies of the Arabs, and from this was founded a new and different civilization. What is the meaning of Islam to us, as wishing to see the world through the prism of a Christian worldview? We cannot, because of our epistemology, take at face value the status accorded by Muslims to the Qur'an, though we can acknowledge Muhammad as being a prophet, driven by the numinous dynamism of his visions and by the beautiful mysteries of those revelations which came welling up inside him so painfully and wondrously.

We can look on Islam as the severest critique of the Christianity of the period. The complexities of theology, the inequality of Christians, the unadventurousness of Christian thought, were all put to the test by Islamic forthrightness, which brought social reform, relative simplicity of belief and a heady new synthesis between religion and classical culture. Its stress on brotherhood was a way of reminding Christians of their divisions and animosities. So from one angle we can see Islam as a mode of prophetically calling into question the values of late Hellenistic Christianity. One aspect of its forthrightness was Islam's attitude to political power and

425

therefore to war. Christianity had a much more ambiguous relation ship to power and violence. Its early pacifism was overlaid by the necessity of political conformity. Now in our "soft" vision we think that the dialectical ambiguity of early Christianity can be resolved in the principle of the minimalization of violence. We consider that often the tensions within the tradition are valuable and part of its dynamic. We thus have a quasi-Hegelian attitude to Christianity and the cultural syntheses it has undergone. This prepares it for a new pluralistic age. But Islam had a more realistic view of the relation of religion and politics in its own hey-day. If we now think that it has problems with pluralism, that is another matter. It once, however, formed the basis for two or three major civilizations, from the early period to the Ottomans. The major difficulty from our perspective is its relative lack of religious tolerance beyond the "peoples of the Book". There is much yet to be worked out by faithful Muslims in adapting their interpretations of the Law to modern conditions and plural society. It is notable, though, that the Islamic tradition has incorporated both numinous and contemplative elements, like the other universal religions. There is the polarity between the *bhakti* of much popular Islam and the inward esoteric Sufi tradition.

Colonialism

Although the colonial period, dating essentially from the great voyages of the 15th and 16th centuries, saw many undesirable consequences, it was important in gradually bonding the globe together into a single or virtually single economic fabric. Even the arrogance of conquering European powers helped to stimulate new forms of thinking in ancient cultures, such as India, China, Korea, Japan, Africa and so on. Some remarkable combinations were achieved, even if they could sometimes end up with a kind of counter-chauvinism, as in the Japan of its imperialist phase. It is the colonial period that mysteriously sets the scene for the true encounter of religions. In this dialogue there is a mixture of ideas – those drawn from traditional natural theology, for instance (which recognizes a natural and transcultural core to varied religious cultures), and those drawn from Enlightenment toleration. When this dialogue is extended to embrace secular worldviews as well, and is given concrete meaning through social cooperation, it promises a new world ethos. Yet at the same time the modern age has seen terrible kinds of intolerance, particularly through the totalitarian ideologies, Nazism and varieties of State Marxism. The decimation of Tibetan religion, the slaughter of Cambodian monks and other elites, the suppression of religious freedom periodically in the Soviet Union and elsewhere are the result of secularism's taking on the evil mantle of the Inquisition. It has taken on the mantle of triumphalist and authoritarian Christianity. This disease is as bad in secularism as it is in traditional religion. So it should be our aim as far as possible to help in the process of the softening of Marxisms.

The Spirit in the World

We have sketched some of the positive aspects of a number of the great religious traditions. It is part of our vision that the Christian worldview can incorporate so many diverse strands of religious experience and social practice. We need to see world history in a comprehensive pattern, and open our vision to the varied values of those cultures. We see the Spirit working in Buddhist piety and contemplative techniques, in Indian metaphysical systems and forms of religious life, in Islamic Sufism and brotherhood, in Japanese Pure Land and Zen, in the Pacific Way, in Iranian eschatology, Classical brilliance and Neoplatonism, in African reverence, in the experiments in living throughout the smaller-scale societies, in the Jewish sense of God and exemplary living creativities of the Renaissance and Enlightenment, in the varieties of Christianity, in Marxist social values, in democracy and pluralism, in the spirit of dialogue in today's world, in the softness of epistemology, and the desire to live together. History has brought us to this: let us all cultivate the same ancestors.

The individual has been created by the modern world. She needs a sense of security in a new community. This is

427

often supplied by the nation. Sometimes it comes with the religion. Gradually the old clans and tribes and extended families are breaking down. We need to prepare the way for a new community, that of humanity at large. Among the visions it can share is the vision which we have sketched. And it can share other great visions too. The Spirit is moving towards a certain critical relationship between the various worldviews of the world.

12
Criteria and Conclusions: the Federal Stance

Reasons for Holding to Our Darśana

While we have generally written in this study as if we were merely presenting our *darśana*, we also of course believe that there are good reasons for it. We do not regard these reasons as building up to a proof, and we reaffirm the softness of our epistemology. But it may be worth looking to the criteria we might employ in thinking about the truth and worth of a religious or other worldview. Naturally we believe that some other worldviews do not match up to these tests. These worldviews occur both within the Christian family of *darśana*-s and outside. But though we would be happy to enter into constructive debate with any of our Christian or other "rivals", we shall not do so here. As we said, the reasons do not and cannot be proofs, so suffice it simply to sketch out ways in which our worldview seems to fulfill the criteria in question.

Thereafter we shall enunciate what may be called the "federal principle" which should so far as possible govern the relations between worldviews and worldview-affirming institutions and movements. And finally we shall recapitulate our systematic theology in the simplest and plainest terms, for at heart our vision is a simple one, and should be able to be expressed not only at the scholarly level but also in another way as relevant to the life of anyone in this world, including children. Christ's teachings were enigmatic and challenging, but there is ample testimony to his regard for the direct grasp of truth that children can have. So our worldview ought in consistency to echo that attitude.

Briefly, the criteria we cite are as follows; (1) richness or comprehensiveness – a religion should embrace as many of the major kinds of religious experience as possible; (2) internal consistency – it should not contain contradictions internally; (3) external consistency with established knowledge and the results of established methods of arriving at knowledge; (4) interpretive power – it should make sense of human history and life; (5) fruitfulness – it should yield ethical, psychological and social results; (6) symbolic power – it should display independent dynamism in society (and not be simply at the receiving end of social and other changes); (7) critical perspective – it should be able to criticize itself and other aspects of society from an original stance; (8) ultimate reference – it should deal with ultimate questions in human life, and should in this sense be "relevant"; (9) intelligibility – it should be open to easy understanding.

Richness and Consistency

We have already shown how the Christian faith in its Anglo-Orthodox form can be seen to incorporate the major types of religious experience – the prophetic and devotional kinds in its history, testimony and *bhakti*; the contemplative kind in its traditional spiritual practises; the world in so far as our position is a kind of panentheism; it is reflective of the *avatāra* type of religion, and of shamanism both in Christ himself but also in the dying and rising to life which is typical of those who pass through the valley of the shadow of death to the experience of the Light. Our vision incorporates not only that numinous Otherness between heaven and earth which is the insight of those who express the majesty of the Divine and the severe power of the great Light, but also the closeness typical of interior experience. Because of its richness our worldview can put out its hands to the Emptiness of the Buddhist experience, the *bhakti* theism of the Hindu tradition, the awful majesty of the Islamic picture of Allah, the love of nature in Taoist philosophy, the sense of divine presence among the Native Americans, the prophetic strand in Judaism, and many other features of the world's religions. It may be thought that our *darśana* does not, at least in this connection, speak to the atheism of the

Marxists or of scientific humanists, or to the world-affirming attitude of the utilitarians. Of course those who reject or ignore all forms of religious experience fall outside of the circle we mainly deal with in regard to this criterion of comprehensiveness: but we only remark that it would be odd to turn our back on so many and so pervasive patterns of human experience. The atheist does not need to buy our metaphysics, but he should ponder yoga, and numinosity, and the panenhenic experience, as possible and important constituents of human life.

Our worldview has internal consistency. We have tried to show that we can in a modern and intelligible way expound the Trinity doctrine, which would be felt by some to be the chief obstacle to seeing Christian faith as coherent. In this we follow many who too have sought to see this crucial and central idea as not involving any contradiction. On the contrary we wish to show that at its root is a view of creation which involves intimately the divine Brahman in the sufferings of this world. We see the incarnation as making sense even apart from the whole doctrine of salvation or liberation. Indeed we try to indicate that the pressure of thought towards thinking of the embodiment of the Divine in creaturely form is virtually necessary. We cannot expect the Muslim and the Jew to agree, for they may find it blasphemous, but we note that our vision gives a partial insight into the solution of the problem of evil.

We may note too that the richness of a worldview in relation to types of religious experience is bound to cause tensions (God is considered both Other and yet within each human being) and these we cannot avoid; but we have tried to show that these connections are not themselves contradictions by our analysis of the concepts of transcendence and immanence, for instance (Smart, 1986, pp. 49–60).

Regarding external consistency, with the results of science and the methods of history, for instance, we believe that our "liberal" perspective allows an easy and indeed fruitful coexistence between the spiritual and secular approaches to knowledge and vision. We recognize that as with scientific hypotheses a certain kind of falsifiability applies to our worldview. It too can suffer from those paradigm shifts that also often signal revolutions in science. Moreover we do perceive that there are some empirical claims which our *darśana* makes which if found out to be wrong would crumble the basis of our vision. We make some historical claims about Jesus and the early Community, of course; but in addition we make claims about the effects of Christian experience. They may be hard to confirm or disconfirm, but they are relevant to the truth of the worldview. In science however, the reference does not run beyond the cosmos. It is of the essence of our worldview that we have this extracosmic focus. This enables us to have a two-aspect view of truth, differentiated not only by the style of the differing spheres (we do not expect spiritual pictures to be technical and precise, or quantified and theoretical) but by their scope.

We have taken the liberal Protestant path in some respects, in relation to questions of the historicity of the Bible. We do so for two reasons. One is so that we can approach Biblical narratives as real history: we do not wish Christ to vanish amid the mists of mythological fancy. The other reason is because we appeal to the modern educated person. It is not possible for us humanly to split our minds. Those who do desperately draw on a literally interpreted Bible, or attempt to suppress the fresh forces of modernism, do us no service, we believe. Faith in our vision does not depend on the rejection of modern knowledge and modern ways. Our worldview, then, is externally consistent with science and historical method, and with both the philosophy of science and the philosophy of history. It similarly is happy to weave into its fabric insights from other sources, from anthropology and sociology, from biology and psychology – as long as these insights arise at the interface between the Beyond and this world.

Because of this external consistency our worldview does not combine easily with some traditionalist or neotraditionalist accounts of the Christian faith. We shall consider this problem later, when we turn to the exposition of what we have called the "federal principle".

Interpretive Power, Fruitfulness and Independent Dynamism

Our soft epistemology, which helps to reinforce the consistency between our approach and the differing epistemologies of other areas of human reflection (and we note too of course in recent philosophical work on science there has been a general softening evident), is one reason why we seek to reach out beyond the confines of the Christian tradition to a world perspective. In doing this we are necessarily faced with the task of interpreting world history, and this we have attempted in outline, as an indication of how we can give positive meaning to the great cultural achievements of the human race at sundry times and in various places. We do not assume the unity of religions, as though we can give an easy sense of the oneness of the spiritual odyssey of the human race. It is of course more exciting to steep ourselves in the varieties of human experience and in the divergent experiments with truth which diverse cultures have been engaged in. So we claim that our worldview has interpretive power, but it does not, of course, claim to be more than one way of looking at history. A Buddhist might look at life differently and see therefore the sweep of human affairs from quite another angle: and the Marxist would certainly not follow our tendencies (as he would see it) to idealism. Once divergent interpretive histories of humanity have been written up, then we can begin to judge between them. But we do claim to have stepped beyond the cultural bounds of the West; and also to have shaken off that narrow sense of salvation history which has so arrogantly focussed so much interest on a narrow range of human historical experience.

We have also sketched ways in which the values flowing from the worldview relate to fruitful human life. Whether our vision moves people (or forms a kind of conduit of that Divine power through which people are inspired) remains to be seen. But at least it attempts to foster various attitudes which should give rise to noble conduct. We look to people and groups to minimize violence, to foster human dignity (for the Light is in our sisters and brothers), to alleviate suffering (out of love which imitates the inner life of the

Trinity), to be tolerant (for that is the consequence of our epistemology), to be realistic (for that flows from our "liberal" attitudes, which are not shot through with fear of modern knowledge and methods), to enhance self-esteem (for the *antaryāmin* nests within the depths of our consciousness), to mobilize feelings for the good (which is where we can draw on Eastern religions in particular, translating our vision into existential reality through yoga), to change behavior (for we insist that ours is not just a theoretical exposition), to give meaning to life (for our doctrine of Creation sees the wondrous everywhere), and to express and stimulate vision (through creativity and the practice of the contemplative life). These values, among others, are those which our worldview points to, and we hope therefore that if it proves to be a powerful worldview it will promote those values.

We have also pointed to the way that the life of the Spirit generates psychological integration and emotional fulfilment. We have been critical of some Christian attitudes which repress feelings implanted in us by the Divine and necessary to a rounded personality. It may be that some of our psychological teachings could be had without our vision (we draw for instance on a number of wise depth-psychologists). But we think that our vision nevertheless gives coherent meaning to the psychological quest. We believe that as well as secular fulfillment the individual can blossom through religious experience and participation in the life of the Trinity, that is to say in a love which has great depth.

We believe too that our worldview, and its accompanying epistemology, will help towards social unity in today's world. This is partly because we espouse the federal principle that people can and should live together with differing cultural and religious customs and beliefs, while uniting in a common desire for peace and the fruitfulness of their lives. Because we do not claim to know in a public sense what is right and wrong and what is true or false in regard to that which lies "beyond" the cosmos and the immediate bounds of human life, we allow room for divergence of belief, provided that toleration is mutually practised. It seems to us that the world is plagued by too many fanaticisms, which often pit religion and ideology against minority concerns, and often involve ethnic bullying. Since most of our current troubles involve ethnic and worldview divergences, it is important to devise political and educational mechanisms which will allow a more federal attitude. While ethnic or even religious loyalty is not ultimate, for our ultimate community is the human race, such lesser loyalties are nonetheless important to people in a world of very rapid and disorienting change, and so we should be easy-going in our acceptance of other ways of looking at life, and on alternative ethical and social patterns of behavior. That way more unity is obtained (by a kind of accepted disunity) than by trying to enforce conformity, which often spurs revolt and bloodshed.

And so, while we cannot claim that our particular version of the Christian viewpoint has a record of fruitfulness, it does offer a set of values which can well appeal to people of good will in many cultures and following different religious or ideological paths. It is to be noted that the values taken separately or together are in great evidence among ecumenically-oriented Christians, and among many others who are moved by an open and liberal interpretation of their own traditions.

As for the symbolic power and independent dynamism of our vision, we draw on various pictures which may grip those who contemplate them. We look to the omnipresence of the Divine and so to the way God is there in the sunlight and the dust, in the least part of everything we touch and see and feel. We are immersed in the Divine, and the whole cosmos is her body. We are called on to practice this presence, and to seek her in the Light within us. We focus our loyalty on the figure of Christ, transcending categories, mysterious as in the ikons, suffering with us, but also partying and mixing with all conditions of human beings. What is there about our worldview which lacks the potency of older presentations? We do not reinforce the unconscious power of symbolism by staying consciously at the literal level, it is true. And we do not wish our symbolic power to translate into fanaticism. But we hope at least that gently

435

our vision will promote a quiet and determined certitude, and yet leave us open to the critical and fruitful influences of other great traditions. We can see the lotus too as symbol of the sinless Christ and not just of the wholly pure Buddha. We can see the pranks of Krishna by the River Jumna as signs of divine joy and love. We can think of the world as permeated by the spirit of the Tao, and enjoy the ceremoniousness of the Chinese soul. We can read the poems of Zen masters and see the paintings of China as revealing a new freshness in the cosmos which we all love, for all its hard places. We can listen to the whisper of the ancestors in the African elephant-grass, and spur ourselves to adopt the great ones of all the human race as our sacred forebears. We can enter the sweat lodge to pursue a like vision to that of the traditional Chumash. So our symbolic power can in principle spread forth. May it grip the souls of men and women in this hard and sometimes hating world. Above all we center our symbolism on the threefoldness of the Trinity – parent, offspring and the bond of love, existing as one in a triad of centers of consciousness. That symbol breeds love, and as Paul said, that is the greatest of the spiritual virtues. We do not fear for our symbolic power and independent dynamism. For our vision is merely the consequence of the divine Light shining through the cosmos and history, and here refracted by the murky lens of our intellects. At least if the worldview moves we shall have played a little part in the communication of the Light.

Criticism, Ultimacy and Intelligibility

Our worldview fulfills the criterion that it is prophetic and critical, not only because we have used a Popperite perspective but also because our notion of the Transcendent gives a relatively clear basis for thinking of human welfare as going "beyond" the cosmos. We thus are critical of the shallower thoughts of happiness and suffering which pervade today's utilitarianism. We need to have a critical view of welfare, and so, though we do not by any mean despise the material things which bring satisfaction to the poor and those who have been deprived of them, we also emphasize the deeper satisfaction of the peace of Brahman. We look to a stronger bliss than those of the "secular" world. We look to a higher form of nourishment with which to feed the lambs of this world on behalf of the Good Shepherd.

But we also, because we are involved in the whole of human history and the whole world, therefore, need to be critical on behalf of the oppressed and impoverished folk of the planet of the smugness of the Western developed powers – or at least often of their rulers. Ours is a prophetic criticism because we speak out of ethical and social concerns and not spiritual ones alone. They are all fused together. The black man in Soweto is created in the image of Christ, and he has within him the light of the inner controller. Our reverential love for all human beings must be stimulated by our vision, and prepare us to practice a meditation in which we suffuse all living beings with compassion. We can supplement such ancient Buddhist practice with a modern one drawn from the skilled method of structured empathy whereby we learn to enter into the thoughts and feelings of other human beings. It is important for the history of religions, but it can also be an excellent way of laying the grounds for *agapé*.

Our worldview must be restless, and must not settle back into too much satisfaction with the glories of our heritage. That heritage has to be forever tested against the changing world. There are many things to question in the Christian Church – the authoritarianism of the Pope, which stems from illusions about the nature of the open society; the mindlessness of so much Orthodoxy, content to rest upon the Fathers, and to quote Gregory Palamas without entering into the thoughts of modernity; the insensitive establishmentarianism of Anglicanism's Mother Church; the liturgical poverty of much Biblical Protestantism; the hatreds still left among the divisions of Christianity. We have a duty to be critical of our own tradition: and we do so from one central place, namely the Divine Love which is at the heart of the creation and the heart of the faith. So much of the outer life of the Church is merely superficial. The means should not be mistaken for the deeper life, and it is to promote that we composed this sketch of a Christian worldview.

Let it be said that it is much to the credit of Christianity that it has allowed so much criticism, especially from an historical angle in relation to the "sacred" texts. It is of all world religions perhaps the most self-critical. Those who long for the good old days of certainty are crying for the moon, but not gazing upon it. They are immersed in a cloud of unknowing. So we feel that our Neotranscendentalist worldview has the critical powers to prophecy both within and outside of the Christian tradition on behalf of the Light.

Hopefully the worldview fulfills the next criterion, namely as to whether it deals with ultimate and existential questions, for we have tried to sketch something of our understanding of the implications of our vision for our attitudes to sex, death, psychological peace, and personal relations. We have, admittedly, only sketched in these issues here. We have eschewed too precise advice on some practical issues, partly because people have to work out their own destinies, with help from the community. We do not believe in a refined casuistry. We believe it is more in accordance with Christ's teachings, and it echoes some themes in Eastern religions, to emphasize the general attitudes that are important rather than the detailed applications of laws. Our attitude is a consequence of the way Christianity diverged from both the Jewish and Muslim traditions: by and large they have taken the path (impressive in its own way) of the detailed interpretation of a revealed Law. But we hope that our worldview will allow those who follow it to be upright in the face of death and greater immersion in the Light, loving of others and unafraid of the bliss of sex, ready to love our neighbors as offspring of the Divine, and wondering always at the richness and poignancy of human life.

Finally, we believe that a worldview, other things being equal, should be accessible. We admire scholarship, and we like philosophy. But we feel that it is a strange situation where the ultimate meaning of a faith depends on the latest turn in the interpretation of *Acts* or in the deconstructionism of Derrida. You do not need to read Heidegger to be saved.

Still, we cannot reject philosophy and the pursuit in a scholarly way of a religious picture of the truth. We hope that that search can lead us to something which is not too abstruse. We eschew esotericism. We do not deny that some defence of esoteric truth can be mounted: we admire some of its modern Sufi and theosophical exponents. But we do not think that our faith is an esoteric tradition. Naturally, we think some intellectuals have done a lot of good in getting us away from that crude literalism which is so prominent a feature of evangelical religion in our time. Ours has to be a middle path: scholarly, yet intelligible, full of heart, but not mindless, loving but critical, traditional but modern too, loyal but open, Western and Eastern, Northern and Southern. So, as they say, the test of the pudding is in the eating. Let us try to put our worldview into a clear and simple form – a perspicuous credo. We shall do it, but before we do so, let us affirm something of the federal principle.

The Federal Principle

Although we think that the Christian faith, centering on the Trinity as its focus, is dynamic and glorious (even if marred too by many betrayals of its essential spirit), this does not mean that we do not find close brotherhood in other traditions – this we have made plain enough in the foregoing. The organizational implication of this is that the worldviews need to work together as far as possible, where common goals can be agreed. Now as we have also made clear, every so-called tradition is really a family of traditions. There are Judaisms, Islams, Buddhisms, Marxisms, humanisms, and Christianities. It often happens with families that a member of one will be closer to some member of another family than he is to some members of his own. Indeed if this were not so how could marriage be truly possible? So it is simplistic to think that because Christians share the name "Christian" they are obliged to support one another at the expense of outsiders. We have to use judgment honestly and sensitively. Our idea is that we should be committed broadly to the Ecumenical Movement in

439

Christianity, partly because this leaves outside of it some of the shriller members of our family. But we should also work with that broader ecumenical movement across faiths which is represented by various organizations including the World Congress of Faiths. But maybe the organizations are not so important: what is more vital is the spirit of friendship and cooperation. It will be that many movements in other traditions and in our own may repudiate our softness and imagine they have the hard truth. But that need not worry us too much. We have in due course to overcome fanaticism in the world, because it is dangerous and often expresses groupist hatreds. But we shall not overcome it by frontal assault, by being fanatically anti-fanatical. We need the spirit of *agapé* to suffuse our thoughts. We must remember Gandhi and other saints who have given new meaning to loving one's enemies. It may be that through an ecumenical banding together of likeminded religionists we may curl around the fanatics, so that at least the next generation and maybe they themselves will learn to love a softer Light.

A federal approach favors allowing variety to flourish, both internally in any one major tradition, and externally. It is the most effective way of expressing an open pluralism, which in our view is essential in today's world. Even if not all agree, it is an ideal towards which we can strive. So we join together in pursuing certain common objectives. The fruits which we seek to bring forth in the world are: the elimination of poverty, the promotion of deeper values in human life, the spread of peace and the reduction of conflicts, the moderation of groupism. These are not obscure or altogether controversial ends, and they can help to signalize that unity which focuses the plural banding according to the federal principle.

The application of this open and friendly way of expressing religious commitment is bound to result in some mutual influences between traditions. It is impossible to enter into genuine dialogue without having some crossing of boundaries. Already this is happening. But we do not from this deduce that the major worldviews will simply collapse into one another. It is unlikely that we shall easily arrive at a "world theology" or a "world ideology", beyond perhaps the federal principle itself, namely that different cultures, businesses, churches and traditions, should live together cooperatively in a loose open-textured conglomeration. Eventually we may come to see world government, both a hope and a threat, if wrongly institutionalized. But we can at least strive towards a federal *agapé*, a pluralistic *karuṇā*.

Which vision if any will eventually conquer the hearts of human beings remains to be seen. But if our values of love and toleration can be spread, that at least will be a great blessing: it would be at least halfway to that *dharma*-kingdom which so many people yearn for.

Finally, let us sum up our systematic theology in a simple way. Here is a simple credo.

A Simple Credo

Our system, which could be described as Neotranscendentalist, pluralistic, social Trinitarian, universalist panentheism embedded in a soft epistemology, can of course be described without benefit of such barbarous jargon, and as follows.

We believe in a worldview that goes beyond science. This is because the worldview refers to a Divine Being who lies within and beyond the cosmos. She (or he: transparently you cannot seriously talk of gender in the Creator, but he or she is a person, so we do want to use personal pronouns) is creator of the cosmos — made it and still makes it, secretly working everywhere, and so is present in every place, always around us, beside us, present to us. She is in respect of her power and glory, awe-inspiring, and we respond therefore in worship. Our praise is a measure of our recognition of her greatness. But we also find the Divine within us, at the base of our consciousness. In searching inside ourselves through self-training we can find her in the Light which lights our consciousness. The nature ultimately of the Divine is Love.

So whereas science tells us about the cosmos, and our knowledge stems from a struggle between human beings and nature, to wrest her secrets from her, religion is our encounter with the Beyond. But we also must act in the cosmos, and there we see the Divine reflected. The Love which is the Lord's nature is known from the fact that she is composed of three centers of consciousness in one identity, one life. This threefold character of the Divine stems from the fact that God always wishes to create, and yet creation itself implies incarnation. There is for ever the need for the Divine to show her love by becoming embodied in the Son. For us that Son is Christ. The reason why the Divine Being wishes to enter creation is because creation is a wonderful but terrible thing. She creates the world and its living creatures, but the creatures often suffer, and they are bound to be somewhat alienated. This is because to be free they must be veiled from God: the Light is too overwhelming and strong. So ignorance and alienation are inevitably part of the human condition. In blundering upwards from evolution into history the race acquires freedom, so precious a possession. Humans can hope to become mature and free agents in the course of their experience. But they suffer, as do the beings only marginally free, the zebras and salmon, and hawks and vultures. Life cannot go on for free beings without collisions with their environment and rapacious clashes between differing developing species. So creation is the field of suffering, for all its great and delicious wonders. The Creator feels impelled therefore to enter her own world in order to show that she is willing to take on that to which others have been assigned, through the very act of creation.

The inner nature of the Divine is Parent, Offspring and the Bond of Love, or Father, Son and Holy Spirit. Through the three persons there circulates the supreme and blissful life of love. Because this is the essence of God the follower of God should be loving – loving his enemies as well as his friends, and realizing through human love the greatest bliss, which imitates that of the Divine Being. It is through participating in the divine love that we are saved and have the closest relation to the Divine. We see Christ's death as being a sacrifice in which the Divine Being expresses the highest expiation on behalf of living creatures for the alienation (the confusion, hatred and greed) which disfigures human life.

In entering history Christ indicates to us how it is through the sequences of human life that the Ultimate works. It is through the Spirit as inner controller that human beings are stimulated to the creativity and love which help them to form better and deeper joys and insights, and so to bring progress from the life of early humans to the astonishing achievements of the various human civilizations. Christianity itself has played a notable role in the rhythms of human culture, and has helped to vivify the life of the whole planet. But other traditions too display the work of the Spirit, and present noble alternative visions, which in challenging the Christian faith help to keep us honest and to stir in us self-criticism. Though we regard the ritual dimension of the faith as vitally important, for it helps to transmit to us across space and time the life-giving powers of Christ, and though we treasure the conservative nature of traditional liturgy, we also consider that tradition needs criticism, so that the doctrines do not petrify nor the ethics ossify, and so that the sacred narrative is widened beyond its older narrowness. So the critical function is important not only in science, and in the functioning of democracy, but also in the life of the Church. And as the world contracts, so the various great traditions can complement one another by being each other's friendly critics. We see in this, the whole of history, as the sphere of the divine activity and of the Spirit's operation.

We also see history as tending onwards. We have a vision of the end of history, but it is a fanciful picture whose meaning is hard to see. It is however this sense of an end which draws us onward, so that we may build from generation to generation the ideal life, heaven upon earth. And our hope too is that all men and women, whether through our work on this earth, or through progress in levels beyond the grave, may achieve contentment and satisfaction in taking a part of the blissful life of God. As they progress they will be more and more Christ-like, and the way in which humans reflect the nature of the Divine will become ever clearer. So we hope that all humans sooner or later will end up in the divine embrace.

But we do not present this vision as dogma. We see it as a picture for which we can have some good reasons, but we have no pretence that we have somehow proved our worldview, or ever could do such a thing. For all worldviews are open to challenge. Because this is so we seek for inner certitude springing from the experience of the Beyond and the Within. But since we cannot prove our vision, we cannot in the bad sense dogmatize and must recognize how we should tolerate one another. Toleration of other worldviews and customs is one of the offshoots of love, and it is one of the consequences of our observing our small world with its great variegation of religious and ideological belief. And so we commend our vision in hope, but see how its rivals also can be launched in the same way. But we are convinced that our simple credo rests on some good foundations, giving meaning to the life of the cosmos and of sentient beings within it. There is an internal convincingness in our picture of the Divine, and the congruence between our attitudes and the spirit of modern science and more generally knowledge, both humanistic and not, is a cheerful sign that though God is veiled by the cosmos its operations bear something of her imprint.

Our vision has its soft edges, and we do not wish to force it on anyone. But we write this book to make our credo appealing to those who are highly reflective about their faith. We hope it appeals to modern people, products of modern education, who are conscious of today's meeting of East and West and North and South.

At its heart our worldview has the divine threefoldness, the complex way in which the Light is refracted. Complex, but not hard to see: it is the guarantee that the Divine is nothing other than Love. It is this Love from beyond the cosmos which we need to imitate.

We find it easy to talk with the Trinity for we know that she suffered and suffers alongside of us; and takes joy too in our joys. As hidden dweller in our hearts she sees us from within. For her nature is to be an egoless Spirit, an open soul which can merge into the concerns of others. The three selfless spirits as we have called them are unified in the one life.

May those who read this gain a glimpse of what we mean, and may what we mean reflect something of the caring reality which suffuses and embraces this cosmos and with it the whole realm of living beings.

Bibliography

Allchin, 1979	A.M. Allchin *The Kingdom of Love and Knowledge*, London: Darton, Longman and Todd, 1979
Allport, 1950	Gordon Allport *The Individual and His Religion*, New York: Macmillan, 1950
Anderson, 1984	Bernard Anderson *Understanding the Old Testament*, 4th ed, Englewood Cliffs N.J.: Prentice-Hall, 1984
Augros, & Staeuciu 1987	Robert Augros, George Staeuciu *The New Story of Science*, New York: Bantam Books, 1986
Augros, & Staeuciu 1987	Robert Augros, George Staeuciu *The New Biology*, Boston: Shambala, 1987
Aulen, 1961	Gustav Aulen *Christus Victor: An Historical Study of the Three Main Types of the Idea of Atonement*, New York: Macmillan, 1961
Barbour, 1974	Ian Barbour *Myths, Models and Paradigms* New York: Harper and Row, 1959
Barth, 1936	Karl Barth *Church Dogmatics*, Edinburgh: T. and T. Clarke, 1936–1962
Barth, 1959	Karl Barth *Dogmatics in Outline*, New York: Harper and Row, 1959
Berdyaev, 1931	Nikolai Berdyaev *The Destiny of Man* (3rd edn., 1948), London: G. Bles, 1931
Berdyaev, 1948	Nikolai Berdyaev *Freedom and the Spirit*, London: G. Bles, 1948
Berydaev, 1953	Nikolai Berdyaev *Truth and Revelation*, London: G. Bles, 1953
Berdyaev, 1955	Nikolai Berdyaev *The Meaning of the Creative Act*, London: G. Bles, 1955

Boisen, 1955	Anton Boisen *The Exploration of the Inner World*, New York: Harper and Row, 1955
Bornkamm, 1960	Gunther Bornkamm *Jesus of Nazareth*, New York: Harper and Row, 1960
Bornkamm, 1974	Gunther Bornkamm "Jesus Christ" *Encyclopedia Britannica Macropedia*, Chicago: Benton, 1974 edition
Bradshaw, 1988	John Bradshaw *Bradshaw on the Family*, Deerfield Beach, Florida: Health Communications, Inc., 1988
Bradshaw, 1988	John Bradshaw *Healing the Shame That Binds You*, Deerfield Beach, Florida: Health Communications, Inc., 1988
Brandon, 1963	S.G.F. Brandon *The Saviour God: Comparative Studies in the Concept of Salvation, Presented to Edwin Oliver James, Professor Emeritus in the University of London*, New York: Barnes and Noble, 1963
Briggs, 1975	Dorothy Corkville Briggs *Your Child's Self-esteem: the Key to Life*, Garden City, N.Y.: Doubleday, 1975
Buber, 1970	Martin Buber *I and You*, tran. Walter Kaufmann, New York: Scribners, 1970
Bultmann, 1958	Rudolf Bultmann *Jesus Christ and Mythology*, New York: Scribners, 1958
Butterfield, 1950	Herbert Butterfield *Christianity and History*, New York: Scribners, 1950
Chaudhuri, 1960	Haridas Chaudhuri *The Integral Philosophy of Sri Aurobindo; a Commemorative Symposium*, Edited by Haridas Chaudhuri and Frederic Spiegelberg, London: Allen & Unwin, 1960
Clark, 1958	Walter H. Clark *The Psychology of Religion*, New York: Macmillan, 1958
Cobb & Griffin, 1976	John B. Cobb and David Ray Griffin *Process Theology: an Introductory Exposition*, Philadelphia: Westminster Press, 1976

448

Cobb, 1982	John B. Cobb *Beyond Dialogue: The Transformation of Christianity and Buddhism*, Philadelphia: Fortress, 1982
Conze, 1959	Edward Conze *Buddhism: Its Essence and Development*, New York: Harper Books, 1959
Conze, 1967	Edward Conze *Buddhist Thought in India: Three Phases of Buddhist Philosophy*, Ann Arbor, Michigan: University of Michigan Press, 1967
Conze, 1975	Edward Conze *Buddhist Meditation*, New York: Harper and Row, 1975
Conze, 1988	Edward Conze (trans. & ed.) *Buddhist Wisdom Books*, London: Unwin Hyman Ltd, 1988
Da Silva, 1974	Lynn Da Silva *The Problem of Self in Buddhism and Christianity*, London: Macmillan, 1974
Davies, 1988	Paul Davies *The Cosmic Blueprint*, New York: Simon and Schuster, 1988
Davis, 1980	Charles Davis *Theology and Political Society*, Cambridge: C.U.P., 1980
Dawson, 1950	Christopher Dawson *Religion and the Rise of Western Culture*, London: Longman, 1950
Dillenberger, 1961	John Dillenberger, ed. *Martin Luther: Selections from His Writings*, New York: Anchor Bks., 1961
Dobzhansky, 1962	Theodosius Dobzhansky *Mankind Evolving; The Evolution of the Human Species*, New Haven Conn.: Yale University Press, 1962
Dooyerweed, 1960	Herman Dooyerweed *In the Twilight of Western Thought Presbyterian and Reformed*, Philadelphia,1960
De Castillejo, 1967	Irene Claremont De Castillejo *Knowing Women: A Feminine Psychology*, San Francisco: Harper and Row, 1967

Durant & Durant, 1967	Will Durant and Ariel Durant *Lessons of History*, New York, NY: Simon and Schuster 1967
Dumoulin, 1967	Heinrich Dumoulin *A History of Zen Buddhism* (translated from the German by Paul Peachey), Boston: Beacon Press, 1969
Eccles & Popper, 1977	J.L. Eccles and K.R. Popper *The Self and Its Brain*, Berlin: Springer International, 1977
Eccles & Robinson, 1984	John Eccles and Daniel Robinson *The Wonder of Being Human*, Boston: Shambala, 1984
Edinger, 1974	Edward F. Edinger *Ego and Archetype*, Baltimore: Penguin, 1979
Eisler, 1988	Riane Eisler *The Chalice and the Blade*, San Francisco: Harper and Row, 1988
Eliade & Kitagawa, 1959	Mircea Eliade and Joseph Kitagawa *The History of Religions: Essays in Methodology*, Chicago: University of Chicago Press, 1959
Eliade, 1964	Mircea Eliade *Shamanism: Archaic Techniques of Ecstasy*, Princeton: Princeton University Press, 1964
Eliade, 1969	Mircea Eliade *Yoga: Immorality and Freedom*, Princeton: Princeton University Press, 1969
Eliade, 1969	Mircea Eliade *Patterns in Comparative Religion* (translated by Rosemary Sheed), Cleveland: World Publishing Co., 1969
Evans, 1981	Donald Evans *Struggle and Fulfilment* Philadelphia: Fortress, 1981
Eysenck & Wilson, 1974	Hans Eysenck and Glenn Wilson *The Experimental Studies of Freudian Theory*, Barnes & Noble, New York: 1971
Falk, 1985	Harvey Falk *Jesus the Pharisee: A New Look at the Jewishness of Jesus*, New York: Paulist Press, 1985
Farquhar, 1929	J.W.T. Farquhar *Modern Religious Movements in India*, London: Macmillan and Co, 1929

Farrer, 1959	Austin Farrer *Finite and Infinite*, Westminster, England: Dacre Press, 1959
Firth, 1977	Raymond Firth "Sacrifice" in *Encyclopedia Britannica Macropedia*, Chicago: Benton, 1977
Flew and MacIntyre, 1955	Antony Flew and Alasdair MacIntyre *New Essays in Philosophical Theology*, New York: Macmillan, 1955
Fortman, 1972	E.J. Fortman *The Triune God*, Philadelphia: Westminster Press, 1972
Frankena, 1973	William Frankena *Ethics*, 2nd Ed., Englewood Cliffs, N.J.: Prentice Hall, 1973
Frankl, 1969	Victor Frankl *The Will to Meaning*, N.Y.: World Publishing Co., 1969
Frankl, 1985	Victor Frankl *Man's Search for Meaning*, N.Y.: Washington Square Press, 1985
Freud, 1964	Sigmund Freud *The Future of an Illusion* (translated by James Strachey), Garden City, NY: 1964
Fromm, 1956	Erich Fromm *The Art of Loving*, New York: Harper and Row, 1956
Fromm, 1964	Erich Fromm *The Heart of Man: Its Genius for Good and Evil*, New York: Harper and Row, 1964
Fromm, 1973	Erich Fromm *The Anatomy of Human Destructiveness*, New York: Holy, Rinehart and Winston, 1973
Fromm, 1986	Erich Fromm *For the Love of Life*, New York: Macmillan, 1986
Goudge, 1961	Thomas A Goudge *The Ascent of Life*, Toronto: University of Toronto Press, 1961
Gould, 1980	Stephen Jay Gould *The Panda's Thumb: More Reflections in Natural History*, New York: W.W. Norton, 1980
Goulder, 1978	Michael Goulder *Incarnation and Myth: The Debate Continued*, Grand Rapids, Michigan: Erdman, 1978
Grant, 1977	Michael Grant *Jesus: An Historian's*

	Review of the Gospels, New York: Scribners, 1977
Gutierrez, 1976	Gustavo Gutierrez *A Theology of Liberation*, New York: Orbis, 1976
Hall & Lindzey, 1978	Calvin Hall and Gardner Lindzey *Theories of Personality*, New York: John Wiley, 1978
Hazleden Foundation	*The Twelve Steps of Alcoholics Anonymous*, San Francisco, 1987: Harper and Row, 1987
Hardon, 1985	John A. Hardon *A Pocket Catholic Dictionary*, Garden City: Image Books, 1985
Hartshorne, 1963	Charles Hartshorne *The Divine Relativity*, New Haven: Yale University Press, 1963
Hartshorne and Reese, 1953	Charles Hartshorne and William Reese *Philosophers Speak of God*, Chicago: University of Chicago Press, 1953
Heiler, 1958	Friedrich Heiler *Prayer*, New York: O.U.P., 1958
Heisenberg, 1962	Werner Heisenberg *Physics and Philosophy: The Revolution in Modern Science*, New York: Harper and Row, 1962
Hick, 1973	John Hick *God and the Universe of Faiths*, New York: Macmillan, 1973
Hick, 1976	John Hick *Death and Eternal Life*, New York: Harper and Row, 1976
Hick, 1977	John Hick *The Myth of God Incarnate*, London: SCM Press, 1977
Hick, 1978	John Hick *Evil and the God of Love*, New York: Harper and Row, 1978
Hick, 1982	John Hick *God has Many Names*, Philadelphia: Westminster Press, 1982
Hick, 1983	John Hick *Philosophy of Religion*, 3rd edn., Englewood Cliffs N.J.: Prentice Hall, 1983
Hick, 1988	John Hick *An Interpretation of Religion: Human Response to the Transcendent*, Basingstoke: Macmillan, 1988

Hitching, 1982	Francis Hitching *Neck of the Giraffe, or where Darwin went wrong*, London: Pan, 1982
Hodgson, 1944	Leonard Hodgson *The Doctrine of the Trinity*, New York: Scribners, 1944
Homand, 1970	Peter Homans *Theology after Freud*, Indianapolis: Bobbs-Merrill, 1970
James, 1958	William James *The Varieties of Religious Experience*, New York: New American Library, 1958
Jeremias, 1963	Joachim Jeremias *The Parables of Jesus*, New York: Scribners, 1963
Jeremias, 1965	Joachim Jeremias *The Central Message of the New Testament*, New York: Scribners, 1965
Johnson, 1989	Robert Johnson *Ecstasy: Understanding the Psychology of Joy*, San Francisco: Harper and Row, 1989
Jung, 1934	C.G. Jung *The Integration of Personality*, New Haven: Yale University Press, 1939
Jung, 1939	C.G. Jung *Psychology and Religion*, New Haven: Yale University Press, 1939
Jung, 1958	C.G. Jung *The Undiscovered Self*, New York: New American Library, 1958
Kalma, 1988	John Kalma *Aggression*, New York: Wiley & Sons, 1988
Katz, 1978	Steven T. Katz *Mysticism and Philosophical Analysis*, New York: O.U.P., 1978
Kaufmann, 1958	Walter Arnold Kaufmann *Critique of Religion and Philosophy*, New Jersey: Princeton University Press, 1958
Kelsey, 1976	Morton Kelsey *The Other Side of Silence: A Guide to Christian Meditation*, New York: Paulist Press, 1976
Kelsey, 1978	Morton Kelsey *Dreams: A Way to Listen to God*, New York: Paulist Press, 1978
Kelsey, 1986	Morton Kelsey and Barbara Kelsey *Sacrament of Sexuality*, Liberty, Missouri: Amity House, 1986

453

Kelsey, 1988	Morton Kelsey *Psychology, Medicine and Christian Healing*, San Francisco: Harper and Row, 1988
Kraemer, 1938	Hendrik Kraemer *The Christian Message in a Non-Christian World*, London: SPCK, 1938
Kuhn, 1970	Thomas Kuhn *The Structure of Scientific Revolutions*, Chicago: Chicago University Press, 1970
Küng, 1976	Hans Küng *On Being a Christian; translated by Edward Quinn*, Garden City, N.Y.: Doubleday, 1976
Küng, 1979	Hans Küng *Freud and the Problem of God*, New Haven: Yale University Press, 1979
Küng, 1980	Hans Küng *Does God Exist?*, New York: Doubleday, 1980
Küng, 1984	Hans Küng *Eternal Life?*, London: Collins, 1984
Kunkel, 1946	Fritz Kunkel *Creation Continues*, New York: Scribners, 1946
Lasch, 1979	Christopher Lasch *The Culture of Narcissism*, New York: W.W. Norton, 1979
Lasch, 1984	Christopher Lasch *The Minimal Self*, New York: W.W. Norton, 1984
Ladas, Whipple & Perry, 1982	Alice Ladas, Beverly Whipple and John Perry *The G Spot and Other Recent Discoveries about Human Sexuality*, New York: Dell, 1982
Lee, 1949	Roy S. Lee *Freud and Christianity*, Edinburgh: T. and T. Clarke, 1948
Leech, 1977	Kenneth Leech *Soul Friend*, New York: Harper and Row, 1977
Leech, 1980	Kenneth Leech *True Prayer*, New York: Harper and Row, 1980
Leeuw, 1963	Geradus van der Leeuw *Sacred and Profane Beauty: The Holy in Art*, New York: Holt Rinehart and Winston, 1963
Leeuw, 1986	Gerardus van der Leeuw *Religion in*

Essence and Manifestation, Princeton: Princeton University Press, 1986

Leeuwen, 1964   Artend T. van Leeuwen *Christianity in World History*, Edinburgh: Edinburgh House Press, 1964

Leonard, 1989   Linda Leonard *Witness to the Fire: Creativity and the Vial of Addiction*, Boston: Shambala, 1989

Leuba, 1925   James Henry Leuba *The Psychology of Religious Mysticism*, London: Keegan Paul, Trench, Trubner & Co., Ltd., 1925

Lewontin, 1984   Richard C. Lewontin *Not in Our Genes: Biology, Ideology, and Human Nature*, New York: Pantheon Books, 1984

Ling, 1966   Trevor Ling *Buddha, Marx and God: some aspects of religion in the modern world*, London: Macmillan, 1966

Ling, 1973   Trevor Ling *The Buddha: Buddhist civilization in India and Ceylon*, London: Temple Smith, 1973

Linn & Schwartz, 1958   Louis Linn and Leo Schwartz *Psychiatry and Religious Experience*, N.Y.: Random House, 1958

Lipner, 1986   Julius Lipner *The Face of Truth: A Study of Meaning and Metaphysics in the Vedantic Theology of Ramajuna*, Albany, N.Y.: State University of New York Press, 1986

Long, 1967   Edward Leroy Long Jr. *A Survey of Christian Ethics*, N.Y.: Oxford University Press, 1967

Lorenz, 1983   Konrad Lorenz *The Foundations of Ethology*, N.Y.: Touchstone Books, 1983

Lossky, 1976   Vladimir Lossky *The Mystical Theology of the Eastern Churches*, New York: St Vladimir's Seminary Press, 1976

Lowen, 1967   Alexander Lowen *Love and Orgasm*, New York: Coller, 1967

Lowen, 1972   Alexander Lowen *Depression and the Body: The Biological Basis of Faith and Reality*, New York: Penguin Books, 1972

Lowen, 1976	Alexander Lowen *Bioenergetics*, New York: Penguin Books, 1976
Lowen, 1983	Alexander Lowen *Narcissism: denial of true self*, New York: Macmillan, 1983
Lowen, 1977	Alexander Lowen and Leslie Lowen *The Way to Vibrant Health*, N.Y.: Harper and Row, 1977
Lowrie, 1965	Donald Lowrie *Christian Existentialism: A Berdyaev Synthesis*, New York: Harper and Row, 1965
McGarry, 1977	Michael B. McGarry *Christology after Auschwitz*, New York: Paulist Press, 1972
McIntyre, 1977	C.T. McIntyre *God, History and Historians*, London: SCM Press, 1977
Macisak, 1974	Sharon Macisak *Freud and Original Sin*, New York: Paulist Press, 1974
MacNutt, 1974	Francis MacNutt *Healing*, Notre Dame: Maria Press, 1974
Macquarrie, 1977	John Macquarrie *God Talk*, New York: Seabury Press, 1967
Macquarrie, 1977	John Macquarrie *Principles of Christian Theology*, New York, Scribners, 1977
Macquarrie, 1981	John Macquarrie *Twentieth Century Religious Thought*, New York: Scribners, 1981
Magee, 1973	Bryan Magee *Popper*, London, Collins, 1973
Maritain, 1957	Jacques Maritain *On the Philosophy of History*, New York: Scribners, 1957
Mascall, 1967	Eric Lionel Mascall *Existence and Analogy*, Hamden, CT: Archon Books, 1967
Maslow, 1968	Abraham Maslow *Toward a Psychology of Being*, 2nd Edn., Florence, KY: Van Norstrand Reinhold, 1968
Maslow, 1971	Abraham Maslow *The Farther Reaches of Human Nature*, New York: Viking Press, 1971
Maxmen, 1986	Jerrold Maxmen *The New Psychiatry*, New York: Mentor Books, 1986

May, 1953	Rollo May *Man's Search for Himself*, New York: Norton, 1953
May, 1969	Rollo May *Love and Will*, N.Y.: Norton, 1969
May, 1972	Rollo May *Power and Innocence*, New York: Norton, 1972
May, 1975	Rollo May *The Courage to Create*, New York: Norton, 1975
Menninger, 1967	Karl Menninger *The Vital Balance: The Life Process in Mental Health and Illness*, New York: Viking Press, 1967
Menninger, 1973	Karl Menninger *Whatever Became of Sin?*, New York: Hawthorne Books, 1973
Menninger, 1983	Karl Menninger *The Vital Balance: the Life Process in Mental Health and Illness*, Magnolia, MA: Peter Smith Publisher, Inc., 1983
Merton, 1973	Thomas Merton, *Asian Journal of Thomas Merton*, New York: New Directions Publishing Corp, 1973
Moltmann, 1981	Jurgen Moltmann *The Trinity and the Kingdom*, New York: Harper and Row, 1981
Montagu, 1953	Ashley Montagu *The Natural Superiority of Women*, New York: Macmillan, 1953
Montagu, 1966	Ashley Monatgu *On Being Human*, 2nd Edn., New York: Hawthorn, 1966
Montagu, 1971	Ashley Montagu *Touching: The Human Significance of the Skin*, New York: Columbia Press, 1971
Montagu, 1973	Ashley Montagu *Man and Aggression*, New York: Oxford University Press, 1973
Montagu, 1976	Ashley Montagu *The Nature of Human Aggression*, New York: Oxford University Press, 1976
Montagu, 1980	Ashley Montagu *Sociobiology Examined*, New York: Oxford University Press, 1980
Neal, 1975	William-Neal *Harper's Bible Commentary*, New York: Harper and Row, 1975

New English Bible, 1976	Oxford Study Edition, New York: Oxford University Press, 1976
Niebuhr, 1951	H. Richard Niebuhr *Christ and Culture*, New York: Harper and Row, 1951
Niebuhr, 1943	Reinhold Niebuhr *The Nature and Destiny of Man*, New York: Scribners, 1943
Noss, 1980	John B. Noss *Man's Religions*, New York: Macmillan, 1980
Otto, 1958	Rudolph Otto *The Idea of the Holy*, New York: O.U.P., 1958
Owen, 1984	Huw Parri Owen *Christian Theism*, Edinburgh: T. and T. Clark, 1984
Pagels, 1988	Elaine Pagels *Adam, Eve and the Serpent*, New York: Random House, 1988
Panikkar, 1977	Raimundo Panikkar *The Intra-Religious Dialogue*, New York: Paulist Press, 1977
Parrinder, 1970	Geoffrey Parrinder *Avatar and Incarnation*, New York: O.U.P., 1970
Parrinder, 1961	Geoffrey Parrinder *Worship in the World's Religions*, London: Faber and Faber, 1961
Peacocke, 1979	Arthur Peacocke *Creation & the World of Science*, Oxford: Clarendon, 1979
Peacocke, 1986	Arthur Peacocke *God and the New Biology*, San Francisco: Harper and Row, 1986
Peck, 1978	M. Scott Peck *The Road Less Travelled*, New York: Simon and Schuster, 1978
Peck, 1983	M. Scott Peck *People of the Lie*, New York: Simon and Schuster, 1983
Phillips, 1966	D.Z. Phillips *The Concept of Prayer*, New York: Schocken Books, 1966
Phillips, 1958	John Bertram Phillips *The New Testament in Modern English*, New York: Macmillan, 1958
Phillips, 1967	John Bertram Phillips *Your God is Too Small*, New York: Macmillan, 1967
Phillips, 1975	J.B. Phillips *The New Testament in Modern English*, Student Edition, New York: Macmillan, 1975

Polkinghorne, 1987	John Polkinghorne *One World*, Princetown, N.J.: Princeton University Press, 1987
Polkinghorne, 1988	John Polkinghorne *Science and Creation*, Boston: Shambala, 1988
Polkinghorne, 1989	John Polkinghorne *Science and Providence*, Boston: Shambala, 1989
Popper, 1971	Karl Popper *The Open Society and its Enemies*, Princetown N.J.: Princeton University Press, 1971
Radhakrishnan, 1973	S. Radhadrishnan *The Bhagavadgita*, San Francisco: Harper and Row, 1973
Ramsey, 1967	Paul Ramsey *Rules and Deeds in Christian Ethics*, N.Y.: Scribners Sons, 1967
Reynolds, 1977	Stephen Reynolds *The Christian Religious Tradition*, Encino, Ca.: Dickenson Press, 1977
Sanford, 1970	John Sanford *The Kingdom Within: The Inner Meaning of Jesus' Sayings*, New York: Harper and Row, 1970
Sanford, 1977	John Sanford *Healing and Wholeness*, New York: Paulist Press, 1977
Sanford, 1980	John Sanford *The Invisible Partners: How the Male and Female in Each of Us Affects Our Relationships*, New York: Paulist Press, 1980
Sanford, 1987	John Sanford *The Kingdom Within*, 2nd Edn., San Francisco: Harper and Row, 1987
Schaef, 1986	Anne Wilson Schaef *Co-Dependence*, San Francisco, Harper and Row, 1986
Schaer, 1950	Hans Schaer *Psychotherapy and the Cure of Souls in Jung's Psychology*, New York: Pantheon, 1950
Schmemann, 1973	Alexander Schmemann *For the Life of the World: Sacraments and Orthodoxy*, New York: St Vladimir's Seminary Press, 1973
Schrödinger, 1974	Erwin Schrödinger *What is Life?: The Physical Aspect of the Living Cell & Mind*

and Matter, Cambridge: Cambridge University Press, 1974

Smart, 1958   Ninian Smart *Reasons and Faiths*, London: Routledge and Kegan Paul, 1958

Smart, 1964   Ninian Smart *Doctrine and Argument in Indian Philosophy*, London: Allen and Unwin, 1964

Smart, 1966   Ninian Smart *World Religions: A Dialogue*, Baltimore: Penguin Books, 1966

Smart, 1968   Ninian Smart *The Yogi and the Devotee*, London: Allen and Unwin, 1968

Smart, 1969   Ninian Smart *Philosophers and Religious Truth*, New York: Macmillan, 1968

Smart, 1973a   Ninian Smart *The Science of Religion and the Sociology of Knowledge*, Princeton: Princeton University Press, 1973

Smart, 1973b   Ninian Smart *The Phenomenon of Religion*, New York: Herder and Herder, 1973

Smart, 1979a   Ninian Smart *The Philosophy of Religion*, New York: O.U.P., 1979

Smart, 1979b   Ninian Smart *In Search of Christianity*, New York: Harper and Row, 1979

Smart, 1981   Ninian Smart *Beyond Ideology*, New York: Harper and Row, 1981

Smart, 1981   Ninian Smart *Concept and Empathy*, ed. Donald Wiebe, New York: New York University Press, 1983

Smart, 1991   Ninian Smart *The Religious Experience of Mankind*, 4th edn., New York: Scribners, 1991

Smith, 1989   Huston Smith *Beyond the Post-Mortem Mind*, rev. edn., Wheaton, Illinois: Quest Books, 1989

Smith, 1978   Wilfred C. Smith *The Meaning and End of Religion*, New York: Harper and Row, 1978

Smith, 1981   Wilfred C. Smith *Toward a World Theology*, Philadelphia: Westminster Press, 1981

Spencer, 1963	Sydney Spencer *Mysticism in World Religions*, Baltimore: Penguin Books, 1963
St Vladimir's Seminary, 1978	*Orthodox Spirituality*, 2nd edn., Crestwood, N.Y.: St Vladimir's Seminary Press, 1978
Staniloae, 1980	Dimitriu Staniloae *Theology and the Church*, New York: St Vladimir's Seminary Press, 1980
Streng, 1967	Frederick Streng *Emptiness: A Study in Religious Meaning*, Nashville: Abingdon Press, 1967
Streng, 1985	Frederick Streng *Understanding Religious Life*, Belmont, CA: Wadworth Publishing Co., 1985
Suzuki, 1975	D.T. Suzuki *Mysticism, Christian and Buddhist*, Westport, Conn.: Greenwood Press, 1975
Swinburne, 1970	Richard Swinburne *The Concept of Miracle*, London: Macmillan, 1970
Swinburne, 1977	Richard Swinburne *The Coherence of Theism*, Oxford: Claredon Press 1977
Swinburne, 1981	Richard Swinburne *Faith and Reason*, London: Macmillan, 1981
Taylor, 1958	Vincent Taylor *The Atonement in New Testament Teaching*, London: The Epworth Press, 1958
Teilhard de Chardin, 1959	Pierre Teilhard de Chardin *The Phenomenon of Man*, New York: Harper, 1959
Temple, 1935	William Temple *Nature, Man and God*, New York: Macmillan, 1935
Thompson, 1982	Helen Thompson *Journey Toward Wholeness*, New York: Paulist Press, 1982
Thornton, 1928	Lionel S. Thornton *The Incarnate Lord*, London: Longmans Green, 1928
Tillich, 1952	Paul Tillich *The Courage to Be*, New Haven: Yale University Press, 1952
Tillich, 1955	Paul Tillich *The New Being*, New York: Scribner's, 1955

Tillich, 1957	Paul Tillich *Dynamics of Faith*, New York: Harper and Row, 1957
Tillich, 1963a	Paul Tillich *Systematic Theology*, 2 vols., Chicago: University of Chicago Press, 1963
Tillich, 1963b	Paul Tillich *Christianity and the Encounter of World Religions*, New York: Columbia University Press, 1963
Toynbee, 1946	Arnold Toynbee *A Study of History*, abridged in 2 vols. by D.C. Somervell, NY: Oxford University Press, 1946
Toynbee, 1956	Arnold Toynbee *A Historian's Approach to Religions*, New York: O.U.P., 1956
Toynbee, 1957	Arnold Toynbee *Christianity Among the World Religions*, New York: O.U.P., 1957
Underhill, 1962	Evelyn Underhill *Mysticism: a Study in the Nature and Development of Man's Spiritual Consciousness*, London: Methuen and Co., 1962
van Buren, 1963	Paul van Buren *The Secular Meaning of the Gospel, Based on an Analysis of Its Language*, New York: Macmillan, 1963
Vermes, 1973	Geza Vermes *Jesus the Jew*, London: Collins, 1973
Vyshestlavtsev, 1931	Boris Vysheslavtsev *The Ethics of Transfigured Eros*, Paris: YMCA Press, 1931
Wainwright, 1980	Geoffrey Wainwright *Doxology*, New York: O.U.P., 1980
Ware, 1976	Timothy (Kallistos) Ware *The Orthodox Church*, New York: Penguin Books, 1976
Ware, 1986	Kallistos Ware *The Power of the Name*, new edn., Oxford, U.K.: SLG Press, 1986
Whitefield, 1987	Charles Whitefield *Healing the Child Within*, Deerfield Beach, Florida: Health Communications, 1987
Whitehead, 1929	Alfred North Whitehead *Process and Reality, an Essay in Cosmology*, Cambridge, England: The University Press, 1929

Zaehner, 1957   R.C. Zaehner *Mysticism Sacred and Profane*, Oxford: O.U.P., 1957

Zaehner, 1958   R.C. Zaehner *At Sundry Times*, London: Faber and Faber, 1958

Zaehner, 1963   R.C. Zaehner *Matter and Spirit*, New York: Harper and Row, 1963

Zaehner, 1970   R.C. Zaehner *Concordant Discord*, Oxford: Clarendon Press, 1970

Index

Abelard, Peter, 288
Altizer, Thomas, 132
Anselm, St, 233, 287
Aquinas, St Thomas, 40, 82, 94, 217
Arius, 161
Assmann, Hugo, 140
Augros, Robert, 204, 302, 313
Augustine, St, 167, 170, 173, 190, 303, 348, 352
Aulen, Gustav, 284
Aurobindo, 66
Barth, Karl, 25, 110, 111, 132, 138, 157, 165, 173, 186, 187, 189, 190, 191, 326, 327
Berdyaev, Nicholai, 300, 352, 355, 356
Bernard of Clairvaux, 171
Bornkamm, Guenther, 266
Brandon, S. G. F., 266
Buber, Martin, 136, 280
Bultmann, Rudolph, 132, 135, 137, 226
Calvin, John, 244, 354
Chrysostom, St John, 160
Cobb, John B., jr., 143, 144, 183, 184, 288
Conze, Edward, 257
Cox, Harvey, 35, 132
Dawkins, Richard, 313
Da Silva, Lynn, 69, 171
Derrida, Jacques, 438
Descartes, Renè, 233
Dodd, C. H., 286
Dorner, I. A., 188
Dumolin, Heinrich, 144
Durkheim, Èmile, 84
Eccles, John, 304
Eckhart, Meister, 170

Edge, David, 128
Edinger, Edward, 317, 325
Eliade, Mircea, 63
Falk, Harvey, 264
Farquhar, J. N., 144
Feuerbach, Ludwig, 84
Firth, Raymond, 273
Frankl, Victor, 307
Freud, Sigmund, 84, 317
Fromm, Eric, 300, 305, 312, 314, 315, 316
Gandhi, Mohandas K., 106, 373, 374, 393
al-Ghazali, 134
Gray, Asa, 233
Gregory of Nazianzen, 164
Gregory of Nyssa, 294
Griffith, David, 288
Griffiths, Bede, 197
Gutierrez, Gustavo, 140, 388
Hartshorne, Charles, 143, 184, 242
Hegel, Georg W. F., 81
Heidegger, Martin, 136, 144, 438
Hick, John, 25, 133, 144, 179, 180, 181, 183, 281, 288, 289, 290, 291, 294
Hillel, Rabbi, 264
Hodgson, Leonard, 168, 191
Hyppolytus, 160
Ignatius of Antioch, 338
Irenaeus, St, 335
Jeremias, Joachim, 266
John of Damascus, 169
Jung, C. G., 257, 300, 316, 344
Kaufmann, Walter, 280
Kierkegaard, Soren, 226
Kraemer, Hendrik, 110, 111
Kuhn, Thomas, 128

INDEX

Küng, Hans, 133, 144
Linn, Louis, 334
Lorenz, Konrad, 312
Lossky, Vladimir, 154, 165, 167, 196
Lowen, Alexander, 300, 324
Luther, Martin, 354
MacNutt, Francis, 340
Macquarrie, John, 186, 287
Malcolm, Norman, 233
Marx, Karl, 84
Maslow, Abraham, 300, 305
May, Rollo, 347, 356
Meng-tzu (Mencius), 304
Menninger, Karl, 324
Merton, Thomas, 144, 197
Moltmann, Jürgen, 143, 191, 192, 199, 280
Montague, Ashley, 300, 305, 310, 312
Nagarjuna, 93, 257
Niebuhr, Reinhold, 281, 290, 326
Ogden, Shubert, 143
Origen, 295
Otto, Rudolf 69, 133
Palamas, St Gregory, 42, 437
Pannenberg, Wolfhart, 143
Pannikar, Raimundo, 133, 144
Paul, St, 28, 42, 86, 154, 160, 188, 336, 337
Peck, M. Scott, 320, 324, 345, 346
Perrin, Norman, 268
Phillips, Dewi Z., 127
Phillips, J. B., 325
Polycarp, St, 160
Popper, Karl, 11, 128, 303
Rahner, Karl, 25, 144, 186, 189
Ramakrishna, 259

Ramanuja, 60, 77, 106, 185, 203, 209
Ramsey, I. T., 84
Rashdall, Hastings, 288
Reich, Wilhelm, 349
Richard of St Victor, 172
Rubenstein, Richard, 132, 139
Sanford, John, 317, 347
Schleiermacher, Friedrich, 132, 133, 137
Schwarz, Leo 334
Schweitzer, Albert 267, 268
Shammai, Rabbi, 264
Shankara, 170, 175
Skinner, B. F., 314
Smith, Wilfred C., 25, 133
Sobrino, Jon, 140
Spinoza, Baruch, 173
Stanciu, George, 204, 302, 313
Stein, Gertrude, 119
Suzuki, D. T., 257
Swinburne, Richard, 103
Taylor, Vincent, 286
Teilhard de Chardin, Pierre, 66, 143
Temple, William, 202
Thornton, L. S., 157, 191
Tillich, Paul, 32, 173, 186, 195, 254, 300, 308, 320, 329, 343
Toynbee, Arnold, 79
Tracy, David, 133
van Buren, Paul, 132
Vermes, Gregory, 264
Ware, Bishop Kallistos (Timothy), 165, 336
Whitehead, Alfred N., 143, 183
Wittgenstein, Ludwig, 125
Zaehner, R. C. 175